T0116218

"Being a bit of a desert rat, I began *The Immeasurable World* with interest and finished enthralled and grievously enlightened. The strangeness and inhospitable nature of the world's great deserts—and they are so variously singular—have not prevented humankind from assaulting and perverting their inconsolable beauties. William Atkins is an erudite writer with a wonderful wit and gaze, and this is a new and exciting beast of a travel book."   —Joy Williams

"Gorgeous. . . . Atkins is not in thrall to deserts . . . but loves them for their austerity, and the clarity of thought they grant."   —*The Guardian*

"Atkins's richly written account of his travels across deserts around the world brings Bruce Chatwin to mind, along with others who, like Atkins, have explored and have an affinity for the solitude and vast expanse of the Earth's empty places, such as Wallace Stegner, Gretel Ehrlich, and Sara Wheeler. Like theirs, Atkins's prose is gorgeous. . . . He also evokes the spirit of earlier desert travelers, including St. Anthony, T. E. Lawrence, and John Wesley Powell. . . . Atkins's book of journeys will be a modern-day classic."   —*Booklist* (starred review)

"Full of delight and delights. . . . [Atkins] is a seriously fine descriptive writer. . . . A wonderful book."   —*Tablet*

"Atkins's thoughtful book is a wonderfully satisfying travelogue."
                                                    —*Publishers Weekly*

"In sublime prose that veers from startling human and natural history to dreamlike personal experience, *The Immeasurable World* brings apparently barren places to life in a brilliant, revelatory narrative. The author becomes a kind of sensor in the wilderness, electrically gathering together these stories. The result is a book in which to get lost and find another world."   —Philip Hoare,
                                    author of *Leviathan, or the Whale*

WILLIAM ATKINS

THE IMMEASURABLE WORLD

William Atkins's first book, *The Moor*, was described as a "classic" by *The London Observer* and shortlisted for the Thwaites Wainwright Prize. He is a former editorial director of Pan Macmillan UK, and his long-form journalism has appeared in *The Guardian* and *Granta*. In 2016 he was a recipient of the Eccles British Library Writer's Award. He lives in London.

ALSO BY WILLIAM ATKINS

The Moor

THE IMMEASURABLE WORLD

THE IMMEASURABLE WORLD

A Desert Journey

William Atkins

ANCHOR BOOKS
A Division of Penguin Random House LLC
New York

FIRST ANCHOR BOOKS EDITION, JUNE 2019

Copyright © 2018 by William Atkins

All rights reserved. Published in the United States by Anchor Books,
a division of Penguin Random House LLC, New York. Originally published
in hardcover in Great Britain by Faber & Faber Limited, London, in 2018.
Subsequently published in hardcover in the United States by Doubleday,
a division of Penguin Random House LLC, New York, in 2018.

Anchor Books and colophon are registered
trademarks of Penguin Random House LLC.

The Library of Congress has cataloged the Doubleday edition as follows:
Name: Atkins, William (Editor), author.
Title: The immeasurable world : journeys in desert places / William Atkins.
Description: New York : Doubleday, 2018.
Identifiers: LCCN 2017053583
Subjects: LCSH: Atkins, Will (Editor)—Travel. | Deserts. | BISAC: TRAVEL /
Special Interest / Adventure. | BIOGRAPHY & AUTOBIOGRAPHY / Personal
Memoirs. | HISTORY / Historical Geography.
Classification: LCC GB611 .A85 2018 | DDC 910.915/4—dc23
LC record available at https://lccn.loc.gov/2017053583

Anchor Books Trade Paperback ISBN: 978-1-101-87341-0
eBook ISBN: 978-0-385-53989-0

Book design by Maria Carella
Author photograph © Johnny Ring

www.anchorbooks.com

147028622

Three days it's been without a trace of him, his nag, his leather shield, his lance or his armour... It's my belief, as sure as I was born to die, that his brain's been turned by those damned chivalry books of his he reads all the time—I remember often hearing him say to himself that he wanted to be a knight errant and go off in search of adventures. The devil take all those books, and Barabbas take them too, for scrambling the finest mind in all La Mancha!

—CERVANTES, *DON QUIXOTE,* TRANS. J. RUTHERFORD

Contents

PROLOGUE

It was the night of the blood moon. The term was coined by Bible Belt millenarians who believed the phenomenon—a lunar eclipse when the full moon is at its perigee, therefore magnified and pink—portended Armageddon. Joel 2:31: "The sun shall be turned to darkness and the moon to blood before the great and dreadful day of the Lord comes." The timing was just good fortune but it turned out I'd have among the best views on earth. In my ignorance it was its redness I anticipated as much as its bigness or for that matter the fact that it would be eclipsed, and so when it rose into view, more embers than blood, I was disappointed—as disappointed as one can ever be by a new-risen full moon.

By the time I'd rehydrated my noodles and poured my daily half-beaker of wine, the moon had returned from grey-pink to its customary white, like a fingertip pressed against glass, and every cactus and every shrub, and the strawbale cabin, had generated a hard exclusive shadow. It seemed to me that the chief characteristic of night in the desert was not darkness but this light that was not the sun's.

THE CABIN STANDS on a ridge above the San Pedro River sixty kilometres east of Tucson, Arizona. It is a one-room structure about three metres by five, with a door facing north-east. In each of the other three walls is a single window, screened with mesh against insects. It's nice to open the windows to the evening breeze, but during the day they stay shut to keep out the heat. The interior walls are thickly plastered, bumpy and cracked. The floor is packed earth laid with two rugs heavily nibbled by mice. Furniture: a cabinet for cooking utensils, a folding steel cot and mattress, a pine table and matching chairs, and an iron-banded trunk a century old, containing Mexican blankets, batteries and a first-aid kit and dozens of candles. The table resembles an altar. On it, most of the time, stands a storm lantern and a bottle of screw-top Cabernet Merlot ($8.99, Trader Joe's).

Each of the four windows (there's one in the door) gives onto a hillside thick with mesquite, paloverde, creosote bush, ocotillo, prickly pear, barrel cactus, and saguaro, the region's characteristic cactus, the cactus of cowboy films. It is the saguaros' giant candelabra forms that break the line of each hillside and provide landmarks. The tallest for kilometres stands beside the cabin. From the south-west-facing window you can see the Rincon Mountains, with the Little Rincons before them, dropping down to the San Pedro Valley, and the few dwellings of the Cascabel community ten kilometres away. When the sun rises behind me, a blade of light drops from the distant peaks of the Rincons, down the foothills and towards me across the alluvial plain, until slowly, like a lava flow, the threshold where light meets shadow approaches the cabin—and then: there! The warmth as the sun's rays touch the back of my head and my shadow is thrown down long before me.

From a hook fixed to a rafter-end I hang a kettle of water on a bungee each morning, and by 6 p.m. it is hot enough for a shower. On the cabin's opposite side, where there is more shade, lies the two-hundred-litre drum that provides all my water, raised on a bed of rocks and protected against the sun with a jacket of wire-strung saguaro ribs.

The ridge separates two washes (dry, except after cloudbursts): one is broad and shallow, the other is deep and narrow and what they call an arroyo. The ridge rises to the north-east—halfway up this hill, about thirty metres from my door, is a double wooden frame into which two identical square boards are slid, each painted white on one side and on the other red. Every evening, before my shower, though I don't always remember, I walk up the hill along a path marked out with rocks on each side, and slide out the boards, flip them over, and slide them back into the framework. From the ridge near his home down near the San Pedro, my friend Daniel checks each morning with his binoculars, if he remembers; if the boards do not change for a day or two, he'll come and make sure I'm okay.

There are a few books here: a natural history of the Sonoran Desert and a book about the dangerous animals of the region, every one hair-triggered, you'd be forgiven for inferring, to sting you, bite you, maul you, or char you with its fiery breath. My own contribution is a paperback facsimile of John C. Van Dyke's 1901 book *The Desert*. It describes a man's journey, alone, into this desert, the Sonoran, a journey made chiefly in 1898, though its precise course is unclear. He was an accomplished art historian, but trust Van Dyke's guidance at your peril. Here he is, homicidally, on the subject of food and water, for instance: "Any athlete or Indian will tell you that you can travel better without them. They are good things at the end of the trip but not at the beginning." Rattlesnakes he describes as "sluggish." He shoots grey wolves in California, where there were no wolves, and eulogises the purple flowers of the saguaro, which are white (though the fruits are red). Alerted to certain errors by a well-meaning desert ecologist, he graciously acknowledged the mistakes, promised to correct them in future editions—*The Desert* had a long life—and so far as is known made no effort to do so. A note appended to the manuscript of his autobiography spells out his aim: "to describe the desert from an aesthetic, not scientific, point of view."

I no longer sleep inside but, after my sunset shower, drag the cot out to the clearing in front of the door, where I am not disturbed by the lizards in the roof—or, more accurately, where the noise they make is subsumed by the larger racket of the desert at night. I lift each of the bed's feet and slip containers of water under them—tin mugs, a wooden saucer, a saucepan—to keep conenose kissing-bugs or scorpions from joining me. I position the two chairs beside the bed, one at the foot, one alongside my head, and stand lanterns on them. In a row on the ground between them half a dozen candles are stationed. In the mornings the hardened wells around their wicks are black with flying insects. Within this lit perimeter I sleep more easily than I have for months, which is not to say deeply. Waking in the night to the buzzing of cicadas or the yapping of coyotes, I experience a weight of tranquillity that has the quality of a quilt. It might be the peace of the dying.

Most afternoons, as the warmth first intensifies like an oven pre-heating, then levels off at a temperature that permits nothing but sitting in the cabin's shadow cowled in a wet scarf, I try to remember how the song goes:

High on a hill was a lonely goatherd...
One little girl in a pale pink coat heard...

This is my main afternoon work: to remember the words. And day by day, one by one, they return to me, though it's a year since I last heard the song, coming from a cracked Samsung smartphone on the edge of the Worst Desert on Earth, while to the north a massacre was happening.

1
THE DESERT LIBRARY

The Empty Quarter, Oman

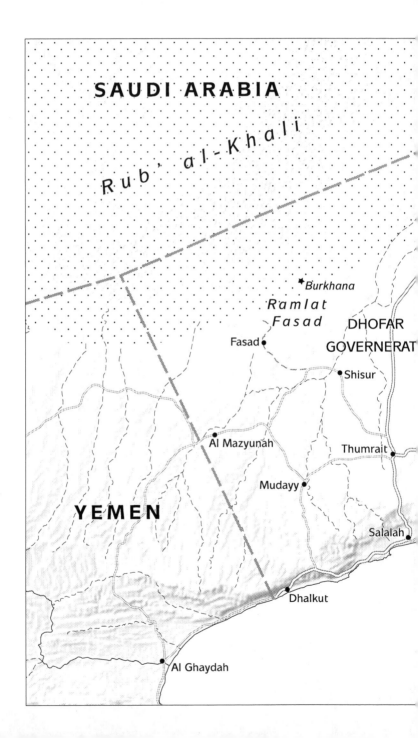

SAUDI ARABIA

Rub' al-Khali

*Burkhana

*Ramlat
Fasad*

DHOFAR
GOVERNERAT

Fasad

Shisur

Al Mazyunah

Thumrait

Mudayy

YEMEN

Salalah

Dhalkut

Al Ghaydah

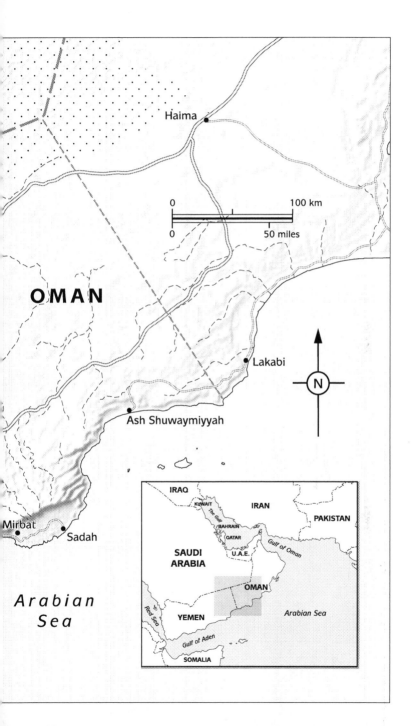

Haima

100 km

0

0

50 miles

OMAN

Lakabi

Ash Shuwaymiyyah

N

Mirbat

Sadah

Arabian
Sea

IRAQ

KUWAIT

IRAN

PAKISTAN

The Gulf

BAHRAIN

QATAR

SAUDI
ARABIA

U.A.E.

Gulf of Oman

OMAN

Arabian Sea

Red Sea

YEMEN

Gulf of Aden

SOMALIA

It seems a long time ago. The woman I'd lived with for four years had taken a job overseas. I would not be going with her. The summer before, in the name of research, I'd spent a week with a community of Cistercian monks on the edge of Dartmoor in south-west England. I attended each of the abbey's sacred offices—matins at 5:45 a.m., lauds an hour later, Mass at 8 a.m., vespers at 6 p.m., compline at 9—and took meals in the vaulted refectory. As the days passed, each office became indistinguishable from the next. I'd sit at the high open window of my room, looking out from time to time to follow the swallows as they spiralled over the cloister roof. When the bell tolled, I would put down whatever book I was reading, and go alone down the long stone staircase, three flights, and wait in the chapel for the twelve monks to enter, one by one, and take their places along the walls on either side. I stood at the back and listened to their plainsong.

It was in the monastery library that I became aware of the connection between Christian monasticism and the desert. I would make a pile of books and carry them up to my small room, and spend the time between offices reading. I learned about the Desert Fathers, the third- and fourth-century solitaries of Upper Egypt, and the first of them, St. Antony. Antony was born in AD 251 in Upper Egypt, the son of a wealthy Christian family. At the age of nineteen, following the deaths of his parents, he happened to pass a church and hear the words of Matthew 19:21: "If you would be perfect, go and sell that you have and give to the poor." Antony obeyed and put his younger sister in a nunnery. To give up your possessions, to remove from your life those you love: these are a monk's first acts, but they might also be described as consistent with grieving.

Artistic depictions of St. Antony—"the Star of the Desert"—fall into two categories, each illustrating a central scene in the saint's life: the first shows him in his nineties meeting the dying St. Paul, having walked fifty kilometres from his cave on the other side of Egypt's South Galala Mountains. It is this scene that Velázquez's *St. Antony Abbot and St. Paul the Hermit* depicts: the dying saint, his beard whiter than his companion's, sits on a rocky outcrop, hands fused in prayer, while Antony looks on in awe. Just above their heads a raven descends with a loaf of bread.

The bird appears in every image of St. Antony and St. Paul, and its presence alone identifies the human figures. The other scenario in which St. Antony is depicted shows an early, more tumultuous period in his life and is much more common on account of its imaginative potency. Having left his home, the young man retired alone to a hut in

the desert—but it wasn't far, hardly the true desert at all, just a place outside the village walls. There he was besieged by the devil's temptations: memories of his former comforts, his abandoned sister, the promise of money and glory, and above all the "spirit of fornication." Hieronymus Bosch's triptych of c. 1500 depicts an army of grotesques crowding its central panel; in the left-hand panel the saint is being rendered away by a squadron of airborne frog-demons; in the right he sits reading, trying to ignore the nude sylph half-concealed in the bole of a dead tree.

He travels still further into the desert, deeper into the devil's domain, like a military scout preceding an invasion. At Pispir, close to the eastern bank of the Nile, he takes up residence in an abandoned fort. When, in Athanasius's account, his friends visit with bread they hear wrestling and yelling from within: "Go from what is ours! What do you even in the desert?" But when he emerges, Antony is "neither fat, like a man without exercise, nor lean from fasting and striving with demons, but...just the same." By now he has become an iconic figure and must fend off acolytes as well as demons. He travels deeper still into the desert, until he reaches the place that would be his home for the rest of his life: the foothills of the South Galala Mountains.

This story of a step-by-step progression into oblivion, from the lush Nile floodplain to the arid interior, became a model for others wishing to renounce society. According to St. Athanasius, "cells filled with holy bands of men who said psalms, loved reading, fasted, prayed, rejoiced in the hope of things to come, laboured in almsgiving and preserved love and harmony one with the other." These communities in turn inspired the establishment of Benedictine and Cistercian monasteries in Europe.

I STARTED ACCUMULATING a library of desert travelogues, mostly by nineteenth- and early-twentieth-century travellers. I read them without system or coherence, least of all geographical. I was impelled by a sort of urgency, as if ransacking their pages for the code to deactivate a bomb. Sometimes I'd resort to Deuteronomy:

He found him in a desert land, and in the waste howling wilderness.

T. E. Lawrence—Lawrence of Arabia—was quoted so ubiquitously that it was barely necessary to own a copy of his first-hand account of the Arab revolt, *Seven Pillars of Wisdom*. But his fellow Arabists—Charles Doughty, Harry St. John Philby, Wilfred Thesiger, and especially Bertram Thomas—joined the heap. A single book, one voice alone, was insufficient to hold my attention for long. It was a modern disease. I'd wake up in bed or on the sofa, ringed by half a dozen old books, each splayed face-down at the point where I'd moved on or nodded off, primed for the next round. As bedfellows went, they were a shabby, irascible, not-always-likeable bunch. Even among the women, the metaphor of sexual conquest was near-ubiquitous: time and again the feminised desert was unveiled, exposed, vanquished and finally penetrated. My bedding was dusty with dried binding-glue.

It was in this way that I came to think of all these accounts as a single narrative: the deserts of the world as one. It wasn't an unprecedented approach.

In his translation of *The Arabian Nights*, I found a footnote by Richard Burton reporting that the "Desert Quarter" in the original Arabic was given as "Rub'a al-Kharáb," which he believed alluded to "the Rub' al-Khali or Great Arabian Desert." In rhetoric, Burton explains, "it is opposed to the 'Rub'a Maskún', or populated fourth of the world, the rest being held to be ocean." Charles Doughty, in the Old Testament prose of his 1888 *Travels in Arabia Deserta*, writes that, in Arabic lore, "two quarters [of the world] divided God to the children of Adam, the third he gave to Ajuj and Majuj (Gog and Magog), the fourth part of the world is called Rub'a el-Khaly, the Empty Quarter."

I had to remind myself that "the desert" was more than a metaphor. For geographers, deserts are simply places where the average annual rainfall is less than 250 millimetres, and where precipitation, by rain or fog or dew, is exceeded by potential evapotranspiration (loss of water through evaporation and the transpiration of plants). The Aridity Index gauges this ratio as P/PET and this formula is used internationally to define the four categories of "drylands": Hyper-Arid, Arid, Semi-Arid, and Sub-Humid. Collectively these areas make up more than 40 per cent of the world's surface. The model desert journey is a progression from the sub-humid to the hyper-arid—from the Nile to

the "Inner Mountain," as the South Galala Mountains were known to
the Desert Fathers—and it was this centripetal tendency that interested me. French travellers in the Sahara in the nineteenth century
sought what they called *le désert absolu*. In the *Vitae Patrum*, the collected sayings and biographies of the Desert Fathers, published in the
seventeenth century, we learn of the *paneremos* (Gr.): at once the place
of uttermost lifelessness, and the locus where the desert's identity was
most purely asserted, and that point furthest from the periphery. Polar
explorers have another term: the Pole of Maximum Inaccessibility.
This it seemed was the ultimate objective of every desert traveller: the
axis where the absolute coexists with the infinite.

ACCORDING TO THE early explorers of the Empty Quarter, the
local Bedouin had not so much as heard of the "Rub' al-Khali." Bertram
Thomas, the first outsider to cross the desert, noted that "they neither use the term nor understand it in its literal sense." When Wilfred
Thesiger mentioned the Rub' al-Khali to his guides, they responded:
"What is he talking about? What does he want? God alone knows." For
them it was only *ar-Rimal*—"the Sands."

A depression the size of France, occupying a third of the Arabian
Peninsula, the Empty Quarter is bounded to the north and east by the
uplands of Qatar and northern Oman, and by the mountains of Oman's
Dhofar governorate and Yemen to the south and west. This tremendous bowl of sand has been stirred, clockwise, for perhaps two million
years, by two great winds: the shamal that sweeps across the Arabian
Gulf from Iraq, and the kharif that brings the south-west monsoon to
soak Dhofar.

In 1904 the Arabist David Hogarth wrote that the Rub' al-Khali
"has yet to be tried by a stranger, and we have no absolute assurance
that even a native has ever crossed the heart of it. It is a name of terror
throughout Arabia." The Empty Quarter was not entirely the virgin
territory that Hogarth and his fellow Arabists perceived it to be, but
during the two centuries of European presence in Arabia it had come
to represent the archetypal desert void, and the archetypal test. Nineteen years after Amundsen and Scott reached the South Pole, Ber-

tram Thomas was still able to describe the Empty Quarter as the "last considerable *terra incognita*." For Richard Burton, travelling in Arabia the previous century, it had been simply an "opprobrium to modern adventure."

Every year perhaps half a dozen expeditions set out in Thesiger's footsteps, completing all or part of his route across the Empty Quarter's eastern edge, north-east from Salalah to the Emirates or Qatar. Of the three formative British explorers of the Empty Quarter—Bertram Thomas and Harry St. John Philby in the 1930s, and Wilfred Thesiger in the 1940s—it is Thesiger whom modern-day travellers follow, and always his first, 1946, crossing, along the desert's eastern edge, rather than the more troubled westerly crossing that he made the following year. It is not just that Thesiger is the more romantic and notorious figure (the better writer, certainly): like the courses of Philby and Thomas, his second crossing ventured deep into what is now off-limits Saudi Arabia, whose border encloses some 80 per cent of the Empty Quarter. If, as a non-Saudi, you wish to cross the Rub' al-Khali, it will probably be in the footsteps of Thesiger.

He was born in 1910 in what was then Addis Ababa, where his father was a British minister. It was those early years, and his experiences in the Sahara during the Second World War, that generated his love of arid places. Published in 1959, more than ten years after his crossings, *Arabian Sands* is full of nostalgia for a way of life—the ascetic nomadism of the desert Bedouin—that, in his view, was doomed by the discovery of oil under the peninsula's deserts. "They are too lovely to last in the utilitarian age." His belief in the fundamental Nobility of the Bedouin echoed the sentiments not only of nineteenth-century European Romantics but of the fourteenth-century Arab historian Ibn Khaldun, who maintained that the "desert people are closer to being good than settled peoples because they are...removed from all the habits that have infected the hearts of settlers."

"It is curious how the desert satisfies me and gives me peace," Thesiger wrote to his mother. "You cannot explain what you find there to those who don't feel it too, for most people it is just a howling wilderness."

But the desert, despite appearances, is not immune to the progress of time. Few desert travellers can bring themselves to conclude their accounts without lamenting the intrusion of mechanised transport upon the desert's sanctity. Or worse yet, other people.

One January evening I attended a lecture at the Royal Geographical Society in London. Two years earlier, the man on stage had crossed the Empty Quarter's eastern flank by camel, with two Emirati Bedouin companions, travelling from Salalah in Oman to Abu Dhabi in forty days. And that was why he was here. The project was called "Footsteps of Thesiger." *Authenticity*, he told us, had been everything—he and his team had planned to carry only what Thesiger had carried, and dress as he'd dressed, in Bedouin garb. And yet, he admitted, he had been obliged, under pressure from the authorities (and his sponsors), to endure the presence of a support crew, which trailed behind in a convoy of four-wheel-drives, bearing the photographer, the cameraman, the soundman, GPS and radios, medical supplies and, of course, food and water; they would also taxi the adventurer to the nearest hospital when he came off his camel. No longer was it necessary to be vigilant for raiders, the "feared puritans of Islam," as Bertram Thomas called them, who would glory in a Christian's slaughter.

Thomas went on to describe the hostile tribes of the Sands as being "of two kinds: that whose tribe and yours have no blood feud [and] that where a blood feud exists. Both want your camels and arms, the second your life as well." Those times were gone. The Bedouin had been enfranchised, after a fashion. It was a further blight on the modern expedition that the Omanis of the desert edge were eager to see the procession as it passed, bestowing unwelcome gifts of yet more food and water, and insisting on feasting the travellers and their entourage each night. The stringencies enjoyed by Thesiger and his predecessors were denied them; you were as likely to gain weight on such a trip as lose it, and the eastern Sands were as footprint-riddled as Clacton-on-Sea.

It has become difficult to be a pioneer. The world has been done. There are only the adventurers now, this new breed of fanatic: rangy large-toothed guys seeking not knowledge or even territory but novelty, managed suffering, "experience," material, sponsorship—K2 by canoe, the Amazon by bike, the North Pole on stilts. And then there are those who seek out the footsteps of the surveyors of the epic era.

Such expeditions might still yield lessons for the budding CEO: "These guys put the team ahead of the individual," said the speaker. He was talking about the Bedouin. He had planned the expedition "like anyone wanting to succeed in business." A question from the audience, the roving mic dispatched: where did he stand vis-à-vis the rumours about Thesiger's "shall we say 'unorthodox' lifestyle"? (The-siger's tender descriptions of his "disturbingly beautiful" guide, Salim bin Kabina, remain unignorable.) A brief catlike rigidifying, then the recovery of sangfroid. "Personally? I firmly believe they were just good friends."

FIFTEEN YEARS BEFORE Thesiger's crossings, Harry St. John Philby wrote to his wife, Dora, "With me, nothing counts but the Rub' al-Khali, and I can find no peace of mind till that is over and done with. Curse!" It was "this beastly obsession which has so completely sidetracked me for the best years of my life."

A Foreign Office functionary since his graduation from Cambridge, Philby had been Bertram Thomas's superior in the British Political Service in Iraq, where both had been drafted in 1917 following the capture of Baghdad. Philby's obsession with the Empty Quarter dated from his earliest excursions into Arabia, as revenue commissioner in Iraq, then as adviser to the minister of the interior. In 1924 he became Britain's political representative to the founding monarch of Saudi Arabia, Ibn Saud. This acquaintance was to prove central to his future expeditions, for it was only with the king's sanction that safe passage into the Empty Quarter could be assured.

It was vital that he should be the first. "To that effort and its conse-quences," he wrote, "I sacrificed everything—the security of an ortho-dox career and the rest of it."

It was not until December 1930 that Ibn Saud gave serious consid-eration to his request, recognising that the success of such an expedi-tion under his patronage would vindicate his claim to dominion of the desert. Indeed, the Empty Quarter, with its vast oil deposits, would soon prove central to the wealth of the Saudi nation. Finally Philby was summoned to the king's palace in Riyadh: "We will send Philby to the Empty Quarter."

But his departure was to be stymied by that old hindrance to adventuring, tribal unrest. As he wrote later, "A year's delay would not be of serious moment—so all thought except myself." For Philby had been made aware that the thirty-three-year-old Bertram Thomas, his onetime underling, was in the south of the peninsula, preparing an expedition of his own.

Thomas's biography prior to the army is sketchy: born in 1892, he volunteered at the age of twenty-two and was sent to Flanders, where he served for two years before being dispatched with his regiment first to India, then to Baghdad. While posted in Shatrah in Iraq he would serenade the local sheikhs on the piano he had brought with him. Their favourite, claimed Gertrude Bell, who encountered him there, was Beethoven's *Sonata Pathétique*.

Having gained a reputation for securing the trust of Iraqi tribal leaders, in 1922 he was appointed financial adviser, *wazir*, to the Sultan of Oman. His appointment was a condition of the British government's agreement to bail out the indebted sultan. Oman might not have been a colony, but its proximity to the strategically vital straits of the Persian Gulf, and its promise of oil, meant it could not be allowed to escape British influence. Thomas was not a particularly effective financial adviser. He was preoccupied, and not with his piano.

From the moment of his arrival, he began to map a route across the Empty Quarter, using his annual leave to make several long recces to the desert's edge. Finally, on the evening of 4 October 1930, he set off from Muscat, aboard a British oil tanker that would drop him along the southern Arabian coast, near what was then the small fishing town of Salalah. As Thomas writes in his account of his travels, *Arabia Felix*, he "avoided the pitfalls of seeking permission," knowing that such permission would very likely be withheld by both the sultan and his own British superiors.

Some six weeks later a deputation of the Rashidi tribe, whom Thomas had been in contact with, appeared from the desert, ready to accompany him across the Sands. At the same time, however, according to Thomas's account, a gunboat appeared offshore, carrying a summons from the sultan. Mr. Thomas must return to his post immediately. He made up his mind: he would send the gunboat back to Muscat without him, while he would "join fortune with those attractive ruffians . . . and take the plunge with them into the uncharted wilderness." In Muscat his British bosses quietly fumed.

Thomas is still elusive. He was the first foreigner to cross the Empty Quarter, but unlike his successors, Philby and Thesiger, his name is barely known. There is no biography. *Arabia Felix*, a bestseller in its day and superior to Philby's turgid *The Empty Quarter*, has long been out of print. In 1944, thirteen years after his crossing, Thomas was posted to Jerusalem as the first director of the British army's School of Arabic Studies. A year later he had resigned to take up a position as Shell's head of operations in the Gulf, tasked with reporting on the movements of rival oil-company representatives and "the aspirations of various Arab rulers regarding petroleum concessions." In 1950 he wrote to a friend: "Tobacco and alcohol are cheap but these I have to go slow on at the moment." Later that year, at the age of fifty-eight, alcoholic and overweight, Bertram Thomas died. I thought of Buzz Aldrin's depression, his alcoholism, the way his existence was at once magnified and belittled by the experience of walking on the moon.

I hadn't any intention of pussyfooting in Thomas's footprints, but I wanted to stand in the desert he had laboured in, and try to imagine what it might do to a person who abandoned himself to it. And of course there was the name of the place.

THE FIRST TOPOGRAPHERS of England, standing on the edge of some boggy realm like Dartmoor, some place that had not been colonised or cultivated, wrote "desert" or "desart" in their reports. From the Latin adjective *desertus*, past participle of *deserere*: "to abandon."

The chief characteristic of such places, then, was not a lack of water but of humankind. And they were not only unpeopled but in the original sense *forsaken*. Shakespeare's "desert inaccessible" in *As You Like It* is not arid, it is woodland; and when Noel Thomas Carrington in his poem "Dartmoor" calls the moor a "silent desert," he doesn't mean it metaphorically. On my shelves was an 1872 book by the French naturalist Arthur Mangin, *The Desert World*, in which he seeks to describe all the regions "where Nature has maintained her inviolability," including the Russian steppes, the "prairies, pampas and llanos" of the New World, the Poles and the Pyrenees, and even Dartmoor itself.

Europeans had no real conception of the world's dry deserts until they started going to them. Look at the paintings of St. Antony. It was not only that vegetation was a requisite compositional device in European landscape-paintings. Even for the most visionary painter, one who had pored over Athanasius's hagiography, the sheer sparsity of the Egyptian desert was as beyond imagining as the moon. Scarcely any of these paintings are without trees, and many show the abbot sitting primly in a landscape as lush as the Apennines in spring. In *The Temptation of St. Antony*, painted around 1560 by a follower of Pieter Bruegel

ceparing the positions

the Elder, he occupies a bosky hillside overlooking a broad river that might be the Rhine. In a painting of the same name by a follower of Hieronymus Bosch, the desert anchorite sits on a lawn, in the shade of what might be an ash tree, overlooking a slow-moving brook, while in the distance the spire of a church rises behind a line of trees.

A kind of paradise, but a Netherlandish one. The desert, then, was European, until Europeans began to conquer it. Only then did a narrowing, an aridifying, of the word's usage begin.

A Dominican friar from Germany, Felix Fabri made two pilgrimages in the Holy Land, in 1480 and 1483. If we are to characterise what the desert is in the cultural, religious and psychological senses, his description remains persuasive five centuries later. I skimmed through the three-volume account of his journey, *Wanderings in the Holy Land*, and found both his retelling of St. Antony's walk to the dying St. Paul, and a description of his own arrival at the edge of the "wilderness of Sin," which lies between Mount Sinai and the Red Sea.

"Holy Scripture tells us in many places about this wilderness, of what kind of thing it is *and what it lacks*" (my emphasis). Fabri attributes to the environment no fewer than twenty conditions:

> Firstly, this country is called the desert because it seems to be, so to speak, deserted by God, as though God had used it to improve or adorn the rest of the universe ... Secondly, this country is called the lonesome place, because no one longs for that land ... Thirdly, this country is called the solitary place, because it is solitary and unfrequented by men. It is solitary because none of the countries which lie round about it wish to have any connection with or likeness to that land ...

He goes on to tell us that the desert is "the image of death," that "nothing grows there," that it is waterless, salt, pathless, inhabited only by serpents, scorpions, *dipsades* (a kind of snake whose bite causes intolerable thirst), worms, dragons, fauns and satyrs; that it is—as St. Antony knew—a place of demonic temptation, "where great merit is acquired," and "where the laws and commandments were given." But it is also, says Fabri, "the place of manna and of Divine comforting," a retreat from the world.

Finally—*twentiethly*—it is a place of devotion and contemplation, "wherefore we read in the Psalms, 'In a barren and dry land where no water is have I looked for thee in holiness.'"

There it was: the hyper-arid zone in all its abundance: solitary, godless, lonesome, deathly, barren, waterless, trackless, impassable, infested, cursed, forsaken—and yet, at the same time, the site of revelation, of contemplation and sanctuary. Amid its horrors, peace—peace *magnified* by those horrors.

The fact that Fabri had set foot upon its gravel plains and slept beneath its stars made the wilderness of Sin no less a symbolic realm for him. It was the wilderness known to Christ, Moses and St. Antony. Fabri's description draws on his own journey, naturally, but his understanding is influenced to an even greater extent by scriptural symbology, and especially St. Jerome's account of the life of St. Paul and the limestone mountains of the Eastern Desert of Egypt, seething with "Fauns, and Satyrs, and Incubi."

To make a pilgrimage to the Holy Land, for Fabri and the thousands of religious tourists who went after him, was less to unscroll a map than to open a book. Even for the twenty-first-century visitor, equipped with satellite phone and Evian, it is very much through that same biblical filter that the desert is comprehended. "I was like Moses," writes Philby, the man who titled his autobiography *Forty Years in the Wilderness.*

BY THE END of winter I'd given up most of my stuff. Apart from the bed, the flat in London was empty. The bed, and some photos—and the books. I'd taken most of them, hundreds of them, to Oxfam, but I kept the desert ones—a library of twenty or so, few enough to fit inside a wheeled flight case. I spent a week accumulating the gear I'd need, or thought I'd need. I bought a "hydration system" called a CamelBak—a blue plastic bladder that slips inside your backpack and has a spigoted rubber catheter that snakes over the shoulder for on-the-go suckling.

I bought sunglasses and two cheap hats and a cotton scarf and three identical beige shirts labelled "Craghoppers." I bought sixty sachets of blackcurrant-flavour rehydration powder. I bought half a dozen family-sized dispensers of factor-50 sunblock (I'm a redhead), which I'd decant into pocket-sized sprays.

During those early days of planning, I came upon an interesting historical document. Written by an American named W. J. McGee, "Desert Thirst as Disease" appeared in a 1906 edition of the *Interstate Medical Journal*. It's a unique study in the stages of dehydration and heatstroke, and no less alarming for being scientifically outdated.

McGee, a doctor and geographer, sets the scene: he has established his field camp in south-western Arizona—close to the Tinajas Altas Mountains on the Camino del Diablo, one of the most feared of the Sonoran Desert's ancient migration routes. "Hardly a mile of the 200 from Santo Domingo to Yuma remains unmarked by one or more cruciform stone-heaps," he writes. The events he goes on to describe take place in August 1905. The subject is a prospector called Pablo Valencia ("one of the best-built Mexicans known to me, albeit lightly burdened with acute sensibility"). With his Sancho Panza, the "erratic and inconsequent and little dependable" Jesus Rios, Valencia passes through McGee's camp en route to an abandoned gold mine, which the two men intend to claim and revive.

Having set out on 15 August, Rios turns back with both horses to fetch more water, arranging to rendezvous with Valencia the following day, an agreement McGee pronounces "inane if not insane." Rios leaves the camp once more early in the morning, only to return exhausted and dehydrated, having failed to find Valencia at the agreed place. A local tracker is sent out to follow "old Jesus's ill-chosen trail," but he too returns to the camp alone.

Four further nights pass. Valencia has been in the desert for eight days, with water sufficient for one day. There is no question but that he is dead. On 23 August, McGee is woken by what he recognises as the roaring of a bull, "an ear-piercing bellow of challenge and defiance." Some distance from the camp, they find him, "the wreck of Pablo," motionless under an ironwood tree.

Pablo was stark naked; his formerly full-muscled legs and arms were shrunken and scrawny; his ribs edged out like those of a starvling horse; his habitually plethoric abdomen was drawn in almost against his vertebral column; his lips had disappeared as if amputated, leaving low edges of blackened tissue; his teeth and gums projected like those of a skinned animal, but the flesh was black and dry as a hank of jerky; his nose was withered and shrunken to half its length; his nostril-lining showing black; his eyes were set in a winkless stare, with surrounding skin so contracted as to expose the conjunctiva, itself black as the gums; his face was dark as a negro, and his skin generally turned a ghastly purplish yet ashen grey, with great livid blotches and streaks; his lower legs and feet, with forearms and hands, were torn and scratched by contact with thorns and sharp rocks, yet even the freshest cuts were as so many scratches in dry leather, without trace of blood or serum; his joints and bones stood out like those of a wasted sickling, though the skin clung to them in way suggesting shrunken rawhide used in repairing a broken wheel.

Desert gothic. It is as if he has been possessed by the spirit of the desert or rendered into some calculus of all its extremes. The impression above all is of an organic being reduced to the mineral—this is what the desert does, before it scatters you. He is half-deaf, half-blind; and there's one last foul detail: "his tongue shrunken to a mere bunch of black integument."

McGee douses him with water, "the skin first shedding and then absorbing it greedily as a dry sponge." From shrunken rawhide to sponge. Valencia's revival from living mummy is in fact remarkably quick: within an hour he is drinking, within two he can manage a little "bird fricassee with rice and shredded bacon." All it takes is water.

In the days that follow he becomes strong enough to recollect his ordeal. Having set out on foot, he became disoriented and exhausted. His canteen was soon empty. "He found some relief—after the fashion of all Mexicans and most Americans in like cases—by occasionally filling his mouth and gargling his throat with urine."

On 17 August, two days after leaving the camp, he lay down in an arroyo and discarded his shoes and trousers. This shedding of clothes is common among those dying in the desert—instinctive but lethal, since clothing is often all that shields you from the sun. The following day he chewed some paloverde twigs and ate some spiders. He became convinced that Rios had deliberately abandoned him (and who knows, perhaps he did), planning to claim the goldmine for himself. It was this conviction that "spurred him on with the aim of knifing his deceiver."

On 19 August he recognised the Old Yuma Trail, which would return him to the camp, but "soon fell under the heat and lay all day long in an arroyo." That evening, as he made his way along the old trail, he glimpsed a coyote following him at a distance. By now the urine he had been carrying in the canteen was *mucho malo*, "very bad."

On 21 August, five days after Valencia's last taste of water, the buzzards which had been monitoring him for two days "came almost within hand-reach." The next day, his urine having ceased to flow, "he felt his last recourse gone." The following evening McGee was woken by those distant bellowings. The dead man was alive, or rather he was not wholly dead.

T. E. Lawrence believed that "thirst" was an "active malady"— "not a long death...but very painful." McGee isolates five stages of what he too calls *thirst*: "normal dryness," "functional derangement," "the cottonmouth phase," "the phase of the shrivelled tongue," "the stage of structural degeneration" and "the final phase"—death. His stages correspond roughly to the three stages used by modern medics in describing dehydration and heatstroke: *mild* (dry mouth, rapid breathing), *moderate* (reduced skin-turgor, sunken eyes and irritability) and *extreme* (cold extremities, no identifiable blood-pressure or pulse).

Valencia was fortunate. Once he was strong enough, he was taken by cart to Yuma, where he "spent practically the whole of August 31 deliberately and methodically devouring watermelon."

TWO DAYS BEFORE flying to Oman, tetchy with waking visions of the desert, I caught a train to Cambridge and went to the Faculty of Asian and Middle Eastern Studies. There, one after another, while the rain pattered on the windows, I was brought the items I had requested from their Bertram Thomas archive. It was the map of his crossing I was interested in, pasted onto thin boards but now so dog-eared and friable that it required painstaking unfolding in order to avoid new tears. It seemed to have been drawn up from his records and subsequently corrected by him. Discredited or misdrawn features had been scrawled out in pencil, and new ones added. The Rub' al-Khali itself, otherwise a blank, was dense with the author's own pencilled features and labels—the courses of the dry riverbeds (wadis), dune formations and plains, as well as blots of what looked like coffee.

In a footnote in *Arabia Felix*, he itemises the geographical features as he and his party move from south to north: "high, red dune country"; "elevated, less-rugged, red sands, with horseshoe hills"; "parallel white ridges with intervening red valleys"; "flat or gently undulating white sands with transverse red hills"; "steppe, salt plain, and red hills alternating." Running from bottom to top of the map was a careful darker pencil line, coursing north-west from the coastal plain of Salalah. It passed over the Qara mountains to the waterhole of Shisur, into the dune regions known as Ramlat Fasad and Ramlat Mitan, before veering briefly west and then, for three hundred kilometres, following the sparse dots of waterholes north to the Persian Gulf.

Also in the collection were Thomas's tables, with columns for *date*, *place*, *hour*, *course*, *rate* and *bearing*: hundreds of entries over five or six pages, drawn up from the notes he took during his journey and recording his party's precise course, hour by hour. As the Sands are entered, the proper names are left behind and replaced by mere descriptions— "white sands," "dune ridge," "dunes and basin," "salt plain," "white plain"—repeated again and again, until place names return as the Gulf is neared.

A WEEK LATER I was standing in Ramlat Fasad opposite someone called Nigel. He was so close I could feel his breath on my eyeballs. He lived in Northampton, he was saying. His life had not been easy, but nor, given the chance, would he exchange it for another.

We had left the peripheral gravel plains behind. Underfoot was a floor of cracked white clay dusted with red sand. Between us and the mountainous pink dunes that formed the horizon were only two salt-bushes, long dead. Nigel was bonneted in a Sahara cap, tied in a bow under his chin, his face crusted with factor-50. The headmaster, he was saying, the headmaster had been "more of a politician than an educa-tor," and it was he who, five years ago, had engineered Nigel's dismissal from the school where he worked. A breakdown followed; divorce; a son's alienation. At the age of sixty, he moved three hundred kilome-tres north and became a postman. As he continued, my eyes traced the tracks of the four-wheel-drive that had left us here, to the brow of a rise. The sand had reddened further, to the colour of a mouth's interior. The land was ablaze.

As retirement approached, Nigel was saying, he began to seek out challenges of a controllable kind: first he ran 160 kilometres along the South Downs; then, in the Sahara, he ran the Marathon des Sables—six marathons in six days. Most recently he had succeeded, after two previous attempts, in completing the Yukon Arctic Ultra, towing a sledge 690 kilometres solo across northern Canada.

And now he was here, to ride a camel in Arabia, alone but for his guide. It was not, on this occasion, about distance, he said. As a young man, he had watched David Lean's film *Lawrence of Arabia* and read Thesiger's *Arabian Sands*. Finally, in his early sixties, he'd joined them, those men. When he looked back on his life, or even as he went about his work next week, he'd be able to describe to himself what he had done.

As Nigel spoke, the realisation was dawning on me that I would die if Hassan, our guide, did not return. Never before had I known so intensely my life's dependence on another. It was as if I had been dosed with a poison whose antidote he alone possessed. And where *was* Hassan?

I HAD ARRIVED in the southern coastal city of Salalah two days before, and was met by Hassan at my guesthouse on the beach. "There's a small problem," he had said, "but you should relax, and then we will talk." I asked him what the problem was. I didn't want to relax, thanks.

The problem was this: he was too busy to take me to the desert. *Right*, I said.

It would be fine, there was a cousin. His cousin knew the desert well, but the problem, the other problem, was that he didn't speak English. I bridled. I was tired from the flight. I came up with an English phrase, the phrase of an Englishman complaining to a call centre: "It's not good enough." I said it again. Hassan said he would go away and give the problem some thought. The solution, an hour later, was that he himself would take me to the desert, after all. I was relieved, but our relationship had been soured. I'd played the monoglot Englishman who knows his mind; he the supplicant Bedu. It was 1914.

For two hours, this afternoon, he and I had followed the tracks of Nigel's camel and the Land Cruiser that was accompanying him, which was driven by Hassan's son, Mohammed. When we had finally found them, Nigel was exhausted. Hassan had driven us both to this spot, ten minutes away, where we were to make camp, and then gone back to help Mohammed bring the camel. I imagined the words they would be exchanging about their English clients.

How long had they been? Twenty minutes? An hour? Nigel had regained his energy and did not seem at all concerned. My eyes scanned the horizon and I cocked an ear for engine-noise as his lips continued to move.

In *The Arabian Nights* is a story entitled "Ma'aruf the Cobbler." Pretending to wealth he does not possess, Ma'aruf is reported to the king by his frustrated creditors. The king's *wazir* (in Richard Burton's 1885 translation) sends Ma'aruf into exile, summoning a jinni, or demon, and commanding it to "take up yonder wretch and cast him down in the most desolate of desert lands, where he shall find nothing to eat nor drink, so he may die of hunger and perish miserably and none know of him." Snatching up the cobbler, the jinni tells him: "I go to cast thee down in the Desert Quarter"—and there, "in that horrible place," Ma'aruf is abandoned.

The thought occurred to me that, while the desert was a sort of heaven—look at it—to be cast down here terminally would be an affirmation of Virgil's idea that hell was a desert. "I'm not *worried*," Nigel said finally, peering out into the dazzling wastes, "but I'm beginning to wonder if they're having trouble with Soran." Soran was the camel.

A DAY EARLIER, Hassan and I had left Salalah, with its date plantations and lawns, for the Qara mountains. On a globe you can make out two unruly hoops of shaggy yellow-brown, almost unbroken but for the oceans, circling the earth thirty degrees north and south of the equator respectively. They are the deserts. Warm air rising above equatorial regions loses its moisture to condensation as it moves north and south, hence the intense rainfall associated with the wet tropics. These poleward-rolling scrolls of circulation are known as Hadley cells, after the English meteorologist (George) who discovered them. As the risen air travels north and south it dries, cools and returns to the surface. In the course of the planet's circling of the sun, it is these bands of dryness, close to the equator and unimpeded by cloud, that undergo the greatest heating. But desert formation is a local process too, and there are other kinds of desert. Along the western coasts of the continents, sea winds cool the air, reducing its capacity to hold moisture and preventing the formation of clouds, contributing to the creation of "coastal" deserts such as Chile's Atacama and southern Africa's Namib. This effect is amplified, in the Southern Hemisphere, by the influence of anti-clockwise ocean gyres, which carry cold water to the west coasts of the continents. Meanwhile winds arriving from the east have surrendered any moisture to the parched land. Moreover the sheer remoteness and size of many deserts—those of Australia and Central Asia, for example—mean that vapour from the sea simply can't reach them. So dryness is partly a factor of isolation. Topography also contributes to desert formation. The deserts of China—the Gobi and the Taklamakan—are bounded by mountains. In Oman fertile land exists in two thin strips: the arable corridor of Batinah, which runs northwest from Muscat; and in the south the Dhofar coastal plain, where Salalah lies. When air confronts a mountain range, such as the Jabl Qara, it cools as it climbs, forming rainclouds that sap its moisture. (In the Empty Quarter average annual precipitation is five millimetres.)

Progressively, as we followed the pass north, the limestone slab that forms the mountains assumed the shallow down-slope that would continue for a hundred kilometres to the edge of the Sands. The legacy of the monsoon—trees, grass, scrub, however sere—resolved into a sequence of pallid landscapes denuded of all but the wiriest black bushes and frankincense trees.

We entered the *nejd*, a rubbled karstland dissected by broad wadis that had not run for generations and scattered with cement-coloured bergs of limestone. Pink sand had been banked along the road's eastern verge by last night's winds. The *nejd* became the semi-arid "rocky desert," the *hamadah*. All along the roadside were discarded tyres. They would still be there in a thousand years. I saw two armchairs, set side by side, a hundred metres from the road and ten kilometres from the nearest turn-off. The alluvial boulders strewing the *hamadah* became rocks; the rocks became smaller black nodules of basalt, laid down in rows upon the paler grit as if by a harrow. The land had been progressively degraded, growing flatter and smoother as it became drier. Hanging a hundred metres up against the electric sky was a pale unmarked blimp.

Hassan was from a mountain tribe, he said. He was in his early fifties and had a neat black beard and a steady, strategising gaze of the kind I associate with both artists and military men. He was quick to judge any situation, and was sensitive to danger. In the boot of the Land Cruiser, I'd noticed, was a giant wooden club, but he carried no gun. He wore a white headcloth, and a white dishdasha, grease-fingered across its front. On his feet were perished black rubber sandals. In the late 1960s, during the Dhofar uprising against the Sultan of Oman, he had trained as a paramedic at an insurgents' school across the border, in what was then the People's Democratic Republic of Yemen. When all of his friends had been killed, as he put it, and the Soviets and Chinese had co-opted the rebellion, he accepted an amnesty offered by the new sultan (who had deposed the previous sultan, his father) and made his way to Salalah. And that was where he lived still. But the mountains, the plains and the desert remained his home, the home of his father, even if the Bedouin as a nomadic people had practically ceased to exist.

In the Sands he couldn't be lost. He became a different man there:

no-nonsense, a figure of authority. And as we put the coastal plain behind us and approached the desert, the unease between us lifted. I might have been a camel. He would lead me, I would follow.

His father, as it happened, had met Bertram Thomas in the late 1920s, when Thumrait—the town above which the blimp was bobbing—was nothing but a waterhole. "The Englishman is crazy," the Bedouin told one another: he had been seen walking in the mid-day heat, stopping every so often to build a small pile of rocks (he was surveying the site). Take him the corpse of a mouse, or a snake, or an eagle, and he'd pay in gold: "The Englishman is crazy." And it was not only animal remains he had an interest in.

Thumrait is the last town before the desert, a stopping-off place for HGVs and camel traders travelling to and from Qatar—at once abandoned-seeming and bustling. Everything carried a sifting of red dust. There was an air of impermanence and urgency. Cats crawled about under the cars, mewling. Unfinished buildings going to ruin stood beside a new Shell garage. The tall palms planted alongside the road appeared to be dead. Outside the al-Khayam Bakery, three pick-ups were lined up, and in the bed of each one, couched under netting, a silent black camel.

Thumrait is the base of the Royal Air Force of Oman and served as a U.S. logistics hub during the wars in Iraq and Afghanistan. The men at the bakery pointed to the blimp and asked Hassan what it was. Its mooring cable could be followed to the grounds of the American base on the town's outskirts, Hassan explained—a radar balloon, surveying Yemen to the west. (American drone strikes against Islamic militants in Yemen were already occurring. A few months later hundreds of Yemenis would be killed when the government in Sana'a was overthrown.)

The road between the town and the desert had been used by Yemeni militants, and as we drove we were twice stopped at roadblocks. The usual portly swaggering policeman, in blue camouflage, checked our papers while behind him his soldier colleague in green stood with his feet planted wide, cradling his rifle. Flanking each checkpoint, fore and aft, were low-slung sun shelters of camouflage netting, and gun-jeeps manned by watchful teenagers.

These last outposts of life were quickly left behind. The landscape flattened. The horizon was lined with low dark hills like spoil heaps. In an hour we reached the *serer*, plains swept free of everything but fine gristle-coloured gravel and occasional black camels in pairs. Placed upon the horizon, twenty kilometres away, were four broad silos with conical tops, perhaps twenty metres tall. "Chicken farm," said Hassan. Of course: highs of fifty-four degrees centigrade; wind speeds of 140 kilometres per hour; five millimetres of rain per year. But there it was, the A'Saffa Poultry Farm: "The third biggest chicken farm in the world!" It was a risky venture: during a heatwave in Oklahoma in 1980, a chicken farm's air conditioning failed, and within minutes half a million hens were dead.

Out of the heat-haze a smear of green resolved: fields of alfalfa, fed by the waterhole at Shisur. Stretching the width of each field, motorised irrigation booms mounted on trolleys travelled back and forth day and night. At the limits of their reach the green stopped dead. There were people alongside the road, Pakistani labourers bare-headed in the impossible heat, as if hitchhiking, but making no attempt to flag us down. They were employed to superintend the irrigators. It was a kind of intensive care. If the watering were to cease for a day, said Hassan, the crop would be ruined. He added something I did not understand at first: "Like African people use creams, to make their skin lighter. But they are still African." Then he said: "The desert stays always desert."

He veered off the road, it seemed arbitrarily, and followed a plait of tyre tracks. As if the green had been only imagined, a fine pale grit extended to the horizon in every direction. Everything else had been ground away. We were travelling at 100 kilometres per hour, but it might have been 60, or 120. The only way of assessing speed, other than checking the dashboard, was the G-force and the intensity of the rattling. There was only the flat plain outside: no trees flashing by, scarcely any rocks bigger than a thumbnail. A stage was being progressively cleared. We would thunder joltingly over an isolated hectare studded with pebbles like blackened eggs. Dust devils shimmied in the middle distance. You blinked and they'd vanished. In the heat-haze the horizon lifted like a page in a draught. For eighty kilometres just these gravel plains, more relentless in their aridity than even the Empty

Quarter's heart. At least in the Sands, for Bertram Thomas and his retinue, there had been occasional waterholes; here, for camel-days, there would be nothing, not so much as a frond of ailing saltbush, and no shelter for anything bigger than an invertebrate.

There had been a quiet sifting of the land as we'd dropped down from the mountains: solid to particulate, coarse to smooth, hard to soft; almost indiscernible.

What was this process of atomisation? It was the desert's forces doing their work. A boulder warmed will expand; cooling, it will contract. Repeated over a hundred thousand days and nights, the opposing pressures will begin to undo the rock's integrity. Tiny fractures will appear and widen; in high-altitude deserts, frost will enter these cracks and jemmy them apart; salt will seep into the rock as a solution and in crystallising expand the cracks still further (a process known as salt-jacking). The boulder thus divides and subdivides, spalling and flaking and crumbling, and with wind and water (such water as there is), the pieces will be dispersed. And so mountains become boulders, and boulders rocks, and rocks stones, then gravel, shingle, grit, sand—ultimately, dust. And the edge of the Rub' al-Khali, a sea of sand, when it came into view, was as unmistakable as the skyline of New York.

Rising from the plains, the dunes were visible from twenty kilometres away. After the hours of ash-like grey and pale cracked clay, it was as if we were nearing a new reality, one that seemed as gorgeous and auspicious, from afar, as the world of dreams. Here was a place for a checkpoint, I thought, a true border. I sensed Hassan's relief.

From the desert's edge, crescent dunes no bigger than whales encroached onto the plain like scouts sent ahead of a vast school clamouring to their rear. Hassan got out and crouched in the thin sand and released a minute's air from each tyre for traction.

WRITING ABOUT the Empty Quarter in 1888, Charles Doughty claimed he "never found any Arabian who had aught to tell, even by hearsay, of that dreadful country." He spent years travelling in the Arabian Peninsula but never reached so far as that dreadful country's edge. Richard Burton was considered "demented" by his Bedouin guides when he proposed entering the region (he decided against it). But in *Arabia Felix*, Thomas's "companions started shouting excitedly, '*ar raml! ar raml!*,' sweeping their canes as they did so along our right front, where in the far distance a sunlit yellow ribbon edged the skyline."

In between accounts of derring-do, Thomas takes an anthropological interest in his escorts—their foods and dialect, their rites of circumcision and marriage, their religious ablutions and sexual practices. A footnote on "the marital bed" he encodes in paternal Latin, but a few pages later he admits, unblushingly, to relieving a Bedouin tomb of its skeleton in order to smuggle the skull back to Britain for analysis. He is equipped with "head callipers to make and record skull measurements, for such measurements are vital to anthropologists."

When Hassan returned to the driver's seat after letting down the tyres, he unfurled and removed his headscarf and I saw that he was bald, his crown as glossy and planar as a club head. Why it came as a surprise I don't know.

We entered the dunes and almost instantly it was impossible to tell in which direction lay the plains we had just come across. To one lost in a maze, the outer passages are indistinguishable from the interior. I was reminded that one of the Arabic words for desert is a synonym of "labyrinth." For two hours Hassan drove deeper into the Sands, looking for his son Mohammed and the other Englishman, cresting one bank of dunes after another, following a trail that was invisible to me.

The dunes at the desert's edge were beach-size but kilometre by kilometre their stature grew. It was like nothing I had experienced save for being at sea. As if Hassan were piloting a skiff over choppy straits, our path up and down the dunes assumed a rhythm: a pass identified; a roar of acceleration; then the momentary sensation of equivocation on the wind-stropped crest, before the sudden plummet. I felt myself being made dumb first by the rhythm and then by the minimalism of the place. It went on: the nearby sand, the horizon—then just sky. It was the desert as pictured by a blind person.

After an hour we found Mohammed's Land Cruiser in the centre of a flat rink of gypsum. Soran the camel was couched nearby. And crouching in the shade of the vehicle were Mohammed and Nigel, the other Englishman, with whom we would be spending the next few days. Nigel was not what I'd expected—a man of my age or younger was what I'd expected. No tan, not especially tall. The first thing he said when we met, as if hailing a celebrity across a river, was his own name. There was a boyish intensity about him that was unusual but which might have been less conspicuous in a British setting.

It was hard to believe Mohammed was Hassan's son—hefty, buzzing Mohammed. Under the seat of his Land Cruiser he kept a ceremonial sword, which he would sometimes unsheathe and, with a glance to ensure you were watching, throw spearlike into a dune.

Hassan set the English down at the spot a few kilometres away where we were to camp, and then drove back to help Mohammed with Soran. It was then that I found myself face to face with Nigel, and learned about the things that had happened to him. When Hassan and Mohammed and Soran finally returned we made camp in the windbreak of a ring of low dunes.

So loved was Mohammed by Soran that the mere sound of his vehicle approaching would send the camel into groans of exaltation. As the day began to cool, I clambered barefoot to the summit of a tall dune nearby. It took twenty minutes. The sand under my soles was losing its warmth, as if life were abandoning it. Like a pond it was cool beneath the surface. I wanted to convince myself of our massive isolation. From there, maybe thirty metres up, the desert laid out before me was brinkless, its colours shifting by the second as the sun went down; but its vastness was not of the "sublime" kind that induces unease. The scale wasn't belittling, because one had no sense of one's own size in proportion to it.

My eyes followed a line of footprints progressing along the dune ridge—mine. For Hassan, Mohammed and Nigel, thirty metres below, the sun had already set, and the flicker of the fire they had made was visible against the darkened sand. The edge of night was reeled away.

Soran, once hobbled at the knees, was docile. Camels' night vision, Mohammed told me, is exceptional. "If your camel looks slowly left to right, it is a fox. If your camel stops chewing and stares into the darkness, something is wrong." Arabian camels come in five colours: white ("fawny cream"—Thomas), red ("gazelle colour"), black ("black-brown"), yellow ("between fawny cream and gazelle colour") and green ("dark wood-smoke"). Soran was a "yellow," with a dark bushy hackle along his spine, smaller than the all-black brutes loitering alongside the road from Thumrait. He wore a smile of beatific forbearance, and was the object of lavish tenderness on the part of Hassan and Mohammed—tenderness born of respect, even love. They would no more shout at or beat him than they would the sagest of grandfathers. When a campsite had been chosen, an empty plastic feedbag was filled with sand and Soran was slackly tethered to it. For hours, as we sat around the fire, he stepped his front feet from side to side, left foot to right, right foot to left. More than once in the night I would wake to that gentle sound, the sound of an old man sweeping his yard.

Nigel seemed concussed. He sat silently in his camp chair in the darkness a few metres from the fire. I went and spoke to him and saw that his face was still caked with sunblock. He looked up at me and I was dazzled by his headtorch. "Have you had a spiritual experience yet?" He was serious. I wondered if that was what he was waiting for. I held a hand over my eyes. "Not yet," I said. In retrospect I shouldn't have been so cynical.

THE MAIN QUALITY sought in a desert campsite, other than shade from the sun as it rises, is shelter from the wind. It's thought that most of the Rub' al-Khali's dunes accumulated some one million years ago, during the Late Quaternary period, when winds even stronger than today's winnowed sand from both the wadis of the peninsula's interior and the Arabian Gulf. The wind continues to be a potent presence: it shapes and reshapes the dunes, and, during the day, is as constant as the sun. The sun heats the morning sands, the warm air rises and must be replaced. Hence the wind ubiquitous in desert literature. Herodotus tells the story of a Libyan army sent into the desert to subdue the lord of the desert wind, only to vanish in its entirety, "into a red cloud of swirling sand." At a ruined fort in northern Syria, T. E. Lawrence and his Bedouin companions "drank with open mouths of the effortless, empty, eddyless wind of the desert." Bertram Thomas recounts the story of a party of the Mahra tribe who pursued a band of camel raiders into a part of the desert unknown to them, only for a wind to rise and obliterate the tracks they had been following. "Six months later one of my own party of Rashidis came upon the seven skeletons and the bones of their camels."

The desert is mobile, and wind its engine. It is the wind that shapes the dunes. To travel in the Empty Quarter is to see their forms—"species," as they are known—in their infinite permutations. The desert is formed chiefly of the *uruq* variety (from the Arabic "vein"), towering parallel ridges sometimes tens of kilometres long; and of crescent-shaped barchans (from the Arabic "horn"), whose tips point in the direction of the prevailing wind. But few deserts, even the great ergs or "sand seas" of the Sahara, are formed of sand alone. In the southern marches you experience not a pure dune-land, an endless beach, but rather a complex of arenas. The sand is quartz; anything softer will be ground to dust and blown away. Each surface grain accumulates a rind of ferric oxide, and it is this that accounts for the Arabian dunes' characteristic redness. Thomas suggests that "Dhofar" means "Red Country." The redness was most conspicuous in hollows, and where the sand was finer; but dig beneath the surface and the colour changed to a cool grey-green.

The dunes are separated by *shuquq*, "interdune corridors"—elongated plains of brown gravel and white gypsum; while the dunes are barriers exhausting to man, camel and vehicle alike, these flat plains are the desert's highways. From their edges archaeologists have recovered the bones of water buffalo, the shells of freshwater molluscs and the teeth of hippopotami. For, some twenty-five thousand years ago, during a cold phase in the global climate, these plains were lakes. Arabia, like the Sahara, became green. Then, as the planet warmed once more, the water evaporated and the vegetation died. The desert returned. Today, even from a small distance, the plains can resemble lakes—it's possible to walk along their shores or between islands of crusty marl deposited by the ancient waters. These honeycombed accretions, sometimes a metre or more tall, are home to desert foxes, and twice I caught a distant glimpse of one—black against the gypsum—ducking into its cave.

To travel here, then, is to move from one lakebed to another, over passes in the intervening dunes. Even for the desert traveller who is not dying of thirst, it is easy to believe, having laboured across the partitions of sand, that what you are beholding as the next plain comes into view, sometimes rippled or blue-tinged and shimmering with heat-haze, is a tremendous sheet of water. Not mirage, not illusion, merely resemblance. At such times the aridity of the desert occurs to you with its full force.

IT WAS WHERE the sand melded into a gypsum plain that two ravens came to inspect me, as I was walking alone the following morning, soon after dawn. They monopolised the attention, as did any living or moving thing. They were a delight—their darkness refreshed the numbed eye. Their vibrancy and their familiarity. Where had they come from? I looked up and they were there, circling against the blue, and only when they were near did they begin to emit their noise, a single bark traded every thirty seconds, thrown casually one to the other. There was a mutual curiosity, I was glad of their coming; but their curiosity wasn't idle.

In explorers' accounts, the raven always appears as one of a pair. Harry St. John Philby, who knew these sands better than any other foreigner, describes every raven he meets—those that visit his camp or which he and his Bedouin party come upon. Finding one wounded at an oasis, he keeps it as a mascot, christening it Suwaiyid, the diminutive form of the Arabic *suwid*, "black." When one of his retinue shoots a hen raven at her nest, "the cock with hoarse cries of anger and distress intervened bravely to protect his wounded mate." Ravens also punctuated Bertram Thomas's crossing a year earlier: "I shot an interesting example with a neck ringed with white feathers. A badu asked for the heart of another pure black specimen which he proposed to eat whole because of some virtue it possessed."

It was hard to think of the ravens as ill omens. I stopped and tipped my face up towards them, and held my breath. The thrash of their pinions was audible—I could almost feel it—as they swung overhead, once, twice, before settling side by side twenty metres away, pecking desultorily at the sand. They stood wide-legged and haunchy, watch-

ing me, showing their gloss to the sun. Each cast a shadow as black as
itself.

It hadn't been my intention to follow in Thomas's "footprints," but
here I was, walking between Ramlat Fasad and Ramlat Mitan, as he
had done: "high, red dune country"; "parallel white ridges with intervening red valleys"; "flat or gently undulating white sands with transverse red hills." The crusty gypsum underfoot had yet to absorb the
sun's warmth. Before the heating ground caused the winds to rise, the
sky was already an intense blue. The horizon dunes were a clean grey-
mauve, the dunes a hundred metres away gaining colour as the sun
rose.

I walked until it was too hot. Every few kilometres I would find
Hassan parked high on a dune-side overlooking my approach, dozing
with his bare feet on the dashboard. I might get lost but he wouldn't
lose me. In the sand under his window, scraps of orange peel would
be scattered; nearby, the double dents where he had knelt to pray. We
would sit and talk for a few minutes, I would drink, and then he would
drive on and I would follow his tracks for another few kilometres.

The desert was not only vast: there was intimacy in its involutions
and granularity—the cool mouth of a tunnel dug by a mouse; the arc
scribed by a windblown strand of vegetation; the campfire's dome of
light. Mohammed and Nigel and Soran were camping elsewhere that
night. In the light of his headtorch, Hassan swept a smooth plaque in
the sand beside our own fire with the edge of his hand, picked a bone-
white twig from the embers, and began to draw.

With darkness the wind drops. In the morning all about the
camp are the tracks of every creature that passed by while you were
sleeping—foxes, hares, mice, scorpions. "The sands," wrote Thomas,
"are a public diary ... No bird may alight, no wild beast or insect pass
but needs must leave its history."

Occasionally, Hassan would stop and place the twig upright in the
sand, while with the tip or edge of a finger he swiped out an unsatis-
factory line, or extended the canvas to accommodate the expanding
picture.

Animal after animal he drew: the hyena, the fox, the oryx, the
hare, the leopard. Mouse, cat, man, camel. The scale and the medium

disallowed fine detail. A frisson passed between us when his quick marks resolved into recognisable form. The drawings of one who knew his subject from life.

Always they were in movement, the active animals of the mountains and the gravel flats, the plains and the dunes. He might take five, perhaps eight minutes to perfect the few necessary strokes: the hyena's arched back must be just so; the angle of its head; its glutted smirk. The angle of the camel's long neck, the extrusion of its lower lip, the length of its tail proportionate to its hind legs. If the sweep of the oryx's horns did not match what Hassan knew to be right, a thumb would be applied and the sand refreshed, the line redrawn. And there, suddenly, would be the complete and living animal.

I was to write its name in the sand. "Camel," say. Hassan copied it alongside and inscribed its Arabic counterpart below, جمل, with the same grace of hand that characterised his drawing. I would attempt to copy the Arabic, the diacritical dot subsumed as soon as it was poked. We would share a moment's appreciation of the drawing and the three iterations of the subject's name, and then, with a flourish, the sand was refreshed once more, and the twig was moving in Hassan's hand, and a new creature was lured into being.

On his mobile phone, a bright window in the windless night, he played me a film of forty minutes, which Mohammed had downloaded for him. It was composed of archive footage from the late sixties showing the build-up to the rebellion: women milking goats; boys stooped in fields with rifles strapped to their backs; lines of troops happily brandishing AK-47s; a British-made Strikemaster jet sweeping low above a distant horizon, then a plume of blast-smoke rising from behind a limestone outcrop. And playing over the footage—a dreadful sound, really, in the desert quiet—a scratchy recording of the rebel marching song.

AS *WAZIR* IN THE late 1920s, Bertram Thomas observed that the Sultan of Oman, Said bin Taimour, "treated Dhofar as a royal domain." When the rebellion started forty years later, this mountainous region, some one thousand kilometres from the sultan's palace at Muscat, remained a dependency of Oman. I had been only vaguely aware of the Dhofar Uprising and Britain's role in it before coming to Oman. It began as a popular rebellion among the tribes of the mountains and desert against bin Taimour. The elderly sultan's conservatism had confined Oman to an antique destitution, while the people—without hospitals, without schools—watched the neighbouring Gulf states prosper on growing oil revenues. The insurgency began in 1964, with a crossing of the Empty Quarter from Saudi Arabia by the leader of the Dhofar Liberation Front, Mussalim bin Nafl, and thirty followers. In a declaration of June 1965, the movement associated the sultan with the "hordes of the British imperialist occupation." The DLF's first act was largely symbolic: a machine-gun attack on an oil-company party surveying the Dhofar desert. In 1967, Britain's chaotic withdrawal from its colony of Aden, in today's southern Yemen, coupled with the Arab–Israeli Six-Day War led to a surge in Arab nationalism in southern Arabia. The influence of the new People's Democratic Republic of South Yemen, Dhofar's western neighbour, and its Soviet and Chinese sponsors, led to a schism within the remaining ranks of the DLF, which prompted the renaming of the movement as the People's Front for the Liberation of the Occupied Persian Gulf. Its fighters were sent to China and Iraq to train in guerrilla warfare. In those days, Hassan told me, "every Omani wanted a gun. An AK-47. If he joined the Communists he got a gun. If he joined the army he got a gun. He wanted a gun. That was his ideology." He'd treated those men as a paramedic.

Oil production in Oman had increased from 88 million barrels in 1967 to some 120 million barrels two years later. The British were not unaware of these figures. When, in 1970, the sultan granted oil-exploration rights in Dhofar to a U.S. firm, his overthrow became inevitable. He was by then virtually impotent, in any case, confined day and night to his palace in Salalah. In 1971 a bloodless coup saw the twenty-nine-year-old Qaboos bin Said depose his father. "My first act," Qaboos promised his people, "will be the immediate abolition of all the unnecessary restrictions on your lives and activities."

He was a moderniser, educated in England, first at Eton and then at the army officer training school at Sandhurst. Former rebels like Hassan were offered amnesty, a resettlement grant. The sultan's armed forces were enlarged. The rebellion became increasingly brutal: oil installations were attacked, oil-company drivers machine-gunned, the road to Thumrait mined and the RAF base in Salalah shelled. Tribal leaders who refused to give the rebels succour or safe haven were thrown off cliffs and "counterrevolutionaries" summarily executed. It was not until 1975, as Britain began to appreciate the strategic threat posed by communism in the region, that British officers and mercenaries were dispatched to Dhofar. The uprising was finally extinguished in December 1975, its surviving fighters "rehabilitated" or absorbed back into the desert. Qaboos the moderniser remains a popular figure among today's taxi drivers and camel farmers, a friend of the Duke of Edinburgh and beyond public reproach. From the wall of every coffeehouse, restaurant and guesthouse in Salalah he gazes down with formidable benevolence. "We could not have asked for a better sultan," said Hassan.

The Americans found oil in Dhofar. Twenty-nine wells were sunk. But the output quickly declined and the remaining oil in any case proved too heavy for commercial exploitation. Fifty million dollars having been spent, the Americans packed up. But prospectors, from Oman and elsewhere, continue to survey the deserts of Dhofar, and the evidence of their efforts persists.

In the firelight I noticed that Hassan's beard was hemmed with fine white where it met his cheeks and neck, as if its pigment were migrating from the edges. I thought of Bertram Thomas's raven, its neck ringed with white feathers. We drank sugary ginger tea in paper cups, softened with cardamom milk from a tin. Dates were prised from a glistening mass. Hassan resumed his drawing. Again and again, between animals, there was the woman. When she first appeared he laughed, as if she had come unbidden; we both laughed. But then, as the face emerged, he became quiet with concentration. The point of the twig moving across the sand was suddenly the desert's centre. The same woman each time; she was wide-mouthed, round-eyed, heavy-browed, cinch-waisted and curvy. His strokes slowed. I did not write the word underneath. When she was finished, we would both admire her for a moment, then a swipe of the hand refreshed the drawing plane. But after a few more animals had been drawn, hedgehog, raven, there she was again, rematerialising line by line. Finally the twig was put aside, he moved from sitting cross-legged to propping himself on one elbow, and we watched the fire. When I dropped a date stone in the embers, he silently reached into the flames, extracted it and flung it into the darkness behind us. No offer of life was to be wasted.

I HAD BEEN in the Sands for two days. We were to meet Nigel and Mohammed, with Soran, at the waterhole at Burkhana, fifty kilometres from the Saudi border. It wasn't far from our camp. After an hour, as the morning marshalled its warmth, I spotted something lying on the gravel five hundred metres away. It was a triangular road-sign on a striped post, felled by the wind: an arrow veering left. Its presence here, fifty kilometres from so much as a camel farm, had the quality of a prank. It had been erected thirty years ago by the oil prospectors who had graded the track across the plain. The triangle's border, once red, had turned yellow. And yet it had remained exposed, as if it had been laid down yesterday. Things on the gravel flats do not accumulate the sand that lies heaped in inordinate masses all around. The sand is blown from the surface, while the heavier gravel and anything discarded upon it remain—rocks, branches, shredded tyres, drinks cans and water bottles and oil flagons. Such was the permanence these articles seemed to possess that to pick one up—a rare length of dead wood to use as a walking stick, say, or a red stone shaped by the wind—felt like an almost profane intervention, an act of vandalism. A few weeks later, at home in my empty London flat, I would pour a pure white sharded grit from my trouser pocket, all that remained of a gazelle's rib, as if, removed from the desert, like some memento from a dream, it could not exist.

I followed the direction indicated by the sign, and, after an hour, stopped and sat cross-legged on the gravel, and peeled an orange. The pungency of its aroma was enough to make me woozy. The previous evening, while I was exploring the dunes around our camp, I became aware of a noise slowly growing louder. Where there had been quiet, a dead bush, thrashed by a jet of wind that had no influence beyond the shrub itself, was letting out a soughing that was overwhelming. This

was not Lawrence's "effortless, empty, eddyless wind." The shrub—a
saltbush gone black years ago—was like something ensnared; in its
fury it had thrown dark splinters of itself for metres downwind.

Even when the wind dropped, you had to work to experience the
silence—had to shut your *self* up, for a start: stop fidgeting, stop the
gulping, the ceaseless tonguing and lipping, the clicking of your jaw,
the blinking of your jellied eyes, the burbling of the nostrils and the
boiling of the guts. Stop breathing. It was easier at night, when the wind
had stilled. I would wake to a full moon so bright it dazzled the stars,
and as I held my breath in my sleeping bag the "silence" was a sharp
hum, and accompanying it, much lower, there was a sound of liquid in
circulation, as of water moving through a pipe deep underground.

Perhaps two kilometres off, a large grey vehicle was approaching.
I got to my feet and watched it, but it seemed to get no closer. It was
a quality of these plains that their selfsameness obscured the passing
of time: a perished tyre thirty metres away might take half an hour to
reach. Earlier I had picked a black rock from the ground and thrown
it as far as I could, and within what seemed like just a few steps, I was
stooping to pick it up once more. "Hour after hour," Thesiger wrote,
"day after day, we moved forward and nothing changed; the desert met
the empty sky always the same distance ahead of us. Time and space
were one."

I resumed walking, and within ten minutes was close enough to
hear that the vehicle was silent, nor had it moved for years. A water
tanker, abandoned while making its way from the waterhole at Burkhana, it had been scavenged of its rear wheels and lay canted in the
middle of the track, its paint peeling and its consignment long siphoned
off or evaporated. Later Hassan would tell me it had been there since
the oilmen came thirty years ago. Its cab, to look at it, might have
been deserted yesterday, apart from the smashed-out windscreen. I
had imagined myself to be many kilometres from the tourist trails, but
the paintwork was strewn with the graffiti of passers-by, from Swe-
den and Germany and Qatar. "We love Oman," a visitor from Switzer-
land had written. Had they carried their marker into the desert on the
off-chance?

I climbed into the cab and sat in the driver's seat, and looked through the glassless windscreen, back down the track that led, fifty kilometres away, to the village of Fasad. The desert's stillness leaves you dazed, and it is hard to find a better word for it: at dusk, from the top of a dune, *stillness*. And yet it quickly becomes apparent that, just as the desert is not silent, it is far from being still. As a shaping force, the wind has a quality that water lacks: the ability to flow uphill. From the pinnacle of a dune a skein of spindrift is spun into the sky; along a dune-brink, a hundred tiny cyclones shimmy in line; a sheet of sand scuds over a ridge like a spool of paper rushing through a press.

The desert is refashioning itself. Nod off in an exposed place and you will wake to find you have been partnered by a buttress of sand, laid down snug beside you. The smallest twig will accumulate a hump in its lee. It is how even the mega-dunes began. In any torch-beam, even on the quietest night, airborne dust is visible. Subtly the desert is in motion.

A COUPLE OF KILOMETRES across the plain, under a dune thirty metres tall, I made out a jerry-built sun shelter. It had been nailed together from timber stanchions and roofed with plywood. The water-hole, Burkhana. The few patches of green seemed like the utmost abundance. Tethered to Mohammed's four-wheel-drive, I could see Soran nosing a bag of feed. I spotted Mohammed and Hassan lying on a rug under the shelter, eating. All but two of the roofing boards had been torn off by winds and lay scattered hundreds of metres across the plain. Then I saw a figure, walking bandily up and down in the sun, some distance from the shelter. Where had his Sahara cap gone? Seeing me, Nigel raised his hand and roared. He was elated, too excited to rest. As I closed in, there was the smell of sulphur.

Bertram Thomas was disappointed to find that the "great brackishness" of the waterholes was "not disguised by desiccated soup." Burkhana didn't exist when he came this way in December 1930. Thirty years ago, a new foray of oilmen had arrived with their rigs, driven in convoy two hundred kilometres from Salalah, directed by those absurd signposts. Four kilometres down, they'd hit a pressurised reserve—not the heavy crude that had been struck in the 1970s, but warm sulphurous water, undrinkable by humans. Today, on the desert surface, were three artesian gaskets and an open concrete tank ten metres square, continually overbrimming onto a border of marshy turf. There is no water so tainted, Hassan told me, that a thirsty camel will not drink it, and Soran had already sated himself. There were birds here, a desert wheatear and a southern grey shrike, but like most desert "oases," the place had been made a tip. It was impossible to tell the age of much of what had been dumped—bottles and oil cans, lengths of metal piping and boles of cement, plastic feedbags, cleated loops of tyre-rubber, and another of the oilmen's felled signposts. Nothing was allowed to corrode in the desert dryness. This was a factor of its timelessness. The shelter might have been put up last year by the local camel farmers, or thirty years back by the oilmen. The camel droppings might be last night's or last summer's. The gaskets, four feet of red steel bearded with mineral encrustations, were ringed by chainlink fencing. Watered by the dripping gaskets and protected from grazing camels, the plants contained within these cages thrived.

We sat in the shade and ate last night's camel stew reheated on a gas stove. Nigel's cheeks and nose were livid. I was worried about him. He seemed exhausted. The man was sixty-five and today he had ridden twenty-five kilometres. He was drinking quickly, one bottle of water after another. He stood up and removed his camera from its case and took a dozen quick photographs of the dunes. Then he sat down. He was a natural camel jockey, Mohammed said, standing over him and clapping his shoulder. Nigel wouldn't glory in the praise, but he had realised a childhood ambition. He had reason to be overjoyed, it seemed to me. It was possible to survive the hardships experienced by Lawrence and Thesiger; he'd earned some kinship with them.

His relief on this his last day in the desert seemed to allow some pent-up emotion to be eased out, and again he talked—as I sensed he'd wanted to talk since I had first met him. In the shade as we ate he spoke about his dismissal from the boys' school, the headmaster who had been "more of a politician than an educator" (that phrase again), and the resentment he'd felt, before his redundancy, at being forced to admit girls into his classes—his belief that the sexes should not be mixed in secondary education. As he continued, he grew angry.

Hassan got to his feet. He was looking across the plain, where dust was rising—a vehicle, careening towards us at perhaps eighty kilometres per hour. He spoke to Mohammed quickly, and for a minute we watched the truck until it skidded to a stop beside Soran, the dust settling in its wake.

In the back were a black plastic water tank and plastic bags of feed and a rope net. Two men got out, slamming the doors. They looked tired and hungry. They were camel farmers and had been driving for two days, looking for fifteen camels that had gone astray. We'd seen nothing. Hassan and Mohammed spoke to them, and the two men sat together with Mohammed on a piece of roofing board that lay on the ground some distance from the shelter. Hassan took food to them, and he and Mohammed stayed with them while they ate. Nigel, after a moment's pause, continued; the distraction hadn't soothed him.

It was not, as I'd first thought, a mere re-enactment of the frustration he must have expressed to his wife and colleagues at the time, but a reigniting of it. He was yelling. I was holding a half-eaten flatbread in my hand. He was like a cyclist who has lost control on a steep, potholed slope. "Of *course* it's a bloody stupid idea! Of course! What did they expect? The boys were fine. The *boys* you knew where you were with. It was the bloody girls. All that ... *emotional baggage*."

The camel farmers and Hassan and Mohammed had stopped eating and were watching us, these red-faced tourists furiously arguing in their metre-square of shade. There was no way to quieten him. When I got up and walked off for a piss, Nigel watched for a moment, then yelled after me, "It's a mess! The system! Christ!"

IN THE CAMBRIDGE archives was a series of telegrams received by Bertram Thomas in Bahrain, where he had stayed immediately after his crossing of the Rub' al-Khali in March 1932. "The King has heard with much interest of your great achievement and offers you his hearty congratulations," wrote George V's private secretary. From Thomas's mentor, David Hogarth, in Egypt: "Congratulations journey." From his friends Mr. and Mrs. How in Edinburgh: "It takes a remarkable fine man to do that." From the literary agent Curtis Brown: "Have firm offer English language book rights story your journey." From Mecca: "Heartiest congrats Philby."

In a letter to his wife, Dora, however, Harry St. John Philby had no reason to rise to diplomacy (it didn't come naturally to him): "Damn and blast Thomas ... I have sworn a great oath not to go home until I have crossed the R. K. twice! and left nothing for future travellers." Then he shut himself in his room for a week.

It was in 1928, Philby claimed, that "the great peace of Islam slowly and surely descended upon me." In that year he wrote to the king, Ibn Saud, for permission to convert. According to his friend Hope Gill, "he made no pretence whatsoever that his conversion was spiritual," but as his biographer Elizabeth Monroe put it, "becoming a Muslim seemed to him the only way of accomplishing the exploit of his dreams." Finally Ibn Saud granted Philby permission to embark. He left the royal palace at Riyadh, reaching the oasis of Hufuf, north of the Empty Quarter, on Christmas Day 1931, some ten months after Thomas had completed his crossing. Nevertheless, for Philby, "the great adventure had begun," and he and his Bedouin guides set off south, into the Empty Quarter, on 7 January 1932.

At Naifa, in the heart of the Sands, Philby's guides rebelled. Their camels were collapsing; there was no guarantee of water to the south. Already they had had to slaughter the newborn calf of one of their camels for food. They would go no further. "The Arab," he reflected bitterly, "clings frantically, desperately to life, however miserable ... I could not, would not, yield." On 5 March, three months after setting out from Hufuf, he and his remaining guides moved west, finally arriving at Sulayil, on the Empty Quarter's western border, nine days later, where they were able to recover sufficiently to make the onward journey to Mecca. "I think," Philby wrote to his wife in England, having completed his pilgrimage, "I have done with desert exploration for good."

A year before his own journey, Bertram Thomas had told the British political agent in Kuwait that he had "every intention of being the first man to cross the Empty Quarter and to live the rest of my life on the proceeds." Following his success he was indeed feted by the British press, and he returned to Britain a hero. He was awarded the Founder's

Medal of the Royal Geographical Society and a CBE; he wrote articles
and lectured in America. *The Times* announced that he had "achieved
one of the greatest geographical exploits of modern times."

And yet, while Philby's and Thesiger's crossings ensured their
lasting fame, Thomas seems to have allowed himself to sink into
obscurity. Today, the first Westerner to cross Richard Burton's "opprobrium to adventure"—a feat compared at the time to those of Scott
and Amundsen—is virtually unknown. In a photo of 1932, captioned
"My Party," the central figure is monkish in Bedouin dress, white and
pale grey against his companions' darker garb and darker faces. He
clasps the crook of his camel stick with both hands, and squints out at
the camera through wire-framed spectacles. A tall abbot or housemas-
ter. His face betrays neither relief nor satisfaction, unlike those of his
retinue. Having arrived at Doha, his account concludes simply: "The
Rub' al-Khali had been crossed."

THAT NIGHT, Nigel was in pain, his inner thighs bruised from the
hours of riding; but he was genial and solicitous, and from time to
time he would get up from his camp chair to speak tenderly to Soran,
to stroke his muzzle and feed him flatbreads. It was as if his earlier
outburst, in the dazzle of the afternoon, had not happened. My skin

smelled slightly of eggs from the sulphurous water at Burkhana (I'd had a dip in the overflow tank). I watched Soran as he stared out across the darkened plain. If your camel stops chewing and stares into the darkness, something is wrong.

"What is wanted is a new master species," wrote Lawrence: "birth-control for us, to end the human race in fifty years—and then a clear field for some *cleaner* mammal" (his emphasis). This was the Lawrence, who, in the Sinai, found his body "too coarse to feel the utmost of our sorrows," and sought "abnegation, renunciation, self-restraint." Thesiger admits in his memoirs that sex had been of "no consequence" to him: "the celibacy of desert life left me untroubled. Marriage would certainly have been a crippling handicap."

True, it *is* partly a matter of old-fashioned, foggy Protestant repression, of a peculiarly English brand. The other desert Lawrence, D. H., reflecting on his transformative time in New Mexico, remembered his native Britain as "an island no bigger than a back garden." For those sweating, leaking, reeking, dreaming travellers in the hyper-arid Middle East, the desert promised *asylum*—both from garden England and from their own body and its cursed fecundity and importuning, its *un*cleanness—at the same time as it consoled those who were denied a true sense of feeling-at-home because of the simple variety of their desires. I remembered that nudge-nudging question from the audience at the Royal Geographical Society, about Thesiger's "shall we say 'unorthodox' lifestyle."

No wonder they preferred it here. Better to be straddling a camel, miles from the nearest waterhole, than hemmed in by men made from beeswax and snuff.

The devil's first attempts to seduce St. Antony from his course in the Egyptian desert having failed, he deployed instead "the weapons which he knows every man carries about him in his own flesh; for here he mostly lies in ambush against the souls of the young." Appearing first as a woman, "the devil threw *filthy thoughts* into his mind" (Athanasius's emphasis).

Who was the woman Hassan had sketched in the sand? You might travel to escape the self, but in the desert of all places, where there is little else, you are thrown back upon your mind and your body with

intensified force. Quietness offers no liberation, after all: there had
been midnights when I swear my libido—whatever it consists of—was
audible (somewhere between a stiff door and a backed-up drain). Nope,
the body was there; the body was there more than ever, and with it all
its claims.

BEFORE DAWN I was woken by Soran whimpering; he was saying good morning to Mohammed, who was reviving the banked fire.
Crouched nearby, Hassan was using the tip of his pocket knife to bore
a hole in a water bottle's lid. I had seen him do this before: it allowed a
jet to be squeezed out for ablutions. He walked away behind a nearby
dune, returning a few minutes later. Then he handed the bottle to
Mohammed, who went behind another dune. Finally, standing some
distance away so as not to wake their guests, father and son performed
the morning prayer together.

The determinists tell us "le désert est monothéiste" (Ernest
Renan); that the inescapable consequence of peoples existing in a
realm deprived of all but trackless ground and cloudless sky is a theology matchingly monolithic and unforgiving. Mohammed was a dry-
land prophet, just as Christ and Moses were.

John Steinbeck, travelling in the American West, noted that the
"great concept of oneness and majestic order seems always to be born
in the desert." Bertram Thomas's mentor David Hogarth reflected
that "the Arab owes in part at least to singular climatic conditions his
strong and simple intelligence which has formulated again and again a
conception of God simple and strong enough to convince alien myri-
ads of mankind." The Japanese geographer Tetsuro Watsuji—whose
language, he tells us, has no indigenous word for *desert*, there being no
conception in Japan of an earthly realm of death—is of the view that
it produces two main characteristics: submission and aggression. "The
spiritual characteristics of the tribe of Shem, its thoughts, its religion,
its polity and the like can all be interpreted in terms of desert living
conditions. This life pattern is that of struggle."

The theologian William Harman Norton, in an essay on "The
Influence of the Desert on Early Islam" (1924), tells us that "the empty

environment offers little food for reasoned thought. Surcharged with emotion, the Semite of the arid lands has turned easily to meditation and contemplation of the supernatural." He goes on to explicate Renan's position: "As the rich scenic profusion of India and Greece led the Aryan to think of gods as many, so the barren simplicity, the endless monotony, the sterile uniformity of the desert, led the Semite to think of God as one."

I could barely make out the words, only Hassan's repeated *Allahu Akbar*, but as they prostrated themselves to the radiant sky, the scene seemed wholly proper to the place, as if it—the desert itself—were the subject of their veneration.

LATER, ONCE THE SUN was risen, the ravens reappeared. Their materialising made me aware they had lives lived out of our sight: they'd have been doing something else when they had been prompted to attend our camp. Had they seen the smoke from our breakfast fire? What had they been doing? What would they do when we were gone? I watched them through Mohammed's binoculars and remembered the ravens described by Thesiger, Philby and Thomas. Thesiger's guide, bin Kabina, seeing a solitary individual, shouts "Raven, seek thy brother!" and explains to the Englishman that "a single raven is unlucky, a bearer of ill tidings." To Mohammed it was a matter of delighted awe that they mated for life. The birds were a reminder that the desert was an ecosystem; that lives in their entirety were eked out within its bounds. It was not just a mausoleum or a museum.

Even as we crossed from the dunes back to the plains and the road to Salalah, I wished we were going the other way, north: deeper, deeper into the Empty Quarter. A person who has visited the desert once, Thesiger wrote, "will have within him the yearning to return." Yet it was impossible to think of him and his predecessors and the brutalities they embraced and not identify in them some grating perversity. Abnegation, renunciation, self-restraint. What I'd come to feel for Thomas and Philby and Thesiger was something like awe, but it couldn't be called sympathy. To seek to prove yourself against this place, forsake the palms and papaya of the coastal plain, seemed like a betrayal of a glorious endowment. It is easy to mistake flight for quest, yes. For all the desert's dreamlike beauty, to travel here, as they had, for months and almost blindly, was not just to pitch yourself into oblivion; it was to grind away at yourself until nothing was left. It was to aspire to the condition of sand.

2

FIELD OF THUNDER

The Great Victoria Desert, Australia

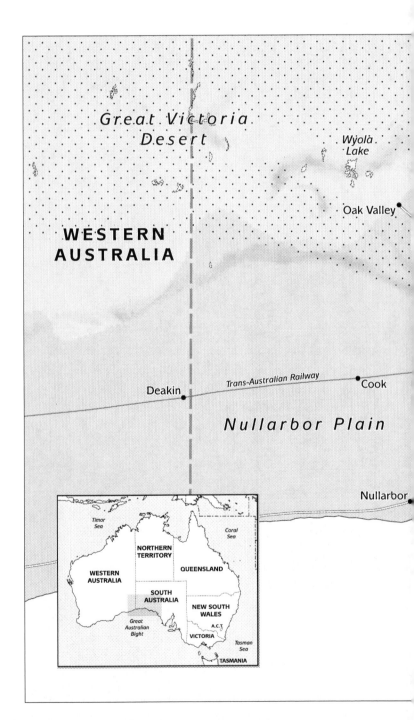

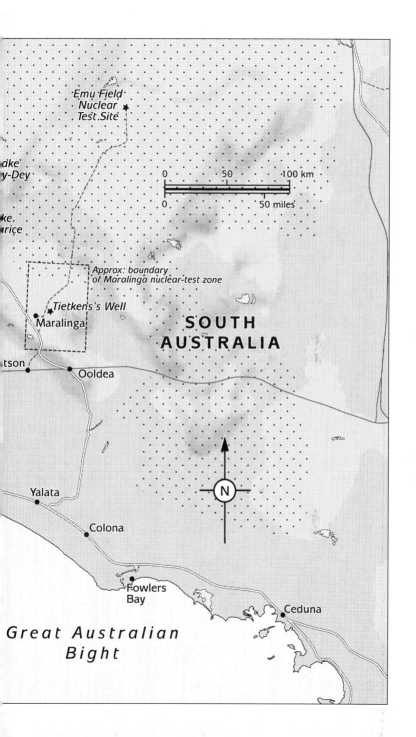

Emu Field
Nuclear
Test Site

ake
y-Dey

ke.
rice

0   50   100 km

0   50 miles

Approx: boundary
of Maralinga nuclear-test zone

Tietkens's Well

Maralinga

SOUTH
AUSTRALIA

tson

Ooldea

N

Yalata

Colona

Fowlers
Bay

Ceduna

Great Australian
Bight

In the early fifth century, the founding father of European monasticism, John Cassian, who had lived for years in Egypt's Wadi Natrun, described the condition known as *accidie*, which, he said, "we may describe as tedium or perturbation of heart. It is akin to dejection, and especially felt by solitaries, a persistent and obnoxious enemy of those who dwell in the desert."

In the months after returning from Oman I sank into a mild depression. I liked the word *accidie*, with its suggestion of tartness, corrosion and dissolution. I could not pinpoint its cause. It was like some virus against which I lacked native immunity. Weirder and more worrying, I developed a condition that began as tinnitus, and evolved, so it seemed to me, into partial deafness, sometimes more prominent in the left ear, sometimes the right. But when I went first to my GP, then to a specialist, even the most sensitive tests showed that there was nothing whatever wrong with my hearing. As I did not think of myself as a hypochondriac, I wondered if it wasn't some reaction to the giant noiselessness of the desert.

I found I didn't want to be in London. In the naked flat, with its scent and its photos. It was not only a case of Thesiger's "yearning to return" or the desert's appeal to loneliness. I'd been thinking about a desert question, which is also a seafarer's question: Without witnesses, how do you conduct yourself? In the secrecy of any imagination, to what extremes, what Poles of Inaccessibility, might the mind wander? I'd found I was drawn to the lawlessness of the desert; not only the way norms might be suspended but how, in the absence of regulation or judgement, the word *good* itself was loosed from meaning. Liberty isn't only for the virtuous. It was in this acidic spirit of enquiry that I bought a flight to Australia.

IN THE DESERTS of Nevada, Kazakhstan and China, in India's Thar and the French Sahara, hundreds of nuclear bombs have been tested, above ground and below, since the first was detonated in 1945, at a site codenamed Trinity in the Jornada del Muerto Desert of New Mexico. Shortly before that event, a storm broke, prompting scores of desert toads to emerge from their holes and fill the air with their song.

When the British government decided to develop its own "capability" in 1947 it was natural that the planners should look to America for a proving ground. In 1946, however, less than a year after the Trinity test and the subsequent bombings of Hiroshima and Nagasaki, the U.S. Congress passed the McMahon Act, which outlawed the sharing of nuclear intelligence even with America's friends. William Penney, the head of the British bomb project, had favoured the testing facilities in Nevada or the Pacific, but now access not just to America's expertise but to its expanses was blocked. There was of course nowhere in Britain appropriate for nuclear testing. Indeed few places in the world were both environmentally suited—flat, vast, unpopulated, isolated, secure, dry—and amenable to British influence. Penney made a reconnoitring flight to Canada but came to realise that, barring a change in American policy, only one place was really satisfactory. "If the Australians are not willing to let us do trials in Australia," he concluded, "I do not know where we shall go."

He needn't have worried. On 3 October 1952 Britain exploded a nuclear bomb aboard a warship, the *Plym*, close to the Monte Bello Islands off Australia's north-west coast. Robert Menzies, Australia's prime minister, sanctioned the tests without consulting his cabinet, let alone the Australian people, and assured Churchill in 1953 that "Great Britain will no more need to worry about Australian co-operation in the future than she has in the past." The following year two land tests were carried out at a place named Emu Field in the Great Victoria Desert, some four hundred kilometres north of Australia's southern coast. Between September 1956 and October 1957 seven more nuclear devices were exploded south of the first two, at a site given the name Maralinga.

After the Emu Field tests, Menzies's minister of supply, Howard Beale, told the Australian people: "The whole project is a striking example of the inter-Commonwealth co-operation on the grand scale. England has the bomb and the know-how; we have the open spaces, much technical skill and great willingness to help the motherland. Between us we shall help to build the free world and make historic advances in harnessing the forces of nature."

I SPENT TEN DAYS in Adelaide, mostly in the library of the Royal Geographical Society of South Australia, acclimatising and planning my journey to the desert. After a few days I started to experience the city's orderliness as stifling, and took to hiking out to the hills and the sea, between bouts of reading. Walking on Mount Lofty one morning, I met Céline, a Frenchwoman from Perpignan, who gave me a lift back down to the city. She had a dancer's lightness of bearing and when she smiled (hardly ever) she displayed a sharkish array of small, sharp, porcelain teeth. She wore sunglasses constantly, and though we met four times, I did not once see her eyes and so cannot say what colour they were. Red possibly.

She was trapped in Australia, she said, because the estranged Australian father of her child refused to leave his homeland. She was half-Algerian, and still found she could be shocked by the offhand racism of even the most liberal Adelaide housewife. She was a masseuse and met a lot of housewives. She longed for Perpignan, whose railway station, she told me, had been designated by Salvador Dalí as the centre of the world. What was it, I wondered, this human urge to stick a pin in the centre? A pin or a flag. Dalí's 1946 painting of *The Temptation of St. Antony*, a more austere vision than Bosch's, depicts a white playa on which a naked, kneeling St. Antony wields a cross at a procession of elephants led by a white horse; each creature walks on hideously extended crane-fly legs, and one of the elephants is surmounted by a statuesque nude brandishing her breasts as if they were mortars. The spirit of fornication.

I went walking or swam in the cold sea in the afternoon, drank cheap local wine with Céline in the evening (sometimes she brought her son, Greg, who was five) and sank each cool morning, hungover, into the writings of South Australia's white pioneers, in the Geographical Society's library.

Here on Australia's periphery was where the people had huddled since the country's founding. The "red interior"—the desert—remained even today a foreign land occupied by a foreign people. There was "the bush"—the bush was part of Australia, part of its idea of itself as a nation of plucky pioneers; but then there was the desert. The desert was something different from either the bush or the "outback." It was not loved, or valued; really it wasn't part of Australia.

"Let any man lay the map of Australia before him," said the explorer Charles Sturt during a lecture here in Adelaide in 1840, "and regard the blank upon its surface, and then let me ask him if it would not be an honourable achievement to be the first to place a foot in its centre." There being no summit to reach, nor any source, the desert explorer's goal is first the centre—to "cross the heart of it," in David Hogarth's words—and then the other side. The earliest explorers of Australia imagined that unseen centre as a green place of abundance. It was in search of an inland sea that Sturt and others embarked. For men of the Enlightenment, the deserts of this new continent, unmapped, undescribed and unnamed, were a slur on national pride. What the Melbourne *Argus* described as a "hideous blank" was, according to one commentator in the 1820s, "staring Britain in the face with a look of askance and regret." As early as 1778 Captain Cook's botanist, Joseph Banks, stated: "It is impossible to conceive that such a body of land as large as all Europe does not produce vast rivers capable of being navigated into the heart of the interior."

What compelled such certainty? Was it just analogy with the provision of river and lake systems in Europe? There was scant evidence indicating the presence of such a body of water. The delusion was not down to excess of imagination but rather its opposite: an inability to conceive of a void, an uncultivable interior being discordant with either God's providence or the equilibrium inherent in nature. The late-eighteenth-century British geologist James Hutton, otherwise a brilliant mind, asserted that there were only two truly arid regions on the planet: "Lower Egypt and a narrow spot upon the coast of Peru."

The British explorer Charles Sturt took his discovery of the Darling River in 1828 as evidence of the great sea he believed lay at the continent's heart. "Everything tends I believe to prove that a large body of water exists in the interior," he wrote. It was the flocks of birds he had seen flying north over Adelaide that convinced him, for "birds which delighted in rich valleys would not go into deserts." In 1844, aged forty-nine, Sturt set out from Adelaide on his final great quest. A public holiday was designated, and crowds filled the streets to see him and his entourage off. So confident was he of the existence of the inland sea that his party carried with it a whaleboat. The expedition missed the continent's geographical centre by a single degree, some 240 kilometres, and discovered scarcely enough water to keep his camels going, let alone float a boat. It wasn't until 1848 that he conceded the possibility that his faith in that body of water's existence had been "fostered by the hope that such would be the case." When Sturt's former surveyor, a Scotsman named John McDouall Stuart, finally reached the geographical centre in 1859, he planted on a promontory nearby a silken Union Jack—"the emblem of civil and religious liberty," in his words—declaring, "may it be a sign to the natives that the dawn of liberty, civilisation, and Christianity is about to break upon them."

Break upon them it would, catastrophically. Any who came upon that flag might, if nothing else, have deemed it a portent. I thought of Stuart and his men, standing by their rag nailed to its pole, and in that godless "void" delivering their three dry-throated cheers to the Queen.

It was not until sixteen years after Stuart planted his flag that Ernest Giles crossed the continent from east to west. It was his second attempt, the first having ended in what he himself called a "splendid failure" following the death of one of the expedition members. His route would take him from the town of Port Augusta near Adelaide, westward across the Nullarbor Plain. Seven months after setting out, Giles's party arrived in the south-western coastal city of Perth. His second-in-command on both journeys was a fellow Englishman, William Henry Tietkens. During the first leg of the journey, the party detoured north from the limestone fastness of the Nullarbor Plain into sandhill country. Giles would name this great expanse the Great Victoria Desert, a dubious honour for his queen: "It was the weird, hideous, and demoniacal beauty of absolute sterility that reigned here," he recalled, and told his companions, "we [are] now in the worst desert on the face of the earth, but that fact should give us all the more pleasure in conquering it."

Following the party's triumphant arrival in Perth in November 1875, Tietkens sailed to England to obtain the support of a wealthy couple, a Mr. and Mrs. Leisler, in mounting an expedition to open up the land north of Ooldea for grazing. He knew the terrain. When he returned, four years later, he would come upon his own tracks.

ON THE EDGE of a red plain six hundred kilometres north-west of Adelaide and two hundred from the sea, a scaffold fence surrounds a low mound from the centre of which a shaft drops deep into the limestone. It is still lined with the grey timbering that was put in when it was dug 150 years ago. The fence is to stop camels falling in (camels are lacking in certain areas of intelligence). This is "Tietkens's Well," which was sunk with the aim of opening up the arid region to sheep-grazing. In the library in Adelaide I read Tietkens's journal of 1879. Whereas Giles writes with the calculation of one who had been a "delighted student of the narratives of voyages and discoveries," Tietkens's report is terse (twenty pages or so), more brutal and more immediate, as if he is getting it off his chest. The desert is never less than a foe, and never beautiful. There wasn't much it could teach you. The location he selected for his well lay some sixty kilometres north of Ooldea on "rich open undulating limestone downs." "I don't," he added, "understand why it is called the Desert." He may indeed have found the land rich (certainly it was more fertile then than it is today) or he may have been exaggerating for his benefactors.

Leaving his two hired well-sinkers to dig, Tietkens went off to explore the land to the west. Returning a few days later, he "had to listen to the lies and growling of the two greatest villains unhung." The men had struck soft sand at twelve metres and the walls simply would not hold. Dehydrated, exhausted, sick of horsemeat, they refused to dig

any further. "It's with difficulty one keeps the pistol in the belt in dealing with such carrion," reflected their employer. Finally, in disgust, he
dismissed them—"clods of infamy"—and returned to Fowlers Bay for
replacements.

On 22 October he was back, and overseeing the digging of
a new well not far from the original one. Conditions as summer
approached became unbearable, even for Tietkens, who was accustomed to the desert's brutality. By November he was nearly blind with
"ophthalmia"—presumably trachoma, a contagious inflammatory condition that continues to afflict Australia's desert-dwellers today. "It is
quite impossible to exaggerate what we suffer from the flies," he wrote
on 21 November (another Australian blight that has not gone away).
Two days later, his eyes were "smarting with intense pain, the flies
feeding off my hands." His hands were peppered with sores. "I thought
the sun never would have set upon this day of horror and pain . . . Darkness and death were a mercy, a thing to be devoutly prayed for for life
is HELL."

Nor were his troubles over. The following day the camp was
attacked by a group of Aboriginal men led by one Wantem, whom
Tietkens had employed to carry his post to and from Fowlers Bay:

> The pistol was out in an instant and off . . . Following up the mail-
> man I fired with the rifle at about 150 yards and he fell . . . The
> screaming of the women, the curses of the men was in a high key;
> the country around was engulfed in smoke, huge dense clouds
> black as pitch showing where they were sending up signals . . . If
> these people make a night attack we are most unhappily situated,
> for my eyes at night are now quite closed.

But there was no repeat attack; the black clouds dispersed.

By mid-December Tietkens's men had dug to twenty-five metres
without striking water. *Deeper*, Tietkens told them. On Boxing Day
1879, at thirty-eight metres, the well finally began to fill. Tietkens had
the water brought to the surface: it was foul—salt, as desert water often
is—but not so foul that livestock would not drink it. He returned to
Fowlers Bay in triumph. Where there had been nothing but bluebush

and mulga and spinifex since the dawn of Creation, there would soon be sheep stations, mines, townships; churches!

When he returned to the well a few months later, with twenty-five sheep, he found that the timber lining had collapsed and fine white sand was filling the shaft. The well was unsalvageable. William Tietkens was not discouraged. In January his men set to work nearby. At eighteen metres they struck an impenetrable floor of granite.

It was, Tietkens admitted, "the most bitter part of my life's history." His well-sinkers might have felt the same way. He returned to Adelaide, the mission to which he had devoted two years a failure.

The plain where he and the men laboured—Tietkens Plain, it is called, in tribute to their failure—remains unpopulated to this day, though you'll see dromedary camels from time to time, descendants, perhaps, of Tietkens's, which in turn were descended from Indian or Afghan herds imported by the British. But whereas the land in Tietkens's time was, at least to his eyes, virgin, horribly so, today it is scarred and littered—perished black cables, concrete balloon-tethering blocks, giant burial pits, hard-standings, the footings of watchtowers, and hundreds of kilometres of roads. A ruined place whose silence is less tranquillity's than that of a battlefield where the killing has just ended.

I HAD BREAKFAST with Céline and Greg before driving west from Adelaide. Much of southern Australia is underlain by a series of gargantuan basins created by the continent's slumping and faulting millions of years ago. Most of the Great Victoria Desert, which straddles the border of South Australia and Western Australia, lies within the Officer Basin, which was formed between 800 million and 350 million years ago. To the south, along the sweep of coast known as the Great Australian Bight, stretches the Nullarbor Plain, a crescent strip of limestone almost undeviating in elevation and covering some 250,000 square kilometres. Once underwater, today it is as treeless as its name suggests. Its northern edge is encroached upon by dunefields, and it was these dunes that characterised much of the country I would see as I travelled north. The plain was a callused web of skin between two digits—that's how I visualised it. At its south-eastern corner, three hundred kilometres west of Adelaide, I spent a night at the port town of Ceduna. The old military outpost of Maralinga, where I planned to be the day after tomorrow, was about three hundred kilometres north-west, in the sandhill country.

Ceduna had a parking lot with electricity hook-ups for RVs, several charity shops, and a single modern hotel whose gaudy-carpeted restaurant-bar was known to the townspeople as "the pub." All day and night the pub was full of white college sportsmen in team tracksuits—hockey and Aussie Rules football—who occasionally broke off from bawling at one another to suck oysters from their shells. "The only people who drink Western Australian beer," I heard one of them bellow to his teammate, "are dark in colour."

Outside it was raining. It rained the whole time I was in Ceduna. Grey rain merging with the grey sea. When I looked out of my window at dusk the streets were scattered with destitute Aboriginal people. They came into the town centre for the alcohol and didn't seek shelter from the rain. A bony girl of about twelve stood barefoot in a torrenting gutter and stared up at my balcony.

When I took off my boots that night a scattering of sand fell out onto the hotel bed; not the red sand of Australia but the fine grey-pink sand of Oman.

In the morning I walked through the rain to the Maralinga Tjarutja office on the edge of town to meet Roger, who was driving a delivery to the Aboriginal community at Oak Valley, four hundred kilometres north-west of here, and had agreed to take me with him. From Oak Valley it wasn't far to Maralinga. Maralinga Tjarutja Inc. was the business founded to manage the affairs of the traditional owners of the Maralinga lands, and it was through them that I'd arranged access to the area.

I wasn't sorry to leave Ceduna. The rain stopped after we'd driven a few kilometres, but the clouds remained. The truck's cabin barely contained Roger's bulk. It would take us all day to get to Oak Valley; he could have done the drive with his eyes shut. He was surly and opinionated and infinitely practical, and once he'd got the measure of me he wanted to talk. Roger, who was mixed race, had been an athlete in his youth; a cousin in Port Lincoln was a pro Aussie Rules player. A few days ago, he told me, the great indigenous player Adam Goodes, a defender with the Sydney Swans, having been booed for years by racist crowds, finally snapped and, with a traditional war cry, mimed throwing a spear at the opposition supporters. The newspapers were bewildered—where did such aggression *come* from?

Roger spoke about the "traditional people" with wariness; he feared them. "There's traditional people at Yalata," he said. "They'll spear you if you break their law. There's a lot of places I'm forbidden from going. Cultural stuff. Sacred sites. You gotta be an initiated man to go down there." Chief among these places were the claypans; it was there that "men's business"—male ceremonial activity—was carried out and ochre for body-painting gathered.

We drove west through the eucalyptus and into the endless grey of the Nullarbor Plain. In every direction grew nothing but knee-high bluebush, saltbush and samphire, a grey sea continuing for fifteen hundred kilometres west. The sky was clumped with small beige clouds that mirrored the clumping of the bushes. The only animal we saw was a halfbreed dingo that had penetrated the dog fence that stretches the length of southern Australia. He was teddybear yellow, limping; perhaps he'd been shot. The fence worked both ways, and I wondered if he wanted to cross back.

We turned off the Nullarbor road and drove north until the saltbush and bluebush gave out to the sandhill country known as the Great Victoria Desert. At a place signposted Ooldea the track crossed the transcontinental railway, which runs east–west along the bottom of the country. A station had been established here by missionaries in the 1920s. The "soak," or spring, nearby had been a sacred Anangu meeting site for as long as anyone could remember. (*Anangu*, meaning "the people," refers to speakers of several languages and dialects of the Western Australian and South Australian desert, including Pitjantjatjara, the dialect used by the people who now live in Yalata and Oak Valley.)

Ooldea had been a place of peace, where warring tribes sojourned in harmony. To serve the railway, built in 1912, a bore had been sunk and a condensing plant built. From the bore 45,000 litres had been drawn each day; the condensing plant, which purified that water, was fuelled by black-oaks felled from the surrounding sandhills. As early as 1930, the water at Ooldea was beginning to run out. The once rich land by now was stripped bare, a bowl empty of all but dust and flies. The mission persisted until 1952 when it was abandoned and its residents relocated to an unwanted sheep station 140 kilometres south, on the edge of the Nullarbor Plain. This place was Yalata; and by now the land to the north—the land the Anangu had walked for at least forty thousand years—was prohibited to them. The white man was busy there.

The glory of the Australian interior is its soil. Its redness is of such ubiquity and intensity that it seems not only to stain the hands and the hair but, after a few days' exposure, to tint the whole world for weeks, as if the cerebral cortex has been injected with a solution of carmine. When the people were dismissed from Ooldea and the desert nearby and forced to settle permanently on the unfamiliar, unstoried limestone plain to the south, which the white man called Nullarbor, they found they ailed. *Pana tjilpi* was what they called it: "grey earth." "We felt lonely about Ooldea," said one old man in 1985, giving evidence to a Royal Commission enquiry into the aftermath of the nuclear tests. "We were sad for all the places that we were related to, and we worried because these places had been spoiled ... We were told we could not go back there."

Ooldea was entirely unpopulated. Once the tests began in 1958 there was to be no return; to this day, Anangu people will only enter the test zone briefly and with reluctance. It was not until the 1980s, long after the last bomb was detonated, that some older citizens of Yalata established a smaller outpost deep in the desert, close to a string of sacred claypans, named Oak Valley: not a mission, but a village run by and for the land's owners.

I had made a detour to Yalata the previous day, before going to Ceduna; it was a couple of kilometres from the northern edge of the Nullarbor Plain. A grid of prefabs set down in the eucalyptus scrub. A characteristic of eucalyptus is that its bark peels off in long ribbons, and at Yalata these ribbons hung from the limbs and swung back and forth under a slight breeze. There was something about it of shed skin. One of the roads had been blocked with boulders and on a wall was freshly painted "Domestic Violence! *Wiya!*" The police station close to the entrance resembled a Belfast checkpoint, bollarded and barricaded behind a chainlink fence topped with barbed wire. It seemed to be unoccupied. Outside the community centre four women sat on a low wall. Seeing me they laughed and waved and a child shouted in Pitjantjatjara. A young bearded man in a neon tabard stood at the door to the community centre. I spoke no Pitjantjatjara and he no English, but it was clear that the person I'd arranged to meet, one of the local administrators, wasn't there. There'd been a murder, it turned out, and she was dealing with the repercussions.

In 1936 the United Aborigines Mission established a camp at Ooldea, and it continued to run a mission there until its closure in 1952. A ration depot was established, providing a ready source of food for the tribes of the desert. There was the school, the church, the children's home. The boys and girls were given three meals a day and on Saturdays a hot bath and a change of clothes: for boys braces and a blue tie, for girls a pink hair-bow. The boys were taught to pump water and cut wood and drive horses, the girls to sew and iron and crochet. In 1944 a mass baptism occurred: "It was no easy thing for them to take this step," wrote the UAM secretary, "renouncing the practices of their forefathers [and] forsaking the superstition of heathenism to follow Jesus." He observed that some of the old men seemed "hard and bitter" and wondered if it was because "many of the young men had stated that they were not going to become men in the old tribal way."

OAK VALLEY IS a hundred kilometres north of Ooldea. The dirt road rollercoasted over the sandhills, a blazing red ribbon cutting through the shimmering green of eucalyptus. Roger leaned heavily over his steering wheel, chewing, and gazing at the corrugated track ahead. "Know what I reckon? I reckon if things keep going the way they're going we'll see the first assassination of an Australian prime minister within ten years."

It was hyperbole—the hyperbole of despair. On the other side of the railway was a sign in red, white and black: "WARNING: NO ALCOHOL / NO DRUGS on the Maralinga Tjarutja Lands."

"We been here *fifty thousand years.*" It was a conservative estimate. "How long you been here?" He meant whites; he wasn't being impolite. "Two hundred and fifty years? God hasn't been in Australia very long."

True, but look around. On the horizon, rising over the sandhills to the east, was the pale mountain of overburden from the Iluka mineral-sand mine—the largest source of zircon on earth. Every day, fifteen 100-tonne trucks left the mine for the port at Thevenard, which had been visible that morning across the bay from Ceduna. All those precious materials waiting in the aboriginal ground.

A few years ago, said Roger, a French oil firm had paid for the rights to survey the Maralinga lands; they were here for months, cutting access tracks for their drilling rigs, inching the rigs in on low-loaders. His friend Shorty, an Anangu man, had been employed by the firm to push its access roads into the bush. The foreman knew little about the country. He'd direct Shorty to take the grader over a sandhill, and if Shorty told him it was too steep, he would insist. Eventually, sick of miring the bloody thing, a solution occurred to Shorty. When the foreman told him to take the road through impassable country, he would frown and shake his head: "Sacred land." And the foreman, not knowing where was sacred and where was not, could only return to his maps and find another route.

We carried on north towards Oak Valley, the fallen leaves at the road-edge glinting like broken glass. There was a spark of reflected sun on the horizon, and a car came jouncing over the brow towards us. "There's young Lancey, my little mate," Roger said, raising a steering-wheel finger to the battered four-door Polo. "He's had about twenty cars in the last five years." The Oak Valley cars were not made for the outback. In the scrub along the way dozens of vehicles lay abandoned—cars and trucks from the sixties and seventies and every year since, scavenged for parts until nothing useful was left.

Beside the road was a white bonnet propped upright on stakes and peppered with rust-ringed shotgun holes, "LIFT EM FOOT" daubed in blue. We were nearing Oak Valley. For two or three kilometres the land was grey and treeless where fire had swept through in the summer. "Kids get bored," Roger explained. A hundred metres from the roadside, ravens and a vulture were circling. Two dingoes stood beside a shot camel, spotlighted by a cluster of sunbeams.

WAITING AT THE STORE in Oak Valley were Pam, Roger the maintenance man (another Roger) and four attentive dogs. We unloaded the provisions and Roger the driver went to drop off a petrol pump that was strapped to the bed of the truck. The nurse from the elderly-care centre, an Anangu woman in her fifties, came to collect some boxes of drugs. With her was a two-year-old girl in a nappy. The little girl gripped one of the bigger dogs by its mane and shrieked "Baby! Baby!" as it dragged her along. Her knee was bleeding but she was too excited to notice.

"Wanna see some camels?" maintenance Roger asked me.

"Of course."

"Good! I'll take you out tonight."

Pam, another of Oak Valley's white employees, was a potter and ran the Aboriginal art gallery in Ceduna. Her husband had been involved in the clean-up operation at Maralinga in the nineties, she said. She held art classes in Oak Valley, driving the three hundred kilometres here and back once a week, staying overnight in one of the prefabs reserved for staff, which were within fenced compounds away from the main community. She was strong and skinny and boyish, with cropped grey hair and an excited, wary smile. "I'll show you the art centre," she said.

The population of Oak Valley fluctuated from one week to the next, with a mean of about eighty, but today the place had been abandoned. Roger and I had passed three cars travelling the other way, as well as Lancey's, each of them containing six or seven passengers piled onto one another's laps. A funeral, Pam explained. The murder in Yalata. A girl had been stabbed, her partner arrested. The graffiti: "Domestic Violence! *Wiya!*" There are two Pitjantjatjara words even the whitefellas know, Pam told me: *wiya*, meaning "no"; and *mamu*. "*Mamu* means 'devil,'" she said. It was a word I'd hear again.

.   .   .

THE ART CENTRE was a corrugated tin building. Inside, sitting at a long table in torn jeans, was Archie, an Anangu man in his thirties, who seemed to be the only resident who had not gone to the funeral; I wondered why. "What are you painting?" I asked. He didn't look up, just carried on painting. Beside him on the table was a coffee-jar lid containing fried witchety grubs. He was painting flowers, black stipples on a red background. Sturt's desert pea, perhaps. He spoke some English, Pam said, but he wouldn't speak to me. I didn't persist; I was not his guest.

The paintings done in the art centre were sold at a gallery back in Ceduna, and this was one of Oak Valley's few sources of income. Passing tourists—the moneyed "grey nomads" in their enormous RVs—would pay well for what they believed to be the real thing. There was after all no employment in the desert other than teaching and doctoring and the maintenance of the village, and those jobs were done mainly by whites.

Oak Valley had been founded when most of the land requisitioned for the British, some 76,000 square kilometres, was returned to the Anangu in 1984 following the Royal Commission enquiry into the nuclear tests and their aftermath. In the 1970s the British had superficially cleaned up the radioactive contamination, but it wasn't until the mid-1990s that compensation was paid to the Aboriginal owners for their dispossession and the ruination of their land, and significant investment made in cleaning up the sites. Even now it was not deemed safe to camp or cook in the test area.

It was in part the British pay-off that had financed the amenities at Oak Valley: the school, the sports centre and the playground, the elderly-care centre, the power station and the art centre. Like Yalata and other Anangu communities, Oak Valley continued to depend on government grants. In November 2014 the premier of the neighbouring state of Western Australia had announced a plan to close 150 of that state's 273 remote Aboriginal communities. In straitened times the taxpayer could no longer be expected to pay for such uneconomic outstations. The PM, Tony Abbott, backed his man: "What we can't do is endlessly subsidise lifestyle choices." There was support for this view. The middle-aged owner of the guesthouse where I had stayed in Adelaide, a model of courtesy and grace, told me confidingly one evening: "They want to screw us for every penny we've got, to get us back for what we did to them."

Pam showed me to the Oak Valley guesthouse, a stilted three-room prefab on the edge of the community. On the bedroom door was a sticker: a composite image of a steel guitar overlaid with a picture of a red sand dune that in turn merged into a waterfall, as if these visions were reflected in the guitar's surface. Over this cluttered image were printed lines from Isaiah, and I did not know what to make of them or their presence here: "Behold, I will do a new thing; now it shall spring forth; shall ye not know it? I will even make a way in the wilderness, and rivers in the desert."

THAT EVENING WE cooked steaks on the fire in the backyard of the house Pam used when she was here. Tomorrow morning she would be driving back to Ceduna, and she offered to drop me at Maralinga. I hadn't seen any black faces since meeting Archie that afternoon; the people were not due back from Ceduna for a couple of days, Pam said. Things were pretty bad. In Yalata they had always been bad, but even in isolated Oak Valley, where the elders had come in the eighties precisely to escape the influence of the cities, alcohol and petrol-sniffing were problems. Just as Pam was telling me this a metallic knocking came from the direction of the store. "That's bloody someone on the roof!" she said, and we listened. And it did sound like creeping footsteps on hollow metal.

Pam marched to the fence and shone a torch towards the store, fifty metres away. The sound stopped, then resumed, but we could make out no movement. Roger the maintenance man—white Roger— had heard the noise, too, from his home across the track. The cabin light of his truck came on and his silhouette was visible moving inside. He pulled across to Pam's fence and wound down his window: "We'll take a look, mate. Little bastards. Then we'll find those camels."

I left Pam by her fire and hopped over the fence and climbed up beside Roger. We spent a minute circling the store but there was nobody there. Roger, in any case, was more interested in his camels. "I've told them before, 'It's *your* bloody store, boys; you want to loot it, that's your business, but you're only stealing from yourselves.'"

He was big and wore a short grey beard on his round face, and tended to begin each statement in that southern Australian way, as if confessing to some regretted weakness: "Ah, look, Will..." We drove out of the community, past the power station and the dump and the water tower and the graveyard on its hill, into the night-time bush— "black as dog-guts."

"You'll usually find them hanging about the road," Roger said. We drove for half an hour, deeper and deeper into the cool desert, the windows open. I looked back and two dogs were running after us, red in the truck's rear lights. Roger was suddenly animated, eager to be interviewed, to share his love for the place where he'd wound up. "I've never felt safer than I do here," he announced. "Nobody here wants to do anybody any harm."

Unlike Pam, he lived in the community, and his son went to the community school. I'd seen a picture of a school group in the guest-house, and there was no question which of them was Roger's boy, all of them bare-chested but him, and he the only white child. "He's lost some weight since then. It's been the making of him, coming here. You wouldn't believe what it's done for his confidence. He was having trouble with bullying at his old school; now we worry *he's* doing the bullying!"

Neither his son nor his wife were here at the moment, he said; they were in Ceduna. It wasn't clear to me if this was a permanent arrangement. "Look," he said, "for some people it's too much. They need a break."

We drove for longer than I wanted, two hours or more, and I was cold by the time we got back to Oak Valley. Pam's fire was out and she'd gone to bed. We'd seen only one camel, an old bull swaying slowly away from the road into the bush. Roger was disappointed, and his reluctance to give up had pushed him on: "Another minute, then we'll call it a night." We must have done a hundred kilometres. "Usually you can't move for them."

He loved the camels, he said; loved the desert, and the old fellers. As I got out, he said: "Truth is, I'd be initiated tomorrow, if they'd let me."

"YOU'LL LIKE NOBSY," said Pam, as we drove towards Maralinga the next morning. "He's an 'outback character.'" Nobsy was what people called Robin, the Maralinga caretaker, though I never heard anyone call him it in his presence. The dogs saw us off, nipping at our tyres, the idiots, and on the edge of the community we passed a car returning from the funeral. The "lifestyle choice"—to live without employment among the glaucomic dust, in a land that could never be truly safe again; to live hundreds of kilometres from the next community and to travel those distances regularly and without hesitation, seven to a car, not in climate-controlled Land Cruisers like ours, but in wrecked Polos and Golfs without glass in the windows, a child dozing on each lap.

Roger had said, "I'd be initiated tomorrow, if they'd let me." They would never let him, he knew; and for all that he loved the desert's freedoms, there were rituals that would forever be forbidden to him as a white man. We could be guests here, or trespassers. Whites understood the land little better than Tietkens had when he arrived with his visions and his sheep and his pistol 150 years ago. It would never be theirs and they knew it; that was the power white Australia could not accept, the power remaining to the people of Yalata and Oak Valley and all the other impoverished communities.

IN 1953, a group of British army surveyors delivered a report to the atomic research facility in Aldermaston: "Beyond the northern limits of the Nullarbor Plain, the country becomes rather more attractive, consisting of low sandhills, thickly covered by mulga and malee trees." They added: "In this country it is very easy to get lost."

As we neared Maralinga, the road climbed towards a high ridge, higher than the sandhills we'd been crossing. The Ooldea Range, it was called. It formed 35 million years ago as a coastal dune system when what is now the Nullarbor Plain was underwater. The turn-off to the compound was tarmacked, unlike the main track or the roads in Oak Valley or Yalata, and still flawless after forty years. "You Brits made sure everything was top quality," said Pam. And there, finally, was the sign: "This land contains artefacts of the nuclear test era, including items contaminated at low levels with radioactivity."

A padlocked chainlink gate blocked the road. Beside it was an upright cylinder of concrete, a metre wide and 2.5 metres tall, a section of water pipe with a doorway cut into it. It was painted blue, with the words "The Tardis" over the entrance. Inside was a black rotary phone from the 1970s; it still worked, apparently, but there was no need to call: we were expected, and within minutes a truck was roaring towards us from the other side of the gate. Pam and I said our farewells. "Tell Nobsy hi," she said.

THE ABANDONED MILITARY outpost was now dominated by the hospital, a long aluminium building whose western flank each evening became a screen of dazzling orange as it reflected the setting sun. It was in the hospital that Robin ("Nobsy") the caretaker lived with his wife, Della, who was from an Anangu family. Robin was white and in his mid-sixties. He had been a shark fisher off Ceduna until Della insisted he pack it in. In the "pub" in Ceduna I'd been told there were Great Whites in the bay: "but don't let that stop you swimming." He was stocky with a stance like a ram, wide-legged and primed, his skin weathered to a reddish-bronze so dark that it was hard to make out his tattoos. He had a straggly pale-grey beard that parted around his mouth before flowing down under his chin to converge with his chest hair. There was a mischievous mobility about that mouth, but his eyes always remained still and watchful. When he'd finished laughing at something his face would turn back to blankness without passing through the usual intermediary stage of the smile.

Sometimes, over the coming days, I would sense he was impatient to be rid of me. There was a subdued fierceness about him—a lifetime of proximity to violence that still simmered away under the bonhomie and the beard. He had spent a lot of time gutting fish, and knew how to drive a road-grader and how to kill a camel: you need to shoot it right in the ear hole. Since giving up fishing he'd worked first for the community up at Oak Valley, then, for the past five years, as caretaker of Maralinga and the bomb sites.

IN 1953 the British search had begun for a "permanent proving ground" in Australia. It had to be at least 160 kilometres from human habitation but close to road and rail communications; there should be an airstrip nearby, a good water supply and a tolerable climate with minimal rainfall, in order to prevent contamination of the water table. X300, as the chosen site was initially codenamed, lay on a flat plain ringed by sandhills (this was Tietkens's Plain) and measured some thirty kilometres east to west and twenty-five north to south. Maralinga was the name of the settlement built to serve the test zone, but it was also used informally for X300 itself.

It took me a while to get my bearings. The best view was from the water tower, Robin told me. Ten metres up a rusted iron ladder. From its gantry you gained a sense of the site's isolation: twenty kilometres to the north, the green thinned to the dull red of Tietkens's Plain; to the south, beyond the railway Roger and I had crossed yesterday, the green yielded abruptly to the blue-grey of the Nullarbor Plain, which extended to the sea. For the British, the most pressing objective in establishing the new site was to carry out an "airburst" explosion, from a balloon, to prove "Blue Danube," its first operational nuclear weapon. A newer, smaller, tactical nuclear bomb for battlefield use, codenamed Red Beard, was also to be tested. Finally, according to the initial plan, a test was to be done to establish the effect of an atomic detonation at ground level. But these tests turned out to be only the start: in total seven nuclear bombs were exploded, followed by some six hundred non-nuclear trials.

In December 1954, Australian and British engineers began building the camp and the airfield and, thirty kilometres away, down on Tietkens's Plain, levelling the test sites and constructing field laboratories. They continued their work through the flyblown furnace of the southern Australian summer.

On the eastern edge of the outpost, visible from the water tower, I could see a stepped platform ten metres across, like a dais for a Roman senate. A signpost read "Pit 68U." At the top of the steps there was only a rectangle filled with rubble: not one of the radioactive burial pits, but the settlement's swimming pool. The sign indicated the presence of nothing more dangerous than asbestos. The diving board had gone, but stainless steel ladders still vanished into the rubble. It had been the centre of the outpost, especially during those stupefying summer months before the tests took place. A swimmer resting with his arms on the pool's rim could gaze out fifty kilometres across those rolling "downs" of mulga (eucalyptus) and malee (acacia) and imagine himself on leave.

To one side of the pool was a crumbling stucco fountain, long dry but once used to filter the pool's mineral-heavy water; beside it was a plastic patio chair on which I'd sometimes sit and read, resting my feet on the wall of the dry fountain. Nearby were a couple of tennis courts. The net-posts and umpire's platform were still standing; but the tramlines were no longer visible and the bitumen was corrugated and cracked and scattered with saltbushes. At first I mistook the low intermittent roar I kept hearing for jets, but I realised that it was only the noise the wind made in the dry boughs of the malee. Although it was not particularly loud, there was somehow a massive suppressed energy contained within it, like the energy of a rally waiting to be addressed.

When Maralinga was abandoned in 1974, the men from Yalata were granted salvage rights. Its onetime buildings can be found today across South Australia: I'd stopped at a campsite near Port Lincoln whose toilet block once stood here; Ceduna's basketball hall had been the range store; Pam's pottery studio, she'd told me, was once a British barracks. Most of the buildings were gone, but from the water tower you could still trace the outlines of the outpost's "roads": London Road, Ottawa Street, Perth Road, Cardiff Road. In the distance, between the settlement and the main gate, with its Tardis, a couple of kilometres away, was the airfield, an expanse of concrete big enough to land the Shuttle on, still maintained and lit up at night. Below the water tower the memorial ground remained, with its flagless flagpole and a cross laid out in white stones; but the church was gone, along with the cinema, the shop, the post office, the barracks and the laboratories. From the water tower I could see the small dry patio beside the hospital where Robin and Della lived, with its pot plants and a sign painted by Robin: FORT MARALINGA.

DELLA'S GRANDMOTHER had been born in the spinifex country south of Maralinga, and had been brought up at the mission station at Ooldea (spinifex is the name given to the various species of sharp, tussock-forming grasses that abound in desert Australia). There she had met Della's grandfather, who was visiting from his homeland north of Maralinga. Della had seemed physically small to me when we first met, but later I saw that it was just that she had the kind of shyness that makes people seem slighter than they are. Robin often spoke for her or amended what she said: "What you mean, Della, is …"; "Why don't you tell him about …?"; "No, Della, remember …?" It was partly instinctive protectiveness.

Her grandparents married and moved to Ceduna, by the sea, where her grandfather—she said it with some pride—was the first blackfella in the town to be issued with a licence, a "dogtag," to buy alcohol and drink in the white pub. Nevertheless, the family was hardly welcomed by Ceduna's white majority. Frequently, "tribal people," as Della called them, would arrive at the house without warning, having walked the 240 kilometres from Ooldea, and camp, fifty or more of them at a time, around her grandparents' home.

The council made her grandfather an offer: give up your home, choose a plot of land anywhere on the outskirts of the town, and it's yours for free, on a ninety-nine-year renewable lease. The plot he selected, a few kilometres along the coast, was sixty hectares overlooking the beach, with fresh water close to the surface. Today it is worth millions, and Della's extended family of twenty households had made the plot their own. It was to the house Robin had built there— "Duckponds," the place was called—that he and Della retreated when they returned to the coast from the desert every week or two. Often their granddaughter, Tori, stayed at Maralinga with her boyfriend, Bobby, and their young children. Tori was prettily snaggle-toothed, with one eyebrow permanently raised. Each evening she brought a meal to my caravan, lovingly made, meat and potatoes and gravy, and always cold. I didn't have the heart to ask her to warm it through. She called Robin "Pappy" and they adored one another. She and her family came here to escape some damaging influence. In the same way, the people of Oak Valley had hoped that their community's isolation would protect their young people.

Sometimes Robin wore a plaid shirt or a hoodie but usually he just wore a singlet. He wore a Royal Australian Air Force baseball cap and smoked Log Cabin tobacco in loose roll-ups that he finished in half a dozen crackling draws. Log Cabin was a good brand to smoke, because it was what the Aboriginal fellas smoked, which meant you could get it in any of the community stores. He had superb recall and was a terrific mimic. When you told him something he didn't know, he'd look at you closely and say, "That right? Well, bugger me dead." He'd been born in Port Lincoln, down along the coast from Ceduna, and on his left bicep a tattoo was just legible: "Port Lincoln Outcast."

After the years of shark fishing, Robin worked on the tuna boats out of Ceduna. In the seventies he'd been employed by the transcontinental railway, stationed at the siding at Watson, Maralinga's main staging post. During that time he'd helped dismantle the settlement, and in the eighties, when the Yalata people moved to Oak Valley, he became their supplies driver, the job Roger inherited (Roger was his nephew, it turned out). As a fourteen-year-old on the shark boats Robin would work each day until midnight, only then repairing to the galley with his shipmates for dinner. This habit had stayed with him for fifty years. While we were camping in the desert, he ate as a kind of soporific, bolting down his meal hours after I'd eaten, then slipping into his swag and falling asleep immediately. He was of the sea first, and then of the desert, and he and Della still lived between the two: between Duckponds and Maralinga. Even in the winter, when the heat at Maralinga was liveable, they would drive down to Ceduna once a week—for a meal at the pub, see the kids, take a boat out fishing. And yet both of them, after a while, found they longed to be back.

. . .

WILLIAM PENNEY, the British scientist in charge of the tests in the 1950s, described the proposed range as "gently undulating and covered with low saltbush and occasional sparse patches of mulga which give it the appearance of English downland." If, as a result, the British scientists and servicemen expected pastoral ease, they were disappointed. Tietkens had used the same word, *downs*, as had St. John Philby describing the dunes of the Empty Quarter (only eight years earlier, but it seems like a different century), as if any land of gentle undulation, however denuded, was merely a version of bucolic western Europe. The pioneer's customary yearning to reconcile his lexicon to the unfamiliar. Describing the first Anglos to confront the American West, Mary Austin wrote that the landscape simply could "not be expressed in terms invented for such purpose in a low green island by the North Sea." It was these same limitations that caused Renaissance painters to depict St. Antony's hyper-arid Eastern Desert as a glebe of dappled knolls.

Next day before dinner I took a walk out to the old rifle range. It was a couple of kilometres away along a track scattered with camel prints and closely flanked by eucalyptus. The eucalyptus each had their own domain, so that their branches scarcely touched. In the trees' shade there was tall white spinifex grass growing in ring or crescent formations (the tussocks die off from the centre first) and inside these "nests" were scattered the empty white shells of snails, as if they had gone there to die, or had been eaten there by sheltering birds. In my memory the land was that simple, and in its simplicity archetypal.

Something like two hundred millimetres of rain falls on the Great Victoria Desert each year: compare that with the Empty Quarter's annual five millimetres. Nor is evaporation anything like as intense. But there was no question that *desert* was the correct word. The dominance of the mineral world—this is a defining characteristic of desert. As defining as the heat and dryness that creates that dominance. The red earth overwhelmed the green of vegetation.

Repetition, the same composition of eucalyptus, spinifex, snail shells and sand, in every direction, generated a sense of infinitude as powerful as a featureless plain. Once I was out of view of the settlement and its water tower, and beyond hearing-range of the generator, and beyond shouting distance, it would require only ten strides into the scrub, and a blind-man's-bluff twirl, to be lost, with no real likelihood, in these thousands of identical square kilometres (eucalyptus, spinifex, snail shells), and in my ignorance, of finding either the track or the settlement. It was a reminder that, for those men based here in the fifties and sixties, the camp was an island, and the tracks serving it pontoons from which it would be suicidal to step.

At the rifle range, the sand berms were littered with hundreds of flattened bullets and shards of brown glass. It had been used for training by the military guard that monitored the test zone during the Cold War. Maralinga's isolation had been a matter of security as well as public safety. Fencing off such a vast area was impossible; but the desert is its own barrier—ask U.S. Border Patrol. Any white stranger was to be treated as a Russian spy. Interlopers were to be shot on sight.

Alongside the rifle range was a doorless wooden toilet hut from the fifties, its floor deep with leaf litter. Unthinkingly, before walking back, I took a photo, one of thousands I'd scarcely look at. When I told Robin where I'd been, he asked, "Didn't go near the dunny, did you?"

"Why d'you ask?"

"Only, I meant to tell you—I always say to the grandkids: 'Kids, don't go near that dunny: king brown lives in there, and a king brown'll kill you, don't worry about that.'"

And sure enough, there in the photo, coiled in the leaf litter, bugger me dead, was *Pseudechis australis*.

NEXT MORNING, Robin wanted to take me to where the Milpuddie family had been found in 1956. On the corridor wall in the hospital he showed me two pictures: a mushroom cloud, black with its hoard of scorched earth; then, from the air, the crater. This was the "Marcoo" test and its aftermath. He also had something to tell me about the "black mist," the cloud of fallout that had been created by the first mainland test, Totem 1, in 1953.

It was chiefly the testimony given by an Anangu man, Yami Lester, who was ten years old in 1953, that led to the setting up of the Royal Commission. He recalled hearing early one morning a giant crack and boom from the south-west, several such noises: it was later that morning, or the following morning, he couldn't be sure, that he and others saw the cloud. It was not a mushroom cloud rising obediently to the heavens, but more like a black wave approaching from the horizon. It was evident that it would engulf anything in its path, and the people were terrified: the men shook their spear-throwers at it; the women dug holes and tried to hide the children. "They reckon it was *mamu*," Lester told the commission.

As we were leaving the hospital, a puppy bounded into the corridor. Crawling after it came Tori's one-year-old son with his beautiful long hair, beautiful in the way of Anangu kids, dark but streaked with gold. Robin shepherded them back into the room before opening the door at the end of the corridor. The morning light charged in, and with it all the sounds of the bush.

OPERATION BUFFALO, which took place on Tietkens's Plain between 27 September and 9 October 1956, comprised four nuclear detonations: One Tree, Marcoo, Kite and Breakaway. The following year there was a second series, Operation Antler, again taking place during the cooler months of September and October, comprising three detonations: Tadje, Biak, and the last and largest on the Australian mainland, Taranaki. One Tree (at fifteen kilotons about the same yield as the bomb dropped on Hiroshima), Breakaway (ten kilotons), Tadje (one) and Biak (six) were exploded on steel towers, and Marcoo (1.5) at ground level. (A kiloton is equivalent to one thousand tonnes of TNT.) Kite, three kilotons, was dropped from a bomber. Taranaki, suspended from a balloon, was twenty-five kilotons. British and American tests of thermonuclear devices in the Pacific Ocean and Nevada were measured not in kilotons but megatons—a megaton corresponding to one million tonnes of TNT. In 1954 the United States exploded a bomb on Bikini Atoll with a yield of fifteen megatons. In Kazakhstan in 1961, on the steppe not far from Almaty, the Soviet's "Tsar Bomb," the largest ever detonated, measured fifty megatons—two thousand Taranakis.

The "minor trials," codenamed Vixen, took place between 1957 and 1963. Cutesy, wink-wink names: Kittens, Rats, Vixen, Tims... They

were designed to assess how a nuclear device would behave in an accident—an air crash, for instance, or an explosion at a weapons dump—
and while they did not involve a nuclear reaction, their effect was to
disperse fragments of radioactive plutonium and contaminated metal
over hundreds of hectares. It was in fact these minor trials that caused
the worst contamination. It remains unclear how much of it was ultimately cleared away or safely buried. I'd done my research. Sixteen
milligrams of plutonium dust caught in the lungs will cause death in
a month.

In 1967, following the official closure of Maralinga, the British
undertook a clean-up. They called it "Operation Brumby." (It might
as well have been done to tuba music.) At Taranaki it had two phases:
the ploughing and grading of the test site to disperse and cover the
scattered plutonium; and the burial of plutonium and other waste in
nineteen shallow pits. In a statement to the Royal Commission in 1985,
the British government's representative, hoping to avoid the expense
of a further clean-up, stated: "Scientific knowledge is not now, and
certainly was not then, sufficiently advanced to enable a complete
decontamination of an area in which nuclear explosive tests have taken
place." But the Royal Commission found that Brumby had been wholly
inadequate, in fact little more than cosmetic. It wasn't until 1999 that
the British assented to carry out a second clean-up, employing "in-situ
vitrification," whereby the ground is heated to temperatures sufficient
to turn it to glass, thus, in principle, containing any pollutants.

IT TOOK AN HOUR to get to Taranaki. We stopped at Tietkens's
Well so Robin could have a smoke, and dropped stones into the darkness, a tribute to Tietkens's fly-maddened well-sinkers. We drove past
two open hangars that had been used to store and decontaminate the
equipment used in the vitrification process in 1999. They were empty
now, their concrete floors gleaming with rainwater. During the Vixen
series, plutonium had been subjected to explosives inside heavy steel
boxes. In 1967 these boxes, along with their concrete mounting slabs,
had been dumped in burial pits capped with concrete. It was these pits
that in 1999 had been vitrified to seal in their poison. Next to the larg-

est of these was a sign: "WARNING: BURIED RADIOACTIVE MATERIALS." It carried two symbols: the three-leafed radiation icon, and a pictogram of a tent and a campfire scored out diagonally. Under this pictogram were the words "*Ngura wiya*." No camping.

At the centre of the site, a hundred metres from the burial pit, was a truncated concrete pyramid about a metre and a half tall. This memorial obelisk had appeared here in 1979, as similar pyramids had been trucked in and lowered by crane at each of the nine desert sites. On one face, cast into the concrete: "A British atomic weapon was exploded here on 9 October 1957"; on the adjacent face: "Warning: radiation levels for a few hundred metres around this point may be above those considered safe for permanent occupation." I clambered up the overburden of limestone rubble that capped the largest burial pit. From its flat surface, about five metres higher than the surrounding ground and the size of a football pitch, I turned and looked down onto the plain—Tietkens's Plain. Robin was rolling a cigarette on the tailgate of his ute. I wondered whether his assurances about the site's safety were to be trusted. There were still zones—Tims, Kittens—where it was unsafe to go. Who knew exactly where the thresholds of those zones lay?

"You think I'd live here if it wasn't safe?"

"Remind me," I said. "How many years did you spend fishing for sharks?"

Beyond him was the harrowed land, and beyond it a verge of mulga, and then, in the distance, red sandhills rolling out to the northern horizon and Australia's "dead centre."

THE ANANGU UNDERSTOOD that there was no transmutation so thorough that it could erase what had been done. The land was spoiled, and it could not be remediated, any more than a heap of kangaroo bones can be made to jump. In 1969, long after the final test, the secretary of the Maralinga safety committee had reassured one of the chief scientists: "The range is a long way from anyone, no one will go there, so why worry?" And with that he spoke for every outsider confronting the native desert. This was also the liberty the desert permitted:

the moral liberty available to us in dreams, the liberty to perpetrate outrages.

For the Anangu there are the Ancestors, then there are the plants and the animals. Finally there is the land; the land that is the nexus between physical and spiritual, temporal and eternal, and whose every feature was created by the Ancestors. Try not to think of these three elements—the Ancestors, organisms and minerals—as separate things.

The Anangu's relationship with the land is a matter of religion. You do not, for example, clear a waterhole in order to maintain a water supply, but because it is your obligation to the Ancestors. Your lawful obligation. There is no founding myth of alienation from nature, no Fall, for the distinction does not exist: there is no "nature" to be alienated *from*. The desert is a place neither of banishment nor of atonement. It is not your proving ground. It is not your sanctuary. It is not St. Antony's realm of demonic temptation; nor, above all, is it the "hideous blank" of the pioneers.

The desert monotheisms tip their heads skywards, seek divinity in the heavens. Anangu know that it is the land—the ground beneath their feet—where the creative spirit resides. To destroy the land is not to deprive a person of their property; it is not a matter of "displacement" or theft. It is to unpick the weft of their being. "The land," Roger the delivery driver had told me, "is like their children." Or put it in Christian terms. To destroy the land is not to, say, burn down a church or even a cathedral. It is not some insult that can be remedied or revenged; there's no rebuilding to be done. Take some holy scripture: cut from it an integral vein, so that the very faith is diminished, so that whatever it is that strengthens or consoles is reduced. Or take the body, the unbelieving body: to have a hand intruded and some organ hooked out, the gall bladder, say, then brandished before you, into the furnace.

And pondering all this, I think first about the words of the secretary of the safety committee—"The range is a long way from anyone, no one will go there, so why worry?"—and then I remember the girl in Ceduna, as I do from time to time, the gutter-water surging around her ankles; stood there, staring up at me on my hotel balcony.

For Tietkens the desert was *terra nullius*: unowned, untenanted, unexploited. An affront to capital and to God. Australia was every man's for the taking, and to take it was every man's duty, no less. *Terra nullius* was more than doctrine. From 1827 it was law. With whom, after all, was a white man expected to sign a treaty? Could a wandering black be said to "own" a claypan or a mountain? Does the dingo own the plain he crosses in search of food? Does the kangaroo own the rockhole he pauses to drink from?

A century and a half after Tietkens sunk his wells, William Penney, the head of the British bomb project, was assured by the Australian government that, while the area had once been crossed by tribes travelling to and from Ooldea, it was now only frequented "by one or two elderly blacks and then on rare occasions."

THERE ARE TWO translations of "Maralinga." When the British named the site, what they had in mind was a word belonging to the indigenous Garik dialect of the Northern Territory, meaning something like "Field of Thunder." Apt for the anticipated drama. But the site was far from the Northern Territory. For the people who crossed it barefoot for sixty thousand years, speakers of the Southern Pitjantjatjara dialect, these sandhills and saltbush plains were a thousand places with a thousand names, and to them "Maralinga" meant something different: "Up above, looking down."

Robin had showed me an aerial photograph of the Breakaway and Biak sites, which lie about three kilometres east of Taranaki. They resembled an eight, the circles overlapping slightly like a Venn diagram. As a teenager in the 1990s, even as the likelihood of nuclear war was apparently diminishing, I would pore over books describing the Soviet targeting strategies of the previous lucky decades; in particular a map of the country where I lived. Two maps, in fact. The first showed Great Britain scattered with red discs. Those the size of a penny were centred on cities of strategic importance—London, Liverpool, Birmingham, Newcastle, Portsmouth and so on. Smaller discs meanwhile overlaid smaller cities, and still smaller discs overlaid large towns, until the whole map was coated in a kind of variegated chainmail.

What struck me most, however, and what today I find most repulsive, was not the descriptions I read of the aftermath of the bombs that were dropped on Japan—people and animals alike "petrified in an attitude of indescribable suffering," in Marcel Junod's account of Hiroshima—but rather the second map. It charted the final phase of a projected attack. Where the edges of three or four discs on the first map touched, there was an unshaded zone, a concave-walled triangle or square of sanctuary, where the blasts could not reach. And it was these omissions that would be the targets of the second phase. Smaller nukes—mere Marcoos—would be dispatched to obliterate any life or infrastructure that had escaped the initial phases. Here was another kind of desert. And I knew, too, even if the book omitted it, that the red discs covered America and France and Germany, and all of Europe and, of course, the Soviet Union; and that the whole world, in the planners' careful phasing, was to be turned red, which was not the red of blood, but of hell.

AS WE DROVE east towards the Marcoo site we passed a mob of six female camels facing into the wind. It was necessary for Robin to cull sick or elderly ones. "You knock one down," he said, "and it'll just rot. Within the test zone dingoes won't touch it; eagles won't touch it. I don't know why, but they seem to know. Look at this place—" He gestured to the red-grey plains on all sides. "The spinifex'll get to twelve inches tall, then it dies."

From the truncated-pyramid obelisk that marked the Biak test site, a kilometre south of Marcoo, you could turn full circle and not see a single shrub above knee height for 800 metres, only the line of low grey mulga that crowded the edge of the zone of sterility. At Maralinga itself, in the winter, Robin would see budgerigars flocking in the trees as they migrated north. But here in the test zone you never saw them. They skirted it as a stream skirts a boulder. And again he said: "They seem to know." The site was safe, he stressed again: "Don't worry about that." But what was it, I wondered, that the animals "seemed to know"? What told the dingo not to touch the fresh-killed camel, or the birds coming north to veer east or west?

At Biak the ground glittered like a lake that has just begun to freeze, and crunched underfoot as I walked. I looked back after ten minutes and could see Robin standing smoking by the ground-zero obelisk. The stuff encrusting the surface was trinitite, named after the place of its first earthly creation, the Trinity nuclear test site in New Mexico. This glassy green substance occurred when the sand was fused by the heat of the bombs; you could fill your pockets with pieces of it, if you wanted. It was the dull black-green of wood mould or the sherbety green of verdigris. In consistency it was volcanic, coarsely glossy, like the hard caramel top of a pudding, or a potter's glaze that has been fired too hot. Some pieces were as big as my palm and had preserved the molten gloopiness of those bubbling hours after the blast. I gathered a handful of beadlike fragments and put them in the pocket of my rucksack. We got back into the truck and made our way north to Marcoo. The camels turned their heads to watch us go. They alone among the animals did not avoid the blast zones, Robin said, and I wondered if it was because they were not native.

At Marcoo there was no trinitite because the crater had been filled in. You wouldn't know there'd ever been a hole here fifty metres across and thirteen deep. Unlike the others, Marcoo had been detonated in a shallow pit, and so it alone had made a crater. Perhaps because the contaminated soil had been diluted by fresh soil when the crater was filled in, there was some vegetable life here, and not only that, a flower: a tiny desert daisy, white with a dash of mauve and a yellow heart. Excavated beside it in the sand was a mulga ants' nest, a circular hole like one dibbed by a finger. Ringing the hole was a raised rampart of sand half a centimetre high, coarser than the surface sand. Around it, slender acacia leaves no bigger than nail-clippings had been heaped by floods. The ring of sand was the ants' dyke against cloudbursts. I was struck, as I often have been in the greener deserts, by lives passing in anonymity—flower, ant, camel, saltbush, raven. Absolute anonymity. A hundred metres away, beyond the crater-fill, I picked out a single modest acacia bush, little more than a metre tall, effectively indistinguishable from the countless others surrounding it; and I imagined all the other acacias and black-oaks and eucalypts, let alone the ants, deep in the desert, far from any track, that would never be seen by a human being. Don't ask why this seemed remarkable: it was not a matter of anthropomorphism—nothing "lonely" about these specimens consoled my quivering heart. It was just a shock to consider that, even in this assaulted place, life was going on as if humankind had never been. It shocks me less today.

THE MARCOO EXPLOSION took place on 4 October 1956, late in the afternoon, watched by a group of Australian parliamentarians. According to William Penney, they were "delighted with their visit—and very friendly." After the test there was "thunder and heavy rain"—those two hundred millimetres of annual rain tend to come violently, as the ants know—and Penney added to his report: "See Ecclesiastes chapter 1 verse 6." ("The wind goeth toward the south, and turneth about unto the north; it whirleth about continually, and the wind returneth again according to his circuits.") It is natural to resort to scripture on being shown hell.

As well as the usual stubbed pyramid marking ground zero, there was a cement obelisk like an anti-terrorist barricade, commemorating the work of the men who'd backfilled the crater during Britain's Operation Brumby "clean-up" in 1967. On top of the obelisk, like pebbles left on a headstone, was a collection of rusted steel fragments: unidentifiable shards, torqued, sheered, buckled. The people at Yalata told stories of hot jeeps, hot bulldozers, hot washing machines, buried a few metres down. All the white man's poisoned booty. I remembered the photos on the hospital wall—the mushroom cloud, black with burnt earth thrown up by the blast, like an upsurge of foul gas rising from the bed of a stagnant lake. And the other photo, the crater with its steep walls, and its base of cracked clay where water had collected.

We walked in circles around ground zero while Robin told me the following story:

"Eight months after the blast, the scientists were coming here doing the experiments, and they saw smoke, and when they got here there was an Aboriginal family on the edge of the crater, camped. They'd actually been going down into the crater, out of the wind, cooking and eating rabbits down the bottom."

He was talking about the Milpuddies, whom I had read about in

the report of the Royal Commission: Edie, Charlie; their kids Henry
and Rosie. The family was from near Ernabella, four hundred kilometres away in the north of the state. They'd been travelling for nearly a
year, heading for Ooldea to trade dingo pelts, unaware that the mission
there had been closed down five years before and the people moved
to Yalata. When the Royal Commission visited Maralinga twenty-

five years later, Edie, whose family had settled at Yalata, addressed the commissioners through an interpreter: "At a waterhole called Unguntju we heard an explosion and the earth seemed to be moving." This would have been one of the first series, at Emu Field. Robin knew the story well; Edie was one of Della's aunts. But his version differed somewhat from the official one. In his version, for example, there were not three dogs but twenty:

"The scientists rang up the range commander at Maralinga, and he said, 'I want you to shoot the dogs, because we can't decontaminate the dogs. And you take the family and you shower them until they're down to safe radiation-levels, then you put 'em in the truck and take them straight to Yalata.'

"That was the idea," Robin added. "If they found people they'd take them straight to Yalata, two hundred kilometres away on the Nullarbor, even if they'd come from the north. Now, to shoot a dog in front of an Aboriginal person is a real big no-no. Because they treat those dogs like children. Literally like children. They sleep with the dogs, they use the dogs for hunting, they use the dogs to keep warm. I've seen a dead bitch with six pups there, and the old girls will walk straight over—the dog might have got run over—and the pups will be looking for the mother for milk. The old girls will walk straight over, grab the whole six pups, and they'll go to the young women, and they might have a baby on the tit, they'll give them two pups, and she'll put a pup on the tit straightaway.

"Then the scientists actually showered the couple and the two kids. Now, these people were naked, and the scientists were all dressed up in the white suit and the big air mask. And they were scrubbing the lady and the man, intimately, to get rid of any contamination. And that would be another hell of a shock. Maybe never seen a white man in their lives. And to be touched by a man in a white suit with a big nose, a big air-mask nose. They would have thought they were being washed by the devil, the *mamu*."

Edie when she entered the shower block was relieved to see another black woman: but when she spoke to her she received no answer; the woman merely stared. It took her a moment to understand that she had spoken to her reflection, that she was alone.

"They were taken to Yalata and left down there," Robin said. "Well, two weeks after, the old girl, old Edie—she was only a young woman then; my wife's auntie—she gave birth to a stillborn baby. And everybody blamed the radiation. But low-level radiation like that, it doesn't work that quick. I blame the shock of seeing the dogs shot, then the shock of being touched by these people. I think that's what shut her system down and killed the baby."

The facts surrounding the health of the Milpuddies and their children and grandchildren, like the number of dogs, are uncertain. Robin maintained that the effects of the radiation itself had "gone to the next generation," that it had not affected the immediate family. The Royal Commission report records that Edie Milpuddie's third child died aged two from a brain tumour, while her next was born premature. As for the two surviving children, Rosie as an adult developed a heart condition, and lost a child herself, while Henry developed tuberculosis and pneumonia in his early twenties, and one of his daughters died of a heart condition.

"Old Charlie, the husband," said Robin, "he passed away in 1974 from pneumonia, but it was indirectly from alcohol—he turned into a drunkard down at Yalata, and he went to sleep in the rain drunk, and got pneumonia and died."

This corruption would be carried onward, and onward. There were Milpuddies living in Ceduna and Yalata. "It's gone to the next generation. But indirectly—" and Robin nodded to the sacred ground, to the great simmering bolus concealed in it, and I recalled that for his wife's people the ground is the dwelling place of the Ancestors, the source of all creation. "Indirectly, it's come from here, don't worry about that."

Robin believed there would have been dozens of Aboriginal families crossing the prohibited area throughout the test period. The task of ensuring that the area—thirty thousand square kilometres—was clear of Aboriginal people had been assigned to one "native patrol officer" working alone and without so much as a radio; he was Walter MacDougall, and his name was still well known among the people of Oak Valley and Yalata. MacDougall had been brought up at mission stations and had spent most of his life working with Aboriginal people. He was tall, pale, red-headed. The Anangu called him brother. In 1955, about two years after the first tests at Emu Field, MacDougall gave an interview to an Adelaide newspaper. "Whenever a white man finds something of value to him in any Aboriginal area the Aborigines are pushed aside," he said. "I believe that what is happening to these natives is contrary to the spirit of the United Nations charter." Alan Butement, one of the Australian government's chief scientific observers, dashed off a letter to MacDougall's boss. This individual, he said, was "placing the affairs of a handful of natives above those of the British Commonwealth of Nations."

THE BRITISH GOVERNMENT, submitting its final argument to the Royal Commission enquiry into the tests, declared that the commission had "found no evidence that any Aborigine has suffered harm from any of the tests or minor trials." And it was true that the council representing Maralinga's indigenous people had failed to prove any link between the tests and the ill health suffered by the Milpuddies and other Anangu. Nevertheless, the commission found it would be "grossly irresponsible of the UK Government if it did not now accept that it has a continuing obligation to clean up the contaminated areas." It was recommended by the Australian government that the British pay 35 million Australian dollars in compensation to the "traditional owners." The British demurred, agreeing only to contribute the same figure to a "final" clean-up of the Maralinga site. In the event, the Anangu of Yalata and Oak Valley received less than half the recommended figure, and that came from the Australian government.

The Royal Commission was set up following public concern about Maralinga's radiological legacy and the safety of the site, which had been largely handed back to the Anangu the previous year as a result of a Land Rights Act. A newspaper had published a leaked report concerning high levels of plutonium at the site, and on Australian TV a deathbed interview had been aired with a veteran who claimed to have seen the bodies of four Aboriginal people at the edge of a crater, presumably Marcoo, since it was the only known crater, though his allegation was never verified. Over the course of 188 days the commission interviewed 311 witnesses in Adelaide, London and Maralinga itself, and concluded that several of the trials were done under dangerous meteorological conditions, including Marcoo, which was "fired in conditions which violated the firing criterion that there should be no forecast of rain." As for the Milpuddie incident, "those responsible for security seemed at least as concerned about the exposure of . . . flaws as the welfare of the Milpuddie family." Operation Brumby, the "cleanup" undertaken just before the British handed over the land to the federal government in 1967, was "planned in haste to meet political deadlines."

It was not until 2009 that the Anangu were finally handed back most of the rest of their land; but by now they wanted nothing to do with it. It was *mamu*, said Robin, and when they visited the Maralinga settlement—as they would from time to time for meetings or, last year, for the ceremony marking the official handover of the remainder of the land—they would lock themselves in the guest caravans and scarcely leave, and would return to their homes in Yalata or Oak Valley as soon as possible. There could be employment here, said Robin, but the tribal people weren't interested. In Yalata even children born fifty years after the tests feared the place. Science was not the answer, there was no answer. The Anangu are a people who can preserve a narrative unchanged for ten thousand years.

WE DROVE NORTH, out of the main test zone, towards Emu Field, across 150 kilometres of peak-and-trough sandhills. Occasionally camels could be spotted milling in mobs between the trees. Towards evening the vegetation began to clear and the land became flat, and ahead of us was the claypan, a two-kilometre-wide disc of red like an unglazed plate glowing in a kiln. Emu Field. The sun was low in the sky, but still dazzling. Once we had set up camp in the lee of a sandhill—dead mulga limbs dragged behind the Land Cruiser and stacked between our two swags for a fire—I took off to the pan for the last minutes of light. In its clarity the air was to normal air as normal air is to water. It was as if I had been given back the vision of childhood. It is a characteristic of arid places, this clarity caused by the absence of vapour. Claypans are ephemeral lakes, basins into which surface water will drain when there is sufficient precipitation, carrying with it fine sediment. In arid environments, where evaporation exceeds precipitation, such basins are usually covered with water only briefly and shallowly for a few days each year. What chiefly characterises claypans—like their counterparts, playas—is their flatness, their surface being graded and swept afresh with each inundation of water.

A raven came to see me, circled, then vanished over the low dunes that surrounded the pan. Seek thy brother. The floor of the pan, scarcely rising or falling so much as a centimetre in elevation across the entire five square kilometres of its expanse, was cracked into irregular polygons and scurfing like a eucalyptus, and each of its palm-sized scales shone with a fine and perfect salt-glaze. It was like walking over the surface of an old oil painting. The gloss added to the illusion of wetness; where it reflected the sky, the ground was blue. A last cruelty to the dying traveller. The appearance truly was of water, even from a fairly short distance, like the ghost of its last flooding.

I followed a line of prints, camel prints made when the pan was wet, gouged deep and messy, the pan-surface littered with the scuffed-up clay. Despite their soggy appearance the prints and the clay alike were, of course, hard and unyielding as terracotta. The pan had been named "Emu" by the army surveyor on account of a footprint he'd found in its surface. The smaller pan nearby was named "Dingo" for the same reason.

I knelt and lowered my head to the varnished surface, suddenly conscious of the enormous flatness expanding around me, and when I looked up, the raven had brought its mate. They quacked and wheeled. I could not see them as ill-omened—as I might were they to alight on the rail of a ship at sea, say. In its lushness their blackness was the opposite of morbid; plus, the presence of other perceptive beings seemed like something to celebrate. I loved them. I walked for two minutes, eyes shut tight, towards the sun. When I opened them the ravens had gone and the sun had sunk behind the horizon. The world was assuming the mauve tinge of night. It was a beautiful place, the constancy of it, and those waiting for the mushroom cloud in 1953 must have found it so too.

.   .   .

WE WOKE BEFORE DAWN. The ground where we were camping was sparsely wooded—mulga, some she-oak, beautiful in silhouette and filled with dovelike birds whose wings squeaked as they took flight— and studded all over with the characteristic raised rings of mulga ants' nests. There are thousands of species of ant in arid Australia. The night before, I'd gone collecting firewood and had returned to the camp to find my hand crawling with them. That was the Aussie desert: a glove of ants and a mask of flies. I ought to have been more careful. A few weeks earlier a man's body had been found in the Northern Territory alongside his bogged car with a note: he'd been collecting brush to put under his wheels for traction, and had been snakebit.

After breakfast we climbed the dune that rimmed the claypan and looked across the flatness. The pan was not the fizzing orange of yesterday evening but a livid purple. Two kilometres away was a column of dust, white in the morning sun, and that dust was being taken up by first one small whirlwind, then a second, and carried across the pan. *Willie-willie* was the Australian term. In the Gobi they are thought to be demons. The cause was a mob of camels, twenty or more suddenly visible through a clearing in the dust, heads hung low, on the move.

The two bombs had been detonated fifteen kilometres south-east of the pan, which itself had been used only as a landing strip for supplies and personnel. The clean-up effort had been more cursory even than that made 160 kilometres south at Maralinga. The eastern shore of the claypan alongside the landing strip was heaped with industrial waste, and beyond it a raised platform of rutted earth covered who knew what. Lengths of bore-pipe; a tank's rusted caterpillar track; a loop of steel rope; an S-shaped rod hung from the stump of a tree; dozens of rusted drums labelled "Aviation Gasoline"; and a mechanic's vice stamped "Made in England." All this crap. It made it easy to forget how isolated you were, two hundred kilometres from the nearest town.

We ate a whole roast chicken, with our hands, off the tailgate of the truck, then drove out to the first site, Totem 1, where a ten kiloton bomb had been exploded on 15 October 1953. We passed a plot of a dozen concrete blocks, tonne-heavy, used to tether Hurricane jets that were brought in to determine the effect upon them of the blast. The jets themselves, intact but irradiated, had been buried along with the exposed jeeps and tanks and mannequins. Crossing the track ahead of us a line of camels snaked away from the proving ground.

In the planning of Totem 1 there was an acceptance that it was not possible to determine precisely what might happen—how high the mushroom cloud might rise, how far or where it might drift, how heavy any fallout might be. It was in the nature of a test, after all, that it was done without full knowledge of its implications, and this was only the second nuclear bomb Britain had exploded, and its first on land. In its report the Royal Commission concluded that Totem 1 "was fired under wind conditions that ... would produce unacceptable levels of fallout. Measured fallout from Totem 1 on inhabited regions did exceed the limits proposed." In its criticism of the decision to fire Totem 1 at that time, the Royal Commission noted particularly that it "did not take into account the existence of people at Wallatinna and Welbourn Hill downwind of the test site." Those stations lie some 195 kilometres north-west of Emu Field, in the northern part of South Australia.

"I was thinking it might be a dust storm," Yami Lester told the enquiry, remembering the black mist, "but it was quiet, just moving through trees and above the trees. It was just rolling and moving quietly." That ghastly, implacable quietness, the quietness of a lava flow; it is this that struck others who witnessed the phenomenon, too, desert people white and black, who were accustomed to the phenomena of the desert and knew that dust storms did not make their approach in windless silence. Lester's stepfather, whom we know only as Kanytji, hearing the explosion, had associated it with Wananpi, the water serpent of the Dreaming, creator and guardian of waterholes. The cloud, he said, "was from the ground and it was black ... there was like a sprinkling rain, like dropping of dew ... We felt cold and shivering." Kanginy, another resident of Wallatinna, said it was "a bit like the sort of smoke when you burn a tyre."

Ellen Giles, at Welbourn Hill station, recalled a "big, coiling, cloudlike thing." In its aftermath "the orange and lemon trees were coated in this dust. It was an oily dust. You could see it on the walls too. We tried to hose the trees down, but they just withered and died."

In Lester's camp there was a searing fear; the vomit was green, the shit was green. There were terrible headaches. *Puyu*, the Anangu called it—"black mist." It is not known precisely how many died, but the camp moved at least twice, a practice undertaken each time there is a death. Like other children who were exposed to the cloud, Yami Lester found he was unable to open his eyes. He had to be led around holding the end of a stick. His eyesight deteriorated over the following years, until he lost the sight in first one eye, then both.

Ernest Titterton, one of the senior Australian scientists, had been present at the explosion of the world's first nuclear bomb in the New Mexico desert in 1945, and helped to devise the system that activated it. It is possible that the weight of that responsibility warped some part of him. In a letter written in the 1980s, when reports of the black mist began to reach the Australian public, he asserted that "the story is laughable from physical, meteorological and medical points of view." In an interview with Australian radio he added that "if you investigate black mists you're going to get into an area where mystique is a central feature." By mystique I don't think he meant mystery, but rather something like the supernatural or allegory or magic or—had he known the word—*mamu*.

The Royal Commission was not inclined to disregard the numerous witness testimonies, and found that the cloud was more than mere "mystique." While it discovered no evidence that the fallout had caused serious or long-term injuries, it conceded that "at Wallatinna the vomiting of Aborigines may have resulted from radiation, it may have been a psychogenic reaction to the frightening experience, or it may have resulted from both these." It was incomprehensible to the commission, as it was to Titterton, that a "psychogenic reaction," or even "mystique," might themselves be catastrophic; that they could kill.

A KILOMETRE FROM the Totem 1 site, Robin and I stood on the promontory from which the detonation had been viewed by Penney and Titterton and the dignitaries who accompanied them. Fixed into the ground were the steel pegs to which the viewing tower had been tethered, and there, across a stretch of glittering ironstone, was ground zero. We walked the rest of the way. Close to ground zero, weathered to near illegibility, there was a yellow sign, its warning in Italian, Greek and Polish, as well as English. The few trees were black and etiolated. A tangle of warped steel was all that remained of the bomb tower.

"I know I'll come across skeletons one day," said Robin. "MacDougall once found seventeen people walking on West Street and turned them back." West Street was one of the grid of service tracks that crisscrossed the Maralinga test zone. "This is recorded in one of his reports. And as he left they were heading back towards Western Australia. Well, those people never made it back to Western Australia, and they never made it to Ooldea, where they were initially going. Those people literally disappeared off the face of the earth. They either were caught in a bomb blast and it vaporised them, or they were caught in the radiation and got very sick and then passed away somewhere in the desert."

That night, rummaging in the pocket of my rucksack, I cut my finger on something—it was a fine, clean, stinging cut. I shone my headtorch into the pocket. Those glassy chips of trinitite I'd picked up glimmered back. There wasn't much blood.

THE FOLLOWING DAY, in the hospital building at Maralinga, Robin played me a DVD, a copy of a publicity reel made by Britain's Ministry of Defence in the 1960s. He wanted one day to set up a museum in one of the mess huts, including a multiple-rocket-launcher that currently adorned the patio, and other artefacts picked up from the ranges. The film would be played as an introduction. He'd like people from Yalata and Oak Valley, whose land this was, to be guides, to "tell the Anangu story." But employment was not enough to tempt them to set foot here. It was not just that Tietkens's Plain and Emu Field had been made hazardous places and places of grief, or that they were haunted, exactly (the *mamu* wasn't like a ghost); it was more that to go there was akin to necrophilia. The land was dead, and only the mad consort with corpses.

And here, in the film, to the sound of quavering strings, was the land being put to death.

"The biological group prepares thirty articulated dummies," says a perky British voiceover, and a dummy is shown being hoisted upright by a cable hooked to an eyelet in the top of its head, "which are to be suitably clad in normal service dress, and will be exposed to the first round at distances up to six thousand feet from the weapon." A dummy is shown "standing in a slit trench to assess the degree of protection," and then pictured gazing manfully from his station. "Others will be exposed in three positions: standing, crouching and prone, with dummies both facing and side-on to the blast." A dummy is shown on its hands and knees. "The object is to confirm theoretical predictions about the distances men in these positions will be thrown by the dynamic blast effect."

We see the mushroom cloud; we see the sky gridded with contrails from dozens of smoke-rockets fired to make the blast-wave visible; the next day, we see the aftermath. It might be footage from an antinuclear campaign:

Two dummies wired upright on posts, their overalls shredded and their hands ripped off, only their gas masks still intact and in place; then a steel crucifix carrying nothing but a singed torso, the ground around scattered with a wreckage of arms, legs and heads; next, a pile of melted plastic and blackened clothing; then a beheaded figure strapped to a pole; sundry others tossed across an acre of ground. And finally, after these visions, the devil, white from head to toe save for that black snout, clutching his ticking box, making his way across the hazard zone.

3

TROUBLEMAKERS

*The Gobi Desert and
the Taklamakan Desert, China*

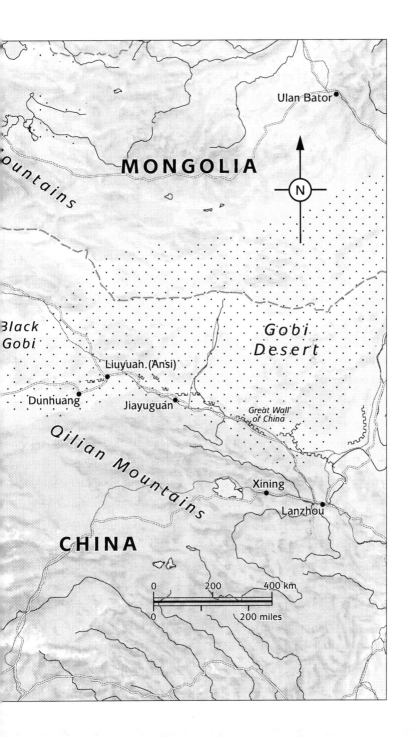

If the desert is a hiding place for human crimes it is also an abyss into which those who shame, disgust or threaten us may be swept. In Australia I had been reading about the Qing dynasty's annexation of territory to the north-west of China in the 1750s. Throughout Qing rule of that region, which continued intermittently until 1911, tens of thousands of criminals and dissidents were sent to the newly annexed land. The threat of banishment to and enslavement in a place so distant and inhospitable, so alien to one nurtured in the watered heartland, was a deterrent; but the tactic was not only penal: such a vital political buffer, it was understood, could be secured only through colonisation and through land reform. The same strategy had been followed by Britain in Australia. Where colonists will not go willingly they must be sent. The severity of a person's crime was reflected in the remoteness of their exile: "very near" (1,000 kilometres from the convict's homeland); "to a nearby frontier" (1,600 kilometres); "to an insalubrious region" or "to the furthest frontier." The deserts of the far west, the Gobi and the Taklamakan, being both insalubrious and as distant from centres of population as it was possible to be while remaining in Chinese territory, were reserved for the gravest cases. Those exiled fell into two groups. First, ordinary criminals, who would usually be sent into slavery. As well as convicts who had committed crimes themselves, this group included the families of those who had been executed for, say, murder, or incest, or treason. The second, smaller, group consisted of disgraced government officials, or *weifei*—"troublemakers"—who had criticised official corruption or had associated with convicted traitors. Convicts on departure would be tattooed on both temples like a double stamp of lading: your crime on the right; on the left your desti-nation. The far west was colonised not only by murderers, thieves, rap-ists, counterfeiters and sectarians, but by bureaucrats, army generals, eunuchs, and *wenzi yu an* or "literary cases." The exiled scholar Ji Yuan, writing to his wife in 1769, described it as "another world."

Whereas for indigenous Australians the desert is an infinite mosaic of symbols and stories, the hyper-arid deserts of China have figured in that country's popular imagination as mere interstices, or collec-tively as a dread realm entered under duress or to reach the next oasis, even among those who populate the desert's edge. One of the earliest recorded crossings is that of the Buddhist monk Xuanzang. Born in 602, he became a novice at the age of twelve and was soon recognised by his elders as a student of uncommon brilliance. Aged twenty-seven, sick of the disputing among his fellow monks on matters of dogma, he determined to travel across the great deserts of north-west China to India, the cradle of Buddhism, where he would retrieve scriptures that would resolve these disagreements. "Dangers and untold difficul-ties lie ahead of him," wrote his contemporary biographer. "He will be sorely tested but he is ready to depart." Xuanzang is warned by a "venerable greybeard" that "the Western roads are difficult and bad; sand streams stretch far and wide; evil sprites and hot winds, when they come, cannot be avoided." As the monk and his nag make their way west, guided only by piles of bones and horse dung, they arrive at an expanse of desert where, according to the monk's biographer, "there are no birds overhead, and no beasts below; there is neither water nor herb to be found." Xuanzang went on to spend fourteen years travel-ling and studying in India, Nepal and Sri Lanka, before recrossing the Taklamakan in 645 with twenty-two horses carrying more than seven hundred works of Buddhist scripture.

I RETURNED FROM Australia to find the living-room window boarded up; I'd been burgled, but my neighbours had been unable to get hold of me. When I tidied up the mess I realised how dusty the flat was: all the surfaces grey with it, and accumulations of grey-blue fluff under the bed and behind the radiators and along the skirting. My laptop had gone, but apparently there was no market for a heap of old books about deserts.

One of those inspired by Xuanzang, 1,300 years later, was a British missionary named Mildred Cable. Among my remaining books was a Virago reprint of her most famous volume, *The Gobi Desert*, originally published in 1942, in which she wrote: "The utter loneliness of the monk's journey … bred a strength and endurance which carried him through every ordeal, and the long silent desert stages taught him the ways of meditation better than any monastic rule could have done."

The epiphany happened in summer 1893. Following some "unaccountable impulse," fifteen-year-old Mildred went alone to a talk by a member of the China Inland Mission. The speaker is unidentified, but seems to have been one Emily Wiltshire. She wore a collar, Cable recalls, embroidered with the words "Jesus He shall save." Afterwards, she took the abashed young Cable aside: "I think the Lord wants you in China." In 1860, thirty-three years earlier and following the Second Opium War, treaties signed by Peking had granted foreign missionaries in China the right to preach and build churches. Five years later, the China Inland Mission was founded in Shanghai by a Yorkshire Protestant named James Hudson Taylor. The CIM, as it was known to its members, would differ from other mission organisations. While the established Chinese missions concentrated on the coastal cities, the CIM's stations would be scattered across the hinterlands—the minority lands; lawless, far from imperial power, far from Christian influence: Inner Mongolia, Tibet, Ningxia, Gansu, Xinjiang.

"Fixed on the objective, which was neither ease, pleasure, fun nor self-expression," Mildred began her training at the CIM Candidates Home in London. The "Principles and Practice of the China Inland Mission" was known to younger members as the Document of Serfdom. Members, it said, must "be prepared to live lives of privation, of toil, of loneliness, of danger—to be looked down upon by their own countrymen and to be despised by the Chinese; to live in the interior, far from the comforts and advantages of society and protection such as they have enjoyed at home."

It seems that Cable had planned to go to China with her husband-to-be. But he reneged. He is referred to only obliquely in her writings, as an absence. Was there an ultimatum? Was it the work itself he renounced, or the marriage? "On a beautiful May morning, when the lilac was in bloom," she remembers in an autobiography, she received "a letter in which that was written which made a goblin of the sun." She broke off the engagement and told herself she would never trust anyone again. But she would go. On 25 September 1901, in the aftermath of the Boxer Rebellion, this unhappy person sailed for China. It was not merely a compulsion; it was escape, and her desert years became the perfect extension of that flight.

When Cable arrived in China, aged twenty-two, Evangeline French, ten years older, had been in her own post for nine years. Meeting the new arrival in Huozhou, a city in the northern province of Shanxi, French wondered: "What possessed them to send such a frail child to our hard inland conditions?" Gansu and Xinjiang, where they would be going, lay a thousand kilometres and more to the west, as far from the sea as any place on earth.

But if the girl appeared frail it was only the strain of the journey and the bleak years that preceded it. She was steely, and throughout her writings you sense an unwillingness to yield to mere circumstances. By some—for instance gentlemen of the Bible Society back in faraway Shanghai—she would become known as "Napoleon."

I WAS BEGINNING to feel there was no way to travel but in the footsteps of others. In early autumn I booked a flight to Shanghai and from there flew 2,250 kilometres west to Jiayuguan, a city on the edge of the Gobi Desert in the province of Gansu. I stayed in a business hotel in a room whose floor, walls and ceiling were lined with the same white glossy laminate, as if designed to be hosed down between guests. Cable found Jiayuguan an unhappy place, besieged by the desert, its people either introverted into lethargy by the horrors beyond the walls, or compelled to violence. "There is nothing to do here all day but sit and listen to that howling wind," the local women told her. The miller's beaten wife killed herself by eating a box of matches; the blacksmith's son was "so profligate that his father took a sledge-hammer and crushed his head as he lay asleep."

A century and more later the mood had changed. Under my window was a beauty parlour, whose dozen employees would file every morning onto the street in front of the store and, accompanied by shrill pop music, perform a synchronised dance in five parts, before one of them unfurled and lit a belt of firecrackers that exploded over the course of a minute, the manicurists vanishing into the smoke.

THE HEXI CORRIDOR is China's throat, a 1,200-kilometre pass squeezed between the Tibetan Plateau to the south and the Mongolian Gobi to the north. It follows a chain of oases westward from the city of Lanzhou, through Gansu to that province's border with the far-western "autonomous region" of Xinjiang. It was at the so-called "Barrier of the Pleasant Valley" in Gansu, where the corridor narrows to just fifteen kilometres between mountain ranges, that the Jiayuguan fort was built in 1372, soon after the new Ming dynasty had driven the last of the Yuan-dynasty armies into the desert. A slammed door.

The fort lies outside the modern city of Jiayuguan, in the "Great Wall Culture and Tourism Zone." Its pale, battlemented walls are surmounted by tiered watchtowers with red-tiled roofs. There were few tourists, and I was the only non-Chinese. From the ramparts you comprehended the setting—how the fort guarded the pass against the desert. It was to repel raids by nomads, ancestors of the Huns, that this stretch of the Great Wall was built in 221 BC. To the north were the dark Mazong Mountains, to the south the Qilian Mountains. Between the two, bracketed by the wall like a locket on a chain, stood the fort. Only the southern, final, stretch of the wall still stands; you can follow it to the ravine of the Badai River—beyond which the mountains of the Qilian massif are visible through the dust hanging in the air. If you were to leave or enter China's heartland via the west, it had to be through this single channel.

The fort has three gates, Cable explains: to the east, the Gate of Enlightenment, through which I had entered the fort; to the south, the Gate of Conciliation; finally, facing west, the Gate of Sorrows. Passing through the Gate of Sorrows I came to a paved incline that appeared to lead only to the sky. This was the exiles' gate, the entrance to the desert, and when Cable was here the parting words of the banished could still be made out, scratched on the walls – "inspired by sorrow too heavy for the careful balance of literary values, yet unbearable unless expressed in words."

To emerge from the unlit tunnel, fifteen metres long and five high, and set foot on that short slope was to go from an intimate, temple quiet to unbounded silence—from cool to heat, stillness to breeze, from shade into searing light. Another world, and the end of your old life. At the top of the slope I looked back east, to the tunnel I'd emerged from, a dark aperture echoing with unseen footsteps, and the fortress whose ten-metre-high wall the tunnel penetrated, with its battlements and bowmen's turrets. I turned the other way, west. West was the Gobi, a rugged, ash-coloured plain coated with grit and low clumps of tamarisk and camel thorn. I thought of the lake and the willows scarcely two hundred metres away on the other side of the fort.

Ahead was a complex of wooden huts (a noodle shop, workshops, toilets), a row of quad-bikes on which tourists could roar around a flag-marked circuit, a shooting range where you could fire a tripod-mounted M16 into the emptiness (west has always been the direction of fire), a mechanical "bucking bronco" under a striped awning and, couched in the sand, eight live camels, sleepily waiting for tourists, like donkeys on an English beach. Their saddles were draped in matching quilts of floral velour, and their eyes serenely closed as if they were listening to a new interpretation of a favourite piece of music. "An undomesticated and savage animal," William Palgrave claimed. It is the imperiousness of camels that people dislike; and it is that imperiousness—that they will not be cowed and cannot be humiliated—that I love.

The M16 squatted unsupervised under its awning. Nobody was riding the bucking bronco or the camels or the quad-bikes. Their proprietors were sleeping, the camel man on a bench, his forearm across his eyes; another was sprawled across the saddles of two quad-bikes. A woman in a yellow jumpsuit with a matching yellow headscarf and facemask sat hunched over an ice-cream chest. She opened the chest and I saw that it contained nothing but bags full of ice cubes. I bought one, and swinging it in one fist, set out into the Gobi.

The explorer Owen Lattimore, writing of his travels in Inner Mongolia in 1927, delineates the Gobi vaguely: "running, on its longer axis, east and west between Outer and Inner Mongolia … it takes an incline south and west, spreading out until it reaches the limits of the Taklamakan." Mildred Cable allowed "Gobi" to stand for the entire extent of her range, from Jiayuguan as far as Urumqi, 1,500 kilometres west. "Gobi" is not only a proper name, however; it's also used locally for the flat sand-and-gravel plains that are distinct from the sand-dune desert of the Taklamakan or the salt-lake desert of Lop Nor. It was impossible to know where one named desert ended and the next began, where "Gobi" became "Black Gobi," where "Gashun Gobi" degenerated into the Kumtag Desert and the salt-fields of Lop Nor, where the threshold was between Lop Nor—a body of water until it was drained last century—and the Taklamakan. And no sooner had I established that one desert lay *here* and another *there*, or that this one abutted that, than I read or was told that, no, the Black Gobi ends *here* and the Gashun Gobi is not *there*, but five hundred kilometres north.

Behind me, beyond the fort, the smoke-churning skyline of Jiayuguan city was visible—coke, cement, fertiliser, the raw material provisioned, like the region's water, by the surrounding mountains. The clinking of a freight train three kilometres away became audible. Under the final stretch of the Great Wall a few kilometres south, a road ran to the border with Xinjiang, flanked by the railways—the old line to Kashgar a thousand kilometres away, and the new high-speed bullet-train line, yet to be opened, that would rush Han Chinese passengers westwards.

Everywhere half-buried scraps of polythene were shivering in the breeze. The place was a dumping ground, as the desert's shore always is, wherever it is accessible and unpoliced. A solitary Christian grave could be made out, with its double headstone, epitaphs sand-scoured to illegibility. Here and there darker stones had been arranged to form Chinese characters. In a land so mobile there are few forms of writing assured of greater permanence, and Cable describes leaving lines of scripture on Gobi hillsides using the same method. For my own part I collected a handful of brown pebbles and arranged them to form an arrow pointing back the way I'd come. You couldn't be too careful.

To the south, the wall proceeded to its terminus seven kilometres away. It remained awesome, insurmountable: the ground dug up and wetted and stamped into a mould, drying to a hardness that has persisted, in places, for two thousand years. And yet from a distance it didn't look ancient; being a kind of concrete, it resembled the concrete walls built to defend the land against the sea, or the European border fortifications of the world wars, or the wall separating the Occupied Territories from Israel. Surrounding the fort there had once been a moat—*tiantian*—containing not water but fine sand raked daily to betray the footprints of deserters. But according to Cable nothing would induce the soldiers garrisoned there to enter the desert beyond the Gate of Sorrows. "Demons, they are the ones who inhabit the Gobi." Cable conceded it was desolate: "but in the silence and solitude God is still there."

SHE AND EVA FRENCH were scarcely apart from the time they met in 1901 until Cable's death in 1952. Evangeline French was born in Algeria and educated in Geneva with her younger sister, Francesca. According to the women's peculiar, third-person group autobiography, "Personal friendships were slightly scorned in the too strong mental atmosphere of Evangeline's home, where anything approaching to sentimentality was anathema." She herself was "robustuous," "obstreperous" and "rebellious" and "convinced that there was something so essentially wrong with the world that nothing but revolution could set it right." When in 1891 the family moved from radical Geneva to staid, working-class Portsmouth, Eva and Francesca were miserable. "For a young lady to hold strong opinions, to be revolutionary in outlook and unusual in small ways, was sufficient to bring her under suspicion."

It was seven years later when, established in Pingyao, Shanxi Province, Eva passed a man hoeing at the roadside. He stopped his work, stood to his full height, and drew a slow finger across his throat. The Boxer Rebellion began in 1898 in northern China. The mantra of its adherents was "Support the Qing, destroy the foreigners." The focus of the unrest was Shanxi, and by the end of 1900, some two thousand Chinese Christians had been murdered there, along with dozens of foreign missionaries and their families. Among the dead, "hacked to pieces," was Miss Emily Wiltshire, who had encouraged Mildred to join the CIM. In early July 1900 Eva was in the city of Jiexiu when the mission station was attacked by Boxers chanting "Kill! Kill the foreign devils! Kill!" Back home in Britain her mother opened a newspaper to see Eva's name among the dead.

In Geneva, while Eva climbed a tree, Francesca would be sitting in its shade with a book. In later life she disdained "the exaggerated or inexact use of words." Her rigour is discernible in the writings jointly credited to her and Cable. She came to believe that "self-expression may easily be a dissipation of strength which, stored and controlled, might accumulate sufficiently to accomplish great things." Her terrifying task was to tame herself in the glorification of God.

During her older sister's long absence, it was she who had cared for their ailing mother. Soon after the announcement of Eva's death, a telegram was delivered: "Your daughter arrived Hangchow safe." Eva had survived the Boxer attack. Shortly before their mother's death in 1908 she returned to England for a furlough, accompanied by Mildred Cable. When they left once more for China, they were joined by Francesca, forming the party that would come to be known by the people of the desert as the Trio: "the three-in-one venerable teachers of righteousness."

In *The Gobi Desert*, which she co-authored with Francesca French, there is a photo of Cable on arrival in Ansi (a city she hated): she's in a dusty courtyard, seated on bales of cotton surrounded by weary camels. She is quite at home, some great ruler enthroned. Napoleon.

THE SILK ROAD: not a Chinese term, but the nineteenth-century coining of a German geographer, Baron Ferdinand von Richthofen. Yes, silk went this way, east–west, but also much more: paper, jade, ivory, ceramics, tea, medicine, furs, textiles and precious metals. Nor was there only a single route, a superhighway, but rather a shifting network of hundreds of tracks, flanking the Taklamakan Desert and twining from east to west between China and—ultimately, so distant as to be unimaginable—Rome.

It was early September 1931 when Cable and the Frenches and

their small entourage set out west from their base near Jiayuguan for the oasis of Dunhuang, in the far west of Gansu. "The Dunhuang journey will occupy at least two months and after that we cannot tell where the Pillar of Fire may lead us." At Dunhuang, Silk Road travellers would prepare for the perils ahead; to ready your spirit was a task no less vital than readying your caravan. Dunhuang huddled on the edge of oblivion, at the point where the southern Silk Road crossed the great north–south passage between Mongolia and Lhasa. Even for the seasoned desert traveller the voyage west was one from which return was uncertain. There were at Dunhuang the famous Mogao Caves, the Caves of the Thousand Buddhas, where prayers would be made, first on behalf of the outward-setting traveller, to protect them against the western wastes; and then, supposing they returned, to give thanks.

My train was crossing the eggshell-coloured plain I'd walked the day before, the easternmost edge of the Gobi. As the train moved west between the mountains, the fort and the remnant Great Wall were briefly visible in the distance, and, hanging over the horizon, the city's haze of pollution. Within forty minutes, habitation and cultivation were left behind, and the only human features of the desert were the endless pylons, gleaming as if new—squatting, hunched or marching humanoids—and the trappings of the railway itself, in the form of fencing, culverts and hills of soil dug a half-century ago. To repel sand the line was flanked by railway-sleeper walls and sawtooth concrete buttresses and by withered ranks of desert poplars. Several times a year the line has to be closed while drifts are cleared. It is the perpetual confrontation of the occupied desert.

The Gobi was not a place of dunes but of flat expanses broken only by low hills and shallow basins and dried riverbeds. The action of water was everywhere visible, even where water itself had not flowed for decades or centuries. The flatness was limitless, or rather limited only by the horizon, or by visibility, the extent of the air's clarity. In my bunk I listened to the low, cardiac double thump of the rails, and this alone gave me any sense of motion; the terrain outside told you next to nothing. Every twenty minutes or so I sat up in my bunk to look at the desert on either side—through the window in my cabin and the one across the corridor—feeling that I was missing something; but the view scarcely altered in character from hour to hour, identical, it seemed, on each side of the train. It was like being on a treadmill. The slightest variation—a darkening or lightening of the desert surface, a clustering of pylons or wind turbines, a derelict cement factory, the threaded bed of a dried-out stream, a rink of inflorescent salt, a dispersal of bones— was enough to arrest the attention. Otherwise, to watch the passing landscape for more than a few minutes required an effort of will: it was partly the weariness of imagining yourself crossing this landscape on foot. Cable, on first encountering the Gobi, asked herself if she might die—"not, as some had done, of thirst or fatigue, but of boredom."

OF THE FOREIGN witnesses to the Hami Rebellion of 1931 few were closer than Cable and the Frenches. The rebellion, which spread across north-west China, followed the Chinese decision to abolish the ancient Muslim khanate of Hami following the death in 1930 of the last khan. With the end of the khanate came an influx of Han migrants (overwhelmingly China's dominant ethnic group) to the largely Muslim city, which stood in Xinjiang, just over the border from Gansu Province, and a hundred kilometres north of Dunhuang. The new regime exempted the migrants from taxes and handed them land that had formerly been farmed by Muslim Uighurs, the largest ethnic minority in Xinjiang. At the same time, Uighurs found that their agricultural taxes doubled, while in compensation for their fields they received unimproved, unirrigated land on the desert's edge. The spark was the marriage of a Han Chinese tax collector to a Uighur woman. At the wedding party, the newlyweds were killed ("with horrible ferocity," according to Cable) by a mob that went on to murder a hundred Gansu families. Their heads were buried in the fertile soil of the fields expropriated on their behalf.

The rebellion was given strength and direction under two ministers of the late khan. One of them, Yolbas Khan, recruited the commander of an infamous Gansu warlord family, a young man of barely twenty who, according to Cable, "terrified north-west Gansu by the violence of his methods of warfare." In the township of Chenfan, Cable alleged, he left three thousand corpses liquefying in the street.

Big Horse, Thunderbolt, Baby General—any warlord's soubriquets are numerous, but his given name was Ma Zhongying. His officers, according to Cable, "obeyed him with a devotion that was almost a cult," and his agents "were everywhere listening and reporting to Headquarters any word of treason against his rule." It was the Swedish explorer Sven Hedin who translated Ma's name as "Big Horse." With the admiration of one who had a soft spot for uniformed tyrants, he described him as "good-looking, tall and slim, with a good figure." But one of the rare pictures of the general reprinted in *The Gobi Desert* shows a frankly stolid, prideful youth in the uniform of the Kuomintang, the Chinese Nationalist Party—forage cap, leather Sam Brown, arms crossed behind his back—staring down the camera with a brattish insolence, as if daring the photographer to discredit him. "Elegant, perfumed and effeminate," according to Cable. She would have cause to despise him.

While the Uighurs of Hami welcomed the rebel army, the non-Muslim Chinese, many of whom had only arrived in recent years, took shelter in the ancient fortified town, precipitating a siege that would last a year and a half. It was an episode mythic in its squalor. The Chinese ate dogs and cats. Boiling oil was poured onto the besiegers. It was only the discovery by the Chinese of a buried eighteenth-century arsenal that allowed them to hold out. Finally withdrawing, Ma rode west to attack the city of Urumqi. He and his troops were met in the desert by Chinese forces supported by White Russian troops and Ma was injured—"shot through both legs," Cable tells us, not without some satisfaction.

AT THE RAILHEAD at Ansi (today's Liuyuan) I boarded a packed minibus bound for Dunhuang, which lay eighty kilometres south across a plain scattered with saxaul, the green-grey bushes that are often the Gobi's only vegetation. At Ansi, the ancient Silk Road split, and the reason for its splitting, like a stream around a boulder, was the Takla-makan Desert, 327,000 square kilometres of sand dunes, and a cause of dread even greater than the Gobi. The longer, greener branch headed north of the Taklamakan, via the oases of Hami and Kucha and Tur-pan, while the shorter more perilous one crossed the jinn-haunted Lop Desert and skirted the Taklamakan's southern shore, passing through the town of Hotan before reconvening with the northern branch at Kashgar, after a journey of a thousand kilometres. For caravans taking this southern branch, the last place of rest and supplies before the Lop and the Taklamakan (weeks of salt flats, months of sand dunes) was Dunhuang. But for Cable and the Frenches, Dunhuang was not merely a site of antique wonder or an opportunity for "gossiping the gospels"; it was their sanctuary, a tranquil, familiar harbour.

When they arrived after two months of travelling, the Trio found the town inundated with Muslim refugees from Hami who "brought a terrible story of slaughter and devastation." The Baby General and his troops having finally been routed, the Chinese soldiers and residents had taken revenge on the Muslims left behind. "Dunhuang became a city of beggars," Cable wrote. "The typhus began to take its toll of victims and the temple entrances were full of men and women mut-tering in delusion." The injured Ma, meanwhile (shot in both legs, you will recall), having been carried by litter from the desert battleground, established his new headquarters in nearby Ansi—"City of Peace." Soon after their arrival in Dunhuang, Cable and the Frenches, with their rudimentary medical knowledge, received a summons to attend the injured general. As they set out for Ansi, a small band of converts came to see them off. "I am weak, but Thou art mighty," they sang.

Again into the desert. "During the campaign," Cable writes in *A Desert Journal* (another of the more than twenty books she co-authored with Francesca French), "there were so many dead bodies left unburied on the Gobi battlefields that during the heat the stench was intolerable, and this winter wolves are rampant." After four days' freezing journey they arrived in the City of Peace to find the general in good spirits, displaying what Cable called "a smiling, cruel sensuousness." She allows herself a note of derision: as she tended Ma's wounds, "his weary voice sharpened in fear, lest the disinfectant should cause a smart to his sensitive flesh."

The road that took us to Dunhuang crossed a land of the severest flatness broken only by sporadic hazy islands of sandstone. Each of the other passengers carried on his or her knees a zippered holdall or an army-surplus rucksack or a cloth bundle bound in twine. The minibus jounced and squeaked and rattled deafeningly: there would be no conversation, no rest. The driver's mate spoke intermittently into his mobile, as if updating someone on our progress. He and the driver had matching seat-covers: Hello Kitty.

Even this, the main highway to famous Dunhuang, was crumbling at its edges, its surface a mosaic of filled and refilled potholes, pocked every few hundred metres with new holes so deep that vehicles had to swerve to avoid them. This was what the desert did to infrastructure, as to stone: the daylight heat, the cold night, the wind and snow and the salt—even the most resilient materials were patiently prised apart. This was the terrain over which Cable and the Frenches moved back and forth—this, and worse. Here at least there was a little vegetation, waterholes, even occasional shade; further west, between Ansi and the Xinjiang border, was the feared "Black Gobi," where you might go five days without fresh water, a region despised even by Cable, who had a genius for finding consolation in places others saw as irredeemable.

The saxaul gave way to sparse lines of poplar and then fields, cotton at first, then the region's famous melons, drip-fed with aquifer water and tenderly wrapped in foam squares against frost even as they grew. The desert was giving way to the oasis—so it seemed. But this was a false dawn, just an outlying island of watered land. As suddenly as the settlement had appeared, the desert and the saxaul, the salt crust and the pink grit returned, the same as far as the eye could see, the same on the other side of the road. The bustling market town of Cable's day when we reached it an hour later was now a tranquil gleaming Oz of designer boutiques and unaffordable hostelries. The streets were sluiced down twice daily to suppress dust. On my pillow when I checked in to my hotel was a pink teddy bear with enormous, brimming eyes.

IT IS IMPOSSIBLE, today, simply to go to the Caves of the Thousand Buddhas. They lie within an enormous fenced sector and you can't visit them without first penetrating the monolithic, newly opened visitor centre, which itself can be entered only during the slot prescribed by your ticket. Until then you will wait in a holding compound resembling a richly endowed Baptist church, a domed hall built around a stained-glass core, where you will buy scarves printed with flying apsaras.

In frigid coaches we were eventually ferried the thirteen kilometres from the visitor centre on a private road. The only noise was the hum of the air conditioning: it was as if we were gliding on oil. To enjoy the ease of our journey, its coolness and comfort, and then to think of the hardships of travel here until only a few decades ago. It had taken Mildred Cable and the Frenches—none of them younger than forty-five—the best part of a day to reach the caves across "fifteen miles of uncompromising sterility," but as Cable wrote, "it was fitting that a few hours of silence and solitude should be imposed on us, for to pass, without transition, from any restless or noisy life to this reliquary would be to offer it an insult."

Viewed from the coach park, the cliff into which the dozens of caves are dug—the "Precipice of the Immortals"—has something about it of a sand-martin colony, a honeycombed skirt of yellow rock fifteen metres high heaped over by a towering brim of sand, like snow on a wall. It's also, tangibly, a sanctuary. Under the cave-mouths in their tiers, poplars shingle in a breeze. Scattered across the surrounding plain are the eroded stone cones of stupas, marking the tombs of monks.

In AD 366, a Buddhist monk named Yuezen arrived. Following "a vision of a golden radiance in the form of a thousand Buddhas," he dug into the soft conglomerate of the cliff-face, creating a cave. In it he settled to meditate. Over the course of nine dynasties, hundreds of further caves were excavated and consecrated alongside. In 1899, 1,500 years after Yuezen's arrival, an itinerant Taoist monk was passing through Dunhuang. Finding the cave site unoccupied and neglected, he selected one of the caves and made it his home. He was born in the far eastern province of Hubei, and had once been a soldier in Jiuquan. According to one account, he established himself as a seller of Tao-

ist spells to the local Chinese. Mildred Cable met him several times, and recognised something in him. "He determined to devote his life to the cultivation of this stony waste," she wrote. Much of his time seems to have been spent touring nearby settlements, raising funds for the caves' renovation. With this meagre income he commissioned the renovation of some of the wall paintings and statuary, and the removal of many tonnes of drift-sand from the cave-mouths.

In the few photographs of him—sometimes he is named Wang Yuanlu, elsewhere he is Wang Tao-shih; Westerners tend to prefer "Abbot Wang," while his Taoist name was Fa Zhen—he is a tiny figure. You can tell, even in the absence of references of scale. In his gaze and bearing there is humour, forbearance. Not the dupe he is often taken for. His robe sleeves hang to his knees, and he is always squinting, as if just emerged into the light. Little is known about him—soldier, spell-merchant, priest, custodian—and yet few figures are more important in the history of the caves. He has been scrutinised by Chinese and foreigners alike; each according to their allegiances: "a very queer person, extremely shy and nervous, with an occasional expression of cunning"; "wary and of a suspicious mind"; "timorous," "diligent," "thief."

In 1900, during the removal of sand from one of the caves (known to modern archaeologists as "Cave 16"), Wang noticed a crack in the wall close to the entrance. He looked closer and found the bricked-up entrance to an antechamber. On inspection it proved to be packed, floor to ceiling, with tens of thousands of ancient documents. If his discovery was to transform the understanding of China's history, it would also redirect the course of Wang's own quiet life. He would find himself courted and exhorted by foreign travellers then vilified by his countrymen. After a lifetime of devotion to the caves, he died—and again we must rely on the most meagre of narratives—impoverished and embittered.

You enter the caves via a network of wooden gantries fixed to the cliff-face. Outside is only the empty anonymous desert, the fathoms of sand and gravel above your head, while in the cool hush and gloom one intimate scene after another is revealed, more intimate still under torchlight, a whole solar system shimmering in malachite, azurite, orpiment, cinnabar, iron oxide, gold leaf, lamp black, kaolin, red ochre, white lead. The sheer opulence of the caves themselves is hardly diminished. The walls and ceiling of each of the hundreds of remaining shrines are crowded with bright paintings: scenes from the life of Buddha; devas, apsaras, yakshas and other divine beings; portraits of the caves' sponsors; niches and platforms crammed with Buddhas and bodhisattvas sculpted in clay and stucco.

Throwing off my mandatory guide, I lingered in the Cave of the Reclining Buddha. A huge recumbent body materialised from the darkness. The Buddha in repose—fourteen metres from head to foot, two tonnes of clay and stucco on a timber skeleton—was imbued with such airiness that a picture came to mind unbidden of him rising to the ceiling. And behind the great body stood his mourners, a fraction of the larger figure's size, looking out across his flank in a line two-deep, like a crowd at a barrier. Seventy-two figures gazing back at me, each bearing his or her individual expression of despair. Levered lips and gritted teeth; brows stunned to fixity; nostrils aquiver, hands clasped not in piety so much as self-comfort. It was as if they were standing at the mouth of a grave—just as they had stood since the High Tang dynasty 1,200 years ago.

He was called the Reclining Buddha, but his rest was the rest of eternity, of liberation from the treadmill of existence, for the statue depicted the Mahaparinirvana, the Great Completed Nirvana. Buddha in death. His face, unlike his body, seemed lifeless; his brows were a black-painted M, his lips taut, his eyes mere slits exposing a slot of black pupil—the eyes of a cat asleep. The red, yellow, green and blue of the mourners' clothing; their pink lips and rosy cheeks; the theatricality of their gestures; the altar, which was a *stage*—it was as if I'd come in at the end of a boisterous piece of theatre, the last notes of the chorus still sounding. The vignettes on the wall behind the mourning statues, skin tones oxidised to tea-and-coffee browns, depicted the continuation of the procession in two dimensions: Buddha's casket shouldered by pallbearers and escorted by banner-wielding kings and priests and bodhisattvas. Sombre, ceremonial, but also quite a jamboree. On top of the casket a rooster, dispelling evil spirits. The god Indra, busily jemmying sacred teeth from Buddha's mouth, as if lifting the marque from a car's grille.

I emerged into bakery heat and icy dazzle. Fresh air soughing the tops of the poplars. The sudden absence of adornment and colour was like a buzzing in my ears. The caves were an assault against the desert's monotony—that was their human glory. Here—in spite of everything, in spite of the weeks of sand, wind and salt that awaited those who prayed here, and the camels and companions left to perish by those who completed the return journey—here was life and replenishment.

IN *BIGGLES IN THE GOBI* (1953) the eponymous hero crash-lands in the Communist desert while attempting to evacuate a party of British missionaries. Meanwhile two of his lieutenants, having parachuted from Biggles's Halifax in order to clear a landing strip, are sheltering with the terrified missionaries in the Caves of the Thousand Buddhas. Aided by a band of Kirghiz nomads, they must fend off a troop of Chinese soldiers, whose nefarious leader, Ma Chang—"a little frog-faced man"—appears to be modelled on Big Ma. The author, W. E. Johns, did not visit the caves himself, but in a foreword acknowledges his debt to the explorer Sir Marc Aurel Stein and his book *Ruins of Desert Cathay* (1912). Stein is an important figure in the caves' modern history. Born in Budapest in 1862, he studied in England, where he would become a naturalised subject. He was as wiry and insatiable as the terriers that were his most constant companions. His moustache frequently froze hard as wood on desert nights. There was none of the sentimentality about him of the Arabian explorers, no desire to emulate the natives, far from it: a European gentleman, down to the hanky poking from his breast pocket. From an early age his heroes were three, and he would shadow them till his death: first Alexander the Great; then those he found himself following in China and India: Marco Polo and above all Xuanzang.

He was forty-five when he arrived at Dunhuang in 1907. He had planned only a short visit to the Caves of the Thousand Buddhas, following his excavation of a previously unknown extension of the Great Wall. But while he was staying in Dunhuang he heard rumours that a huge ancient library had been discovered among the caves. He describes arriving at the site and seeing the "multitude of dark cavities...honeycombing the sombre rock in irregular tiers." It was a scene that recalled for him "fancy pictures of troglodyte dwellings of anchorites such as I remembered having seen long, long ago in early Italian paintings." (Who knows, but perhaps he was thinking of the Master of the Osservanza's portrayal of St. Antony embracing St. Paul.) It was not the last time he would be reminded, during his time at the caves, of the lives of the Desert Fathers. When he finally left the site and returned to Dunhuang, "the oasis looked delightfully green and refreshing, and I greeted it like an anchorite set free from another Thebaid."

The shrine, he noted, "was in the charge of a Taoist priest"—Wang, who at the time of Stein's arrival was away on a "begging tour" with his acolytes. The priest, when he returned, was wary. In *Ruins of Desert Cathay* Stein notes his "occasional expression of cunning" and adds: "he would be a difficult person to handle." Initially the very suggestion that the Englishman might *buy* one of the specimens was met with "such perturbation" by Wang that the subject was temporarily dropped. What finally changed his position, in Stein's narrative, was the explorer's invocation of his "patron saint," Xuanzang. "Very soon I felt sure that the Tao-shih...was quite as ardent an admirer in his own way of [Xuanzang] as I am in another." Stein went on to tell Wang that he had followed in the pilgrim's footsteps "from India over ten thousand *li* across inhospitable mountains and deserts." Wang led Stein to a modern temple he had built among the poplars in the shadow of the cliff: its veranda walls were adorned with newly commissioned scenes from Xuanzang's journey, including one that showed the monk on the bank of a river, preparing to lead across his horse laden with manuscripts—a reference, Stein realised, to the twenty-two ponyloads of sacred books and relics Xuanzang had removed from India.

That night Stein's assistant and translator, Chiang, came to his tent bearing a bundle of scrolls in Chinese, which Wang had given him in secret, "carefully hidden under his flowing black robe." Chiang returned in the morning, having spent the night translating the material. Stein was astonished: the scrolls were printed with sutras and colophons that showed they had been brought from India and translated into Chinese by none other than Xuanzang, a coincidence of which

Stein believed Wang "in his ignorance could not possibly have had any inkling."

The tens of thousands of manuscripts and scrolls, written and printed not only in Chinese but in Tibetan, Sanskrit, Sogdian and Uighur included what would prove to be the world's earliest printed document, the "Diamond Sutra" from AD 868, as well as numerous tightly folded temple banners and silk paintings from the Tang dynasty. "Nowhere," wrote Stein, "could I trace the slightest effect of moisture. And, in fact, what better place for preserving such relics could be imagined than a chamber carved in the live rock of these terrifyingly barren hills, and hermetically shut off from what moisture, if any, the atmosphere of the desert valley ever contained?"

Wang was induced to allow a selection of the manuscripts to be removed to a "temple of learning in Ta-Ying-Kuo" (England), in exchange for a "substantial subscription" to the upkeep of the caves. As Stein remarks upon striking a deal with the priest, "when I surveyed the archaeological value of all I could carry away for this sum, I had good reason to claim it a bargain."

When I went there the library cave was empty. Other European and American antiquarians had followed Stein, and its treasures have been dispersed across the world. Only a century ago it had lain in utter darkness, unknown even to Dunhuang's monks. In his foreword to *Biggles in the Gobi* Johns writes: "It was implied recently in an American magazine (which should have known better) that Sir Aurel Stein stole some of these books. That is untrue. It is correct that he brought some home with him, for no one on the spot could translate them...But he paid for them with a sum of money sufficient for the Abbot to develop the productivity of the oasis." A Chinese history of printing published in Beijing in 1961 records that the Diamond Sutra "was stolen over fifty years ago by the Englishman Ssu-t'a-yin, which causes people to gnash their teeth in bitter hatred."

Mildred Cable recalled the words of a woman who'd met Stein while he was excavating near her village: "He was searching very hard for something or other, but he never found it. I think it was dragon's bones to grind down for medicine. He was a nice man, but peculiar. He would never let anyone watch him eat."

. . .

ONCE I LEFT behind the cool, swept streets of the tourist city, Dunhuang began to seem like the oasis it was: palm trees and poplars growing from the dust; a verdancy that felt provisional. Turn a corner and, a few kilometres away, pale as a daytime moon, the Mingsha dunes, an immense range known locally as "the mountains." At the edge of town I climbed the steep slipping flank of a thirty-metre dune, knowing that, to the west, five kilometres away, lay the Crescent Moon Lake, a natural spring ringed by dunes, "small, crescent-shaped and sapphire blue," according to Cable, who recognised it as a sacred place.

The dunes extended about twenty-five kilometres west to the Gashun ("bitter") Gobi, beyond which lay the Lop Desert and the dry lake of Lop Nor, where China's nuclear-test zone was located. I walked along the dune crests, a foot either side. Finger-sized orange lizards scattered like fish in a boat's wake. I was conscious that my steps obliterated the cleanness of the line, so that the ridge resembled the crimped edge of a pie—though no sooner had prints been made than they were obliterated. The wind was constant. Sometimes a slope would feel solid as concrete underfoot, then an infinitesimal change in gradient would cause me to sink ankle-deep with every step. I rested astride a dune's brink, horsemanlike. In a shallow depression, a handful of chaff, helixing in the wind; then a dozen seedheads jostling a couple of metres above my head; suddenly a shadow—a butterfly, cadmium yellow against the near-white sky. There was a low tearing noise, shifting in volume and pitch. And *there*, maybe a kilometre away, clambering across the flank of a dune—I was not alone: a figure, a man in black.

FINALLY ALLOWED TO return to Dunhuang following their summoning by the Baby General, Cable and the Frenches found that Ma's troops—whose comrades in Ansi they had just been nursing—had turfed them out of their quarters, stolen their best mules and ransacked their medicine chest. Homeless in the Gobi's midwinter, the women and their small entourage took the road between the "Singing Sand Dunes," to the Crescent Moon Lake.

"All around us we saw tier on tier of lofty sand-hills," Cable wrote, "yet when, with a final desperate effort, we hoisted ourselves over the last ridge and looked down on what lay beyond, we saw the lake below, and its beauty was entrancing." Adding to the scene's grandeur was the famous "*lui-in*" emitted by the surrounding dunes. On one occasion the Trio was "awakened by a sound like a roll of drums." Fearing attack by brigands, Cable was reassured by the resident priest: "Don't be anxious, Lady. It is only the drum-roll of our sand-hills. Rest your heart." It was a phenomenon recorded by Marco Polo when (he tells us) he crossed the Gobi seven hundred years earlier, though he attributed it to "spirits of the desert," which, he adds, "are said at times to fill the air with the sounds of all kinds of musical instruments, and also of drums and the crash of arms." Wilfred Thesiger described a "low vibrant hum, which grew in volume until it sounded as though an aeroplane were flying low over our heads," and Cable reminds us that "we also read of 'singing sands' in the Arabian desert where Dr. Bertram Thomas and companions heard a loud noise, which he describes as being like the sound of a ship's siren." The sound continued for about two minutes, Thomas reported, "and ended as abruptly as it had begun." The cause remains unexplained, despite the efforts of scientists. The sand can be coarse or fine, hard-packed or loose, quartz or carbonate, though it occurs only when the surface is disturbed—by someone sliding down the face of a dune, for instance, as the French sisters do in Cable's description—and in the driest of dunefields. There are two schools of thought as to the cause: the first says it is produced by the vibration of air between sand-grains, the second by the friction of grains one against the other. Harry St. John Philby found he could "play" the dunes using a glass bottle: "I then thrust the bottle deep into the soft, moving, singing sand and, as I drew it out, I noticed a remarkable suctional sound as of a trombone."

The noise had gained in volume and pitch; a shadow swept across the arena of sand far below: it was not the *lui-in*, the "thunder-roll," but a tourist microlight; and its noise was joined by the growing buzz-roar of dune-buggies. The sand was streaked with their exhaust smut. From the next summit I looked down on a parade of mounted camels fifty strong, filing along the foot of the dunes. It was an ancient scene; apart from the single loudspeaker on its stand beside the camels' path, its cable snaking away between the dunes, playing Chinese pop; and apart from the riders' calf-length fluorescent orange booties. You could hire them at the ticket office if you didn't want sand in your shoes.

I had an hour before sunset, and veered south, deeper into the desert. After a kilometre or so I had left the noise behind and only the distant humming of the microlights was audible under the wind. And there, on the summit of the dune I was climbing—there he was, the fellow in black, sitting with his back to me, looking out to the horizon. As I got closer I heard that he was singing to himself. Black shirt under a black suit, and flat black office shoes. No dayglo shoe-protectors for him. He was in his thirties, an engineer at the Tuha oilfield in Xinjiang. (I would pass through the Turpan–Hami oilfield the following day on my way to Urumqi.) I asked him if he'd ever heard the *lui-in*. "You must come when it's quiet," he said, "when no one's here. But someone is always here!" He laughed. It was Saturday, and this was his leisure-time stroll, a quest for quiet. The municipal desert. I didn't detain him for long, but every now and then, as I approached the Crescent Moon Lake, we would spot one another across a kilometre-wide dune valley and each raise a hand.

From the surrounding dunes the lake thirty metres below revealed itself as a kidney-shaped slick presided over by a pagoda tower and modern pavilions. As dusk approached, the temple was still busy with visitors. It was no longer possible to stay there, as Cable had a hundred years ago, but such was the immensity of its setting, a hundred coach-loads of bright-bootied tourists wouldn't have diminished the tranquillity. Between the terrace and the water was a band of rushes and desert willows, and as I settled on the steps that led to the shore I became aware of sounds I hadn't heard since I was in England: chatter of finches, lapping of water, kids. It was here on the banks of the Crescent Moon Lake that Cable "began to see that the acceptance of a severe rule of life is an integral part of the absolute freedom which is theirs whom He makes free." The life, in other words, that had been promised to her all those years ago: privation, toil and loneliness. Recalling her arrival in the desert fifteen years earlier, far from "conventional, snobbish" England, Cable wrote: "My first feeling had been a sense of liberation which was intoxicating. I threw up my arms as if to take flight, saying: 'I have the freedom of the spaces and I can go anywhere.'"

Bertram Thomas, when he left Arabia, drank himself to death back in England, in the house he'd been born in. For Cable and the French sisters, it was a 1936 decree against foreigners that finally forced them to abandon the Gobi. The Trio moved together to a hamlet in rural Dorset, to a house called Willow Cottage. Where could be more pastoral-sounding, more English? Jasmine, honeysuckle and mignon-ette bloomed in the garden. Cable died in 1952, aged seventy-four; the sisters within a month of each other, six years later. The dream of home had never quite been quellable. But sometimes in Willow Cottage, thinking of the "thunder roll" of the Mingsha dunes, Cable tells us—whether we believe her is immaterial—she would "take up a handful of Crescent Lake sand, and try to make it sing."

AS SEPTEMBER BECAME October, I went west, over the border from Gansu Province into Xinjiang. Around this time, another hostage video was uploaded to the internet. To the layman the setting could have been any dry and rocky place: a pale grey-beige dustland, and apart from a few fist-sized volcanic rocks, quite featureless—selected, indeed, for that very feature: its featurelessness. It had nevertheless been identified by U.S. military geographers as a certain tract near a certain Syrian town being held by the militants. It was a backdrop, but it was more than that. Death was a slim creature, almost svelte, stand-ing wide-legged and costumed in snug black battle-wear, black from head to foot. Only the pale slits of his eyes were exposed. Part of his horror was his affectedness. Before him, kneeling as if at an altar, the white man, standing in for all white men, shorn, pale from lightless-ness and stress, and attired as always in the vestments of today's politi-cal prisoner: the oversized fluorescent orange jumpsuit. Death's hands, unlike his captive's, were free, and in one of them he held, almost casu-ally, like a decorator's brush, his knife. I had recently read a Russian soldier's account of his time in Afghanistan in the 1980s in which he observed that the colour of blood on sand, once it has dried, is not red-brown but grey.

It was partly this association—between blood and sand, which is to say life and death—that accounted for the anxiety I felt as I travelled to Urumqi to catch my flight to Hotan. I wasn't much soothed, true, by the fact the train was full of teenage soldiers rampaging up and down the corridors, queuing for the samovar, queuing for the toilets, smoking in the vestibules. All of them were crew-cut and wearing camouflage T-shirts and baggy green trousers tied off with a ribbon at each ankle.

Pinned to their T-shirts was a badge bearing the initials CAPF. Not, in fact, strictly soldiers, then, but the new intake of the People's Armed Police, whose primary mission was "internal security." It turned out they too were going to Urumqi. The excitement was infectious—the excitement of those heading to a front line.

The new railway line to Xinjiang, the so-called New Silk Road, was still being tested. It could sometimes be seen running alongside the old line. It had cost $23 billion dollars and would cut the journey-time between Lanzhou and Urumqi from twenty hours to eight. There was talk of its being extended to Kashgar in the far west, into Uzbekistan and as far as Turkey and Bulgaria. The vice-chairman of Xinjiang's regional government had said: "Xinjiang will be the biggest beneficiary of the Silk Road. It will help it open up further, increase trade, tourism and other exchanges with neighbouring countries." An official in Xinjiang's Development and Reform Commission stated that a branch to Hotan, my destination, would "help the ethnic groups become more open and modern ... We can't leave them alone just because their way of thinking is backwards."

Above the constant thump-thump of the train were the occasional Tannoy announcement and panpipe covers of Lloyd Webber favourites, and the clamour of the CAPF boys. Meanwhile the desert rolled out on either side. Each time one of the boys passed my compartment he'd pause and dip his shorn head for a better look, and I would raise a hand and say hello. Then, from behind, a shove and a boot in the arse from his friend, and he'd be gone up the corridor. After an hour or more of this, two of them came and spoke to me, sitting, arms over each other's shoulders, on the foot of my bunk. We exchanged a few words, and they went away and came back with two of their fellow recruits, with whom I had the same conversation, and these two in turn fetched two more, and so on, until the whole compartment was full of them, ten, twelve, crammed onto the lower bunks, legs dangling from the upper ones. They were dressed identically, heads shaven, but the effect of this uniformity was less to diminish than to emphasise individuality—faces, physiques, posture. They wore digital camouflage, the most effective camouflage for desert conditions. What they had in common was that they were without exception ethnic Han Chinese. Did they know that they were being posted to Urumqi as the trial of Ilham Tohti was beginning? It would have been unwise to ask. Ilham was an economics professor, a scholar of Uighur culture, and an advocate of Uighur rights in Xinjiang. You could hardly call him a radical, he was scarcely even a spokesman: his misdeed had been to question publicly the official response—violent suppression, mass imprisonment, "crackdown"—to recent street protests by Uighurs in Xinjiang.

The Xinjiang Uighur Autonomous Region is China's largest administrative division: 1.66 million square kilometres—Germany, France and Italy combined. In the south are the Kunlun Mountains and the Tibetan Plateau; in the north, the Altai Mountains and Mongolia. The province is split horizontally by the Tienshan—the Heavenly Mountains—north of which lies the fertile Jungar Basin. Occupying the south of the province, below the Heavenly Mountains, is another basin, the Tarim, which is dominated by the Taklamakan Desert, my destination: 327,000 square kilometres of sand, where annual precipitation can be as low as ten millimetres. One cause of this aridity is the Tibetan Plateau, which acts as a barrier against the Indian monsoons. But the dryness of Xinjiang is also a product of its sheer isolation: few places on earth are further from the sea. The nearest body of water to the capital Urumqi, the East China Sea, is around 2,500 kilometres east. The region's ailing tourist industry attempts to make a virtue of these superlatives: furthest, driest, hottest, highest, lowest...

For centuries the Chinese called it *Huijiang*: "Muslim Land." Only in 1884, with its reconquest by the Qing following a local revolt, was this fragmented region incorporated as a province and the official Chinese name changed to Xinjiang. Today veils and beards (among the young, at least) are outlawed, and state employees and students are banned from fasting during Ramadan. On the doors of mosques there were signs prohibiting entry to men under eighteen. In January Ilham Tohti had been taken from his home in Beijing to Urumqi, where he was held in shackles and denied halal food. Eat what you're given. He ate nothing for ten days. In July the charge was announced: "separatism." He was the founder of a website that—to quote the police—had been used to "make rumours, distort and hype up issues in a bid to create conflicts, spread separatist thinking, incite ethnic hatred, advocate 'Xinjiang independence' and conduct separatist activities." His attitude, the state news agency reported, "was utterly vile, and therefore he should be heavily punished."

The boys started, two by two, leaving my compartment and returning with gifts: a handful of nuts, a sachet of instant *chai*, a cigarette proffered from a Tupperware box. They rolled up their sleeves to show their biceps and performed muscle-man poses. I did the same. They came from Shanxi, five hundred kilometres east of Jiayuguan, they said; some of them had known each other since school. No, they had never been to Urumqi before. Had never left Shanxi. They were not sure exactly what they would be doing, but one of them thought training. He made as if to fire a machine-gun, and did the noise; the others followed, until the whole compartment was full of these good-natured lads firing at one another and imitating the noise of automatic gunfire, a sound I doubted they'd heard outside *Call of Duty*.

Warning Mildred Cable against entering the Black Gobi, a soldier told her, "everyone fears that place." Owen Lattimore, passing this way in 1927, describes a "desert of black gravel . . . like shattered slate in formation, laid thickly over yellow sandy clay." The cause of the blackness is "desert varnish," a micrometre-thin rind of windblown clay and manganese that accrues, over the course of millennia, on the exposed surface of desert stones. A stone picked up from a desert plain might be pale underneath and near-black on top. Occasionally, from the train window, paler underlying sediment was exposed where a flash flood had washed away the black gravel, or in parallel looping tracks where a vehicle had passed perhaps years before.

The train slowed interminably, then halted. I sat up. Scattered across the desert, governing the landscape entirely, dozens of twenty-metre-tall drilling rigs, the Tuha oilfield mentioned by my friend in Dunhuang, and between them, moving with an up-down regularity that seemed both inexorable and primordial—primordial as the workings of the heart—hundreds of the oil-pumps known in the West as nodding donkeys, and in China as *ketouji*: "kowtowing machines." From the *Selected Works* of Mao: "We say China is a country vast in territory, rich in resources and large in population; as a matter of fact, it is the Han nationality whose population is large and the minority nationalities whose territory is vast and whose resources are rich." Black on the surface, black beneath.

AT URUMQI I caught a flight to the city of Hotan on the southern edge of the Taklamakan. I watched from the window as the glaciers of the Tienshan sloped abruptly to desert, vertical to horizontal, solid to particulate—and then nothing but diffuse beige sand, as uniform as the dark blue of space overhead. After an hour a thread of green emerged, a river, leading to a city pressed on all sides, it seemed, as we circled: between the two rivers running east–west, and between the desert to the north and the mountains to the south.

It is from the Tarim Basin's bounding mountains that most of the Taklamakan's sand is winnowed. In Hotan, dust hung in the air as in the minutes after a demolition; it made everything vague and insubstantial. I had a strange sense of the city disintegrating. "Nobody cares!" is what Absalom, whom I met at the airport, said as we buzzed about on his scooter or sprinted across roads. The only way to stop traffic as a pedestrian was to walk in front of it, he explained. "Nobody cares." At the airport he'd offered to act as my guide, and since I liked him and he was cheap, I agreed. Absalom was not his name, but it is the name I think of, now, when I picture him. He was young, educated, though his English was self-taught. His first language was Uighur, his second Chinese. Throughout the week or so I spent with him he wore the same blue jeans and navy-blue sweater, a canvas satchel slung across his back. His favourite things were ice cream and computer games, and several times we went to a parlour near Hotan's main square, where we sat down to glutinous cream-less sundaes among the city's better-off youth.

Founded by immigrants from India around 200 BC, Hotan was a major Buddhist city state and remained a centre of Buddhism until 1006 when it fell to the Muslim khanate of Kashgar. The Islamisation of what is now Xinjiang was triggered in 950 by the conversion of Satuq Bughra Khan. According to legend, he met a talking rabbit, which turned into a sheikh and bade him repeat "There is no god but God, and Mohammed is his prophet." Satuq promptly ousted (and beheaded) his father, the Bughra Khan. Oasis by oasis, Islam replaced Buddhism, hastened by Sufi missionaries. By the seventeenth century, Xinjiang was largely Muslim. The *Huijiang Zhi*, a Chinese history of the region composed in 1772, recorded: "Muslims' natural character is suspicious and unsettled, crafty and false." Nevertheless, while "hard-drinking and addicted to sex," they were able to "endure hunger and cold, and will take any insult." In common with most Chinese names for "barbarian," the written character for "Muslim," *Hui*, until recently contained the canine radical, the sign for "dog." Hotan maintains its reputation for obduracy. In Unity Square armed police stood under a dull statue the colour of wet clay depicting a bowed Uighur peasant shaking hands with a man who has the distracted air of one thinking about his lunch—Mao. The peasant was Kurban Talum, a symbol of ethnic unity favoured by Beijing.

The city is situated between two rivers, the Yurnkash (White Jade) and the Karakash (Black Jade), which converge to its north, exhausting themselves in the Taklamakan as the Hotan River, whose green-brown thread my flight from Urumqi had followed. Jade continues to be eked from the rivers and the Kunlun Mountains. If you see a BMW, Absalom said, it belongs to an official; if you see a Land Cruiser it belongs to a jade dealer. In either case, keep your distance.

OUTSIDE THE JADE MARKET on the bank of the Yurnkash next morning an ox was being trussed. The scene was watched by four uniformed CAPF men who stood in formation under an awning, one in the centre resting the tip of a studded lathi between his feet, the others clutching their automatic rifles in an outward-facing ring around him. They stood like statuary or ghosts, unseen among the throng, and unhappy, it seemed to me, as ghosts are said to be. The ox bucked, once, against its restraints. Behind the jade market's iron fence hundreds of men surged between stalls as if subject to underwater currents. Some of the stalls were loaded with boulders of jade as big as a person's head; others were scattered with no more than a handful of tinted shingle, black, white, green, gleaned from the broad bed of the White Jade River that ran alongside. Each stallholder constantly sprayed water from a plastic mister to heighten the jade's shine so that even among the heat of the crowd the market was the coolest place in the city. I bought a single pebble of green jade, the size, shape and texture of an earlobe. It would be my talisman. When I looked at it again later, in my hotel room, its gloss had dried to the dull finish of sea glass.

Released from the crowd, I stood outside under the brazen sun and there was the ox still, all four legs trussed with a single knot, while a man stooping over it sawed at its throat with a knife that seemed too short for the purpose. The ox, kicking its four trussed legs as one, silently released its blood onto the road. All of this was watched by three captivated toddlers. There was nothing appalling about it; it could hardly be described as violence: the ox seemed like a participant. The man went on sawing. I turned away and walked back to my hotel, past the policemen under their gazebo.

SINCE 11 SEPTEMBER 2001, Beijing has characterised Xinjiang as merely another front in the global struggle against militant Islam. Its actions there, it explains, constitute nothing more than the commensurate duties of any responsible government. Even those living in the towns and cities where riots or demonstrations or massacres had happened were denied the facts. Two? One hundred? Two thousand killed? And by whom? Han or Uighur, civilian or police or army? There was little news, and when such information as existed seeped out, officially or underground, it was liable the next day to be revised by the authorities, or withdrawn or gainsaid.

In Urumqi, where Ilham Tohti's trial was commencing, there had been a commotion as I left the station for my flight to Hotan, the turning of heads, a crowd gathering. I saw a man, a Uighur, yell and raise a fist to a Han policeman and strike him in the jaw. The policeman only turned his head with a frown, as if to avoid a disagreeable draught, replying with a temple-blow that knocked his assailant unconscious.

But the police presence in Hotan was experienced less as a force of law than as an occupation. The wailing of sirens was continual but did not indicate urgency: the white or black police vans moved at walking pace up and down the dusty streets, sirens blaring, and nobody drove too close or overtook.

In the bazaar the next morning the stallholders were opening the grates of their stalls and laying out their wares. Metalworkers and wood-turners; rug merchants and grape-vendors. Even at this cool hour the cuts hanging at the meat stalls were as thickly infested with flies as a hive's combs with bees. In front of each such stall on the ground was the head of a horse. They had been freshly removed, but there was no blood. The eyes were closed. The tongue lolled, as if it had been slipped out deliberately, as if it were part of the trader's routine to lay out each morning, like a signboard, this symbol of his trade—a finger pushed between the bared teeth, the tongue hooked out. The tongue was not glossy or pink, but had already been dulled by the dust in the air. This in turn made me conscious of my own tongue, and the chalky taste that had been discernible even indoors, even at night with the windows closed and the air conditioning off.

The oases of the southern Taklamakan have always been dusty—the lungs of two-thousand-year-old desert mummies are clogged with it—but there was an understanding among those I spoke to that the increased frequency of the dust storms, more than two hundred days per year, was due to human activity. Xinjiang's five hundred reservoirs contain some 8.5 billion cubic metres of water, more than the total annual discharge of the region's rivers. Ninety-six per cent of water-use in Xinjiang is agricultural. Following China's economic reforms in 1978, huge areas of cotton were planted across the region, cotton being a lover of sunshine and sandy soil. Since cotton consumes great quantities of water, the effect in a region so arid was inevitable: rivers ceased to flow, the forests of poplars they sustained died, farms were surrendered to the sand.

It has been estimated that desertification affects a sixth of humankind and 70 per cent of all arid areas. The image often given is the desert "marching" on the fertile land, advancing like a necrosis. But this is to misunderstand the process. The main causes are unregulated irrigation, overgrazing and deforestation. The desert has neither hunger nor jealousy, but in forcing resources from impoverished soil, we render that ground not only unproductive but antibiotic. "Desertification," in fact, is a misnomer, for whereas the natural desert—*le désert absolu*, so to speak—is, for all its superficial minimalism, a network of largely self-regulating equilibria (think of the sand at first light, crisscrossed with tracks), desertified regions more closely approach desert in the original Latin sense: not just impoverished but forsaken. A desertified landscape is not a *desert* landscape but rather a zone of human making, and often the result of our inability to reconcile ourselves to the arid.

Lop Nor, once China's second largest salt lake, has all but dried up due to the diversion and damming of its source river, the Tarim. The Crescent Moon Lake, celebrated since antiquity for its miraculous permanence, is shrinking as industry and agriculture day by day exhaust its aquifer. The earth having been denuded of vegetation, the dust that has settled on the desert edge over millions of years can simply be swept up by the wind. Nor have the effects been confined to Xinjiang—and this was of some satisfaction to Absalom; each spring, he said, Beijing, the seat of government, was choked by this curse from the insalubrious west.

THE TRANSLATION OF "Taklamakan" favoured by Western explorers—"You go in and you don't come out"—bemuses the locals. It's known that the name was given to at least one of the desert's sand-drowned cities, and it's possible that it was just extended to the desert itself. "Old home place," some say; or "end place"; or "place of grapes." One theory is that Taklamakan is a Uighur form of the Arabic for "leave alone"; another associates it with *toghrak*, the Turkic word for the desert poplar. A modern British adventurer who crossed the desert east to west titled his account *The Worst Desert on Earth*. "It was mine," he wrote, in 1995: "I was its conqueror and my footsteps would *strip the virginity from the ruffled layers of sand*." My emphasis.

But it is an earlier account that served to mythologise the Takla-makan in the Western mind as a place as fearsome as any frozen Pole. In the collection of the Royal Geographical Society is a measuring tape, its case inscribed as follows:

LEFT BY

DR SVEN HEDIN MARCH 1901

NORTH OF LOP NOR, CENTRAL ASIA

FOUND DECEMBER 23 1906

BY DR M. A. AUREL STEIN

The Swedish explorer Hedin made an earlier expedition into the Taklamakan in 1895, having just turned thirty. He and Stein met only once—at a dinner at the RGS in 1909, Stein handed the recovered tape to a delighted Hedin. Hedin's maps had proven invaluable to Stein, just as Stein's would be to later travellers, but Stein in turn did Hedin the service of verifying the accuracy (unerring) of the measurements he'd taken. Hedin's 1895 expedition was to cross the Taklamakan from south to north. This first venture was almost Hedin's last; and the horrors he endured shaped both his own reputation and the Western image of the Taklamakan. Of the four local men who ventured into the desert with him, according to his account, only two returned. "To my eyes," he wrote, as they set out from Merket, on the western boundary of the desert, "the desert ocean was invested with a fascinating beauty. Its silence, its unbroken stillness, exercised a magic charm over me." It was a charm that, for Hedin, even the events of the coming weeks were hardly to diminish—he rhapsodises the desert even as he lies dying. "I knew nothing of hesitation, nothing of fear," he wrote, words echoed by Harry St. John Philby as he faced death in the Empty Quar-ter thirty-five years later: "I would not, could not yield."

Hedin's account reminds us that sand is not merely sand, but to the desert traveller an element as mobile and impulsive as water. He glosses the Uighur names for the high dunes they must cross as they move deeper into the desert: *ighiz-kum*: "high sand"; *chong-kum*: "big sand"; and, increasingly as they move north, *yaman-kum*: "hateful sand." Fifteen days into their journey to the desert's northern edge he realised that his men had brought water for only two more days. But assured by his guide, Yolchi, that the River Hotan was within two days' reach, the party continued. At least that is what Hedin tells us. A frisson of "hesitation" or "fear" might have served him well. "What suffering, what loss, what sorrow would have been spared both to ourselves and to others if we had retraced our steps." But such a reversal, even in the face of unmistakable death, would have been anathema to him.

They were being slowly killed by the desert, he felt, and yet "deeper Sabbath peace never brooded over any graveyard." As they negotiate dunes sixty metres high, one of the men cries "*Karga! Karga!*" and points to the sky: a lone raven, circling the caravan. Then the skeleton of a vole; a withered *toghrak*. "We believed we were nearing 'land,'" Hedin admits, but from the next high dune nothing was visible in any direction but endless stages of *yaman-kum*. Three days had passed without water. "Men, as well as camels, are extremely weak," he wrote in his journal: "God help us!" On 1 May, wild with thirst, he forced himself to drink the flammable spirit from his Primus stove; it burnt his throat "like oil of vitriol" and nearly killed him. This he presents as the act of one determined, heroically determined, to prevail, but the more I learned about Hedin, and the more I sensed his disregard for the lives of others, the more I wondered if it was not an act of self-destruction.

IN THE CAR on the way to the desert, Absalom looked anguished. I could hear the camel man barking, camel-like, from his mobile: if we were late, he was saying, he would not be there. Three o'clock, no later. It would mean driving through the heat of the day. It being Friday, it would also mean driving through the hours reserved for prayer. Absalom hung up, and wrung his hands. Actually wrung them, as if washing them under a tap. He removed his thick spectacles—their prescription severe enough that he was all but blind without them—placed them in his lap and wiped his face with both hands. He removed his spectacles case from his satchel and from it took a cloth and wiped each lens, then returned his spectacles to his face.

We were to meet the camel man at the edge of the desert thirty kilometres north of Hotan. From there we were to spend two days travelling into the desert before circling back south to the ruins of the stupa known as Rawak, a Buddhist reliquary and sanctuary built sometime around the fourth century, prior to the Islamic conquest of Hotan. Aurel Stein first visited Rawak in April 1901, six years before his second expedition and his famous discoveries at Dunhuang. Rawak, or "High Mansion," which Stein's guide had spoken of only as "an old house" half-buried in the sand, turned out to be "the most imposing structure [he] had seen among the extant ruins of the Hotan region."

For two hours the driver hardly went faster than twenty; he used the quiet roads, the narrow roads lined with poplars, the farm roads between lines of date palms. There were things it was not possible to discuss, even inside the car, thirty kilometres from the city. Each time we passed a row of houses Absalom would press a finger to a button and my window would be wound up. "I will tell you," was all he said, by which he meant "later," although he never would. He and the driver, his friend's father, hardly exchanged a word, just glances. The driver slowed further until the sound of the tyres on grit was louder than the engine, and it was possible to hear the steering wheel squeaking in its column; until it seemed that our very slowness was showy. I was a carnival-float princess; a despot on his progress; a sugar baron. For fifteen kilometres we went on like this, at jogging pace, the windows sealed. Absalom and the driver stared at the road ahead even when villagers came to their doors and watched us pass. "We must go slowly," he said finally, turning to me. "To keep you safe."

We pulled up at a noodle shack and the owner came out and watched us. Absalom got out and shook hands with him. The driver stood by the bonnet. I was to stay where I was. Don't open the windows. Absalom handed some notes to the noodle man, who went and spoke to another man who was standing at the darkened door of the shack. He in turn summoned two children, a girl and a boy of six or seven. Once they had been detailed, they skipped off into the maze of buildings and alleyways and fields behind the building.

I sat in the hot car. I had no idea what was happening. When I looked back, Absalom was standing there alone, passing a hand slowly though his hair, and holding it there, awfully, on top of his head as he gazed at the gravel. The road was not a small one but no other cars passed. The children had not returned. In a cage above the stall were two blue canaries and a lovebird. There was silence. It was a strange characteristic of the desert's edge: even the cage-birds did not sing.

The children reappeared hand in hand and the boy passed something to the man, who pressed it into Absalom's hand. It was like a drug deal. The children's faces and clothes were filthy; both had shaven heads, girl and boy.

Only when he sat down in the car did Absalom turn to me and open his fist briefly to show off the two objects the children had brought: translucent plastic lighters, one red, one yellow. He thumbed the red one and the flame flared. He smiled. "To be honest, it's very hard to buy lighters here."

There had been an escalation in violence between the Han Chinese authorities and Uighurs in Xinjiang since riots in Urumqi in 2009 had left two hundred dead, mostly Han civilians, according to the official account. Thirty-one people had been killed last May (2014) when a car was driven through a Han market in Urumqi and explosives thrown. Three months ago the pro-government imam of China's largest mosque, in the far western city of Kashgar, five hundred kilometres north-west of Hotan, was stabbed to death. Ninety-six died in the violence that followed in nearby Yarkand—though who had died and the nature of the violence was, as usual, unclear. Even knives were difficult to obtain these days, Absalom said, and matches and lighters could be bought legally only with a certificate of permission or from certain sanctioned individuals. Vouched-for men. It had been like this since the mass killings in Yarkand. To possess the belts of firecrackers I'd seen in Jiayuguan would mean arrest, and a vehicle entering a petrol station must first drop off any passengers at the entrance. For rural Uighurs the creation of fire had therefore become a daily trial. But we would need fire in the desert. The driver started the engine and eased onto the road.

The sand was loud on the side windows, drowning out the radio's Arabic pop. The whole substance of the land was in motion—not a constructive force but one of obliteration. A veneer of sand was blasting low across the straight road ahead. Out of the back windscreen the road we had passed over was already hard to distinguish from the flanking dunes. The desert was closing behind us. If the road were to be covered, only the occasional signpost or fencepost would indicate the proper course.

We passed a walled farmstead then plantations of cotton and dates. The roadside ditches were brimming with stagnant pumpwater. Left alone, these hectares would revert to sandy scrublands of saxaul or tamarisk. At each corner of each field, visible through the dust was a scaffolding watchtower from which during the harvest an overseer would monitor lines of labourers. The military farm has been a tool of Chinese border statecraft since the Han dynasty. Between 1952 and 1954 some 150,000 Kuomintang soldiers, demobilised following their defeat by the Communist Party of China in the civil war, were deployed to Xinjiang to form the Production-Construction Military Corps, the *Shengchan-sanshe bingtuan*, know colloquially as the *bingtuan*. The *bingtuan*'s tasks were resettlement and land reform, to turn the languishing desert to use. During the Cultural Revolution the *bingtuan* absorbed hundreds of thousands of Han migrants. Today its ranks are believed to number between two and three million, a seventh of Xinjiang's population. Under its aegis, the Qing's treatment of the New Dominions as a zone of penal expulsion was revived. Prison farms were established across the region. Between 1949 and 1961 the cultivated area in Xinjiang expanded from 1.2 million hectares to 3.2. million. The *bingtuan* owns a third of Xinjiang's arable land and controls paramilitary units whose efficiency in the suppression of unrest is proverbial. Absalom would hazard one detail about the *bingtuan*: "It produces a third of the world's tomato paste."

As we were passing these fields I noticed two black BMWs a hundred metres ahead, facing the same direction as us but idling side by side, blocking the road, as if the left-hand car had flagged down the other. Our driver slowed and looked across at Absalom. The left-hand car carried no number-plate. The car directly in front of us sped off; but the other one stayed where it was, on the wrong side of the road. As we approached, it too started moving, keeping on the wrong side of the road, until it was going at the same speed as us, its front wheels level with our fender. Our driver did not accelerate. The other vehicle only dropped back when two motorcycles, farmers, approached on its side of the road. Finally it turned off into a farm compound, but I wondered about the other car. After a kilometre or so, I said, "Absalom?"

He didn't turn but nodded.

"Okay?" I said and he nodded again.

TWENTY MINUTES LATER we stopped at a squat castellated tower where we were to meet the camel man. It was newly built of black stone. Was it a *bingtuan* watchtower? A confection for tourists—not that there were any, apart from me—to survey the desert? Absalom didn't know. It had been built about three years ago, the driver thought. The cement between the stones was white, like the grouting between bathroom tiles. The foundations having been exposed by the wind, the tower stood on a mound of coarse cement rising from the sand. People had been here: the ground was heaped with plastic bottles. "Nobody cares, you see!" Absalom was sweating, still wearing his pullover despite the heat; edgy. He looked at the driver then said to me, gesturing to the tower, "Go." The driver looked at him. I climbed the steps and they followed.

From the battlements we looked out at the shrub-covered sandy plain. The beginning of the desert. No livestock, no buildings or fences, only the low dunes and the empty road, and now just a sigh of wind. We climbed down and waited in the tower's shadow. A fly settled on my wristwatch. Absalom took his phone from his pocket and poked its shattered screen, bringing up a photo of a government poster showing two men's faces. The first man had a thick black beard of the prohibited kind, the second a goatee—sanctioned. I recognised the first man. "Isn't that—?" I said. Yes, said Absalom, it was Keanu Reeves, the Hollywood actor, his image used by the designer solely because of the exemplary impropriety of his facial hair. "*Abu Keanu!*" Absalom whispered.

He tapped the screen again. "Listen."

There was no sound. He turned it off, powered it up. "Listen."

Only the buzz of flies.

The driver had walked off into the dunes, and when I went for a piss I found him lying buried in sand, only his head exposed. His eyes were shut, then they opened, and he smiled. Therapeutic.

"Listen," Absalom said again, when I returned. This time there was music, surprisingly loud. It was "The Lonely Goatherd."

"*The Sound of Music!*" he said, and he played it to the end, smiling and nodding.

An hour later, around 4 p.m., hearing a distant engine, we climbed the tower again: a kilometre away a motorcycle was crawling towards us between the dunes, four Bactrian camels leashed behind it in a line.

THEY WERE NOT the lithe "yellow" Sorans of Arabia or even the coddled seaside donkeys of Jiayuguan—these stared at you balefully and squealed in outrage each time they were mounted. Their fur was like a bear's after a long hibernation, pale and oily, each hump tousled with a whip of black hair. They were spotted with sores where the wooden saddle frame, or rope, or chain, had chafed away the fur and bitten into the skin beneath. Disobedience was punished with a cane slammed across the face, which brought another plaintive cry. But this treatment was reserved only for the junior animals, as a child might be spanked, and the older ones were treated with tender reverence— spoken to sweetly, prompted to sit by a leash swung gently against the haunches.

After we had ridden for two hours the camel man dropped from his saddle and delved among the branches of a tamarisk. These dunes, for all their mobility, were as familiar to him as those of Ramlat Mitan in the Empty Quarter had been to Hassan. Older tamarisks and saxaul are often found growing from the summit of a low cone of sand— known as a *nebkha*—accumulated around the plant's tap root. Islets rising out of the sand sea, these mounds are home to scorpions, lizards, flightless sand-jays. The lower branches will be clogged with wind-blown sand, and the slope of the mound scattered with dead twigs. From the heart of this specimen he extracted something—a blackened gridiron, which he knocked with his palm to shed the sand and hooked over the steel horn of his saddle. He had stowed it there who knew how long ago.

The camel man's name was Mr. Abdul Rasheed Mohammed; he wore grey flannel trousers, black flat-soled plastic shoes and a white shirt with cufflink holes. He wore a white sunhat pulled down low on his brow and, once the sun had set, a white *dopa*, the skullcap worn by some Uighur men. When answering a question he looked at the ground, but when addressing a camel he went close, placed a hand on its muzzle, and gazed into its wet eye. He had once crossed the Taklamakan from west to east, one and a half thousand kilometres. What was it like? He gestured to the surrounding dunes. *Like this.*

The sand was grey, cool even on the surface, not at all like the vivacious "red country" of Arabia. Formed chiefly from quartz and feldspar, the Taklamakan contains little iron. From afar, even in late-afternoon sunlight, the dunes were the pale dishclout tone of an autumn sea. A soft disc of molten white, the sun vanished without flourish, and did not sink behind the line of dunes so much as melt before it reached them.

AFTER WE HAD EATEN, I scooped out a bed, as Hassan had taught me in Oman—working from head to toe, pushing the sand outwards from a central line. In the museum in Hotan, I remembered, the prize exhibit was a mummy disinterred from a desert cemetery; such is the dryness of the desert that your body will scarcely decay: merely shrivel as all moisture is drawn from it. This process may commence before death. The mummy's jaw was bound, but between his lips a grey cat-like tongue extruded. His nostrils were like knife-jabs in his papery face. His hair was wiry black. He was about two thousand years old. And what was most touching, each night the vitrine in which he lay was covered in a velvet blanket, which each morning was rolled back and folded neatly at the foot of the vitrine.

On the eastern horizon the sun's soft afterburn disintegrated; but then, an hour or so later, the sky where it had set suddenly lightened once more, as if—impossibly—the moon was rising where the sun had set, or the sun was backing up. When I propped myself on my elbows and looked back at the camp, I saw that Absalom was awake too, sitting cross-legged in his blankets, looking out at the same area of light. He said he suffered from amnesia. He corrected himself—*insomnia!* Insomnia. He had not consulted a doctor. There was no point. "It is because of the pressures in my life."

"All the same," I said.

"A doctor cannot help."

This accounted for his harried look, the expression he wore of one who has just been jolted from deep sleep and whose facial muscles have yet to activate. It could sometimes look like disdain, his tiredness; and sometimes, I think, disdain was what it was—for someone who would come here willingly, who would spend money, perhaps six months' wages for him (not much less for me), to not only abandon a land of greenery and freedoms but to forgo the opportunity to visit those *desirable* places—New York, Berlin, Paris—that were forbidden to him, and instead come here to dusty Xinjiang. Some of his friends had been able to go to Shanghai to study. Others had married. "But I'm different." It wasn't just poverty; he was a son of divorced parents, a taint attached. His mother remarried—"for money." As for his father, "He sees me occasionally," and then, to clarify, "Abandoned."

He said it "abandon-ed"; and when he said it—"abandon-ed"—it was easy to comprehend a feeling of forsakenness, desertion, that was about more than his father. Often, and without pride, he repeated that self-characterisation he'd come to accept: "I'm different."

The dim yellow glow on the horizon remained for five minutes before fading quickly to darkness. It was only later that I came upon Mildred Cable's description in *The Gobi Desert* of "dancing magnetic light, which bewilders the inexperienced with its suggestion of men and camps in a region which is wholly deserted. The light flickers on the horizon, appearing and disappearing suddenly and unaccountably." I got into my sleeping bag in its sand trench and listened to the camels slowly munching at the tamarisk. Their slow, scuffling dance. If your camel looks slowly left to right, it is a fox. If your camel stops chewing and stares into the darkness, something is wrong.

Mr. Abdul Rasheed Mohammed had begun snoring as soon as he

lay down. Silently Absalom was watching a movie on his iPad—it would be something American and dreadful: his face was aglow with it. Hour by hour the stars inched across the sky, and I did not sleep. The sand preserved none of the day's warmth. Soon after midnight the quiet was broken by a low mechanical hum, and this was joined by another, as of two flying insects, and I sat up, with a start. The light, the yellow light on the horizon, had returned, and was growing stronger as the volume of the noise grew. Not Cable's "dancing magnetic light" or an illusion. Absalom had put his iPad back in its box. "Motorcycles," he said; and when I asked him where they were coming from and where they were going, he said, "Passengers"—by which I supposed he meant travellers, or smugglers (why else travel at night?)—and added, more mysteriously, that their destination was "Shangri-La," a word he used without irony. Later I remembered that the fictional Shangri-La of the 1933 novel lay in the Kunlun Mountains that towered over Hotan. All night, every hour or so, I heard these or other "passengers" on their motorcycles and saw the shuddering lambency projected by their headlights low in the sky, like a lighthouse beam from far out at sea; but however often I heard them, and however close they seemed to come, not once were their lights directly visible, only their influence on the sky.

Towards morning the crescent moon became visible above the horizon. As the sky lightened, the wind picked up. Within an hour it was too cold to sleep, though it was barely five. I got up and went to a thicket of dead tamarisk and tugged branches and roots from the sand and built a fire that roared in the wind but gave off hardly any heat.

WHEN SVEN HEDIN'S mobility returned after his self-poisoning, he crawled through the sand following the caravan's tracks and came upon his men encamped, too weak themselves to go further. "Who would be the unhappy wretch that should die last—whose lungs would be filled with the pestilential stench from the corpses of his comrades." The cockerel they had brought with them was finally killed and its blood drunk. His retinue tried to slake their thirst with camel's piss flavoured with vinegar and sugar but were soon doubled up with nausea. "Mohammed Shah was perfectly delirious, laughing to himself,

weeping, babbling, playing with the sand." A sheep they had brought with them was slaughtered, but Hedin, unlike his men, could not bring himself to drink its coagulating blood, he who had drunk the fluid from his stove. "Gaunt and wild-eyed, with the stamp of insanity upon him, Yolchi sat beside the tent, gnawing at the dripping sheep's lungs. His hands were bloody; his face was bloody; he was a horrible sight to look upon." Finally, leaving Yolchi and Mohammed Shah to die ("Water, sir!" Yolchi pleaded. "Only a drop of water!"), Hedin and the two remaining members of the party, Islam Bey and Kasim, made a final desperate eastward foray in search of water. Islam Bey by now was retching so violently, Hedin "thought he would bring up his very intestines." And yet, if we are to believe his account, Hedin himself began to rally: "I was buoyed up by an abounding energy and the joy of life. I *would not* die in the desert. I was too young." Finally he and Kasim abandon Islam Bey and the remaining camels with the ruins of their caravan and march east in search of the River Hotan. It was the following day when they came across the first remnants of blackened tamarisk and reeds extending from the sand, and finally, on 5 May: footprints! They follow the trail to the top of a dune; Kasim drops to his knees. Somehow they have walked in a circle. "They are our own footsteps!" To follow your own footprints endlessly—the classic desert ending.

I TOOK THREE EGGS from a plastic bag—miraculously they had survived our journey intact—and placed them in the fire's embers and heaped the embers around them. Absalom and Mr. Abdul Rasheed Mohammed were still sleeping. The camels began to stir. When I had asked their names Mr. Abdul Rasheed Mohammed had shaken his head: only numbers, and these were branded deep in the rump of each one. The senior animal was munching slowly on the saxaul to which it was tethered. Proper light was coming, not seeping from the east but (such was the haziness) infiltrating the whole sky at once, evenly, so that no region of it seemed brighter than any other. Low on the horizon, a pale centre evolved, and became a sun—the same extinguished, moonlike sun that had set the night before. A lone raven circled once, low, battling the wind, before vanishing over the brink of a dune.

The wind was noisy in the dead tamarisk and in the fire's flames. I took my scarf from my pocket and wrapped it once, twice around my head, so that only my eyes were exposed, and pulled my hat low on my head to keep the scarf in place. As the eggs hissed, the wind picked up, Absalom pulled himself from his pile of blankets and came and crouched beside me wordlessly, a blanket still cawled over his head. There was a crack, loud as a pistol-shot in the dull silence. One of the eggs had burst. A shout of shocked laughter and the blanket slipped from Absalom's head. The noise had woken Mr. Abdul Rasheed Mohammed; he was sitting up in his nest of blankets staring at us as if concussed. He spilled water on his hands and there was the familiar mutter of prayer. Absalom didn't join him.

We mounted the camels. It would take us three hours to reach Rawak. As we left the camp I saw the twin dents in the sand where Mr. Abdul Rasheed Mohammed had knelt to pray. He sat on the lead animal, not astride it but side-saddle, as if on a bench, his short legs crossed at the ankle as he led us into the wind. If you opened your mouth it filled with dust. After a kilometre or two, he slipped off his camel, removed the gridiron from its hook on his saddle and lodged it back in the heart of a tamarisk. I couldn't tell if it was the same specimen he'd taken it from the day before.

The dunes had none of the towering grandeur of their Gobi or Arabian counterparts—and yet it was possible, occasionally, to glimpse a distant vista and suddenly to gain a sense of the Taklamakan's vastness. We would be riding in a basin ringed by dunes, and following a ridge to a dune-top we would see the selfsame dunes (so it seemed to me) rising and falling to the horizon. It was like finding yourself enclosed within mirrored walls, the same scene extended to infinity in every direction.

It was inconceivable that life could exist here any more, and yet over the next ridge was a poplar tree three metres high and seemingly thriving. In the hollows between the dunes were raised plateaus of cracked clay, clay which had once formed part of the bed of a lake or river and which Hedin identifies as "the last surviving fragments of the bed of the great Central Asian Mediterranean." Over thousands of years, being more solid than the surrounding sand, they had been exposed by the wind and now stood like crumbling plinths or podiums, as flat and square as the ruins of buildings, ringed by their own rubble and the dry reeds that grew wherever there was any moisture.

The sun was cooled and dimmed by a gauze of dust. The wind was of such force—or rather so unrelenting—that all you wanted to do was to *stop*; stop, and find shelter, and yet it is in the nature of the *buran*—the notorious wind of the Taklamakan—that its direction shifts continually. The air was thick with dust, clogging the nose, the heavier grains skimming or tumbling across the dunes' rippled surface and in turn disturbing further grains. Any shelter could be no more than momentary. Aurel Stein called the deserts of the Sahara and Arabia and southern Africa "tame": tamed by their waterholes, however sparse, that enabled the existence of nomadic tribes. In the Taklamakan, as in the Black Gobi, there were no nomads: "the absence of moisture bans not only human existence but also practically all animal and plant life."

A Muslim legend of the sixteenth century tells of a Sufi preacher,

Khoja Jamal ad-Din, who came to a town named Lob Katak, unknown today but situated somewhere in the Taklamakan. Refused water by the town's citizens, he warned that Allah would visit a punishment upon them. With that, he left, accompanied by his sole acolyte, who was also the town's muezzin. The muezzin decided to return to the town (why is unclear), and it was while he was delivering the call to prayer from a minaret that a sand storm blew up, a *karaburan*, or "black storm." The air cleared to reveal a silent infinity of sand from which nothing extended—nothing but the top of the minaret, upon which stood the stunned muezzin, like the last survivor of a scuttled ship clinging to its crow's nest.

The lost settlements of the Taklamakan are not just mythical. Four months before reaching Rawak in the winter of 1900, Aurel Stein excavated the ruins of the Buddhist city of Dandan-uilik ("Ivory Houses"), which lies under the sand a ten-day trek north-east of Hotan. "Pregnant with death and solitude," as he put it, the city had not been consumed, like Lob Katak, by some scriptural cataclysm, but fifteen hundred years before had simply been conceded to the desert due to the failure of a stream from the Kunlun Mountains.

SVEN HEDIN'S DESPAIR was short-lived. The next day a darkening of the horizon-line betrayed the existence, finally, of vegetation, living vegetation. His man Kasim being too weak to go further, Hedin on his own crawls towards the poplar forest that marks the valley of the River Hotan. "I do not think I at all exaggerate, if I say that during the first ten minutes I drank between five and six pints," he writes, and there is euphoria in his description of his resurrection:

> Every blood-vessel and tissue of my body sucked up the life-giving liquid like a sponge … My blood, which had lately been so sluggish and so slow … now coursed easily through every blood-vessel. My hands, which had been dry, parched, and as hard as wood, swelled out again. My skin, which had been like parchment, turned moist and elastic.

I'm reminded of W. J. McGee rubbing water into the skin of the dehydrated Pablo Valencia in the Sonoran Desert, fifteen years later, "the skin first shedding and then absorbing it greedily as a dry sponge." The sheer thirst of organic matter. Removing his boots and filling them, Hedin returns to the dying Kasim: "Would you like some water?"

His account of this expedition, more so than his subsequent triumphs, established his reputation for hardiness and a ruthlessness that was indistinguishable from sadism, a willingness to sacrifice lives— camels, livestock, men—to his ambition. Only one of the three men he abandoned survived. It was not until later in his life, however, that these characteristics came to be associated with his political stance. Remember his admiration of the "good-looking" tyrant General Ma. "By temperament Hedin was a Nazi," wrote Sir Clarmont Skrine, the former British consul general of Kashgar (in an obituary), "to whom exploration was a *Kampf,* a struggle not only against the forces of nature but also on paper, against rival explorers. It is not surprising that he espoused in turn the causes of Kaiser Wilhelm II and Hitler." And indeed there is a photo of Hedin, a smirking old goat full of good wine, shaking the hand of the Führer. What did T. E. Lawrence write of the Bedouin? "His sterile experience robbed him of compassion and perverted his human kindness to the image of the waste."

WHENEVER AUREL STEIN describes his arrival at a new destination it seems to be accompanied by a howling sand storm, and when he reached Rawak on 10 April 1901, "the season of *burans* had now fully set in, and the gales...were blowing daily." His excavations would reveal a rectangular courtyard measuring forty by thirty-three metres, within which the remains of the stupa's cylindrical tower rose nine metres above the sand's surface. Built of mud bricks and dating from the peak of Xinjiang Buddhism in the fourth century, the structure was cruciform in plan, with staircases leading to the tower's base at each of the four cardinal points. Even in photographs from ten years ago, you can make out the boundary wall and corner steps. The tower, its dome long collapsed, had once been a reliquary. Like the reclining figure at Dunhuang, its statuary and paintings had represented the Buddha's nirvana. Surrounding the courtyard wall, buried in the sand, ninety-one man-sized stucco statues were uncovered by Stein and his workers. They had depicted the Buddha and bodhisatt-vas, some still bearing scraps of their original 1,500-year-old paint. "Those on the inside face of the wall could still be expected to be in a fair state of preservation," writes Stein in *Sand-Buried Ruins of Khotan*, "owing to the depth of the sand, which was in no place less than seven feet." However, "the heavy stucco statues threatened to collapse when the protecting sand was being removed." The threat was heightened by the *buran*, which "carried away the fine sand which had filled the interstices between the statues and the wall behind, and thus placed the friable masses of stucco in danger of sliding down through their own weight to immediate destruction." It was this process, in Stein's view, that explained why so many of the colossal statues were missing their heads; these had extended above the sand and therefore had been deprived of its preserving support. While he and his men did remove a cache of small relics for (where else?) the British Museum, he recog-nised that the statues themselves were too large and fragile to survive such a journey, and so, having described and photographed them, he went about their reinterment. "It was a melancholy duty to perform, strangely reminding me of a true burial."

When we reached the site and dismounted, the stupa that had so delighted Stein emerged from the dust as a drum of pale eroded bricks four metres tall. Only the top few centimetres of the courtyard wall were exposed. Nothing could be seen of the celebrated reliefs or fres-coes. When Stein returned six years after his first visit he was told that a band of jade diggers had visited the site two years earlier in search of "treasure" and had stripped the wall of its stucco images. I spent half an hour walking around the site while Absalom sat in the shade of the storage shed amid a mass of plastic bottles. Strewing the sand were bricks fallen from the stupa; a stringy tamarisk was growing from a corner of the tower's stump. I stood and listened to the prickle of sand being blown against my trousers. A car's horn sounded from a nearby track; our driver.

A *buran* had descended on Hotan when we returned. The air was freighted with dust. In the oases, *sand* storms are rare—sand has a mass that means only the most powerful winds will lift it above head-height. It is dust, finer and lighter, that forms the clouds that hang over Hotan. As we crossed the Black Jade River once more and passed the empty jade market, the city had taken on the cold pallor of the desert. I thought of the grey fuzz of a disconnected TV. Visibility was reduced to a few hundred metres, and you could taste it, chalky on the lips, and feel it in your eyes like the onset of a stye. The tiled steps leading to the entrance of my hotel were covered in footprints, as if they had been forensically dusted. The leaves of the few trees were pale. The dust lacked fog's coolness but seemed to sit on the city like a fog, with a fog's power to dissimulate and deaden, so that your voice was deprived of its resonance, and with a fog's miasmic strangeness. The whole land was mobile: the dunes inched windward year by year, smothering roads and railways, farms and cities. The stuff of the earth was swirling in the air. The only solidity was the oases, and even their permanence was illusory. For two days the dust grounded all flights. I was trapped in Hotan. "We're used to it," Absalom said, as we ate ice cream in the parlour overlooking the main square. That was not to say he didn't hate it. The dust—it was possible to speak about the dust. The way it infiltrated your life and dictated your movements. It had grown worse even in his lifetime, he said. Moreover it was experienced by the citizenry as a deliberate plague, a collective insult, and more than just a quirk of nature. Remember the people of Lob Katak, entombed under a hundred metres of sand, with their livestock, their children. *That*—a mere act of God—would be tolerable. The cause of the dust (articulated in a whisper) was the "tests"—meaning the nuclear tests that had taken place at Lop Nor, five hundred kilometres north-east. The base, covering some 100,000 square kilometres, was established with Soviet assistance in 1959. China's first bomb, codenamed 596, was exploded there in 1964. It has been claimed that cancer rates in Xinjiang are up to 35 per cent higher than in the rest of China. Contamination from the tests has been detected more than a thousand kilometres west in neighbouring Kazakhstan.

I'd assumed the dust was a natural phenomenon exacerbated by desertification until I saw the official footage from the underground tests of the 1980s: the earth's sudden heaving, then the instant transformation of static matter to swirling airborne matter, as, from the surface of the desert as far as the horizon, a dense blanket of dust was thrown up—as if a beater were being taken to the back of an old rug. I remembered the "black cloud" that had blinded Yami Lester at Emu Field. When I told Absalom I thought the tests had ended in the 1990s, his terseness was so uncharacteristic it took me aback—"You think they would tell *us*?"

From my hotel window the white armoured personnel-carriers were everywhere and the sound of sirens constant. At the time, I knew nothing about the massacre that was said to have been committed in Luntai County on the other side of the desert. Initially the Chinese state news agency would report that "at least" two people were killed during riots. It was not until a week later, when I was in Shanghai, that it admitted that fifty people had died in gunfire and explosions, forty of them "terrorists." What did forty terrorists look like? Did they look like rioters? Exiled Uighur-rights activists put the number of dead in the hundreds. I wondered if it was this incident, rather than the dust storm, that had caused my flight to be cancelled. Ilham Tohti, on trial in Urumqi, would be sentenced to life in prison for his "separatist" activities, and all his assets seized. According to Radio Free Asia, he is held today at "Xinjiang No. 1 Prison" in Urumqi, five thousand kilometres from his Beijing home—the "furthest frontier" among the Qing Dynasty's zones of exile.

Half a block from my hotel, the upper storeys of the city's police headquarters were lost in the pall; only when the air cleared the next morning, as we drove to the airport, was its roof visible, bristling with antennae.

4

BASTARD STURGEON

The Aralkum, Kazakhstan

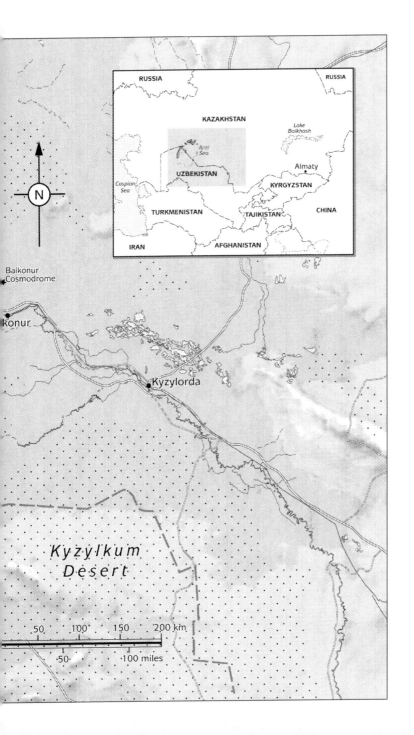

RUSSIA

RUSSIA

KAZAKHSTAN

Lake
Balkhash

*Aral
Sea*

UZBEKISTAN

Almaty

*Caspian
Sea*

KYRGYZSTAN

TURKMENISTAN

TAJIKISTAN

CHINA

IRAN

AFGHANISTAN

N

Baikonur
Cosmodrome

konur

Kyzylorda

*Kyzylkum
Desert*

50   100   150   200 km

50   100 miles

In the landlocked city of Orsk, in Russia's far south, Commander Alexey Ivanovich Butakov commissioned the construction of a fifteen-metre schooner. At the end of April 1848, the *Konstantin* was transported seven hundred kilometres south into the Central Asian desert.

Unlike Charles Sturt's men hauling their whaleboat towards Australia's centre four years earlier, Butakov knew his vessel would be used. The caravan's destination, to which it was transported in pieces, was the Russian fort at Raim, sixty-five kilometres from the mouth of the Syr Darya on the Aral Sea's north-eastern coast, in what is now Kazakhstan. Crossing steppe, crossing desert, the caravan comprised two hundred infantrymen, two companies of Cossacks, six hundred cavalrymen, 2,500 carts and 3,500 camels, forming a train extending beyond the horizon. In Raim it took a month to unpack the *Konstantin*'s thousands of components and rebuild her.

Alexey Ivanovich Butakov: "the Magellan of the Aral Sea," Alexander von Humboldt called him. The navigation and mapping of what was then the world's fourth biggest inland body of water—at 67,000 square kilometres, smaller only than lakes Superior and Victoria and the nearby Caspian Sea—were his life's work. The charts he produced were in use as late as the 1950s. In his appearance there's not much to note—the uniform, the standard moustache. That he was exceptionally robust can be inferred from his deeds. As a young senior officer he'd spent two years aboard a military transport navigating the world.

In a letter to Sir Roderick Murchison, who read it to the Royal Geographical Society, London, on 13 December 1852, Butakov described his expedition. Supporting the *Konstantin*, he explained, was a smaller

schooner, the *Nicolas*, which had been transported to Raim the previous year. Under Butakov's deputy, Pospeloff, her crew was charged
with surveying and sounding the eastern coast, while Butakov in the
Konstantin would cover the northern coast. On 20 July 1848 they cast off
upon the Syr Darya. Six days later they reached the open waters of the
uncharted Aral. The *Konstantin*'s crew numbered twenty-seven, among
them two topographers, a surgeon and various non-commissioned officers, including Taras Shevchenko, poet, artist and exiled enemy of the
state.

The first voyage lasted two months. On 23 September the *Konstantin* anchored off the small island of Kos Aral at the mouth of the Syr
Darya, waiting for the river to unfreeze. The crews spent a cold six
months on the island in wooden huts. It was the winter of European
revolutions, but for the captain "the only remarkable incident of my
wintering there was a tiger-hunt in our near neighbourhood." It was
not until May that conditions improved sufficiently to allow the expedition to resume. "Our labours," Butakov writes, "were crowned with
the most complete success; notwithstanding manifold risks and dif-
ficulties, inseparable from an exploring expedition on waters so boisterous and so completely unknown." As for the climate, "I shall only
say that the summers are exceedingly hot and the winters very cold."
The coast was "a perfectly dead and barren desert," and yet Butakov is
able to list an abundance of wildlife: "immense quantities of pelicans,
cormorants, sea-gulls and sea-swallows" and "a great many wild hogs."
The principal fish "are the sharp-nosed sturgeon and the Silurus, or
bony pike." On occasion, finding themselves far from shore, the crew
were obliged to drink the waters in which they floated. The water was
salt, said Butakov, but less so than the oceans, whose flavour after all
he was familiar with: "Its taste resembles that of the Gulf of Finland, at
about a hundred *versts* from Cronstadt."

I ARRIVED IN the city of Almaty in eastern Kazakhstan as the
World Weightlifting Championships were starting. Kazakhstan's hope
was Zulfiya Chinshanlo, who'd set a world record in the clean-and-
jerk at the 2012 Olympics. The city was full of nervous giants in white

tracksuits, and at the public baths it was possible to feel diminished. There I met a man in his fifties whose duty it was to tend the saunas and steam rooms. His was one of the few jobs, it occurred to me, that require you to be nude from the moment you clock in. Nude apart from rubber sandals and a conical towelling hat. The Russian sauna, fiercest of them all, had in its wall a quarter-tonne iron door opened and closed by a bolt operated by a broom handle. He would open the door and a great blast of heat would be unleashed. Unfazed, balls swinging gladiatorially, he'd throw four ladles of water from a pail into the firebox and push the furnace door to. The heat became intolerable.

I thought of him afterwards at the Cathedral of the Holy Ascension. It had been reconsecrated in the nineties having spent forty years as the national museum of the Kazakh Soviet Socialist Republic. Flanking the door to the nave were murals: on the left the chorusing entrants to heaven; on the right, cartoons of the greater mass of us, naked and shrieking, flabbergasted to find themselves subjected to the innovations of hell's furnace-tenders. A young novice was standing with her back to me, a vestal finger extended towards one of the icons that clad the narthex walls. She was a figure from an icon. There we stood for perhaps ten seconds, I with one hand still on the open door, she with an arm outstretched, seemingly abandoned to her devotions. But then she made a hook of her finger, and drew it slowly towards her. "*Pauk*," she smiled, noticing me. Dangling on a thread from her fingertip was a spider—*pauk*—that had been hanging across the door. I went in and, among the headscarfed babushkas, lit a candle and placed it before Christ Pantocrator.

THE TRAIN FROM Almaty to the port town of Aralsk, 1,300 kilometres west, shadowed the Syr Darya River and took almost twenty-four hours. For most of the time I was sharing my compartment with a group of four—three teenage sisters and their grandmother, who was swaddled in layer upon layer of richly coloured velvet and wore a black lace headscarf. They were going to a funeral in the city of Kyzylorda; they seemed to be looking forward to it. Every few minutes they would hand me sweets or pastries or tiny cucumbers and, sitting in a line, watch me eat, occasionally exchanging smiling remarks with one another, as if pleased at a new dog's obedience. Having stuffed my face obligingly, I fell asleep. I imagine I snored. Seldom had I met such attentive strangers. I woke when the train stopped at Kyzylorda, and said goodbye to my velveteen family and their bags full of pastries. They left seven small cucumbers for me lined up on the fold-down table below the window. The train continued west through Baikonur, which serves the Soviet-built cosmodrome nearby, from which men continue to be sent into space.

Two hundred kilometres from Aralsk, we moved from steppe to desert-steppe to semi-arid desert. There were no longer the distant spinneys of elms that had scattered the steppe west of Turkestan; the few railside villages, too, were bereft of trees, the roofs of the houses whitewashed against the sun; and where cattle and sheep had been the livestock until Kyzylorda, as the train neared the Aral Sea there were no sheep, and the cattle were outnumbered by camels. The cows, when the train passed, did not look up; but the camels—dark, double-humped Bactrians, shorter-legged than the dromedary—turned their heads as one, switching their tails eagerly. The train halted for a few minutes beside one sparse township. No human beings, but in a back-yard white with dust was a black goat; and standing on a black road nearby, a white dog.

IN 1552 Ivan the Terrible commissioned his subjects, if *commissioned* is the word, to "measure the terrain and make a drawing of the state": the resulting description, not published until 1627, includes a discrete body of water named *Sinee More*: the Blue Sea. A hand-drawn map made during Peter I's march to Persia in 1772 shows the sea as a circular blob labelled "Oralsky Lake that loses its waters, while the shores are filled with cane. The water is fresh, but in the middle of the lake the water is saline and bitter." It was salty because the Aral Basin in which the sea sat is endorheic, a closed hydrological system like Xinjiang's Tarim Basin or America's Great Basin, having no out-flow to external bodies of water. The Aral Sea's waters, in other words, are regulated by evaporation alone. The first of its two feeder rivers finds its way three thousand kilometres from the Tienshan: known to Alexander the Great as the Jaxartes, today it is called the Syr Darya. The second river, born to the south, in the Pamirs of Tajikistan, is the Greeks' famed Oxus, today's Amu Darya.

If Yuri Gagarin, the first person in space, blasting off from the Baikonur cosmodrome in 1961, had been able to look down on the Kazakh Soviet Socialist Republic diminishing beneath him, what would he have seen? Two hundred kilometres west of the launch pad, a body of water, a jagged oval in outline, measuring some five hundred kilometres from south coast to north, and set largely amidst sandy desert. *Aral* means "island," and from above it would be obvious: of course, an island of water within a sea of desert.

From the sea's northern shore, the Aral Karakum Desert extends northwards, gradually merging with the colder steppe of southern Siberia; between the Amu Darya and the Syr Darya is the Kyzylkum, the "Red Sands"; while south of the sea, extending into Uzbekistan, are the dunes of another "black" desert, the Karakum. Finally Gagarin might (let us allow him some downtime) observe the hairline of a railway, shadowing the Syr Darya across the Kyzylkum and terminating at the water's north-eastern corner. A cluster of buildings. A port, ships coming and going.

SNOW HAD FALLEN the day before—the moonlit steppe was aglow with it—but when we reached Aralsk at 3 a.m. only a rind survived in the gutters. After the ravishing heat of the train, the air, barely above freezing, was a shock. In the waiting-hall, lit by a single yellow light, was a mosaic celebrating Aralsk's donation of fish to famine-struck Mother Russia in 1921. In front of a sea of blue and green, the monumental fishermen hauling nets and sealing barrels; the railwaymen and the proudly smiling boys; a solitary woman watching, hands on broad hips. All the dynamism of labour gladly given, and each gazing towards the local functionary, who is holding in outstretched arms a sheet of paper as big as *The Times*—a letter from Lenin, whose disembodied head, like a head on a coin, floats behind him. "The only hope of the starving of Kazan, Ufa, Samara and Astrakhan lies in the great proletariat solidarity of toiling men, like themselves, with toil-hardened hands," he wrote on 7 October 1921. "So please set aside part of your catch for the old men and women bloated by starvation." It is surprisingly importuning in tone, and not concise. The famine, which mainly affected the Volga and Ural regions, was caused partly by drought, but it was also a result of Lenin's policy of *prodrazvyorstka*, the confiscation of grain from rural peasants at a fixed price and its allocation to the urban poor. As with most famines, it was as much a question of distribution as supply. After a year an estimated six million people were dead. The fishermen obliged with fourteen wagonloads of salted fish. (Twenty years later they would send thousands of cans of carp to the German front.)

Aralsk would be my base for the next week. As I looked out from the station forecourt, there was a sense of great darkness beyond the lit town. Mirrored in a puddle were three billboards in a line, lit by a streetlight, memorialising the president's opening of the new freshwater works ten years earlier. Until then the people had made do with a pump in each street. The flag-waving women of the fish-processing factory; the president clasping his hands before banner-wielding crowds; and, the centrepiece, grave-faced, cyan-eyed President Nazarbayev cupping water from a gushing standpipe, and, Photoshopped behind him in such a way that the president seems to be emerging from the blue waters, the reborn Aral Sea. In preparation for Nazarbayev's visit, apparently, two live carp to be tagged and released by the president were transported by chartered helicopter and Mercedes from the more plentiful waters of the Caspian.

The other passenger who'd disembarked, a waddling faun engulfed in furs, ducked into a Lada and was driven away, and I listened as the car descended into the town. A bank of traffic lights silently maintained its cycle. Across the forecourt was a white steel sculpture of a sailboat set down on an arch. After ten minutes a Land Cruiser pulled out of the night and blinked its lights. The driver, Serik, lived in the centre of Aralsk, near the marketplace, with his mother, his brothers and their wives, and his wife and two children. Over his day-clothes he wore hooded hunting overalls in a camouflage of crisscross rushes. On his phone he showed me a photo of his friend lifting the head of a stag by its antlers. He'd been employed by a Danish NGO that, among other things, promoted the fishing of flounder—a saltwater flatfish that had been introduced into the Aral Sea as salinity increased and fresh-water species ceased to reproduce. The local fishermen, unaccustomed to bottom-feeders, required retraining and suitable nets; the towns-people needed to be convinced that such strange-looking creatures—a kind of pallid flatbread with both eyes on top—were edible, let alone palatable. They had never been entirely won over, he said. The Danish NGO was defunct, but Serik was now employed by its locally estab-lished successor, which co-ordinated World Bank grants to pay for infrastructure, equipment, legal aid and training in the region's strug-gling fishing villages. There was a kind of wary avuncularity about him that I liked; he was hospitable, but he knew he owed me nothing beyond what I was paying for: driving, introductions, interpretation. Aralsk was not a healthy town, but he was glowing. He had a wide, straight, puppetlike mouth, soft skin and glossy, thick hair. If he had an occasional air of distraction it was because his mind was on his home, his family, and his baby daughter. In the days ahead, each time we returned to the town, and then his street, and then his house, he invariably grew progressively more at ease and talkative. Home, it seemed, was the only place he ever really wanted to be.

IN ARALSK there were no birds, not even gulls. On sunny days, children emerged, and young women arm in arm; but the town I remember is as male as a barracks. Even the dogs were all male. The ground they were sniffing had been dust in summer but was mud now, in early November, and would remain mud till May. Only the new streets around the station and the squares were asphalted; when rain fell, the town's unsurfaced roads or those surfaced only with gravel (the roads people lived on) became oily wallows impassable to all but the GAZ utility trucks, giant Soviet six-wheelers, forty years old but still running faultlessly long after the Russians had left. The trick, for those in ordinary trucks, was to drive on the firm ground on either side of the road—until day by day the wallows broadened to subsume those strips and then the ones beyond them, until there was no solid ground

between the buildings, only canals of mud, and an alternative way to
your destination had to be found. The residential blocks, with their
blue-fenced compounds, became islands. The Central Asian desert
in November, the *drylands*: the constant towing and cleaning of your
vehicle, the scraping of mud from your boots, the relief of returning to
the dry car or home.

As we progressed through the town and the crouching mud villages over the coming days, Serik would every few seconds have to
raise his hand or stop and wind down his window to greet someone,
usually a friend of his late father's. With me he was watchful, at least to
start with; unforthcoming. He could sit out an hour in easy silence. But
whomever we met in the streets or in shops or village homes greeted
him with joy. He was from an old Aralsk family; his father, whose picture adorned the reception room in his home, had been well loved and
the family still suffered from his loss. It was partly the pleasure Serik's
presence manifested in others that made me warm to him. Like all
Kazakh men, he smoked at every hiatus and every encounter and was
munificent with his Kents. Not to smoke in this world of smokers—it
was a sign of infirmity or a failing, like childlessness or bachelorhood
in this country of giant families. He dropped me at a guesthouse where
silently in a near-dark dining room a woman served me tinned ham
and a fried egg and hard bread with tea whose syrupy sweetness I
associate, looking back, with her careful laying down of each piece
of crockery before me, and the kindness of her smile. In the pebbled
pane of a closed door the flicker of a TV played. I slept, and when I
woke it was late morning. Watery light was flooding in through a gauze
curtain.

"THE CAPITALIST CLASS has always used the toiling man's hunger
to enslave him. They now want to make use of our famine to destroy
the freedom we have won at the price of our blood ... Dear comrades,
fishermen and workers of the Aral Sea, I urge you to give with a gener-
ous hand!"

I found the copy of Lenin's 1921 letter the following day in the
museum, a corrugated-iron structure on the outskirts of the town.

Inside, on a table by the door, was a relief map showing the Aral Sea as it was when the museum was founded in 1988. It was not intended for the purpose of comparison—no "now" map stood alongside this "then"—it was just that it had not been updated since the museum was opened. And yet the blue had been refreshed. Indeed the border between Kazakhstan and Uzbekistan, which crosses the sea horizontally, had carelessly been painted over, and was visible only where it crossed islands, and as a pale line below the surface. You wouldn't know you were in an ecological disaster zone. It was just another Kazakh provincial museum with its odious taxidermy that billowed dust when patted, its sharks' teeth and ammonites and ill-lit dioramas, its corner of reconstructed yurt, and its hall dedicated to Kazakh independence.

The museum was low-ceilinged, windowless and subaqueously murky; from a far room desultory conversation was audible. A young woman appeared with a blonde girl of seven or eight. In silence the woman went ahead from room to room, switching on the lights; as I moved to the next room, guided by the light, her daughter would reach up and switch off the light in the room I was leaving, skipping past me to catch up with her mother. Beyond a kapok-leaking badger that surely had never contained a beating heart, and a fish cart once owned by a Hero of Socialist Labour, was the section of the museum concerning the recent history of the Aral Sea. Here was the before-and-after, painted by schoolchildren (perhaps by the light-switch girl), even if the sea's current shore had receded further still since the two paintings were done. The boundary of the sea in each was identical, but one was coloured in blue to the edges, while the other was yellow with only a blue disc floating in its centre; this, the yellow, was the new desert. They called it Aralkum, *kum* in Turkic meaning "sands."

On the floor of the museum, lining the skirting, were a dozen demijohns and cuboid glass vats. Drum-skinned across their mouths were squares of greaseproof paper, like seals on jars of jam. The vessels were backlit by floor-level spotlights, so that the gone-off formaldehyde within glowed medicinal yellow, revealing each one's horrible occupant: specimens of the former fish of the Aral Sea. Aral barbel, bastard sturgeon, shovel-nosed sturgeon, bream, roach, carp, snakehead, pike perch, and a hulking whiskered catfish, its tail dislocated to fit, like a corpse wedged into a too-small coffin. Each fish hung nose-down in its bottle, gazing at the floor with a semblance of alarm. On the lid of one jar, containing a flaking sturgeon, was a label: "Currently efforts are being made to reintroduce this species." It didn't seem hopeful. Before the 1960s the Aral Sea supplied fifty thousand tonnes of fish per year. By 1975 the figure was three thousand. Commercial fishing ceased in 1980 and had only been revived, tentatively, in the past ten years. On the corridor wall was a line of blanched squares where paintings by local artists had hung; most of them were on loan to the museum in Kyzylorda. Only one was left—overlooked or rejected—a bright gouache of a busy harbour: cranes discharging ships, trawlers at anchor, a timber landing-stage, and—pretty detail—sculling in the calm ultramarine water, a young couple in a rowboat, the man in a white open-necked shirt, the woman facing him holding a pale-blue parasol. It might be any municipal boating lake. The sun is out—the tender sun of May. It had been painted recently: the harbour of Aralsk envisaged as it once had been, and yet there was no regret in the depiction, no darkness daubed on the horizon: *this is how things were; now they are different.*

The girl turned off the last of the lights, and walked me to the door. She stood and watched me with her head tipped to one side, then seeing Serik waiting said in English, "Good afternoon!" And Serik, whom she knew, replied in kind, and she ran back into the museum hollering with delight. Whenever we were outdoors Serik wore his hunting overalls. I could imagine him stalking prey—his quietness seemed born of calculation rather than subdual. His movements, too, had something of the hunter about them. As we walked, he had a tendency to watch the ground immediately ahead of him, as one might to avoid stepping on a twig whose snapping would spook the deer or boar. It was sensible to watch your feet, of course, in a place where the pavements and streets were rutted and potholed.

At the harbour, five minutes' drive from the museum, two trawlers of the Aral Fish Industries fleet, the *Toktarev* and the *Alimbetov*, had been repainted and set in dockside cradles, at once monuments and, one of them, a viewing platform. Serik waited while I clambered up an iron companionway and stood on the booming drum of its wheel-house roof and looked out. Until the railway between Orenburg and Tashkent was built and the station opened in 1905, Aralsk was only a fishing village around a few wells. With the railway came men; fishing co-operatives were established and factories founded. From Ushsai and Muynak on the Aral Sea's southern coast, five hundred kilometres away, the Central Asian State Shipping Company transported fish, canned goods, watermelons and cotton, while in turn timber, grain and fertiliser were shipped back from Aralsk. A sea, after all, is more than a larder or a well; it is also a road.

A few of the wooden and concrete wharf buildings—the town's own cannery, the refrigeration plant, warehouses—were still intact and two giant cargo cranes, the cranes from the painting, languished with their arms swung out over the basin. But the cranes were rusted and immobile. Aralsk's harbour had been accessed from the sea by a broad channel. Where its water had once been deep enough for ships of five metres' draught, now there was only a gaping dry recess scattered with retarded saxaul and an infinity of dumped waste. It was becoming a landfill. Lining the far bank were more derelict warehouses; others in the midst of being knocked down. To the south the empty channel, broad as a glaciated valley, receded to the horizon. You stood here for a while, you had your photo taken; for this (this absence) was the town's main attraction. Its emptiness was as starkly alarming as a socket deprived of its eye. "Some people in Aralsk, even adults, have never seen the sea," Serik had told me.

You could say it started as long ago as 1882, with the words of A. I. Voeikov, the esteemed Russian geographer and climatologist: "The existence of the Aral Sea within its present limits is evidence of our backwardness and our inability to make use of such amounts of flowing water and fertile silt which the Amu and Syr rivers carry." The Aral Sea was "a mistake of nature." I thought of vanished Lop Nor and all the cotton-drained lakes of Xinjiang. Where Chinese Confucianism had advocated *tianrenyii*, "harmony between the heavens and mankind," the Maoist apothegm had been *ren ding sheng tian*, "man must conquer nature." It was a Chinese adaptation of another slogan, Lenin's

"We cannot expect charity from nature, we must tear it from her!" How did Yuri Gagarin describe his trip into space, on returning to Baikonur? "An unprecedented duel with nature."

IN 1918, a year after the Russian Revolution, Lenin signed a decree "On the Allocation of 50 Million Roubles for Irrigation Development Works in Turkestan and on the Organization of these Works." As in Xinjiang, national self-sufficiency in cotton was the aspiration, but while cotton thrives in heat, its thirst is such that 750 millimetres of water per year is necessary to keep it alive; this, in the Aral Basin, where annual precipitation is at most 350 millimetres, and usually much less, even in the slough of Aralsk. A decree signed by Lenin was not to be ignored. It was those rivers identified by Voeikov, futilely debouching into the Aral Sea, that would be caused to furnish the required water. Decree after decree followed. In 1927 the Soviet Union imported 41 per cent of its cotton; six years later the figure was 3 per cent. President Nazarbayev maintained in a recent interview that "nobody thought to calculate what would happen to the Aral Sea." But the calculation was done, profit set against loss—the continued existence of the world's fourth largest lake and the sixty thousand livelihoods it supported vs. national self-sufficiency in cotton—by Voeikov, by Lenin, by Khrushchev and Brezhnev. These so-called "virgin lands," steppe and desert alike, must satisfy the national need, just as the Aral Sea and its labour had been called upon in 1921 to feed the starving of the Volga. In 1968 an engineer said shruggingly: "It is obvious to everyone that the evaporation of the Aral Sea is inevitable."

In Kazakhstan and its southern neighbour, Uzbekistan, 32,000 kilometres of irrigation canals were dug to supply water for cotton and wheat. In the early 1960s the first centimetres of the sea's recession were recorded. Over the following decade the level continued to fall, by on average twenty centimetres per year; during the 1970s it was fifty centimetres per year; between 1980 and 2000, eighty centimetres per year. It was as if a breach in a dyke were widening itself. By 1982 the Amu Darya had been so heavily diverted that it ceased, for a time, to reach the Aral Sea at all, while the Syr Darya's flow had been reduced to 10 per cent of its former volume. The vast mass of that diverted water was squandered—soaking into the deserts from unlined canals (trenches shovelled in the sand) or evaporating from undrained fields. In 1989 the Aral became two separate bodies of water, the Large Aral to the south and the Small Aral to the north, divided by the now dry Berg Strait. By 2004 the sea's former area of 67,000 square kilometres was reduced to a combined 17,000 square kilometres. Today it is smaller still, and south of the Berg Strait the water has all but gone.

But it was not that the fish were left gasping on the exposed sands, like guppies in a cracked aquarium. Reduced to a third of its original area, the water became correspondingly saltier. The fishes' coastal spawning areas were the first to be affected. Algae, zooplankton, phytoplankton perished. Fish like the barbel and the sturgeon, which can tolerate only low levels of salt, migrated to the interior and its remaining enclaves of fresh water, until even these were contaminated. Of the twenty edible species in 1960, thirty years later, in 1990, there were only four, all saltwater-dwellers: bullhead, sprat, stickleback, atherina, plus the introduced flounder.

Serik was standing under the *Toktarev*, smoking and checking his phone. He barely registered the absurdity of it any more: visitor after visitor gazing into the vacancy, trying to understood what it meant, reluctant to concede that it meant only what they'd known it to mean even before they got off the train. An eyeless socket—but the organ gouged out not by accident or malice, but by its owner.

THE FOLLOWING DAY we drove towards what had once been the sea, south along a ten-kilometre dirt road that served a "fish-receiving station," as Serik called it, where the day's catch was landed and weighed before being transported to Aralsk for gutting, freezing and canning. As we passed under the white steel archway that marked Aralsk's boundary, the surfaced roads coarsened to rubble and mud. Serik stopped for a smoke beside a field of rubbish: kitchen waste, construction waste, broken furniture, clothes, bones, the ubiquitous, uncountable vodka bottles of Central Asia. It was the town's tip, and of course it was where the desert began—the desert that itself was viewed as little more than one giant tip. And this was a description that might be extended: to the oblast of Kyzylorda, of which Aralsk was a part; but beyond that, in the Kremlin mind, to Kazakhstan itself. There were the deportees of the Second World War—the mistrusted millions of Greeks, Volga Germans, Chechens, Ingush, Kalmyks, Turks, Tartars and Koreans, dispersed across the republic. There was Solzhenitsyn, banished to Ekibastuz in the north-east; Trotsky to Almaty; and Dostoevsky to Semipalatinsk (then Semey) in Kazakh Siberia, a thousand kilometres north of Almaty. And there was the steppe close to Dostoevsky's exile, the so-called Polygon, where between 1949 and 1990 Moscow carried out six hundred nuclear explosions—detonations that made those at Maralinga and Lop Nor seem like firecrackers. For days after each aboveground test steppe eagles would be seen standing motionless on their telegraph poles, blinded.

With the appropriation of the sea's water came a drop in the volume available for evaporation. Rainfall decreased, and the lowering of the Aral waters accelerated. The restraining effect of the sea on the local climate diminished. Summers became hotter and longer, winters shorter and colder. Humidity declined, drought-days multiplied. The powdery seabed became a repository for dust storms. Millions of tonnes of matter each year are whipped from the surface and taken up in towering plumes to be broadcast across the Aral Basin as far as Lithuania and Afghanistan. Unlike the *burans* of the Taklamakan, these dust storms are tainted, containing not only sediment but the sea's residual salt, which, settling on the already sickly land, has caused it to sicken further. Sometimes water itself causes desertification. Excessive irrigation, especially in areas of high evaporation, causes dissolved salts to accumulate in the soil until nothing will grow. Poorly managed and improperly drained, Kazakhstan's new cottonlands became tepid swamps. The water, standing vainly on the surface, evaporated, leaving only a rime of salt on the cotton and in the soil. As the Aral Sea shrank, the crops that its waters had been diverted to sustain failed. Thus the new desert that has emerged on the onetime bed of the Aral Sea is itself surrounded by desertified land. And meanwhile the toxins of that same failing agronomy—those mountains of fertiliser, defoliants, herbicides and pesticides that were required merely to maintain crop yields—have seeped into watercourses and into the land, their residues filtering into the Syr Darya's delta lakes and contributing to the dust-load swept into the atmosphere from the dry seabed. The blood of Kazakhstan's children contains DDT at levels twenty times higher than their European counterparts. Oesophageal cancer, congenital deformities, jaundice, anaemia, impaired immune function, gastritis, heart disease, hepatitis—all have burgeoned locally since the 1960s. Average life-expectancy in Central Asia's cottonlands is twenty years below that of the former Soviet Union as a whole.

Troops of swaying Bactrian camels hung about at the roadside, the colour of old bronze. For Serik there was little distinction between steppe—*dala*—and desert, *shōl*. You can seldom step across the desert's edge as you might from land to sea, let alone from one political jurisdiction to another. Say you're driving across steppe dense with succulent grass, perhaps blooming with tulips—then, look around, and it has become something else, you are somewhere new: drier, the vegetation sparer, the birds gone. This is how the desert tends to come upon you.

As we sped towards the sea the camels at the trackside bucked and galloped briefly like dead leaves thrown up by a passing gust, before settling—becoming still as only a Bactrian can be still, displaying the same immense imperiousness with which, you suspect, they would watch an onrushing tidal wave—and surveyed us, fixedly. These were the "undomesticated and savage animals" William Palgrave described. The farmers would no more ride one than they would a cow; they were everything but pets and steeds—haulage; meat and milk; hide and hair. You would follow with your eyes a branch line of telegraph poles to a low cluster of shacks that was a camel farm—a smouldering scribble on the pale land, as if scratched in by a splint of charcoal—and tracing the line of poles to or from the farm would be a parade of thirty camels. Lost in snow or heat, the best advice, Serik said, was to follow the wires: they'll take you eventually to a farm, a village, a camel man's bivouac, sure as river to sea.

Even far from the original shore, where it had been above water for a million years, the land resembled a former lakebed: not only the sand and the alluvial grit, but the flatness and the occasional knolls like islands. On the summit of each one was the spiked formation of a family cemetery. The fish-receiving station stood at the end of a narrow spit branching from the track where the land shelved off to the south. For the first time the vast drained depression was comprehensible rolling out ahead; thirty kilometres off, the soaring cliffs of the Aral Sea's one-time shores. The station today resembled a naval fortification shelled and overrun; it was impossible to rebuild it in the imagination: only a slumped stack of concrete slabs bristling with exposed reinforcement rods. Why, I wondered, had it been demolished? Serik didn't know. Where once water had lapped a loading wharf, now the tumble of concrete stood three storeys above a salt lake no bigger than half a hectare and no deeper than a puddle. Only thirty years ago on any unfrozen afternoon boats would be discharging their day's catch here, the place glad with the clamour of the day's end. Edging down the embankment, I stood, finally, on the dry seabed. In the distance was a shimmering rank of saltpans. I left Serik and walked south.

The seabed expanded before me, a plain of grey porridge, of doused ashes, and within ten minutes the horizon on all sides had pulled back to no more than a paler or darker line battening land to sky. The first kilometre was strewn with scalloped off-white shells little bigger than a thumbnail (you could scoop them up in handfuls) and hummocks of low vegetation, near-perfect circles of glasswort and smotherweed. Step by step these hummocks and the shells became fewer, as if the plain had been swept from its centre to its edges, until nothing was left but the frailest driftwood twig, rolled across the surface by the wind; or a rusted enamel mug, half-buried and packed with shell-shards; or a wedge of glass from a bottle dropped into the blue waters fifty years before. And then nothing, no appeal to the eye.

My boots got leaden as a deep-sea diver's. Every few minutes it was necessary to stop and scrape the mud from my soles with the piece of glass, kept in one hand as I walked. When the fish-receiving station had been left behind there was nothing to advise you of your progress. If desert evokes thoughts of the sea, it is no coincidence— after all, often you will be walking on an ancient lakebed. But this was different: in terms of the sea's lifespan, the water had gone in an instant; and in that abruptness was a terrifying violence. Standing in a place where water has once been, you are alert to the threat of its rushing back, like an unparting Red Sea, no matter how improbable its return. I looked back and there were my footprints, a darker procession backing away; there was the rain-dimpled lakebed, the sky with its cruising clouds.

Under the horizon shimmered those plaques of white—salt—that I had wanted to reach before turning back (dusk was coming). It was a reassurance to have a destination in sight, even if the saltpans appeared no closer than when I had seen them on setting out half an hour ago. As I went on, pausing to pare the scurf of mud from my boots, the broken white line seemed to recede correspondingly. A place devoid of landmarks or way-markers can be as confounding as any maze. I walked for another half-hour, mud-shackled, and still the salt flats seemed to be no closer, and when I turned to look back again, the derelict fish-receiving station, and Serik and the Land Cruiser, were no longer visible on the horizon, and thus the line of my footprints, like a caver's safety-twine, was the only way of knowing where I'd come from and how to get back. The sky was darkening; I turned around, tracing my own footprints, so that to one coming across the double rank it would look like someone had been to harvest something beyond the horizon.

As I neared the fish-receiving station, I noticed again those low circular hummocks that had encroached, over the years, spot by spot, from the shores of the former seabed; this was how life retook a place divested of it. "Primary succession"—the commencement of biology on a slate wiped clean: a cooled lava field, or the rasped track left by a glacier, or a drained seabed... There are few places so antibiotic that seed and substrate will be permanently put off. One place becomes another. These button-shaped islands of vegetation had been populated by pioneers. I stepped onto one to scrape my soles. Around the plants' stems a new soil was trapped, windblown sandy soil, loess, and in turn the young humus laid down as the first generations died. These isolated discs—each no more than a pace across—would multiply and coalesce further, just as they had at the plain's edge, as raindrops on dust multiply and coalesce. Small bands of birds treated these discs as islands, flitting from one to the next. When I was two hundred metres from the fish-receiving station a dull slap carried across the sediment, then another—Serik, in a cloud of dust, holding a rubber floor-mat from the Land Cruiser, beating the dried mud from it. Seeing me, he raised his hand, as if hailing a returning trawler.

THE FOLLOWING MORNING we drove out to Zalanash, one of the old fishing villages, sixty kilometres south-west of Aralsk. The village was signposted from far across the plain by twin conical hills plastered with snow and called locally "the tits." Again, those bristling cemeteries raised on their hills, assemblages that sometimes had the appearance of an encamped army—the panorama afforded by their station; their defensibility. You felt surveilled. Alongside the track, at every bend and crossroads and junction and blind hill, a monument or several monuments had been erected to the road-dead. Usually these were slender pyramidal towers of rusted sheet steel and not much taller than myself. The appearance they had of rudimentary rockets did not seem inappropriate, and not only because the cosmodrome was nearby. Scarcely so much as a metre of verge, I noticed, was clear of empty vodka bottles thrown from passing vehicles. There was a connection between the glass and those steel towers.

It was a coastal landscape, and the skies were coastal; cloudless, not blue but powdery white like fired lead. Along the road were the endless telegraph poles, and at the base of each pole a heap of spoil. And alongside the road, where drains had been dug, further heaps of spoil a metre high, one after another, kilometre after kilometre. And this repetition—the telegraph poles with their spoil heaps, then the closer unbroken line of spoil heaps—became hypnotic, and in their repetition was a sense that the road might go on like this for ever. The spell was broken by a large bird perching on one of the roadside heaps, a steppe eagle, Serik said, the same hard burnished bronze colour as the camels. It was watching, but seemed to watch nothing in particular, neither us nor any special point on the steppe, but everything, as if its alertness were universal.

. . .

ZALANASH MEANS "NAKED," and naked it was, as a person raised by wolves. In the distance was a rise of rocky land beyond which, Serik said, lay the waterless sea.

Under the steel arch that heralded every village, and down the hard-packed earth of Zalanash's broad main thoroughfare we drove, white housing compounds hunkered on either side. On the edge of the street were more billboards hailing the president. We drove on, the roadway tipping down towards the sea and Zalanash's onetime landing berths and slipways—and then the wind slamming against the vehicle's flank, and once more the colossal dry crater.

I climbed out of the Land Cruiser. A cliff-face, perhaps twenty metres high, a couple of kilometres away to my right; another, snow-topped, ten kilometres away to my left; and ahead nothing but the dry lakebed corrugated by spits and sandbars. But not lunar or stripped, not a saltscape or sandscape: camels had been put out to graze on the carpet of halophytes that had developed since the great reversal of thirty years ago. The track, deep-cut into the surface, as if a monolith had been dragged across the desert, was leading me towards a dark mechanical constellation in the distance, eerie as the abandoned craft of a failed invasion.

Serik, as usual, stayed in the warm Land Cruiser. I walked until I could no longer hear the radio. Apart from the scattered camels, swaying on their splint legs, there was the shrilling of the pale finches that skimmed in mobs between denser patches of vegetation, the same birds I had seen near the fish-receiving station, less like things flying, flap-flap-glide, than projectiles collectively blasted from one point to the next. More abundantly there were the "great gerbils" (thousands per hectare, there must have been), tawny rattish things whose burrow-holes cratered and honeycombed certain plots so densely that all vegetation was discouraged, and to inadvertently walk across one meant collapsing the animals' tunnels and sinking ankle-deep into the sediment. Occasionally one of them would sight the intruder from a dozen metres and, rather than ducking instantly into its burrow, would pause in scrutiny—neither eagle nor fox nor wolf, but predator, *predator*; and—blink—vanish, into its subterrain of fishbones and clamshells. As so often in the desert, there was a sense of being watched: the birds, the gerbils, the camels, not one of them was unaware of you.

As I remember it, the ship is a terrific edifice, as big as an oil tanker; but then I look at my photos, and it's just a rusted conning tower no roomier than my London flat, stilted on an array of bulkheads corroded to a filigree. The ground around the hulk, if hulk was right, had been eroded and manured by the camels that used its shade, and, it seemed, treated by the farmers as a mausoleum, for the ground was scattered with bones and bundles of wool scarcely identifiable as lambs or camel calves save for a few triskeles of hoofed legs rooted to a blackened bundle of organs. Perhaps it was simply that here, where it was sheltered, the foxes and jackals brought their food. Twenty years ago a flotilla of a dozen ships was foundered on this low bank—these few ruins all that was left of that graveyard (that's what Serik called it, "the ship graveyard"). The rest had been cut up with acetylene torches and sold to the Chinese for scrap. It was hard to visualise the vessel as it once had been, in its entirety; to fix the bridge I was looking at upon the vanished hull. It was natural to imagine some 1970s seafarer gripping the taffrail that still crowned the wheelhouse, facing off a spumey wind. I was not the first to picture the grounded ship's onetime crew. Someone had spent a day or more here, but just as nobody in Zalanash knew the ship's name, nor could they say when the graffiti had appeared; they knew for certain that it was not the work of locals, who had better things to do. It was a landmark, and distant from authority, so naturally we got out our aerosols and markers and defaced it. The bulkheads had been crewed by life-size Russian sailors painted in white emulsion, uniformly dejected-looking and skeletal, as if confined on this grounded vessel for eternity: this one sitting on a crate, his chin propped on a fist; this one slumped in a hammock; another, a vodka bottle grasped in one hand; a fourth, facing away, elbow crooked to suggest masturbation.

On the way back to the car I noticed on the cliff-top, two or three kilometres off, yet another cemetery, a handful of domed tombs whose view must once have been the coming and going of fishing boats and cargo carriers to Zalanash and Aralsk. There were those still living,

said Serik when I got back to the car, who had visited the graves since
childhood and had watched as, decade by decade, the water below first
withdrew, then further withdrew, until the vessels in their obsoles-
cence were abandoned, circumscribed by a shrinking pond and then,
as the water vanished, set down in the dry sediment, canted there as if
by an ebbed tide that had failed to come back. The slow change from
deep water to shallower, to marsh, to puddled silt. And then, over a
decade, to this new environment of sand, dust and sagebrush. Everything was someone's resource. Serik saw the selling-off of the hulks
as a new failure. He'd tried to persuade Aralsk's mayor to preserve by
statute those that remained, as a "monument"—where would tourists
be taken otherwise? What would Aralsk's schoolchildren be shown as
proof that a sea truly had existed, when even its ghosts were expelled?
"The mayor listened to me very carefully," he said. And? "He was not
interested."

WITH COMMANDER BUTAKOV on his crossing of the Karakum
Desert 140 years ago was an erstwhile member of the Third Company
of the Russian army. Unlike the other soldiers he carried no rifle, let
alone ship components; nor did he wear a uniform. In his diary he
wrote: "When I was a child, as far back as I can remember, I showed no
interest in soldiers, as is common with children. When I was growing
up and grasping the rational order of things, I began to feel an innate
irresistible dislike for Christ-loving soldiers."

I'd seen his picture in Aralsk's museum, his moustache resembling
less a walrus's whiskers than an eagle shot and mounted: this, said the
label, was the Ukrainian poet and artist Taras Shevchenko.

Shevchenko had come to the attention of the Russian authorities in
1847 as a member of the secret Society of Saints Cyril and Methodius,
which promoted the so-called Little Russian language, Ukrainian, and
called for the unification of the Slavic nations and the end of serfdom
(Shevchenko himself had been born a serf). Following the society's
denunciation, he was arrested and his pro-revolution writings came
to light:

Oh wicked tsar, accursed!
Oh crafty, evil, grasping tsar!
. . .
Inhuman monster vile!

Nicholas I laughed at this depiction of him in Shevchenko's poem "The Dream." What he did not laugh at were the lines about the tsarina, Alexandra, with her famous tic:

Every time she steps, her head
Goes jiggling on her neck.
Is this the beauty rare they praise?
Poor thing, you are a wreck!

"I suppose he had reason not to be on terms with me," he complained, "but what has she done to deserve this?" In a report urging Shevchenko's exile, the tsar's aid, Count Orlov, wrote: "Because of his insolence and rebellious spirit, which are boundless, he must be considered as one of the most important criminals." (It was Orlov, head of the secret police, who would cause Fyodor Dostoevsky to be exiled to Semipalatinsk six years later.) Approving the sentence—recalling his nervy, maligned wife—Nicholas duly inscribed on the report: "Under the strictest surveillance, prohibited from writing or painting." To the failure of his overseers to uphold that prohibition we owe some of the best descriptions we have of the Aral Sea region as it was before the Soviet era.

On the first day out of Orsk, in May 1848, before the desert proper was encountered, Shevchenko—more accustomed to the fertile plains of the Dnieper—swooned from heat exhaustion. On the second day, crossing terrain as flat and colourless "as if it had been covered with a white table-cloth," he found himself surrendering "entirely to quiet sorrow and the observation of nature." It was as evening neared that he saw clouds on the horizon. But not clouds: smoke. An "indescribable, magnificent picture of fire," according to Shevchenko, the blaze had been kindled by herdsmen to encourage young forage for their sheep. In front of the line of flames appeared a long line of camels,

Shevchenko wrote, a vision "which disappeared, like Oriental shadows in the reddish mist." The scene reminded him of the smiting of Sodom and Gomorrah as depicted by the English painter John Martin.

Shevchenko made a watercolour sketch—one of his most famous works, and the first of some two hundred he would complete during the next eighteen months of exile. It shows the evening camp, scattered yurts, a train of carts and wheel-mounted skiffs; a gowned Kirghiz outlined before a glowing tent; a horseman crossing a shallow salt pond. The following night was spent at the ancient grave mound of the Kirghiz warrior Dustan. Again Shevchenko paused to make a drawing. Nearby, the party found a scene of butchery. This he does not draw:

> Since time immemorial,
> The desert has hidden from the people,
> But we have found it:
> We have built fortresses,
> And soon there will be graves.

In the sand lay dozens of mutilated and headless corpses, wolf-torn and made leather by the sun, all that remained of a Russian patrol routed by the troops of the rebel khanate of Khiva, south of the Aral Sea. Leaving behind the grey bloodied sand, the party followed the fire to a "light-pink plain"—a dry salt lake whose dust, Shevchenko was warned, caused blindness, and indeed he did lose his sight, as the salt-talc billowed up under the horses' hooves. Picture Shevchenko, then, far from his motherland, cowering under the sun of the "Kirghiz Sahara," exhausted and fretful, the heat intensifying, his moustache turned white with salt-dust. Now blind.

When sight returned to him, the convoy had entered a dazzling new place, a plain of sand "marked with a white row of horses" and camels' skeletons—further casualties of the expedition against Khiva. The way to desert hell, from Xuanzang's Black Gobi to the migrant trails of Arizona, is verged with bones. Finally there appeared on the horizon "a faint blue line."

The company regained its cheer after those hundreds of *versts* of blinding salt flats and sand strewn with the blackened organs of their countrymen. The sea breeze was as salutary as a dose of oxygen to a mountaineer. They camped on the coast and bathed in Sarichaganaku Bay sixty kilometres north of the Syr Darya. The euphoria of cold water on parched skin. On 19 June, more than a month after setting out from Orsk, they reached the Russian fort at Raim.

The shore of the Syr Darya, as painted by Shevchenko in the days before their boats embarked, is a lush idyll, thicketed with reeds and bulrushes, the river itself placid and inviting. In the background of one painting can be seen the *Nicolas* already bobbing on the unruffled water, and the *Konstantin* in her cradle, awaiting masts. Six weeks after arriving at Raim the expedition set sail. Butakov appointed Shevchenko, whom he called "comrade and friend," to the crew of the *Konstantin* as expedition artist. Apparently he had no qualms about ignoring the tsar's orders that the exile be prevented from writing or drawing. The delicate sketches and watercolours that resulted are an exquisite visual diary of the *Konstantin*'s thirty-eight-day voyage: tender, doctorly attention to sparsity (every crack in every rock, every stem of every shrub), intimate regard for bleakness. Like a surveyor's sketches of a planet assigned for colonisation.

FROM ZALANASH the desert crossing to Tastubek was marked only by a plait of puddled ruts. The plain was olive-brown, and smooth and sticky as the surface of a pudding. We were going to the next village, Tastubek, to stay with Serik's friends, fishermen. Two kilometres from Zalanash the Land Cruiser lost traction; of course it did. I got out and braced myself in the mud and pushed; the vehicle slewed and jinked. I put my shoulder to it and rocked the car with each acceleration and soon we were moving again, thundering across the clay, and once again I had arrived at that place where the horizon had retreated so far it was evident that the world was only a ball. And not that big. This was the *takyr*, the poorly drained plains of clay that roll north and west from the Aral Sea's former shores. As we entered a thin plot of saxaul Serik slowed and drove more circumspectly, skirting the puddles, riding the ridges, but finally bumping to a halt from which the car would not, no matter how he jerked the gas, be jolted. He killed the engine and slumped in his seat and lit a Kent, offering the packet to me, though he knew I didn't smoke. When he had finished he looked at me, and I got out again, and planted my feet in the morass behind the car. I pushed and he accelerated, and we continued like this for ten minutes. The car moved a little, found some traction, then ceased to move, and I pushed again, pushed so hard that I would feel it for mornings to come, and the wheels as they spun only drove deeper into the mud. Serik turned off the engine; in flooded the silence.

From the boot I took a shovel and two short planks and sliced a trench in front of each back wheel and into each placed a plank, and when Serik accelerated again one of the boards split in two and the other was spat out between my shins and skittered twenty metres across the desert behind me. This went on for an hour and a half, until I was bruise-eyed with tiredness, and golemed to the waist in frigid mud. So much for sunblock. Inside the car Serik was exhausted, too, though perhaps I was more exhausted, and he was lighting another cigarette. It was almost dusk. We were twenty-five kilometres from Zalanash and sixty-five from Tastubek. On a distant island of rocks something glinted in the low sun; some Turkic monument or camel man's hut. We were here for the night. We had half a bottle of vodka, eight (Serik thumbed through them) Kents, and for dinner a near-empty carton of Smints.

Serik went to sleep almost immediately—like he'd been hit by a sedative dart—though it was barely seven o'clock. I drank some of the vodka, then the rest of it. My boots were wet but it was better to keep them on: the foot wells were ankle-deep in mud. I pushed my seat back as far as it would go, and hunched up on one side using my rucksack as a pillow, cowling my hood low and wrapping my scarf around my face, and there I waited, alert as a great gerbil, while Serik snored gently and night settled upon the plain, settled like a silk scarf dropped from someone's hand: no sunset afterglow, no celestial unveiling or astonishing moon, merely grey darkening to black. We'd turned the heater off to preserve the battery. A chill began to creep in as the engine ticked. I lay there beside this near-stranger and saw, as if from above, the vehicle stranded in its ruts amid that disc of sparse vegetation, surrounded in turn by the plain's vastness, perhaps two hundred square kilometres.

I probably dozed off; at any rate I became aware that something had disturbed the blackness beyond the windscreen. There it was again, a pinprick starburst intense as a lighthouse. It was impossible to know how far off it was; but several kilometres, certainly. A solitary light—a motorbike, then, hazarding the journey from Tastubek to Zalanash. *Passengers*: the word Absalom had used in the Taklamakan.

It was then, as Serik was roused by my shifting, that the light that had maintained a steady level on the black windscreen appeared to rise, before powering first to the right then to the left and finally drifting back to its original level and resuming its journey towards us once more, if indeed it was coming towards us—only to repeat that strange dance, suddenly shooting heavenwards and flitting from side to side, before settling once again. Was it a jet? A helicopter? Some will-o'-the-wisp? I opened a window but only a gentle desert wind was audible. Serik turned the key and flashed the headlights. "They will help us." The oncoming light continued but did not return our signal. He flashed the lights again, clicking them on and off. The light vanished.

He stared out at the blackness and flashed the lights again. "Strange," he said finally, lying back in his seat with an executive air.

"What happened to them?"

"They think they will get stuck."

So it was not the other vehicle that was the lighthouse.

Lights continued to appear intermittently throughout the night, but no sooner would we flash them than they would vanish.

At 6 a.m. I woke to a sky the colour of sacking. Serik started the engine and accelerated. The car rocked back and forth, cradled in its ruts. The idea was that the overnight cold would have hardened the mud enough to give purchase; but the wheels simply spun and spattered. I got out and pushed again. Futile; we knew it would be. Serik locked the Land Cruiser—you couldn't be too careful, apparently—and we traced the tyres' tracks from yesterday, back to Zalanash. No one else had been this way.

"Tits!" Serik said, as the twin monticules came into view five hours later. The track hardened, as if a skin had grown on the pudding of the plain, and the verges acquired a camel-grazed fuzz of green. A kilometre away a boy on a red dirtbike was bouncing across our path. As we reached the edge of the village a two-man helicopter reared skywards and thundered over us, heading towards Tastubek. Ten minutes later, to the barking of dogs, we were standing on the broad main street. Stepping across the mud, arms linked, was a party of little girls in puffy yellow dresses. They were old hands—the hems were spotless. They looked at the two fugitives from the mud and tightened their grip on one another. "Where is Tabin Alenov?" Serik demanded.

ALENOV HAD BEEN president of Zalanash's fishing co-operative. He would be able to arrange for the Land Cruiser to be towed from the mud: what was needed was a GAZ or a tractor. Over the next hour, while we looked for him, Serik stopped three Russian jeeps full of young men and explained our difficulty to the driver, and each time the driver would smile and shake his head before winding up his window and speeding off. A man's transport was his livelihood. I couldn't blame them for being reluctant to take the risk. We'd been stupid to attempt the crossing when the plain was so wet, and this was a reasonable penalty, to be cold and hungry and tired for a day or two. And we still hadn't found Mr. Alenov.

We'd learn that it was a bad day to have got stuck: the helicopter we'd seen was carrying the regional mayor (he went everywhere by helicopter), who'd been attending the opening of the village's new kindergarten. Most of the adults had already gone to a party at one of the village homes. Serik rang his friend in Tastubek; he wasn't in. He left a message. They had grown up in Aralsk on the same street, and he had a jeep.

Mr. Alenov was at the party. We found the house and Serik went in while I waited at the wicket gate. A minibus pulled up and ten men in their early twenties got out—smart shoes, suit trousers, white shirts and cufflinks, all of them smoking, queuing up to shake the hand of the stranger as if he were a doorman, before they stepped through the gate. Village boys who'd moved to Aralsk for the factories, back for the afternoon boozing. After ten minutes Serik came out with a tall man in his fifties, black shirt and black tie and immaculate soft black leather shoes polished to brilliance, and with black hair and moustache. This was Mr. Alenov. Like all the men of the fishing villages he had the reach and grip of a prize-fighter. No problem: come, he'd find someone to tow us. We followed him away from the compound. The mud was scattered with camel bones. There was the odd hypodermic needle (livestock inoculation). Hay and firewood were stacked high in fenced compounds. A young camel, eyes tipped wide to the sky, galloped in circles, bucking as if to rid itself of some ghost rider. Mr. Alenov raised a fist as it approached and it shied off, thundering up the street towards the onetime seashore.

There was a tractor parked beside one of the camel pens but the owner was not to be found. A jeep passed by and stopped (you stopped for Mr. Alenov); but no, ruefully, not today, even for Mr. A. Another jeep, overshooting us, skidded to a halt on seeing who it was, and reversed, only to inform us that they could not help, either. Word seemed to have spread. It had barely risen above freezing last night, and I was weak from the cold, made inept by it. I might as well have been on a leash. Mr. Alenov took us to his home. At the threshold he looked at my caked trousers and said wait, returning with a pair of his massive tracksuit bottoms and sending me to the shed to change.

In the house's main room two sleeping mats had been rolled out on the carpet alongside the wall. The wall, as in all the older steppe houses, was deliciously heated, and nothing was more comforting than to pass your palm back and forth across the rough pinkish plaster. It was about 1 p.m. Serik and I lay head to head and dozed. Mr. Alenov went back to the party. The scent and sounds of cooking came from the adjoining kitchen. When I woke it was dark outside and the table had been laid.

With our hands the three of us ate scalding pasta and the tender-est camel meat. The hump, cubed: soft and salty. A bowl of greasy broth. The body isn't hard to satisfy. There was sweet tea, bread, a bowl of stiff cream, wrapped sweets on a tiered cake-stand. Mr. Ale-nov explained the Soviet system. The fishing villages, like the farms, had operated as either self-governing collectives, *kolkhozes*, or as satel-lites of the regional co-operative, the *sovkhoz*, of which the largest in the Small Aral region was Aralrybprom, "Aral Fish Industries," whose escutcheon I'd seen fixed to the boats dry-docked at Aralsk. While the *sovkhozes* were state-controlled and their directors often outsiders appointed from Moscow, the *kolkhozes*, such as the one that had existed at Zalanash, were smaller autonomous collectives that elected their own chairmen.

In 1991 the *kolkhozes* were superseded by a free-market system that divided the various fishing sites—some of which were now thirty kilo-metres from the onetime harbours—into a series of ten plots, *uchastki*, each owned by a "nature-user" like Mr. Alenov, who issued fishing licences and ran the receiving-stations to which each brigade's daily haul must be delivered for weighing and refrigeration. There were quotas but the fishermen weren't interested in quotas. If the official monopsonies were honoured and "poaching" prevented entirely, then the people of the Aral's shores, whose forebears for centuries had fed from the sea, would never taste fresh fish. What mattered were the markets in Europe and Russia and the day's catch. Since 2005 the fishermen had learned to believe that a small haul today did not mean a small haul tomorrow. It was in that year that a dyke, the Kokaral, had been built across the Berg Strait in order to stall the shrinking of the sea. The sea north of the dyke not only ceased to shrink, Mr. Alenov said, but was slowly refilling. The salt content was levelling off, the old fish species had returned. So long as the market held, the fish-receiving centres—at least those close to the new shoreline—would remain viable. But who was to say that the villages would not one day be left marooned and gasping again? The farmer dreams for the year, the fisherman for the day.

We finished eating and went outside to smoke in the darkness of the yard. The moon looked enormous. A subdued collective howling carried from far beyond the village boundary, from some steppe-bound camel farm; but otherwise just this tremendous weight of quiet.

ABOARD THE *KONSTANTIN* in 1848, the food supplies putrefied. "The dried bread became mouldy," Shevchenko reported; "the fat turned pink; butter was rancid. Only the peas remained wholesome." Wind from the north-west was near constant and would leave the schooner rocking for hours. On 23 September the crews finally docked for the winter at Kos Aral island. The expedition had been a success, but after Shevchenko's lonely months at sea, no letters! Not one. Throughout his exile, his longing for Ukraine takes the form of griping about his friends' failure to write. Not merely exiled, he would come to feel, but *abandoned*, even by those he loved:

> At one time they swore
> Eternal friendship with me,
> But now they have vanished.

A quarter of the poetry he produced during his ten years' banishment was written that winter. There wasn't much else to occupy him.

> Boredom and autumn
> Surround me in a foreign land.

Dear God! Where shall I hide?
What shall I do? I walk along the Aral
And secretly write verses. I sin,
And I recall other times
In my soul and write about them.

A man in a hut, on an island, in a sea in a foreign desert, asks: Where shall I hide? It seemed absurd until you came here and understood that nowhere were you more exposed. Those cloistered months were otherwise enlivened only by sketching and, in November, the hunt mentioned by Butakov: "Tigers roam constantly in the vicinity of Aralsk," the commander explained. The creature in question "had recently devoured four cows...two weeks afterwards I heard from the Kirghiz that the same animal had devoured two men and a number of sheep; and on the 21st Nov. the foreman of the fishery reported that this tiger had killed their horse at only 3 *versts* from our fort."

The hunt occupied half of the garrison's men. The animal was trapped and shot. "It was a real royal tiger, of a beautiful orange colour with broad black stripes, uncommonly fat, and 6 feet 4 inches long from the nose to the beginning of the tail." In Shevchenko's painting it is far from regal; it might be snoozing, a fairground toy invoked from the

frosted sands. His pen-and-ink sketches of the fort on Kos Aral show a
slum of smouldering huts and tents, a few yurts, a black poodlish dog
and a stack of firewood; in the distance, ice-trapped, the schooners
Konstantin and *Nicolas*. As winter tightens, the drawings depict not the
terrain but interiors: smoky, orange-lit yurts and huts, men and boys
gazing heat-drugged into incandescing stoves.

IN THE MORNING Serik's friend came from Tastubek and in his
jeep we returned to the Land Cruiser and towed it from the mud. We
spent an hour in the village shovelling out its foot wells and sluic-
ing down the mats. After yesterday's exertion and the cold I felt as
if I'd been pushed down a flight of stairs. By noon we were back in
Aralsk. I was being educated in the varieties of mud. As the Uighur
had many names for sand, and the Rashidi for dune formations, did the
people of Kazakhstan, I wondered, have a lexicon of mud? Whisked by
spinning tyres, in the streets it had developed a velvety smoothness,
like melted ice cream. Only the dogs chanced the wallows, packs filing along the shallower ridges. Everywhere cars were being towed or
pushed while men looked on. They went about this as part of their
routine; delay was factored in when meetings were arranged, or else—
more often—lateness taken for granted. There were ten petrol stations
and in winter and at harvest-time supplies ran out and queues formed,
further degrading the ground, until even those stations with petrol to
sell could only be accessed by the envied, guzzling GAZ utility trucks
with their shoulder-high chassis. We crossed the town to the main
highway leading south. Our destination was the sea's current shore.
Finally we would see water. At a checkpoint three men marched from
a shipping container and asked to see my passport. Hoods pulled over
police caps, the army escort cradling his AK-47, they approached as
a unit, as if shackled together. The black paint on the gun's stock was
flaking. *Your name. Your name. From.* They were on the lookout for lorries carrying contraband vegetables to Russia—turnip-smugglers—
but I was a novelty, and the senior policeman was enjoying himself.
Serik was used to it and smiled, but he was subdued afterwards.

For eighty kilometres we drove south on the new highway that led to Kyzylorda, so new that its central markings had yet to be painted. On the verge was the night's reaping of dead dogs and camels, the usual glitter of broken glass. On either side were kilometre upon kilometres of low yellow dunes scattered with saxaul and camelthorn. The camels seemed to have acquired no wariness of vehicles; they crossed the road with impunity and didn't hurry even in the face of the heaviest lorry. Ahead of us for a couple of kilometres a jogging-pace jalopy, piled six metres high with steppe brush, swayed under a column of black smoke. We left the highway and the silent bitumen continued for a hundred metres before breaking off to potholed grit.

We passed alongside Lake Kambash, one of the Syr Darya's delta lakes. At its edge was a holiday camp for Soviet Young Pioneers, long derelict, a cluster of peeling blue cupolas. Until the water vanished thirty years ago, children from across the union had swum here. On dressers in Almaty and Orenburg stood framed sepias of children playing among the dunes. There was a beach—coarse sand dotted with the crinoline skeletons of yurts hireable by the day in summer. And there was water—returned water! The lake was ten kilometres long and two wide, its far shore distance-hazy; but it had not reclaimed its former size. On the horizon, what had once been an island was now a peninsula—and the water, like all the region's surface water, was a broth of agrochemicals. There were fish here, swarming in the shallows, but the surface stillness was less that of tranquillity than of stagnation. Serik was at ease, and he sat on his haunches and gazed out contentedly. For once he didn't smoke. Kambash held fond memories for him—he'd come here as a child, he said, and brought his own children—and he thought it a pretty place, in spite of last summer's litter embedded in the sand.

An hour later we reached the Syr Darya, and looking down on its slow surface I recalled those paintings of Shevchenko's when he first arrived at the fort on this river, when the world was lovable again after those weeks of blinding desert—the richness of his pigments, the charge of his line. And now before me, 150 years later, the waters of all Kazakhstan's steppes rendered into this broad grey procession channelled between cliffs of pale mud. What I took at first for ducks turned out to be floating vodka bottles. But the river wasn't, actually, lifeless. Rounding the corner, against the flow, a two-man skiff was puttering, laying nets: "Poachers!" said Serik approvingly. They looked up at us and one of them raised a hand. We waved back. There were penalties, and the fisheries inspectorate in Aralsk occasionally patrolled the river, but enforcement was light, and even the "nature-users," who owned the fishing rights, were indulgent when it came to a man feeding his family from ancestral waters.

IT WAS TO the fishermen of the village of Bogun, thirty kilometres away, that Lenin's 1921 letter was addressed: "Russian and Muslim, nomad and settler—all are equally faced with cruel death unless help comes from their comrades…"

The village was a scattering of low earthen houses concealed behind hoardings. At the centre of each circle of four or five compounds were a shared camel pen, stacks of straw, heaps of steppe-wood for the hearth, and an outhouse. We would be staying with a fishing family, friends of Serik's. The younger two of the three Dilzhanov brothers, Maksat and Mukhtar, were rangy and red-faced, a head taller than me. They walked with a swagger, their potency unspent, their legs given an oedemic appearance by trousers doubled against the cold. They were fearless, imperious, and thought nothing of having a foreign stranger in their home. Zeinolla, the older brother—"Zikon," he was nicknamed—carried a pot belly of natal roundness, an attribute that was conferred upon every village man to mark the birth of his first child.

Maksat was spading sand over the septic tank buried outside the family compound before it got dark. Nearby were two green GAZ six-wheeler trucks stacked with empty fish crates. All three brothers drank continuously while they worked, from two-litre bottles of Coke—this, it seemed to me, was the national drink, more so than vodka (they drank vodka too, though I'd been instructed by Serik to conceal from their father the bottles I'd brought as gifts). I rarely saw anyone drink water. The cold was coming, said Maksat, you could feel it on the air. Fog attended each morning—sea fog, though the sea was twenty-five kilometres away—and did not disperse till noon or later. If the septic tank wasn't given this extra blanket of sand its contents would freeze solid when the snow came, and then you had a pleasant job.

NEXT MORNING Serik and I followed the track that went along the top of the dyke built in 2005. The ridge was only eight metres high, but it had been enough to cause the level of the Small Aral to rise, and the waters that had withdrawn as far as a hundred kilometres from Aralsk were now just twelve kilometres away. In the year it was built, 695 tonnes of fish had been taken from the Small Aral; nine years later the figure was 5,595 tonnes. A reversal had been engineered, but only in the Small Aral. Surplus water was dispensed into the Large Aral. The volume passing through the sluice, when we stopped alongside, was enormous—tens of thousands of cubic metres per second. We had to shout to be heard. A huge river—as voluminous as the Syr Darya itself, it seemed. And yet within a few kilometres it vanished into the desert to the south, soaking into the ground or evaporating. All that power, dissipated. Unless the Syr's contribution was one day matched by the Amu's to the south, the Large Aral would remain a desert. Uzbekistan, in whose territory much of the Large Aral lies, has shown no willingness to desist from diverting the Amu Darya for cotton. In 2006 the government signed a production-sharing agreement with a consortium of oil and gas firms from China, Korea and Russia. Prospection of the former seabed was under way. And when the oil and gas were gone? Then means would be found to exhaust the sun and the wind, and empty the tides of their energy.

Next to the sluice was a helicopter pad and a wooden-decked viewing point under a white awning. Both had been installed for a presidential visit years before. For some reason (nobody knew why) Nazarbayev had cancelled and the facilities were never used. Next to a white guardhouse by the dyke lay the carcase of a camel, still partially swaddled in its skin. Its teeth were as white as a newscaster's, its eyes as lightless. It would make a punchy photo, grainy black-and-white, the sky filtered to a gradated grey. But the Aral Sea was not a graveyard. Granted, to our left, south, there was the Aralkum—for five hundred kilometres little but sand and saxaul until you reached the defunct Uzbek port at Muynak. But then, to our right, thickets of bulrushes clamorous with waterfowl.

The whole scene shimmered with a shifting, elastic light. A stork wheeled overhead, and it was this, not the dead camel, that I photographed, a speck against the steely sky. This was the Aral Sea that Butakov and Shevchenko recorded; the shores a busy community, frenzied almost, frenzied as life before man; the habitat of "immense quantities of pelicans, cormorants, sea-gulls and sea-swallows."

Finally, on 22 April 1849, an audible cracking from the sea. Two weeks later, Butakov's second exploratory voyage set sail. An unshackling for the men: all the fresh fish you could eat, the sun glinting off the blue chop. But they found themselves released to another kind of prison. For two weeks storms trapped the *Konstantin* far from shore and the men were forced to draw water from the sea, with its taste of the Gulf of Finland. Kos Aral's bedbugs and boils were replaced by scurvy, vomiting and what Butakov termed "a strong diarrhoea." Peas and pike; pike and peas. Barbel and snakehead and bastard sturgeon. So despairing did Shevchenko become during the voyage that when, in calmer weather, he was despatched with a party to survey a minor island, he wandered off alone in an attempt to get "lost." Naturally he was found. There'd be no getting lost, no "hiding."

Finally, in late summer, the schooners returned to the Russian fort at Raim. As they sailed back to the Syr Darya, Shevchenko dispensed an ambivalent farewell to the island that had been his prison: "I grant / Neither praise nor blame for your desert."

But as this phase of his exile ended, he could not see the Karakum as anything better than a "wasted wilderness, forsaken by God." Still he would not be permitted to return to Ukraine; only when he was dead was he repatriated. Then he could go home.

WHEN WE RETURNED to Bogun the sky was red. In a dark toolshed Zhaksilik and four other men were gathered, the older men of the village, as they always gathered at this time, in a circle, sitting on

a log positioned for the purpose or squatting around pages of news-paper spread out on the ground. Lumps of salt fish were passed from man to man, a shred torn off, the raw guts pinched out and flicked onto the newspaper, cigarettes doused in the gore. A plastic beaker was filled and refilled with cold vodka. "Schnapps," they called it; and I said "schnapps"; and from outside a passing woman, the wife of one of them, overhearing, said witheringly: "*Schnapps...*" We laughed at her contempt. They would not allow me to leave without a second, a third beaker of vodka, and more fish. The fish was delicious in its saltiness; delicious, somehow, in its disgustingness.

Bogun had been a waterside village; old Zhaksilik had been born to the sound of lapping waves, he said, and he had watched as year by year the water withdrew, further and further, until the shore was two days' walk away, and the water when you got there all but dead. All hope had been lost, said another man, rolling a cigarette in bloody fingers. A depression had settled on the land when the first dykes failed, he went on; but then the new dyke had been built, and though it had seemed impossible, the water had begun to return, and with it the fish, and fathers had reason once more to teach their sons how and where and when to fix nets.

When I left the shed, I did not feel drunk. I took a walk around the village. It was deserted apart from the dogs and the camels; and quiet save for the roar of an open standpipe, which fed a narrow lagoon whose surface was broken by the ribs of old boats. On the village's northern edge was a three-storey building, shiplapped and whitewashed. Abutting one wall, buttressing it just below the second-storey windows, was a sand-dune, its spine stretching away to the horizon. The building, now abandoned, had been the village school. The Karakum advanced to occupy the ground quitted by the sea, and in time—any day—the dune's oncoming weight would bulldoze the building. A replacement school had been built on the other side of the village, but while efforts had been made to slow the dunes' progress—geotextile netting, stabilising planting—it was understood that, in time, once it had flooded the classrooms and corridors of the old school, the wall of sand would move across the village, house by house, nudging the settlement ever southward towards the sea.

As I was trying to find my way back to the house, a jeep roared towards me and pulled to a halt. Behind it was another. *Get in*, and Mukhtar—Zhaksilik's middle son, who was driving—put his foot down. The land, the former seabed, between the lagoon and the fishing site at Shagalaly was sandy thicket, which gave way to a broad strip of powdery sediment the colour of pigskin, and it was across this, ten kilometres, that the jeeps raced, three members of the brigade in each, the other one driven by Mukhtar's older brother Maksat, following the hundreds of twined tracks made by their previous comings and goings. Where Serik was I didn't know. At eighty kilometres per hour, ninety, we thundered over this open land towards the sun, the other vehicle jostling and rattling alongside five metres away. A shunt would have been disastrous, would have meant death and maiming; but we were going to the sea, and in my drunkenness the feeling was not peril; the boys in both jeeps were howling—with the familiar excitement, and pride, and love for their home and one another. The racetrack gave way to a maze of reeds three metres tall, which went on and on, flocks of birds rising, until the vista opened out, and the sky expanded, and everything was bright-lit and shimmering as happens near great expanses of water.

Amidst the reeds close to Shagalaly was a cloister formed by three shipping containers in which the boys slept when the boats were late back. Clothes hung on a line strung between containers; a black dog trotted out of the shadows to watch us pass. The sea when we reached its edge was still and hyper-reflective. It was the sea depicted in the rowboat-painting at the museum in Aralsk, tranquil and alive. From the beach, a narrow wooden jetty extended into the water. No far shore was visible, just water and sky.

It was as if this had always been the shore; nothing indicated that the place where we stood was new; that until thirty years ago it had been fathoms underwater. The boats were home and had been pulled onto the sand. Folded on the deck of one of them was a pink floral duvet for when it got cold. Serik, it turned out, was somehow here already. Looking out at the waveless water, we stood in a circle while the boys unknotted nets and spiralled them into rubber buckets. First the blunt heaving of the fisherman's day, then once the catch was landed and before you went home, these hours of unpicking with numbed fingers. One of the men put a cigarette lighter to an empty Coke bottle to breach the plastic then carefully tore the base off to make a drinking vessel. (Vodka is never to be drunk straight from the bottle.) I'd drunk enough, God, but I downed what I was served. And okay the next. The aim was not to get drunk, or even to drink, but to get the foreigner drunk.

Two brown horses, farmed for meat, appeared on the track behind us, and stood side by side between an upturned boat and one of the Russian personnel carriers. They dropped their muzzles to a puddle and began to drink, raising their heads every few seconds to monitor us. Others stepped out of the reeds, two or three at a time; finally the mothers with their young, until a party of twenty or so was milling about the puddles, sipping, watchful. Glossy and gorgeous, and baulky. Sixteen hands; taller, some of them. Two approached, keeping close to the edge of the reedbed, wavering when they sensed our eyes on them. Others joined the line, treading behind the leaders. Mukhtar dropped the net he was working at and picked up an empty vodka bottle from the sand and with a roar pitched it at the lead animal, striking its flank.

It turned and galloped back to the rest of the herd still waiting by the GAZ. Scanning the sand, he picked up another bottle and threw it at the second horse, missing, before turning back to his work untangling the nets. The herd found its confidence. The line broke up and began to gallop towards us. At the last moment they charged away and splashed along the shore to some hidden bay where they would spend the night.

5

BETWEEN GREAT FIRES

The Sonoran Desert, USA

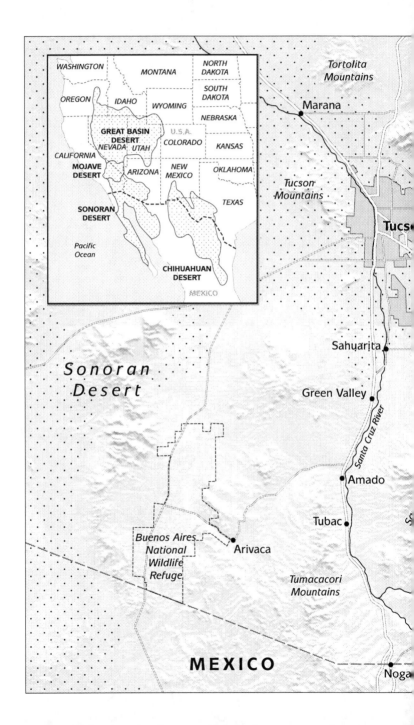

I moved to Tucson, Arizona, in the summer. The afternoon heat in this city enclosed by mountains was too much even for the hummingbirds. The feeder I put out for them dripped agave untouched on to the dry concrete. The world can be cavalier with its metaphors. In London I had checked each room of the flat before locking up and posting the key through the letterbox. When you have exhausted the resources of a place you move on or perish. There was a desert lesson.

It rarely rained in Arizona but when it rained it rained explosively and with atrocious, ecstatic ferocity—less like a tap turned on than a bucket flipped. More than once the street adjacent to my hundred-dollars-a-week casita would be ankle-deep in rushing water while the rain had not even dotted the dust of my yard. The Sonoran Desert, in which Tucson is situated, occupies much of southern Arizona and eastern California and extends over the border into Sonora, the Mexican state it takes its name from. With up to thirty-eight centimetres of rain per year, it is the wettest and greenest of the United States' four desert regions (the others being the Mojave in California, the Chihuahuan in New Mexico and the Great Basin in Nevada). Like many deserts, the Sonoran is largely enwalled by mountains: to the north and east, the edge of the Colorado Plateau, the Rockies and the Sierra Madre; to the west, the Sierra Nevada. It is the last that is responsible for much of south-west America's aridity, removing the moisture from the Pacific's clouds as they are drawn up its western flank. Annual precipitation on the western slope might be seventy centimetres, while a kilometre away on the eastern slope it won't exceed twenty. They call it a rain shadow but the effect is not so much a shadowing as a milking. It is from the low-lying south—the jungle south of Central America—that the monsoon comes, and the result is a desert in which dozens, perhaps hundreds, of people die each year, but which often feels fecund.

One morning I cycled on the rutted suburban streets to the path that follows the Santa Cruz River through the city. The banks were three metres high and vertical, so it was not possible to get close to the riverbed. To look was enough. It was dry grit save for a seam of silver threading down its centre like a zip. When I returned the following day the water had gone. Later someone told me it was likely effluent. The Santa Cruz was not always like this. Without a perennial river, as it once was, the Native Americans would not have settled on the plain they called "S-cuk Son" ("at the base of the black mountain"); without it the Spanish mission at San Xavier del Bac, south of today's Tucson, would not have been established nor the presidio that replaced it. The Native Americans dug many kilometres of drainage ditches to irrigate their beans, squash and maize, but for white farmers and miners the fitful Santa Cruz, with its meagre 0.7 cubic metres of water per second, was not enough, and the valley is too broad to dam. It became clear that the visible water was a fraction of the actual river. When, in the 1890s, steam pumps began to "mine" the aquifers beneath the basin's alluvium, the water table sank, and by 1940 the volume being removed from the aquifer exceeded the rate of recharge from precipitation. As early as 1910 an Arizona hydrologist described the Santa Cruz as "ever a dwindling stream." Wells that in 1902 needed to be no deeper than six metres, by 1920 had to be sunk to thirty metres. By the 1950s the river no longer flowed except in times of flood or where treated sewage was discharged into it. When the Santa Cruz ceased to be perennial, the habitats it supported dwindled: first the cattails, then the cotton-woods, then the mesquite; until finally the onetime river was flanked by nothing but desert scrub. The existence of Tucson is vouchsafed by nothing but the vanishing mass of water banked in the ground. Today the open-pit mines south of modern Tucson extract some 30,000 acre feet of water annually—37 million cubic metres (an acre foot being the amount of water it takes to cover an acre of land to a depth of one foot); the pecan groves near Sahuarita are similarly exacting. As the ancient reserves were pumped, the land shrivelled and slumped and buildings collapsed. Interstate 10, the road from Tucson to Phoenix, became rucked and cracked. Completed in 1993, the Central Arizona Project canal was dug to supplement Tucson's and Phoenix's groundwater, running 540 kilometres across the desert from a dam on the Colorado River. Look at it on maps and the canal's straight lines, especially where it runs near-parallel with the channel of the Santa Cruz, are reminiscent of the cannulas and catheters attending a body in intensive care.

In 1878, John Wesley Powell, a one-armed Civil War veteran and confidant of Ulysses S. Grant, published his *Report on the Lands of the Arid Region of the United States.* It caused outrage, and remains among the most influential treatises on the American deserts. "The Arid Region begins about midway in the Great Plains," he wrote, "and extends across the Rocky Mountains to the Pacific Ocean." It was an area so dry, he warned, that "many droughts will occur; many seasons in a long series will be fruitless, and it may be doubted whether, on the whole, agriculture will prove remunerative." Nor was the question merely of dispersing what water the region possessed: "When all the waters running in the streams found in this region are conducted on the land, there will be but a small portion of the land redeemed."

For Powell understood that lack of water was not the only problem: there was also the frost, the alkaline soils, the poor drainage. You could not live here as you lived in the east. Above all space was needed. The Homestead Act of 1862 granted 162 acres to each homesteader, but that was a dispensation calculated by men in cloudy Washington. In the desert it would suffice for about two self-possessed cows. Powell suggested an allocation of at least 2,560 acres per ranch. He advocated unfenced common pasturage, co-operative labour and federal grants. The implication, some felt, was this: the West was inimical to capitalism. For the report's readers in Congress it was, at best, a council of capitulation. (Nobody used the word socialism.)

For "boosters" of the American West such as an influential land speculator named Charles Dana Wilber, Powell's desert was simply a myth: "The Creator never imposed a perpetual desert upon the earth," he wrote in 1881, "but on the contrary, has so endowed it that men by the plow, can transform it, in any country, into farm areas." No preponderance of scientific opinion sufficed to sway those gripped by the doctrine of Manifest Destiny. Wilber was also an evangelist of the notion that agricultural activity itself would alter the immediate climate, an idea first articulated by Josiah Gregg in 1844; "The extreme cultivation of the earth might contribute to the multiplication of showers," he wrote. The mechanism of this process remained unclear—some speculated it was connected to the increased absorbency of ploughed soil—but there developed a conviction among settlers and boosters that the desert, such as it was, might be routed to the very foothills of the Rocky Mountains. One booster claimed that upon every yard of rail put down across the desert an extra gallon of rain would fall each year. But we know it was not the desert that was routed. "Rain follows the plow" was to prove a catastrophic motto for homesteaders who established landholdings on the desert's eastern edge, only to see drought follow drought as the century drew to a close. Those leaving the dustblown plains painted on their wagons "In God we trusted, in Kansas we busted."

In 1890, one Robert Dyrenforth was charged by a worried Department of Agriculture to conduct a series of "experiments in the production of rainfall." This involved the firing of explosives into the desert skies from cannons, balloons and kites. In the view of the *Chicago Times*, the twenty thousand dollars would have been "less ridiculously employed if it were devoted to the manufacture of whistles out of pigs' tails." Dyrenforth was duly dubbed "Dryhenceforth."

In May 1957, eighty years after Powell's report, an essay appeared in *Harper's Magazine* by Walter Prescott Webb entitled "The American West, Perpetual Mirage." It was the cover story: "The West's leading historian uncovers the one overwhelming fact which seventeen states have been trying to hide for the last century." His subject is the persistent failure of America, even into the twentieth century, to concede the extent and severity of its desert. The West, Webb argues, setting out his stall, extends from a "line drawn from the southern tip of Texas to the further boundary of central North Dakota"—significantly further east than the threshold of Powell's Arid Region of 1878. He slices this vast strip into three north–south segments: the Pacific coast, the mountains, and the Great Plains. The "overriding influence," the

"dominating force," is the desert, and in his description it is a kind of
ruthless god: "It shortened the grass on its borders before destroying
it in the interior. It never permitted trees on the plains it built; and
where it found them it beat them down to sage and brush, reducing the
leaves to thorns and the sap to grease and oil." He pictures the desert
as an inferno. "In the centre will be an area where all life has been
destroyed, a charred mass such as may be seen in parts of Utah, Idaho
and Nevada. Beyond that will be a series of concentric circles where
the destruction decreases as the distance grows." When he studies a
selection of school textbooks on American history, he finds that the
Great American Desert is invariably given no more than a few pages.
This is partly because "the West is in comparison to the east a land of
deficiencies."

The most provocative element of the essay is the map outlin-
ing Webb's incendiary geography. "Let us be realistic and divide the
West into the two categories, Desert States and Desert Rim States."
Labelled "DESERT STATES, THE HEART OF THE WEST" are not only Ari-

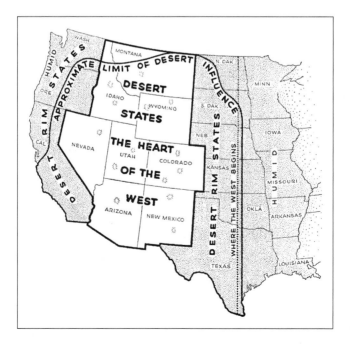

zona, New Mexico, Nevada, Utah and Colorado, but northerly Idaho, Wyoming and Montana. The "desert rim states" meanwhile comprise all or part of California, Oregon and Washington to the west, and, flanking the desert's eastern edge, Texas, Oklahoma, Kansas, Nebraska and the Dakotas. Webb's line marking the "approximate limit of desert influence" therefore impounds well over half the nation's landmass. The desert, he writes, "emerges in its true character as a great interior force—repelling to people and repulsive to wealth in nearly all forms."

IN LONDON the mouths of pundits and politicians had been full of the "migrant crisis" and here in Arizona was another of its grim centres, the U.S.–Mexico borderlands. I began attending weekly meetings in a church hall not far from my casita, organised by an activist group called No More Deaths, which provided food, water and medical care to undocumented migrants trying to cross the desert between the Mexico border and Tucson eighty kilometres to the north. Once a week, James, a senior member of the group, would pick me up at 5:30 a.m. He was a former high-school principal with a buzzcut and an army bearing that belied a great sweetness of temperament and the kind of regretful quality found in those who struggle to reconcile a belief in their own basic cheerfulness with a suspicion that hope is implausible. It is a common enough tension. Lois, another elder of Tucson's migrant-aid community, joined us one morning. She had the stature and alertness of a teenage girl; a girl's interrogative glare too. She'd just turned eighty and was glowing bones and sinew, healthier than someone—me—half her age. Even a child-size T-shirt was baggy on her. It bore the No More Deaths logo, a single plastic water canister marked with a green cross and the word "AGUA." She sat in the back of the car dispensing homemade muffins and barbed commentary. As the morning went on, as we moved into the desert, her frown softened. She carried in her backpack food parcels and fresh socks in ziplock bags; she could no longer carry water in the quantities she once had. This she admitted with some embarrassment, this woman of eighty, who marched into the desert at a pace that left me constantly a hundred metres behind. On either side of Lois as we drove south from Tucson along Route 19 were Ryan, a new volunteer in his early twenties, who was studying astronomy at U of A in Tucson; and John—John with his long white hair and his desert bonnet and neckerchief, all ironic east-side softness and transatlantic teasing. John, a birder, loved the desert at this time of day, he said; loved it for its birdsong that would die off as the sun rose, and loved especially its TVs—turkey vultures—even if their collective circling did indicate something dead.

Dropping south on the Nogales road, past the Santa Rita Mountains and their alluvial fans, through Sahuarita and the retirement enclave of Green Valley, we took a right at Arivaca Junction, past the Border Patrol checkpoint on the other side of the road, and the small settle-ment of Arivaca where No More Deaths has a first-aid outpost. The drop site in the San Luis Valley lay within the Buenos Aires National Wildlife Reserve. There was a period of preparation: the rolling-down of sleeves, the slow winding of scarves, the fitting of sunhats and sun-glasses. Sunblock slathered on, two-handed, like a potter. Travelling in the Sonoran Desert in 1909, the Norwegian explorer Carl Lumholtz wrote that "the sensation was that of walking between great fires."

Our backpacks were loaded up with four-litre plastic flagons of water from the trunk. We'd barely set off into the dry creekbed before John and Lois had vanished into the dense ironwood forest ahead. The ground was dominated by prickly pear cactus, and ironwood and mes-quite trees. The creekbeds were dry, but thick with wildflowers, and as we moved, a shoal of grasshoppers moved ahead of us from tree to tree, with a dreadful massed shrieking. We stopped at one of the many dumps of discarded possessions. It hadn't been there more than a few days. It included a "fruity shine" lip balm and a pair of chrome-plated nail-clippers. As if their owners believed they were going somewhere else entirely, a visit to aunty. When, after an hour, we reached the place where the supplies were to be left, John and Lois were waiting, sitting a few metres apart on boulders that strewed the dry creekbed.

Lois looked up at us as we put down our water containers and unloaded our backpacks. "They've all gone."

Hanging from the branches of the mesquites were a dozen nooses of blue twine, from which we'd tied water containers the week before (hanging them off the ground keeps the ravens from pecking holes in them). It wasn't the disappearance of the water and food that was concerning Lois so much as the cleanliness of the site: no litter, no empty bottles, none of the signs of desperate consumption she was used to. The site had been cleared out, cleaned up, not by migrants. Lois blamed the reserve's rangers. They had served citations on No More Deaths in the past for unlicensed activity on this protected land—littering, in other words, in the form of water containers. Water containers were sometimes slashed and the cans of food split and tipped out. As well as Border Patrol there were hostile ranchers and militias, vigilante boy-scouts armed with automatic weapons who hunted undocumented migrants and believed that to leave water for the dying was an act of treason. Some time ago No More Deaths had left a motion-activated video camera hidden in a bush to try to establish who was vandalising one of their drop sites, only to return to find it had been removed. Another camera, this one undisturbed, recorded a Border Patrol agent slashing bottles.

In the breeze the bare ropes swung. John had brought three Sharpie markers with him, black, blue and green. On the food-tubs and the water bottles he drew hearts and flowers and messages of greeting in Spanish. There is a belief among some migrants that the food and water are set out by Border Patrol or other hostile bodies as traps, or poisoned. Neither the BP nor the militias would be able to bring themselves to draw love-hearts and flowers, John reasoned. And yet it was not only a ruse; the expression of hospitality was heartfelt. *Comida + Calcetines.* Food and socks. *Que le vaya bien.* Hope everything goes well. *Nuestros corazones no tienan fronteras.* Our hearts recognise no borders.

John went on with his flower-drawings, his messages, and I thought he was right; it was something their enemies would be incapable of.

In the church hall at the end of each weekly meeting a minute's silence was observed for the lost.

I'D SEEN PHOTOS of Jim Corbett on the jackets of the few books he wrote, a toothy-smiled, knobbly-handed, sun-wrinkled scholar with big glasses and wire beard—a goatee. In his book *Goatwalking*, published in 1991, he advocates a form of pastoral nomadism—the lead-

ing of goats from pasture to pasture and living off their milk—as the
lightest-footed way a person can live in an arid environment. "From
the Alps to the Empty Quarter, Java to Baja, with the goat as a partner,
human beings can support themselves in most wildland environments."
He lived much of his life in Tucson, and would often go into the desert
for weeks at a time with only a small herd for company and sustenance.
To goatwalk was to re-enact "the history of the prophetic faiths"; it
was the desert nomadism of Arabia, and of the Chosen People. It is
the animals' cussedness and their association with anarchy—"foraging
in garbage, raiding clotheslines, and butting the unwary"—that Corbett loves, as much as their self-sufficiency and loyalty. Goats, he adds,
never make the mistake of thinking they're human, but "they will
allow properly behaved human beings to become fully accepted members of the herd." That is, they will allow humans (properly behaved
ones) to be goats.

While Corbett was tending a herd in south Baja during the drought
summer of 1980, the bucks climbed towards a line of cliffs in pursuit
of a herd of does (goats favour high ground). Once they reached them,
Corbett knew, the bucks would follow the she-goats rather than him,
and the animals would be lost. The way to regain control of a herd
of goats is to panic it—signalling alarm and then running so that
the animals follow you. After sprinting for miles and finally bringing the herd under control, he found himself exhausted, overheated
and dehydrated in the full heat of an Arizonan summer afternoon—
thirty-seven degrees-plus. The only water source anywhere nearby
was a small hollow fed by a spring much used by vultures, whose white
droppings coated the surrounding rocks. "The greenish water smelled
of carrion and seethed with putrefactive bacteria." Knowing that it was
all that lay between him and an unpleasant death, he drank about four
litres, which revived him for long enough to enable him to lead the
goats to fresh water. "I spent the night drinking water that took just a
few seconds to go through me," he recalled, "but nightlong diarrhoea
was much better than being dead."

As well as a goat, he admitted that as an older man he resembled
the other constant presence in his life, Cervantes's Don Quixote,
whom he calls his "daemon." It was from Don Quixote that he learned

what he calls "errantry," a guiding principle of his life—"sallying out beyond a society's established ways, to live according to one's inner leadings." When Corbett was in his late twenties, his marriage of five years ended and his ex-wife was given custody of their children. He withdrew alone to the slope of Black Bear Mountain in the Arizona–Mexico borderlands. "The first lesson is where everyone starts: despair that clears the way." On Black Bear Mountain he taught himself Malay—"a language I'd never heard, spoken on the other side of the world by a people I'd never met."

After an unspecified time, he went alone—but for his copy of *Don Quixote*—to Sinaloa, Mexico, and from there to a boarding house in Berkeley, California, where he "considered fitting in," but then thought better of it. He had planned to become a philosophy teacher, "but the main thing I learned from studying philosophy was that I knew nothing to teach." It was there that the epiphany occurred: he was certain that his heart stopped. "Out of the stillness that I thought was death, love enlivened me—or something like love that doesn't split, the way love does, into loving and being loved." It was not death; it was something more significant. He gave away everything he didn't need, and took to the road.

"Disobeying the government is like failing to keep a promise," he wrote: one should not do so lightly. When eventually he came into conflict with the state it was because he saw that the state itself was contravening or failing to uphold the law; that is, failing to keep its promise. Among those promises, mandated not only by international law but by U.S. federal law, was the obligation to provide sanctuary to refugees.

In the early 1980s the civil wars in El Salvador and Guatemala were at their most grotesque: even at the time, the atrocities committed by government death-squads in both countries were well known in America. In a letter written in January 1982, Corbett recalled a story he had heard in the border town of Nogales, of a baby boy whom Guatemalan soldiers had mutilated and slowly murdered while forcing his mother to watch. In order to maintain its stance that escapees from the violence were not refugees but economic migrants, the United States government was required to deny that human-rights abuses were occurring in Central America. To make such a concession would also have rendered illegal the military assistance it was providing to the regimes in El Salvador and Guatemala.

In June 1981 a twenty-four-year-old Salvadoran named Santana Chirino Amaya, found to be living without papers in Los Angeles, was deported. Two months later he turned up in Amapulapa, El Salvador. He had been beheaded. Neither state-sponsored atrocity nor deportation of Central Americans fleeing those atrocities was new. In December 1980 a planeload of forty deportees was reportedly massacred on arrival in San Salvador. As a Salvadoran, it was said, you had three choices: join the left and be killed by the right; join the right and be killed by the left; or escape, knowing that flight too might mean death.

It was not until 1981, after he and his second wife moved to Tucson, that the plight of Central American refugees entered Jim Corbett's consciousness. In May that year, a friend of his gave a lift to a young man close to the border, who, when they were stopped at the Border Patrol checkpoint on the Nogales–Tucson highway, turned out to be a refugee from El Salvador and was detained. Hearing about the young Salvadoran, Corbett took it upon himself to look into his fate, and was told by Border Patrol that they did not divulge information about detainees. He rang a senior official in the Immigration and Naturalisation Service and with an air of authority said, "This is Jim Corbett, here in Tucson. I need a name, A-number, and current location of a Salvadoran male you picked up" (an A-number is an "alien registration number"). As Corbett had hoped, the official assumed he was another Jim Corbett—former Mayor Corbett of Tucson—and duly divulged that the person was in Santa Cruz County Jail, in Nogales, Arizona.

Corbett obtained a copy of the form, a G-28, that detainees needed to complete in order to designate a legal representative. On arrival at the prison he found a number of other unrepresented Salvadorans, and went out to obtain more G-28s. When he returned, the authorities, having gathered that he was not *the* Corbett, told him the Salvadorans had been moved, and refused to say where. A court injunction eventually allowed Corbett to bond the Salvadorans, meaning they were released from incarceration under his supervision, while rulings were awaited on their asylum claims. In the meantime, he and his wife put up twenty or more of them in their converted garage. The numbers swelled further when he began to bring Central Americans over the border himself. For each individual act of assistance, he was committing a felony punishable by up to five years' imprisonment. Many of those brought across the border at this time were aided by a goat-milking co-operative, "Los Cabreros Andantes," of which Corbett was a member. They knew the Sonoran borderlands better than most. The name can be translated as "the goatherds errant," and was a punning allusion to the archetypal *caballero andante* or "knight errant," Don Quixote.

PICTURE A MAN standing on a volcanic spur near the Baboquivari Mountains, a few kilometres south of Tucson. His name is José Salazar Ylarregui and the year is 1851. He is a senior member of the Joint United States and Mexican Boundary Commission, responsible for surveying the newly defined border. Until then there was no line, no fence, no wall. It was war that created the line, the Mexican–American War of 1846, or rather the Treaty of Guadalupe Hidalgo that followed it. Salazar Ylarregui, jointly responsible for a hundred men in the unspeakable heat of the Sonoran, on constant guard against Apaches, made a note (maybe he pictured his superiors in their Mexico City drawing rooms): "On paper one easily draws a line with a ruler and pencil."

In the east, that line followed the natural barrier of the Rio Grande; to the west it travelled originally from El Paso along the Gila River to its confluence with the Colorado, thence in a straight line to San Diego Bay, placing much of today's southern Arizona in Mexico. The Gadsden Purchase of 1854—when, following disagreement over the line drawn by Salazar Ylarregui, the United States acquired some 77,000 square kilometres of land from Mexico—caused the western section of Arizona to be repositioned further to the north. Tucson became American, and the border, rather than following the course of the Gila, followed a straight line from El Paso to the Colorado. Upon an expanse of desert where there were few natural features, and fewer names on the maps of either nation, significance was conjured.

The process by which the border would function did not escape those tasked with making it a reality on the ground. One member of the 1851 survey, considering the newly designated borderlands, asked simply: "Is this the land we have purchased, and are to survey and keep at such cost? As far as the eye can reach stretches one unbroken waste, barren, wild, worthless." Another described a "sterile waste, utterly worthless for any purpose than to constitute a barrier."

In the town of Nogales, which straddles the U.S.–Mexico border south of Tucson, I would see a five-metre-tall rusting blade snaking unbroken over hill after hill. The wall looked impassable, as if conceived to rebuff a military assault. But until the twentieth century it was little more than notional: a line on paper echoed by a constellation of obelisks on the ground, each one separated from its neighbours by some three kilometres of desert, or even more where conditions were harshest. Mexicans crossed it daily; the people of the border region had always circled from one area to another, according to the economic patterns of season and climate. Not until 1924 was the U.S. Border Patrol founded, and even then hundreds of kilometres continued to be realised by nothing more than the surveyors' obelisks. In many places you could still, in principle, move back and forth unregarded, even if the towns and villages that had emerged along the border were more heavily controlled. There was no need to build a wall, it was understood, when one already existed: a "sterile waste, utterly worthless for any purpose than to constitute a barrier."

A year before Santana Chirino Amaya's deportation, on 5 July 1980, a group of thirty mostly middle-class Salvadorans had been led into the desert north of the Mexican border town of Sonoyta by three paid guides—*coyotes*, as they are known—having already crossed Guatemala and Mexico. This happened not far from where in 1906 W. J. McGee found the near-dead Pablo Valencia, his skin dried to "shrunken rawhide." From Sonoyta, the Salvadorans, accustomed to their homeland's tropical conditions, were walked north overnight for fifty kilometres. Next day, as their water supplies began to dwindle and the heat of the morning increased, two of the *coyotes* left to "find water." Hold pebbles in your mouth, one said: it will stave off the thirst.

Understanding they had been abandoned, all but one of the remaining men went to find water or help. With no idea where they were, they simply walked away in the direction the vanished *coyotes* had taken. Nor did they return. There were ten women in the group, including three sisters aged twelve, fourteen and nineteen, travelling unchaperoned to Los Angeles where they were to meet their mother who had paid for them to be smuggled out of El Salvador. One of the older women died soon after midday. As the afternoon went on, another woman became ill. She had taken the *coyotes'* advice, and one of the pebbles she had been sucking had become lodged in her throat. The remaining man, the third *coyote*, named Rivera, jammed a stick into her throat, as if clearing a drain. The woman coughed up blood and died.

Rivera had been with the group for four days—across Guatemala, across Mexico, and now the Sonoran Desert. The fee, per person, for this service? Twelve hundred dollars. The surviving women reported that he raped two of the sisters, though this was not borne out by the later autopsies. The group, the living and the dead, were found by U.S. Border Patrol two days later, near-naked and huddled in the meagre shade they had formed by strewing their clothing across the branches of paloverdes. They were caked in make-up, which they had used to protect themselves against the sun. One of the surviving men, found a few kilometres away, had daubed himself with toothpaste. In the night the tablet of his face was a beacon to the Border Patrol agents. In total, thirteen of the original group were found dead, with Rivera and the three young sisters among them.

IT WAS JOHN FIFE who mentioned this story to me. I was introduced to him at a book launch in Tucson. He had been a keystone in the so-called Sanctuary movement, and it was to him and his church, Southside Presbyterian, that his friend Jim Corbett had turned when more room was required to accommodate the migrants the Goatherds Errant were bringing over the border. Fife was a white-haired six-footer, 80 per cent leg. He was straight-backed, but his posture was less the chest-thrusting rigidity of the man in uniform than the supple uprightness of the horserider who knows slouchers get thrown. We met again the following day at Southside Presbyterian, a compound of halls and kitchens and accommodation blocks surrounding a church. After recollecting some instance of horror or injustice—he had frequent cause—he would utter a quiet, dry, appalled chuckle. The modulations of his voice were deft, honed over a lifetime of addressing his congregation. The church we walked through to reach his office was circular, with the pews laid out concentrically. It had no pulpit, just an altar table built by a man Fife knew, a guy from the desert out near Bisbee, ironwood with the bark left on.

Fife had dedicated much of his life to this impoverished part of the city; to his congregation, and, for more than thirty years, to the people crossing the border against the wishes of the government. National policy was an abomination, intolerable. Simply that: not to be tolerated. "Look at the failure of the church in Europe to protect Jews in the thirties and forties," he said. *There* was his modern-day lesson, the lesson to which lip-service is so often paid. But he had acted on it. And then there were the older lessons. There was Numbers: "The Lord spoke to Moses, saying: Speak to the Israelites, and say to them: When you cross the Jordan into the land of Canaan, then you shall select cities to be cities of refuge for you." There was Leviticus: "When an alien resides with you in your land, you shall not oppress the alien. The alien who resides with you shall be to you as the citizen among you; you shall love the alien as yourself, for you were aliens in the land of Egypt."

By the end of 1982 fifty Guatemalans and Salvadorans could be found sleeping on the floor of Southside Presbyterian on any night. At the church gate he placed a sign: "This is a Sanctuary for the Oppressed of Central America." It was not a "movement" when it started. It was just a succession of actions born of uncomplicated faith. But those actions were the roots of a phenomenon that moved from Arizona to the wider United States and beyond. Sanctuaries for Central American refugees were established in places of worship and universities as far away as Germany. Border Patrol, realising what Fife was doing, threatened to indict him. "None of us wanted to go to jail for Jesus." But there had been little turning over of pros and cons. His government was allowing people to die in the desert; or it was delivering them—"rendering" them, in modern parlance—to torture and rape and murder.

"We learned later that they had a meeting at the Washington Justice Department about what to do about this dinky little church in south Tucson. And the conclusion of the meeting was, 'Well, we're not going to indict them, because that would just call attention to this issue. If we leave them alone, they'll fade away.'

"The whole international community was telling the United States: 'These people are refugees; they need to be protected by law.' It's the same as what's happening in Europe now. You guys keeping talking about a great tradition of caring for refugees: well, you're not doing it." There it was again: the sea, the desert; to die due to water or its lack. Geography enlisted as both cordon and executioner. Notifying the Attorney General in March 1982 that his church was declaring itself a sanctuary, Fife wrote: "We believe that justice and mercy require that people of conscience actively assert our God-given right to aid anyone fleeing from persecution and murder. The current administration of the United States law prohibits us from sheltering these refugees from Central America. Therefore we believe that administration of the law is immoral as well as illegal."

Southside was infiltrated by undercover FBI agents and paid informants, and in 1985 the recordings those individuals secretly made were used to indict Fife and fifteen others. As well as himself and Jim Corbett, the accused included two Catholic priests, three nuns, and two other Quakers—"the usual desperados." Two days before the trial, the defendants' attorney was advised by the judge that he could say nothing in the group's defence about refugee law or conditions in El Salvador or Guatemala. "I used a lot of four-letter words." The sixteen, sentenced to five years' probation, immediately resumed their work, and in the meantime sued the Attorney General. "The next day we get a call from the Justice Department, saying, 'Wouldn't you like to negotiate a settlement?' They agreed to stop all deportations. And they agreed to give everyone who was here without documents temporary protected status. And then the peace accords were signed in Central America in ninety-two, so we called an end to the Sanctuary movement. And quite frankly I was exhausted. I'd thought we were going to be dead meat hanging in the town square."

In 1992 the leaders of the United States, Mexico and Canada signed the North American Free Trade Agreement, NAFTA. That same year, Operation Gatekeeper was instituted by the government. Beginning in Texas and California, its purpose was to "harden" security in the vicinity of towns and cities close to the border. The intention was to usher would-be crossers into more "hostile" areas—into the desert—as a form of deterrence. The strategy was subsequently extended across the entire border, but the immediate effect was an increase in corpses in the desert south of Tucson. "I thought: damn, here we go again," said Fife. The networks that had created the Sanctuary movement in Tucson were reactivated and various groups created to survey the desert between Tucson and the border, leaving water, food and other provisions along the migrant trails. One of these groups was No More Deaths.

The opening up of U.S. markets to Mexican consumers instituted by NAFTA ruined many small Mexican farming communities, which could not compete with America's subsidised agricultural giants. It has often been men and women from rural areas—tropical Veracruz, the cool mountains of Oaxaca—whose lives end in the desert. "It's a war against the poor," said Fife, and even this he uttered with a low outraged chuckle. "If you look at it overall, the United States is conducting a low-intensity conflict against the poor, with *thousands* of casualties. In the eighties, when we were smuggling people across the border, there were 284 Border Patrol agents for the whole Tucson sector. That's why we got away with it. Now there're 4,300. And all of the technology and the helicopters, and drones; all the crap that's out there."

The surviving Salvadorans from the group found by Border Patrol in 1980 had eaten sand. Like Pablo Valencia they had removed their clothing. One had jammed his head into a fox hole. They had already drunk their piss, naturally, and when it had ceased to come, perfume and shaving oil. What was more haunting? Their unwitnessed desperation, or their city innocence? That their satchels contained *shaving oil*? The work continued, said Fife: the desert would go on consuming those obliged to cross it. Congress was deadlocked on border policy. He added as I was leaving: "I have a friend, a Latino ethicist. He says: 'You guys are doing it all wrong. You keep talking about hope: there is no hope! Are you kidding me? You think your little project out here is going to deal with neoliberal economic power? Bullshit! You just need to stop telling people that it's hopeful. What you need to do is realise it's hope*less*: they're going to *win*.' So therefore you're *free*!" said Fife. "You're *free*—if you realise it's hopeless—to just fuck with the system!" He laughed again, but loud and liberated this time—"And I think he's right. Just fuck with the system any way you can! Just go fuck with it."

SINCE THE 1990s a doctrine known as "prevention through deterrence," inspired by the success of Operation Gatekeeper, has been practised by the United States Border Patrol. Only 565 kilometres of the country's 3,145-kilometre southern border are effectively fenced, 18 per cent. The stretches in between are marked by nothing more than a triple strand of cattle wire, or barbed wire, if by anything at all. Increasingly Border Patrol is deploying remote electronic surveillance technology, the so-called virtual wall—infrared cameras, motion-sensors, pressure-sensors, drones and radar blimps—but in many places you can still pass from the southern side to the northern with a single step. Even if that step must be flanked by a million others. "The overarching goal of the strategy," goes a congressional report, "is to make it so difficult and so costly to enter this country illegally that fewer individuals even try."

Still the desert border remains largely unfenced, but by obliging those who are determined to cross to do so in the most isolated areas, the strategy has become one whose efficiency can be measured not only by the number of would-be migrants discouraged from embarking (which is anybody's guess) but by the number of human remains recovered from arroyos and bajadas and the shadows of ironwood trees. Between October 2000 and September 2014, in southern Arizona alone, this number was 2,721. Among these people—who succumbed to heat exhaustion or dehydration, or fell from cliffs or died of snakebite or heart attacks—some eight hundred are unidentified. And we must add to this number—perhaps doubling it, perhaps tripling it—those remains that have *not* been found, either because of their remoteness or, more likely, because they have simply been erased.

Sometimes the desert preserves—remember the Hotan mummy with her small grey tongue. More often it obliterates. Those shapes helixing high above, shuddering on their huge wings, are turkey vultures, and with the coyotes and the foxes they will strip a body of meat and disperse its bones over several square kilometres in the course of a few days. As you wait in Nogales or Sonoyta on the Mexican side of the border before trying to enter the desert, therefore, you do so in the knowledge that it is not just your life you will be staking, but—in the absence of your corpse or, if your corpse is recovered, any way of identifying it—your loved-ones' opportunity to properly grieve for you.

ONE MORNING Dan Millis and I drove out to the border to meet a rancher he knew, Tony Sedgwick, whose three hundred hectares lay east of Nogales in the Santa Cruz Valley. Dan worked for the Arizona chapter of the Sierra Club, the environmental organisation. He'd also been involved with No More Deaths as a volunteer. He was young, younger than me, shaven-headed, friendly, sceptical. For the first hour he watched my face as I spoke. But then he made a decision about me, I suppose, and we grew easy in one another's company. In 2008, while walking in the desert, he had found a body. A fourteen-year-old Salvadoran girl, Josseline Jamileth Hernández Quinteros. She'd been reported missing by her parents in Los Angeles, whom she had been trying to reach. She was wearing a pearl bracelet, Dan recalled. Two days later, returning to the spot to leave provisions for other crossers, Dan was confronted by National Park rangers, and cited—cited for littering (plastic bottles, buckets full of fresh socks and biscuits). Declining to pay a fine, he was convicted in federal court and given a suspended sentence. This was how you became a system-fucker—seeing how it ranged against kindness.

We met Tony Sedgwick outside a diner on the edge of Nogales. He wore a spotless white Stetson and his hips had a castered looseness when he walked. What you get for fifty years on horseback. Tony had been a lawyer, and once, years ago, ran for political office (Republican, who else?). "It was a lot of fun, but I was not successful," he said. "Mexicans don't vote; if they're illegal, they can't vote; if they come into the country as registered aliens, they're not *allowed* to vote. And besides, they don't *want* to vote, they don't *care* about voting, they're just glad to be working. Today, blacks have way more power than Mexicans. I'm not saying black people aren't totally screwed, but think of a single Mexican politician. Marco Rubio? Marco Rubio can barely speak Spanish."

We spent the morning on his ranch. Tony had been fighting the Department of Homeland Security's positioning of one of its surveillance towers on the highest hill on his property. They had asked his permission and when he refused they had gone ahead and installed it, citing the law of eminent domain and handing him a few thousand dollars. The hilltop was now the government's. What had begun as a personal disagreement had swollen to a broader awareness. He had come to understand that those frustrations he'd experienced as an affluent white rancher, a man with influence and reputation, were as nothing beside what was meted out to Mexicans and Central American migrants. He had been given a taste of powerlessness. But the tower was not what he wanted to show me.

The border wall cut across hills of sweetgrass, Fremont willows and creosote bush. You could see it from many kilometres off, a close-set rank of rusted palisades five metres tall. Tony's gorgeous steers lounged in the shade of cottonwoods. The sound of birdsong was constant. This too was the desert. In the wall's shadow, the grass was tall and flowers seemed to grow more abundantly than elsewhere. Blue flowers, especially, asters and flax. Perhaps they fed on something leached from the iron or concrete, or simply preferred the shade. As we descended into the valley and the vegetation thickened and became taller, the wall ended. You could still follow the line—barbed wire and steel tank traps—but there was little to keep a person on foot from crossing from one country to another, and indeed the purpose of the remaining barrier was to control cattle and the narcos in their cocaine trucks. But drugs, like water, would find their way. Here, fifteen kilometres from one of the main international ports of entry, you could edge along the banks of the Santa Cruz and duck under a fence into the United States with little more inconvenience than wet feet. "It's interesting," said Tony, meaning: "It's ludicrous."

That afternoon, as we approached Nogales, Arizona, in Tony's truck, the wall was a disorienting aberration; as if it had been drawn on acetate and laid over an image of the city by some speculative planner. Its geometry seemed warped, dislocated; like an Escher print. What is the function of this black blade, the eye asks, pressed down into hills and streets? To look east onto the broad green valley of the Santa Cruz was to see, instinctively, a corridor—where water flows, so will clouds, seeds, Harris hawks, jackrabbits, javelinas.

"The traditional migration pattern to this country was to come here and create a new world," said Tony: "New Jersey, New York, New you-name-it." We'd stopped for quesadillas in a roadside diner. He was getting into his stride. "People who come here now, they would rather *not* come; they would rather stay home. They didn't burn their boats like Aeneas. They come here, and they work—and what do they do with their money? They send it home. Home is *over there*. *This* is not home."

We drove on into Nogales. *The wall*, they call it, though it is not the blind concrete monolith of Israel or China. As it crosses Nogales, it is an array of steel girders set a few centimetres apart, each triangular in cross-section and five metres tall. The wall is prefabricated in ten-girder sections, each crowned with an unbroken blade a metre high and five long. The sections are planted in a concrete block that reaches to waist height and bears the grain-pattern of the timber form it was cast in. The steel above, untreated, is red-brown with rust, and this rust in turn has leached into the paler concrete, and drained down its sides to the ground.

"Our country is based on the concept—at least our judicial system—that it's better for a hundred guilty guys to go free than an innocent man to be convicted," said Tony. "That's what we've always heard. And this type of structure, this says exactly the opposite."

Wherever there is a dip in the terrain, the foot of the wall is fitted with a line of low floodgates secured with a single massive bolt, a bolt that can be slid out with nothing lighter or more mobile than a fork-lift. Pressed up along the Mexican side, like fish in a net, are clothing and litter and rubble and vegetation—Nogales, Sonora's flood-trash. When the monsoon floodwaters come—and they come from the Mexican side—debris accumulates in Nogales, Sonora, until the water can no longer flow between the palisades. The slope nearby, on our side, showed the violence of the water's sudden escape, the ground sluiced back to the bedrock. For the wall is also a dam. The previous year's floods toppled sections of it and in 2008 the waters rose so high that a neighbourhood of Nogales, Sonora, was devastated, with eight million dollars' worth of damage done to homes, businesses and vehicles. Two bodies were recovered, unidentified, but believed to be men trying to enter America through an underground storm tunnel.

On one of Nogales, Arizona's slopes, where there were few houses, the wall's concrete base had been used as a shrine. Ranged along an iron reinforcement joist that slanted from the concrete were some burnt-out tealights in glass jars. Knotted to the vertical palings above were a curling length of yellow ribbon and, tied in place with the same kind of ribbon, a bunch of dirty plastic daisies turned brittle by the sun. Nogales, Sonora, lay on the other side, six metres below, and I realised that the wall stood on its own ridge—steep on the Mexico side, like a castle dyke. In order to climb the wall you first had to climb the slope. About twelve metres. Between the steel posts that made up the wall, I could see—in Mexico—a white windowless building and a sign: DESPACHO JURIDICO, legal office. Stencil-sprayed on the adjoining wall, a young man's face—a boy's really, in its chubbiness—repeated over and over, like a crude Warhol. An image of martyrdom. RIP JOSÉ was penned in black on the rust-stained concrete. José Antonio Elena Rodríguez. He died in Mexico; the bullets that killed him were fired from the United States. It had happened on this spot on an October night, Tony said. Border Patrol had been called to a report of men climbing the fence. As the agents converged, the men climbed back over to Sonora. A crowd gathered on the Mexican side and began throwing rocks over the fence at the patrolmen. Among the rock-throwers was José Antonio Elena Rodríguez: this is the official version. José Antonio Elena Rodríguez threw no rocks, he was merely walking past the fence on the way home from basketball: this is the unofficial version, the version told by Rodríguez's friends and family and other civilian witnesses. José Antonio Elena Rodríguez was sixteen. That much everyone seems able to agree on.

Atop the six-metre bluff, behind the five-metre fence, stood the Border Patrol agents, eight of them. Among the agents was Lonnie

Swartz. At the foot of the bluff was José Antonio Elena Rodríguez, walking home from basketball, or throwing rocks—both, perhaps— throwing rocks over the top of the fence, twelve metres above him. Again there is no question that Lonnie Swartz approached the fence, and drew his firearm, and shot down on José Antonio Elena Rodríguez, hitting him ten times.

"They call it a bollard wall," said Tony. "The agent stood right here, put his firearm between the *bollards*, and shot Rodríguez eight times in the back."

It is not an easy target, a sixteen-year-old's back, at that range.

"Imagine trying to throw something over that. It's very difficult to understand."

The federal case rested not only on whether Swartz's actions were reasonable—he feared for his life, rocks big as pomegranates raining down—but on whether the killing could even be described as criminal when the kid was a Mexican in Mexico and his killer an American in America.

AFTER 9/11 the Department of Homeland Security evolved a new method of "prevention through deterrence," which it called "enforcement with consequences." Until 2001, those apprehended in the desert were processed and dispatched to the nearest port of entry without prolonged detention. This was called "voluntary departure," as the migrant waived his or her right to a judicial hearing. Naturally, once removed from the country, they attempted to cross again as soon as possible—the next day, why not, since you've come this far? Part of "enforcement with consequences," since 2005, has been Operation Streamline. Instead of being allowed to leave the United States under the terms of "voluntary departure," apprehended migrants are instead processed through the federal criminal-justice system. Under Operation Streamline, first-time offenders can be sentenced to up to six months in jail, repeat offenders to up to two years.

Tucson is often the first objective of undocumented migrants trying to cross the Sonoran Desert. It is also where those who are picked up by Border Patrol are taken for trial. Given the very large numbers of people—tens of thousands—apprehended each year, it is not possible for due process to be applied. This is the nature of streamlining, and it can be seen if you go to Tucson's federal courthouse on any weekday afternoon.

"Please rise," said the judge.

A massed jangling as sixty young men got to their feet. They were manacled and fettered. It was an old, old sound, this jangling, not new to the USA or anywhere else. It was nauseating. "When your name is called, please rise and say 'Present.'" They were tired, and slow. They had come, most of them, directly from a cell, having been picked up in the desert in the past twenty-four hours. Who knew how far they had walked or how long since they'd slept? They looked around. The courtroom was cool, high-ceilinged and bright, its walls lined with pastel-coloured fabric. How strange to find yourself here: perhaps days spent trudging over the hills and arroyos, your clothes shredded by cacti, the birds circling overhead; and then to be transported first to a cell and then to this hushed theatre with its air of order and privilege, itself symbolic of what you have been seeking, and your appointed attorney placing his bejewelled hand on your shoulder.

"Jesús Manuel García," read the judge.

"*Presente.*"

They were called up to stand before the bench in groups of five or six, the same formulation repeated again and again.

"Mr. Manuel García, did you enter the United States illegally near the town of Nogales?"

This one had the build of a fourteen-year-old; he was smirking shyly as he lifted himself to his feet. The earphones through which proceedings were being interpreted for him were not working. His attorney intervened. The attorney was a big, bearded man, and, like his colleagues and the Border Patrol representatives, spent most of the hearing fingering his iPhone.

There was a delay while replacement headphones were found.

"Gentlemen," said the judge, "if you don't understand, please stand, or speak privately to your attorney." Nobody stood or approached his attorney. They were young men, self-conscious among their peers.

"Mr. Manuel García, did you enter the United States illegally near the town of Nogales?"

There was a pause as Jesús Manuel García listened to the translation.

"*Sí.*"

"You have been charged with illegal re-entry after deportation. Do you understand the charges and the maximum penalties that you are facing?"

A pause.

"*Sí.*" He glanced at the men alongside him.

He was wearing a thin hooded jersey in a camouflage pattern, the kind worn by many of his fellow defendants, bought from the stalls catering to migrants on the Mexican side of the border. This is also where you buy your black plastic three-litre canteens and your electrolyte powder and the plimsolls soled with carpet that leave no prints.

"Mr. Manuel García, you have agreed to plead guilty to the petty offence of illegal re-entry. In exchange, the government agrees to dismiss the more serious felony offence against you. Do you understand?"

"*Sí.*"

"Mr. Manuel García, please speak up."

There was a pause, he said it loudly this time, almost shouted, and the other defendants laughed.

"Thank you, Mr. Manuel García."

She asked him how he pleaded.

He listened, and said quietly, "*Culpable.*"

"Thank you, Mr. Manuel García. You are going to be deported and removed from the United States. The charge will always be on your record."

Others, repeat offenders, were sentenced to time in jail—nine months, a year. Yet there was little palpable tension in the room. When Manuel García's group of half a dozen had received their sentences they were led from the room. One of them wore a T-shirt with the words "Keep Calm and Chive On." I didn't understand what it meant. One of them was wearing a white facemask. One of them was on crutches. "Bring 'em down!" came a warehouse holler.

And so it went, *"Culpable," "Culpable," "Culpable," "Culpable"* ... until, after an hour, the process achieved such momentum that it seemed unstoppable, and indeed once those sixty had been processed, another sixty shuffled in, and tomorrow the same, and the next day; and there was nothing in the fashion of the proceedings to give one hope it would ever ease, this filing of people.

I ARRANGED TO meet one of the agents. The thing about Border Patrol is the solitude, he told me. Once you're trained, you're on your own—stationary in your truck, watching the line for eight, nine hours at a time. You need to know how to take that, Tom said, as we drove south from Tucson into the desert the next day. As well as being a Border Patrol officer, Tom was the agency's local PR rep. He had been well briefed; he was compassionate and reasonable. Nobody wants anyone to die out there. The comedian Billy Connolly, he said, was recently a guest. Took him and his crew up in a chopper to film the wall from above. That's a funny guy. Tom himself had been a patrolman, quite senior, but he no longer spent much time in the field, and he missed it. I got the impression that handholding the media and chaperoning pasty British writers was not real work, to his mind; wasn't the kind of work his father would have admired. The PR front dropped a notch when we stopped for a burger at a Wendy's on the Nogales road.

"If I was in their shoes? Maybe I'd want to cross, too; but I'll say this: I wouldn't cross in the desert; I wouldn't cross where it's *impossible* to carry enough water to keep me alive. I'd cross in one of the towns. Sure, you're more likely to be apprehended, but you're a heck of a lot less likely to die."

His father? A strict man who required academic excellence of his only child. Tom, no scholar, was punished for his poor grades with long periods locked in his room. He did not become, therefore, a sociable boy, and grew up to experience solitude as if it were normal. It is what made him effective, before he was singled out by his employers for his manner, his diplomacy. It's a kind of strength, isn't it, being able to abide solitude?

Following Iraq and Afghanistan and Border Patrol's corresponding expansion, more and more ex-soldiers joined up, Tom said. But BP is not the military; it's a very particular thing; there's nothing "kinetic" about it (the army word: *kinesis*). The job, in essence, is to sit, to watch—and only then, sometimes, to track and to apprehend. You are a security guard, you are also an agent of punishment. To be alone, furthermore, is to be unwitnessed. It is the perennial test of the desert: when you can do whatever you wish, without anyone there to censure you, how do you behave? Take a man who has seen action in one desert and put him in another, on his own. A man who's shot at nameless foreigners and seen those same foreigners shoot back. The way blood can stand on sand for minutes before it sinks in. Put him on the line.

Even in this relatively lush desert there is only so much to occupy the gaze—limestone outcrops, prickly pear, paloverde, mesquite; the sky and its carnivorous birds—before that gaze turns inwards. In the patient desert once again you will find the familiar silence, save for the radio crackle and the wheeling hawks. It is those men who either crack up, said Tom, or, alert to the danger within themselves, quit.

Coming back from Nogales I'd passed through the checkpoint at Amado on Interstate Highway 19, a dozen agents halting vehicles under a hangarlike white canopy that bridged the northbound road, a secondary line against those who had illegally crossed the border thirty kilometres south. It was the scrubby badlands flanking the checkpoint that Tom and I searched, though I was aware it was mainly a performance for my benefit. For him, the trek was not, as it was for me, a mere succession of obstacles. He was barely conscious of its physical demands: he knew an ankle-turning rock when he saw one, how to negotiate a steep scree slope (crabwise). I tried to see the desert through his eyes. His focus was the mark that betrayed a human's recent presence; the aberration: broken or pushed-down grass, overturned stones, the slightest darkening of the sparse soil where it had been kicked. It was unforthcoming ground, this shattered limestone; even our own prints were impossible to trace when we turned back. This was the work, then, the daily work. The country scarcely changed. A week might pass without your apprehending anyone. But that, Tom said, is not a week of failure. There were, he assured me, no quotas. Sure, a beautiful place to work. Not that you think much about its beauty.

The ground was littered with discarded belongings. People had been coming this way for years; for generations, in fact. It was one of the great Sonoran routes, following the course of the Santa Cruz that once, before its water was pumped and diverted, snaked between the Santa Rita Mountains and the Tumacacori Mountains. The artefacts lay there under the ironwood tree where people had rested for shade, along with empty water bottles and plastic bags and clothes. All of it slowly being drawn into the rocky ground. It was hard not to be reminded of the aftermath of a great flight; or a rush burial. I looked at Tom with his sidearm in its holster; and, reflected in his Ray-Bans, myself in my sunhat and my desert-wear. Our breathing was audible. Back in the truck, we rolled slowly along a dirt track, Tom leaning from his window as he drove, scanning the verge for prints, kick-marks, flattened vegetation. *Cutting sign*, they called it. Some of these tracks were regularly raked smooth with the aid of three tractor tyres dragged behind a Border Patrol truck. I remembered the *tiantian*, the moat of sand that ringed the fort at Jiayuguan on the edge of the Gobi, smoothed each evening to betray the footprints of deserters.

You hardly needed to leave your vehicle, if you knew the roads well enough: just noted where the trail crossed the track, and drove to the next road along to see if the trail reappeared there. If not, you waited; they would come to you, too tired to run. They had been here, of course, the young men in their hundreds, but not lately. High above us on a knoll, enclosed within a gleaming cyclone fence, stood one of the new line of watchtowers designed by an Israeli defence firm. We walked to the fence and I looked up at the watchtower. Its gaze was fixed southwards: radar, high-res video. It was alert to the slightest lateral movement, and in Nogales officers were stationed at their screens, ready to send agents.

In 2014, José Antonio Elena Rodríguez's mother, frustrated by the slowness of the federal investigation into his killing, sued Lonnie Swartz in federal court. It would come as a surprise when he was indicted for second-degree murder. I hadn't mentioned the case, but Tom wanted to talk about it. A rock, if you think about it, he said, delivered with velocity and precision, is a lethal weapon. Ask the Israeli Defence Force. "People think, 'Hey, that jerk shot him for throwing a little stone.'" Next to the track stood a lollipop sign warning of rough conditions ahead. "I don't know what happened, but I know what a rock can do"—and he crouched, selected a fist-sized chunk of volcanic rock, stood and pulled back his arm and with all his strength launched it at the sign. It hit it in the centre, with an explosion of dust and a bang that echoed from the hills.

SOME DAYS LATER, in the car park of John Fife's church in Tucson, fifteen men were waiting, Mexicans and Salvadorans and Guatemalans and Hondurans. They had entered America illegally; many had been deported several times. Not all of them were young. On church property they could not be apprehended by the police or Border Patrol. Citizens of Tucson needing day labour could come here and liaise with the manager, Ereberto, who would allocate the appropriate worker or workers for a set daily fee. For six days a week the men were able to earn a living, at a fair wage and with minimal risk of arrest and deportation.

I sat among a group of them on the kerb, in the shade of the church wall, and handed out cigarettes and cans of San Pellegrino lemonade. Occasionally a truck or car pulled in and one or two of the men were called away by Ereberto to go with the driver to mow a lawn or tile a roof or lay paving or clear a dead person's house. After an hour, only one guy was left, and in the absence of the others he became talkative. His name was Enrique. He was in his early twenties and wore a young man's clothes—oversized baseball jersey and jeans, backwards baseball cap over his frizzy ponytail. He lived in the future, when things would be better. After all, his life today was better than it was a year ago, wasn't it? He was quickened by his own words.

It was approaching 2 p.m. and the light had an astringency to it, a penetrating quality that differs from heat. The lemonade was gone, the cans lined up on the kerb between us. He was from Honduras, he said. Like thousands of others each year he crossed Mexico on the roof of *la Bestia*—the Beast, *el tren de la muerte*—the notoriously perilous network of freight trains. It took him twenty days to reach Monterrey in the north-east of Mexico. He had already been deported from that city three times, he said. "A lot of people die, you know. You can see a lot of crows beside the tracks. Sometimes on the train people are asking for water or food or money. Bad people. You don't have money, they push you off the train. I see that kind of people."

He and two friends from Honduras caught a lift to Sonoyta on the border, and it was from there that they entered the Organ Pipe Cactus National Monument. "No fence," Enrique said. "Only desert. Only desert." It took him nine days to reach Tucson. "For three days, no water, no food." He became separated from his friends when he left them to search for water. "I almost died. I was looking for them everywhere. I was screaming, asking names. And I never found them."

He repeated himself: "I spent three days in the desert, by myself." He could scarcely believe it. He wasn't one of those wide-eyed Salvadoran farm-boys with no conception of the desert's hardships, the sort who tries to cross wearing flip-flops and carrying a few bottles of Coke. He had heard the stories, and there he was in the middle of one. He found a rancher's water tank. "I couldn't believe that. How God is." Then he came upon a can of beans. A can of beans, sitting there in a dry wash! "God is the only one. The only one. The beans were bad, but anyway I ate them. They give me energy for two more days. I got lost but then I find a town, I don't remember the name. A truck driver had a flat tyre. I helped him, and he gave me a ride to Yuma."

From there he hopped a train to Tucson, hiding in the restroom to avoid the guard. The friends he lost in the desert? They too survived. They were now in Indiana, working as roofers. He was saving for a bus ticket to join them. A car pulled in, and Ereberto was calling him, but he didn't stand up. "I'm feeling like I am in the middle of my road," he said. "God is the only one. The only one. The one who choose. If God wants me to go back, I'll go back."

6
MATTER OUT OF PLACE

The Black Rock Desert, USA

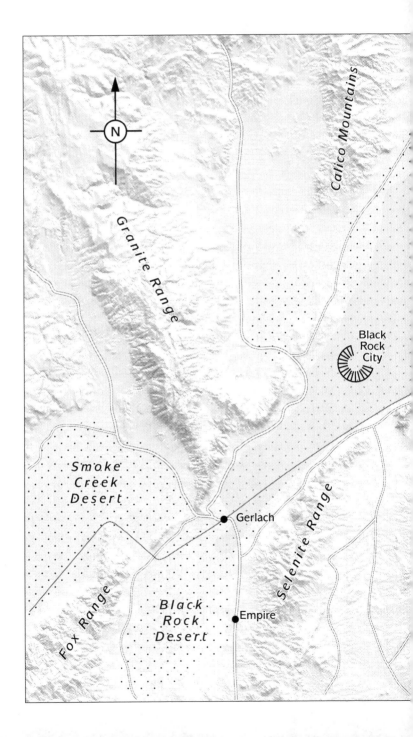

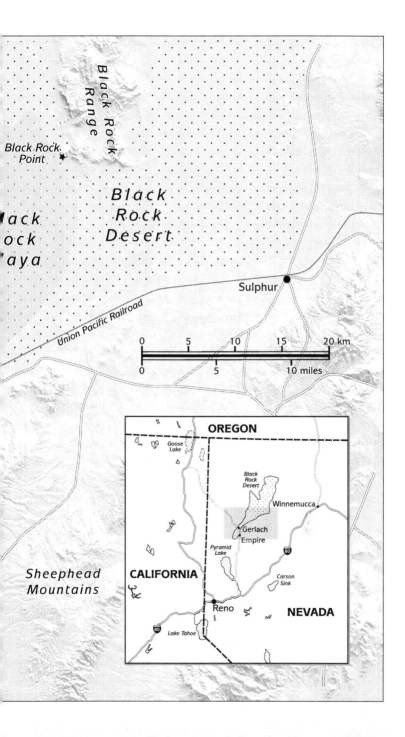

Black Rock
Range

Black Rock
Point

ack
ock
aya

Black
Rock
Desert

Sulphur

Union Pacific Railroad

| 0 | 5 | 10 | 15 | 20 km |

| 0 | 5 | 10 miles |

OREGON

Goose
Lake

Black
Rock
Desert

Winnemucca

Gerlach
Empire

Pyramid
Lake

Carson
Sink

CALIFORNIA

Sheephead
Mountains

Reno

NEVADA

Lake Tahoe

I'd been living in Tucson for a month, periodically going out into the desert with No More Deaths, when I took a flight 1,200 kilometres north to Reno, Nevada, the heart of Walter Prescott Webb's "charred mass." I'd arranged to meet a man named Papa La Mancha in a casino hotel in nearby Sparks. I myself stayed at the only hotel I could afford, the Reno Sands, which was occupied by a mixture of "Burners" and gamblers who coexisted in a state of strained equilibrium, like prison gangs. Floating in the swimming pool was a white patio chair. When Raymond, the maintenance man, came to my room to remove the hairdryer that had exploded (I was trying to dry some socks), I asked him how many rooms they had. "You know, it's funny," he said. "Nobody seems to know. I asked maybe ten people and I got ten different answers. One guy said five hundred, another guy was like eight hundred. Someone said a thousand. But I keep asking, and nobody knows for sure."

At 3 a.m. I was woken by crazed screaming. It was nearby, outside. When I looked out at the city shimmering far below my window, I could see nobody in the parking lot. It's strange, I thought, how plate glass can sometimes seem clearer than air. The scream came again; it was a man's, giddy and defensive. It was coming from *above*, ten storeys above my room and therefore twenty-five from the ground. The little bastard was up on the roof, smashed out of his gourd, being gently berated by some voice of authority—cop or security.

"Just drop what you're holding and come down."

"Hey man, howja like it if I took a back-flip *off* of this thing?"

A pause, then a girl shrieking—then idiotic laughter. Then it was quiet again.

Next morning, at one of the windowless twenty-four-hour bars, a muscled young Dutchman and a gaunt gambler in her fifties were admiring one another's tatts. There was an abundance of wheelchairs and oxygen masks, and two amputee friends, one without an arm, the other without a leg. The names of the gambling machines were Midnight Eclipse, Lobster Run, Wolf Mania, Jumpin' Jalapeños, Wild Aztec, Lotus Flower, Lucky Beans and Moby Dick. I felt that the whole flashing, beeping, chiming arena was on the brink of something hysterical—violence or sobbing or orgiastic sex. In that sense, it prefigured what was to follow. Gliding through it all, the people about to head out to the desert, with their wheeled cases and rucksacks, their boas and fur coats and spandex and piercings and wolf masks, were like some imperial mission from another planet. "Please respect OUR playa," said a sign in the lift.

THE DESERT HAS always been a permissive space. For the Mormons who settled in Utah in 1847 it was a refuge for the free expression of faith, just as it had been for the Christian anchorites of third-century Egypt fleeing the persecutions of the Roman emperors. But while the desert could be both a sanctuary and—God knows—an unassailable barrier, it was also, in Mary Austin's words, a "land of lost borders," where the sureties of civic life evaporated along with its impositions. If for some the desert promised liberation from the rancorous body, it also offered—in its seclusion and boundlessness—sovereignty of the spirit, bodily freedom, and an almost overwhelming provocation. In any void, after all, potential is infinite. Not just a blank canvas but the biblical darkness.

Until recently I'd known only that Burning Man took place each year at the end of August, two hundred kilometres north of Reno, on the Black Rock Desert playa (a dry lakebed, and one of the largest flat expanses on earth) and that it culminated with the burning first of a huge human effigy, then, on the final night, a structure called the Temple. The burning, it turned out, was not really the point of Burning Man. Although there was lots of music, constant music, most of it electronic dance music (EDM), it was less a music festival than an arts festival. But it was not exactly an arts festival, either. I wasn't sure it was really a "festival" at all. There was no roster of performances. It wasn't a "show." You did not generally need to be anywhere at any particular time in order to see a particular thing happening. The point was that, in Black Rock City, as the encampment was called, something was occurring everywhere, all the time, and it was likely to involve you. Seventy thousand Burners, as we were called, camped for a week in one of the harshest environments on earth. That would be spectacle enough.

As with most cults, Burning Man's foundation myth is fugitive. I had read that Larry Harvey, the Stetsoned founder, guru and spokesperson, was the adopted son of "Exodusters," refugees from the Nebraska Dust Bowl. Shy, they said, socially awkward and impractical. My kind of guru. The story goes that Burning Man began in the 1980s as an act of expiation following Harvey's abandonment by a woman he loved. He denies this narrative. The first "burn" was purely an exercise in "spontaneous self-expression," he insists. It took place not in Nevada, not in the desert, but on a beach, Baker Beach in San Francisco. Papa La Mancha, a model of equability and tolerance, and a Burning Man aficionado, had seen Harvey give a talk in London: "It was the single worst talk I've ever seen," he said as he drove. "It was *incomprehensible.*"

I pulled out my ticket and read the back: "You must bring enough food, water, shelter and first aid to survive one week in a harsh desert environment. YOU VOLUNTARILY ASSUME THE RISK OF SERIOUS INJURY OR DEATH BY ATTENDING."

PAPA LA MANCHA and I had been driving for two hours. We were about thirty kilometres from the edge of the Black Rock Desert. He and Mama La Mancha, who would be arriving later, were middle-aged Londoners who'd met at Burning Man years before. He was not an anarchist or a hippy; he was a London Underground station-manager and this was his annual holiday. His dream, he told me, was to one year lay a temporary branch-line to Black Rock City across the playa from the Union Pacific freight line, which skirted the edge of the Black Rock Desert. Burners would be able to travel by train direct from Reno and it would reduce the traffic jams that blighted arrival and departure. He was a practical-minded fellow.

The road followed the Truckee River along the floor of a series of broad basins dense with grey-green sagebrush, Nevada's dominant flora. In its greyness it reminded me of the shrubby chenopods that covered the Nullarbor Plain, the knee-high, clumpy saltbush and blue-bush. Ahead of us was a convoy of Burner vehicles: RVs, station wagons packed with barrels of water, bicycles strapped to the roof; a trailer full of plastic unicorns, an old yellow school bus with a couch roped to the roof on which sat a bare-chested man in a Viking helmet. A friend in London had told me to look out for "the guy with two dicks." I'd know him when I saw him, I supposed.

There were thousands of "theme camps" at Burning Man. A few months earlier, on the internet, I'd come across one that called itself La Mancha's Bar and Cabaret. There were about twenty members. The La Manchas seemed appealingly errant, and I didn't want to go alone. I emailed the address on their website and offered to help behind the bar, which in practice would mean ladling pre-mixed margaritas from a bucket.

Close to the defunct gypsum-mining community of Empire, twenty-five kilometres from the Burning Man site, the locals had set out their wares—dust goggles, feather boas, leggings, el-wire, the faux-fur coats that were a playa uniform during the cool nights. I was glad they were making something out of the invasion. Since a claim was established here in 1910, Empire's lifeblood had been gypsum, a mineral evaporate of the vast lake that had once covered the region. The United States Gypsum Corporation—"the Gyp," as they called it locally—had produced dryboard for the construction industry, but with the recession production had slowed until, by 2011, the plant was no longer viable. It had been a company town, and when the company left, so did the citizens, two hundred in total. Empire had become a ghost town, like the defunct nineteenth-century silver-mining enter-prises scattered along the desert's edge. The streets were filling with dust; the zip code had been discontinued. Apart from seasonal hikers tackling the old migrant trails, few outsiders passed through.

The great yearly event on the playa twenty-five kilometres away would not start officially till tomorrow, but the chaos was beginning; the excitement was building and the locals were a contented part of it. The last hamlet before you hit the playa is Gerlach ("Girl-lack," the ranchers call it), where dozens more stalls had been set out. "Absolutely Everything Playa!" read a banner. The sheriff's men standing around their cars at the roadside did not smile; there was no banter. The new sheriff of Pershing County was less tolerant of Burning Man than his predecessor. "Burning Man taxes this county," he had told a local newspaper. "Pretty much everything they buy, they buy outside... they leave Pershing County high and dry." The advance guard of Burners was more welcoming. In the town's store a stranger in the queue introduced his baby daughter to me, and proffered a hug: "Welcome home, man." It was a kind of mantra, *welcome home*, and if there was a currency at Burning Man it was the embrace. One of the theme camps, the Hug Bank, offered a "menu" ranging from "businesslike" to "awkward."

As we left Gerlach and approached the playa, the local radio station was playing Bowie's "Space Oddity." "Take your protein pills and put your helmet on."

LAKE LAHONTAN, which once filled the basin of the Black Rock Desert, no longer exists, but water draining from the surrounding ranges each winter has continued to flood the dry surface periodically, adding millennia of sediment to those layers deposited by the lake. This is the playa. In places the sediment is deeper than the mountains around it are high—mountains from whose very substance, weathered away, atomised, and washed down canyons, the playa is largely formed. It is these processes, similar to those that formed the claypans I'd seen in Australia, that account for the evenness of the playa's surface, as year after year it is swept and scoured and polished by water.

Once we left the road that followed the foot of the mountains, it took an hour to reach the entrance to the site a couple of kilometres from the edge of the playa. In the dust thrown up by the vehicles I did not appreciate the vastness of the setting, a three-hundred-square-kilometre plane whose solitary concession to the vertical—when Burning Man is not happening—is the occasional dust devil. Only the bones of the city grid were in place when we reached the site allocated to our camp: the edges of the streets marked out with mini surveyors' flags, the lorries and shipping containers of the major camps waiting to be unloaded, the portapotties unsullied in their ranks. (Each line of toilets was signposted with a red light on a six-metre mast. Somebody, in the prankster spirit of the event, had had the forethought to weld a red-lighted mast to an adapted golf cart, which over the next week they drove about each night, trailed by anxious Burners.) The rest of our campmates had yet to arrive. There was hardly any music and the silence of the desert hadn't yet been driven out. The city had no coherence; it was just scattered clutches of half-naked people and half-built scaffold structures, as if there were some doubt as to our continuing presence here. It was impossible to imagine what it would become, the feeling of permanence, even of decline, it would acquire.

Like most deserts the Black Rock Desert has historically been a place to skirt or to cross as quickly as possible, even for the indigenous Paiute tribes. Seldom before has man hung around here without necessity. The reports of those who encountered the place as explorers or migrants testify to its hardships; precisely the hardships that we—ketamine brats, Oregonian coders, pale scribes from the drizzly shires—were exposing ourselves to at such leisure. (Not that the experience was leisurely exactly.) In 1843, at around the same time as Sturt was seeking the inland sea of Australia, the explorer John C. Frémont set out to find another nonexistent body of water, the San Buenaventura River. In the course of his journey he mapped an immense desert realm encircled by mountain ridges, some 427,000 square kilometres including most of Nevada and western Utah: he called it the Great Basin. Like the Aral Basin, the Great Basin is endorheic, having no outflow of water to external bodies of water. It is partly this circumscribed geography that accounts for its thirty-five playas. The Great Basin is also basin-and-range country, a landscape of faults and scarps, filled with lesser basins. Its crust, stretched like toffee by the movement of tectonic plates millions of years ago, broke into lateral ridges trending north–south: basins separated by ranges. The first thorough geological survey of the former Lake Lahontan was carried out by Israel Cook Russell in 1882. Folded into a flap at the back of the resulting volume, published by the United States Geological Survey one year later, is a large map of the Great Basin, showing the land as it was during the Pleistocene when the lake was at its height, a body of water intruded upon by islands and spits, stretching north-east from today's Lake Tahoe in the Sierra Nevada all the way to Oregon. The valleys of the Carson, Walker and Humboldt Rivers are shaded blue to their brims, and today's deserts—the Carson, Smoke Creek and Black Rock—likewise are underwater.

It was possible to see, even today, the ancient lake terraces etched into the slopes of the ranges on either side of the playa. I was sometimes reminded of the dry bed of the Aral Sea—the flatness, the whiteness, the winding contour lines of gravel that marked its onetime shoreline. But while it had been hard to overcome the sensation, when strolling among the ruins of its grounded boats, that the Aralkum was Felix Fabri's "image of death," the Black Rock Desert, in all its lethal starkness, seemed fully alive.

BY MORNING the rest of our campmates had arrived. Bob was dressed as a badger, and it suited him. Occasionally he would appear as Tiffany from Accounts in her green miniskirt, or Consuela, who was a chambermaid and had been known to vacuum the playa. She was delightful, but with his beard and middle-aged paunch he made a more plausible badger. Beaker was a fire juggler and a member of something called the fire conclave; he was wiry and wired and in fire-juggling he'd found the activity for which he was born. Hawthorn was an academic with a magnificent heap of purple dreads piled high on her head and a leather utility belt jangling with carabiners. She was forthright and practical and hilarious. Some Burners adopt a "playa name," an alter-ego moniker, and I assumed this was the case with Brocket; but Brocket, it turned out, was the name he used in daily life in San Francisco, just as Beaker and Hawthorn were also called Beaker and Hawthorn back in Britain. Call me Dryhenceforth.

Carabinered to a belt loop you carried a tin mug, and all day and night you went from camp to camp and got your mug filled with whatever happened to be on offer, which tended not to be anything so essential as water, and was very often a concoction whose only identifiable chemical was alcohol. There was a lot of nudity, lots of what Papa La Mancha called "shirt-cocking." If you walked out of a dust storm and came across a couple screwing on the ground, they'd barely give you a second glance. Black Rock City was sometimes called a Temporary Autonomous Zone, a term coined by the anarchist thinker Hakim Bey, who defined the "TAZ" as "an uprising which does not engage directly with the State, a guerrilla operation which liberates an area (of land, of time, of imagination) and then dissolves itself to reform elsewhere/ elsewhen *before* the State can crush it." Burning Man was temporary, certainly: a key principle was "leave no trace." Two months after the last Burner had left, the only sign that the thing had happened was a slight compaction of the playa surface. It was a condition of Burning Man's licence that the playa be restored, but it was also part of its ethos. If it was not dust it was MOOP, and must not be allowed to remain. Matter out of place.

But Burning Man was hardly an uprising, and if autonomy meant a lack of social impositions then it was far from autonomous: the state, and the organisation's interactions with it, were essential and visible everywhere. Not only Pershing County Sheriff's Office and the Bureau of Land Management but the State Health Department and Highway Patrol and the Department of Transportation and the federal administrations of aviation and communication. In order to receive its Special Recreation Permit, Burning Man had each year to submit an operating plan to the Bureau of Land Management. It was a vast civic collaboration, even an achievement of capitalism, and while you were largely free to imbibe whatever drugs you pleased and walk about wearing nothing but a shirt ("shirt-cocking"), or, say, a leash, you were not at liberty to cross the fence that separated Black Rock City from the rest of the playa. Then there were the ten principles drawn up by Larry Harvey, principles that might be called rules, or laws. These were Radical Inclusion, Decommodification, Radical Self-Reliance, Radical Self-Expression, Communal Effort, Civic Responsibility, Gifting,

Leaving No Trace, Immediacy and Participation. You were responsible for keeping yourself alive, and everyone contributed to maintaining the city and creating the spectacle. There was no advertising and, in theory, no spectators.

On Baker Beach, back in San Francisco, in 1987, the Man—Harvey's first wooden man—had been maybe three metres tall, knocked together in his garage. Soaked in gasoline, it was gone in minutes. This was nearly thirty years ago, when there had been eight participants, including Harvey. Today something like ten thousand times that number were here. Tickets were hard to come by, and cost hundreds of dollars; some people paid thousands, and there were the so-called turnkey camps, which offered package tours to the Silicon Valley millionaires who wished to fly into the desert and stay in dustless luxury for the price of a Nevada ranch.

By 1990, the Man was more than nine metres tall, and eight hundred people packed the beach. The police began to take an interest. The Man was raised that year, but by agreement with the authorities he was not burnt. Harvey began to look around for alternative venues. One of his friends had visited a huge playa on the other side of the Rocky Mountains, beyond Reno, best known as a venue for landspeed records: the Black Rock Desert. In 1990 a flyer circulated in San Francisco: "Bad Day at Black Rock (Zone Trip #4)...the Zone Trip is an extended event that takes us outside of our local area of time and place. On this particular expedition, we shall travel to a vast, desolate, white expanse stretching onward to the horizon in all directions." Burning Man has continued to take place annually on or near the site of the 1990 Zone Trip. This year the Man was eighteen metres tall and Black Rock City's population, dispersed among hundreds of camps, was bigger than that of Nevada's capital, Carson City. Arriving at the playa edge in 1990, the leader of the Zone Trip, whose playa name was Ranger Danger, reportedly stooped to draw a line in the dust. One by one, goes the founding fable, the participants stepped over it.

BROCKET HAD A tufty Mohican dyed in rainbow colours. He held his weight with daintiness, and walked with a patient, deliberate languor, as if carrying something that might spill. He would not be hurried. "This used to be a gay camp," he told me mournfully, "now it's a geek camp," and that explained its location in Black Rock City's gayborhood. I was one of La Mancha's geeks, but he hadn't meant it unkindly. He was a designer for Google, and dressed beautifully—with the absurd, coherent eclecticism of a celebrity drag queen. He had a new costume for each day: on one occasion a pink chiffon tutu so vast it was barely possible to make him out within; another night he was costumed as an orange, with a tiny orange cocktail hat; on Friday a dreadfully snug evening dress that might have been blue-and-black and might have been white-and-gold. He'd been a member of the San Francisco Gay Men's Chorus, and one night in the cabaret tent performed a karaoke rendition of "Close to You" that, at the time, seemed like the most exquisite thing I had ever heard. It was Brocket who would be my mocking guide to the city—mocking my reserve and my explorer's attire. One evening I met him by chance on the open playa: "I used to be a bit witchy," he confided. He'd been some kind of San Francisco wicken, he gave me to understand. "But then this one time I saw a malevolent presence in the mirror. That was that."

On that first morning we set to work pitching the tents and canvas carports and shade structures that would make our time here tolerable. Papa La Mancha knew how to direct a workforce and saw no reason to accept discomfort. Every afternoon he would magic up an array of rare cheeses, prosciutto and good cold wine. It was one of many miracles of civility in the heat and dust. At one of the other camps, lobster was dished up nightly, first come, first served.

Our camp's tents and yurts were pitched beneath a three-metre-high horizontal canopy. Ordinary tent pegs were useless; they'd bend when you hammered them into the hard playa, and would hold nothing against the gales. Everything was tethered to the ground with thirty-centimetre lengths of steel rebar. There were a dozen large iceboxes to keep the food fresh, a generator, three 2-ring industrial camp stoves and a shower with an evaporation pit lined with tarp. There were six plastic 120-litre barrels of drinking water, and three for washing-up and showers. From 9 a.m. we worked solidly for five hours, knowing that in six days' time we would dismantle what we had built, just as the

Man, erected over the course of weeks, would be destroyed. All those millions of hours and dollars. This was the point of Burning Man, of course—it would all be obliterated.

Over the mountains to the north-west, that first day, a terraced stack of lenticular clouds towered watchfully in an otherwise clear sky. It was a Martian sight. The clouds seemed gravid with something more than water, and they scarcely strayed over the following hours. As noon passed, however, and the wind strengthened, the clouds began to shred, until the dust in the air was so heavy that the sky was no longer visible. Our first dust storm. Already my skin was coarsening. A tightness in my head. By 2 p.m. it was impossible to work, to build our camp—we'd only had time to set up a canvas carport before the gale hit in its fullness, winds of eighty kilometres per hour, and under this cover eight of us cowered miserably and in silence but for the odd grunt of hangdog despair. *Six more days.*

Mark Twain, crossing the playa of the Great Salt Lake Desert in the 1870s, described it as "that species of deserts whose concentrated hideousness shames the diffused and diluted horrors of Sahara." It was a hellish sea whose far shore it seemed his party would never reach: "The alkali dust cut through our lips, it persecuted our eyes, it ate through the delicate membranes and made our noses bleed and *kept* them bleeding—and truly and seriously the romance all faded far away and disappeared, and left the desert trip nothing but a harsh reality—a thirsty, sweltering, longing, hateful reality!" The taste in my mouth was the pall that had hung over the city of Hotan in Xinjiang. I'd heard that a New York firefighter who'd come here after 9/11 had suffered debilitating flashbacks—much of the dust in the wake of the disaster was formed from obliterated dryboard.

Bob the badger had removed the plastic bladder from a box of white wine and was carefully easing its remaining fluid into a beaker. His fur, I noticed, had turned from black-and-white to grey.

But the wind died down after a few hours, and there was a moment late that night, my stomach full, when I went out onto the open playa between the Esplanade and the Man and stood apart from the lights, within a small ring of unpeopled darkness, and looked around me and beheld it all—the lights, the fire, the music—and was drenched by a wave of sheer astonishment and delight at the scale of the creative enterprise, its audacity and superabundance. Its splendour. It was at night that Burning Man happened. During the day the beauty was a natural beauty: the vastness of the setting, the distant mountains on either side, and the sun arcing murderously from one range to the other. But in the dark the city asserted its humanness. You set out with a destination in mind—the Man, say—and within seconds were distracted by something else, by a great flare of white flame a kilometre away, or a twenty-metre yacht gliding past, packed with people dancing; or the form of a standing woman made of steel mesh, thirty metres high and lit from within; and every item aglow within its apportioned sphere of darkness. An hour later you had forgotten where you had set out for in the first place—was it the Man?—and you were dancing on the battlement of a green-lit Celtic castle with a thousand others, necking spiked Gatorade from a tin mug.

Within twenty-four hours most of the camps had been built. On one side of ours was Li'l Crack Whores, whose communal shelter was made of sewn-together T-shirts, and on the other Weiner Zoo, whose keepers served hotdogs and oversaw something called a dildo ring-toss, a kind of pornographic hoopla. Barbie Deathcamp, Polegasm, Bloasis, Celestial Bodies and Beaverton all lay within the Gayborhood. Nearby was Milk & Honey, a Jewish camp where, on the Friday before the Man was burnt, Shabbat was observed. Bitch 'n' Tea advertised itself as a "place to share your trivial woes in exchange for some delicious tea"; Get Nailed offered the opportunity to "get nailed to our crucifix"; passing Mudskippers, I was invited—rather, commanded—to attend "the world-famous Camel Toe Fashion Show." This was the desert, after all.

The city plan was a horseshoe, with its central point the eighteen-metre wooden man positioned on his giant stage. Between the Man and the innermost street of the horseshoe, called the Esplanade, was a stretch of empty playa 800 metres wide. Twelve successive streets receded concentrically from the Esplanade, each with its own name and intersected, like wheel-spokes, by seventeen further streets, numbered clocklike from 2 to 10, with "half-hour" increments. This arrangement of blocks had been agreed with the county police, as the population grew, meaning that each point within the city could be given an approximate address in case of emergencies. La Mancha's was handily central, on the corner of 7.30 and Carny, moments from the Ass-Stamping Tent and the Genital Portraiture Studio, and conveniently located for Comfort and Joy's Pink Gym. It was also close to a block of portapotties, which were suctioned out each morning by Mexican labour, almost the only dark faces you saw on the playa. It was the Mexicans, too, who drove the water tanker that each morning sprayed the streets to subdue dust, a parade of nude whites behind, cavorting in the mud.

JOHN C. FRÉMONT had no desire to settle the desert, nor any expectation that it might be made to bloom as the boosters would promise; he wished only to find the safest route from one side to the other side by land or by river. His party of thirty-nine left Kansas City on 23 May 1843. Two thousand five hundred kilometres from here. "Our cavalcade made a strange and grotesque appearance and it was impossible to avoid reflecting upon our composition in this remote solitude." His objectives were both to map the Oregon Trail to the Pacific coast and to locate the course of the San Buenaventura River, which, the best maps informed him, represented "a connected water line from the Rocky Mountains to the Pacific Ocean." It was a kind of mirage.

In Frémont's wake, some 300,000 migrants would follow. His party entered the Black Rock Desert from the north on New Year's Day 1844: "The soil in many places consists of a fine powdery sand, covered with saline efflorescence; and the general character of the country is desert. During the day we directed our course towards a black cape, at the foot of which a column of smoke indicated hot springs." This was Black Rock Point, which they reached the following day. Other than tufts of coarse salt-grass, Frémont beheld a "perfect barren," while the "jagged, broken point" towering over the hot springs had "a burnt appearance—cinders and coal occasionally appearing as at a blacksmith's forge." He was right: Black Rock Point—180 metres and the only dark point in a world of pastels—is an intrusion of volcanic andesite weathered into something resembling an ironworks' slagheap. He woke to find the desert covered by snow and a thickening fog. "The appearance of the country was so forbidding, that I was afraid to enter it."

WHAT I USUALLY want to do at parties, after an hour or two, is lie somewhere quiet and read a book; here, at the most excessive party on earth, that instinct was intensified. It made me uneasy to be in a setting that was fundamentally tranquil—that was in fact the apogee of tranquillity—but which had been occupied by an administration that trapped its participants in a state of constant stimulation. Maybe it was partly this unease, this desire to flee, that caused my awkwardness, along with the knowledge—which neither I nor my campmates could quite ignore—that while they were here to be Burners, I was here in a more speculative role. Whether I liked it or not, I was precisely what Burning Man discouraged: I was a spectator, although my mind was less on what was happening in Black Rock City than on the desert and the mountains *outside* the trash fence. My instinct, often, was to escape the music and the people and the excitement, and the closest thing to escape was to cycle far beyond the Man and the Temple, to the perimeter of the site, which was marked by the trash fence. The fence was designed to catch litter blown from the city, but in fact there was barely anything alongside it but the odd cigarette butt that had been rolled across the playa by the wind. Its more important purpose was to mark the limit of the permitted zone. The Black Rock Desert on the other side might be public land for the rest of the year, but for the duration of Burning Man it was off-limits, and to be found there was a federal offence.

As well as a desire to safeguard Burning Man LLC's investment by preventing unpaid access, there was the question of safety. This wasn't San Francisco: despite its flatness, it was easy to lose your bearings on the playa, even to lose the city itself, and the dangers of dehydration and heatstroke were real. These were exacerbated, of course, when everyone was fucked up. We had to be watched like toddlers on a beach, stoned toddlers. Somewhere far out on the site, between the Man and the outer fence, I nearly cycled over a skeleton, a full-sized anatomical model half-immured in dust and adorned in pink boa, tutu and fur legwarmers. This was what would happen to those who strayed.

Bicycle was how you got around in Black Rock City. I would sit at our camp over breakfast and watch as, minute by minute, the flow of bikes crossing the adjacent crossroads grew denser, until it seemed impossible that there should not be a pile-up. And yet the intersecting flows continued smoothly as a military display. The bicycles were mostly second-hand or fifty-dollar models from Walmart and were as much a part of the scene as the mutant vehicles. It was sensible to lock your bike to prevent it from being misappropriated by someone who wanted to get somewhere and whose own bike had been misappropriated by someone else. My own, a lady's, was one of a lorry-load brought to the playa by Badger Bob and was garlanded with plastic flowers and holographic tape from a previous year's Burning Man. Three soft toy turtles were tethered to its basket and it was lit by a string of battery-powered fairy lights.

To reach the fence you had to cycle for twenty minutes or walk for twice that. On the way I passed three words four metres tall standing in a circle: BELIEVE, LOVE, DREAM; and a yellow rubber duck the size of a house; and a canvas chapel crowded with naked people in wedding veils. As I left the Man behind, the artworks and mutant vehicles became fewer and fewer, until there was just the playa and the occasional lone cyclist suddenly emerging from the dust. Sometimes the dust would close in, and your ambit of vision was reduced to a mere disc; there was nothing to see but the dust and yourself and the playa surface under your wheels, which was not featureless: it was cracked, tessellated; here and there were miniature crescent-shaped dunes, "playa serpents," raised only a few centimetres but enough to bog a bike to a standstill.

The fence was fifteen kilometres long and encircled the site in the shape of a pentagon. Outside each of the pentagon's corners was a Land Cruiser occupied by Bureau of Land Management agents or Black Rock Rangers. I would sometimes raise a hand to them, but they would never acknowledge me. The Black Rock Rangers had been established by Burning Man as a search-and-rescue body in the days before the containing fence and the scrutinised perimeter. Their role—the name alluded to the Texas Rangers, the old border guard—was to "ensure the collective survival of the community" and "address situations...that would otherwise require outside intervention." To that extent they were Black Rock City's police; but the police of Pershing County and wider Nevada were present, too, of course, as certainly were the FBI, even if they did not advertise their presence. You rarely saw a police uniform or vehicle, but you were warned never to accept drugs from a stranger, who might be an undercover cop, and along with your tin mug it was invariably necessary, even for those of us whose beards were turning white, to present ID when being served at a bar. La Mancha's had been stung, years before, when an undercover agent two months below the age limit had been handed a margarita. The police, having other priorities, failed to show up to the court hearing in Reno and the charge was dropped, but it had still cost the camp hundreds of dollars. It was part of my duties as barman to ID people. It felt incongruous, but this was not another planet; it was not even an island. On the first day a woman from a nearby camp was apprehended at the gate with the entire cohort's drugs for the week concealed in her car, thousands of dollars' worth of Ecstasy, LSD, GHB, ketamine and coke. The camp would suffer a straight week (a prospect as horrifying to them as scuba diving without an air cylinder); she, on the other hand, a trans woman, would be in prison for years.

The Black Rock Rangers were not operatives of the state, but they enjoyed the authority we granted them and, as a subdivision of the city's Playa Safety Council, took their duties seriously. They went around coupled in golf carts, and dressed like scouts, in khaki and beige adorned with badges, albeit they had more piercings than is common among scout leaders. There were those Burners who wished to disrupt the smooth running of the week, anarchist factions disapproving of Burning Man's increased orderliness and commercialisation. At each of the city's intersections, road-signs had been installed at the start of the week by the Department of Public Works. The DPW was the Burning Man institution responsible for building and dismantling the city's infrastructure and ensuring the playa was spotless afterwards. Within days the signs had been surreptitiously erased or painted over or removed altogether, as happened every year, so that by the end of the week it was often necessary to stop and ask where you were ("Black Rock fucking *City*, man!"), especially when the Man himself was no longer there to mark the centre. Those responsible for the vandalism were not admired (it was annoying), and were taking a risk given the DPW's reputation as meters-out of extrajudicial punishment, but their lawlessness was truer to Burning Man's founding spirit.

From the east came a mournful horn, a sound I had heard the morning before but had not identified—a freight train on the Union Pacific railroad three kilometres away. The playa's surface was cracked into irregular polygons, like the claypans of Australia, and as I looked out at the jigsawed surface beyond the fence, I was again reminded that in uniformity and repetition can be an intimation of the infinite. But then from the west, where the city lay, a snatch of idiot techno reached me, carried across the playa like a migrant bird blown off course. With it came a whiff of barbecue; a whiff of piss.

There was no real respite; only if you accepted the chaos could you forestall despair. Trying to keep the dust out of your tent, for instance, was futile to the point of madness. You could duct-tape the seams and lay down a protective sheet before zipping up each morning, but the dust was as invasive as water, as air. "It's so fine," Papa La Mancha assured me, "that it'll permeate the membrane of your lungs and enter your bloodstream. It'll seep from your palms for months. You'll see. It'll stay in your body forever." He was exaggerating, but weeks later, back in Arizona, it was still trickling from my ears like sand from a conch shell. The dust was part of Burning Man mythology; as much as the heat: the way it penetrated you and ruined your skin—"playa foot," "playa hand"—and caused your hair to stand on end and your nasal membranes to scab over and bleed. It was easy to forget what the dust was: the mountains crushed and washed down into this basin, winnowed by wind and water and laid down thousands of metres deep. This was what we were breathing. Again this feeling that the desert sought to assimilate those who entered it, to turn them from organic to mineral, as marine organisms are turned to limestone.

On the way into the site, I'd been pulled up by a Black Rock Ranger who, identifying me as a Burning Man virgin, instructed me to lie face-down on the playa and flap my arms to form a "playa angel" in the dust. I rose, spitting and caked in white, and looked at the shape I'd made: a drowning person, waving for help. A man in blue rubber chaps embraced me. "Welcome home, brother, welcome home."

I DIDN'T FEEL at home. For the first few nights I got barely any rest. The dust, but mainly the music. Earplugs would have been laughably pointless. But after a day or two I found I was able to sleep. It wasn't as simple as being exhausted, though I was exhausted; it was a kind of swooning, my mind rejecting consciousness. Stirring at 3 a.m. to the sound of a mutant vehicle beside my tent, blasting out some brutal variation of German house, I acknowledged its presence with a muttered "fuck you" before turning over in my sack of dust and returning to sleep. The mutant vehicles, along with the thousands of bicycles, were the only means of transport in the city. They spent most of the week trundling up and down Black Rock City's increasingly rutted streets and crossing the open playa between the Esplanade and the Man. The many wheeled boats—yachts and galleons, slavers— seemed especially at home on the former lakebed. The vehicles were remarkable by day but they were designed for the night-time, and then they were dazzling. There was a fifteen-metre-tall amphora, tilted on its side and pulsating with coloured lights. There were several dragons, fire-breathing. There was a giant polar bear, there was an electric-green Pac-Man, and a mechanical flaming octopus, and a flying carpet packed with people lounging on cushions. There was the set of gaping comedy teeth, three metres tall, zipping about with its glossy red lips and two drivers within, which seemed to follow me around the playa, appearing as I turned a corner or thundering past me in the night. All of the mutant vehicles played EDM at incredible volume and if there was room on board—as there usually was on the bigger boats—you just jumped on and off as you pleased.

To the west, the mountains were obscured by the dust rising from the city. I cycled slowly back towards the Man and came across a single black signpost with two lights attached: "I am 2.6 miles long and I rule the earth," it read. Two hundred and seventy-nine more of them had been positioned regularly in a straight line across the playa, and the line could be seen vanishing into the dust. "I am a ruler that shows the curvature of our planet. At my north-west end the curve of the earth has dropped away 1.42 metres."

IN THE SPIRIT of participation, I joined the Earth Guardians, who worked with the Burning Man organisation to minimise the environmental impact of the city with all its RVs and its waste and its fire. They weren't here to have fun. In the course of my duties I spent a day in the company of a woman who told me her playa name was Acumen. She was a veteran Black Rock Ranger with cropped golden hair and wrists weighed down with bangles. Our job was to drive around the city in a golf cart, following up on environmental infractions that had been recorded the previous day by another pair of Earth Guardians. In practice this meant crouching to examine oil or waste-water leaks from RVs and other vehicles.

We were not exactly unwelcome at the camps we visited—that would be unthinkable on the playa—but nor were we greeted with smiles when, following co-ordinates recorded on a GPS unit, we pulled up at a previously cited camp, with our clipboards and cameras, and began asking the dazed, stoned, half-dressed inhabitants who was in charge. Our hugs, exchanged without eye-contact, had all the mutual warmth of a policeman's handshake. Invariably the oil-drippers or grey-water leakers had done nothing to address the issue since they had been warned about it the previous day (had probably in fact quite forgotten) and so we could only tell them, with another hot hug, that if the problem had not been addressed when another pair of Earth Guardians returned tomorrow they would be cited for a second time, which would mean involving the Bureau of Land Management, which effectively meant the cops. As we trundled away over the playa, the people we had just hugged farewell would watch us go and Acumen would wave and holler, "We *love* you guys! Thank you *so* much!" and they in turn would raise a hand, but silently, and I would watch Acumen's face relax into unsmilingness.

It went on like that, from street to street, for the rest of the morning, until, shortly before noon, a dust storm hit, and after driving blind for a minute Acumen pulled to a halt, the GPS having gone haywire. We sat there in our goggles in the stifling whiteout. "We've not seen as many camps as we should have," she said, flicking through the documents on her clipboard. "If we don't follow up, they'll just go on infringing, and we don't want that, do we?" The dust cleared for a moment up ahead, and it was possible to see a giant set of comedy teeth trundling away, and two women wearing nothing but dragonfly wings walking hand in hand, and behind them a man in his sixties in Bermuda shorts and a Stetson, who I told myself might be Larry Harvey. "We're done," Acumen was saying, as the dust closed in once more. "If anyone asks, I'll blame you for slowing us down." I looked across at her in her goggles; she wasn't smiling.

I WOULD OFTEN cycle out to the Man at dawn to enjoy the sun and look at him standing on his platform, eighteen metres tall, the city's static centre. To enjoy the relative tranquillity, too. The Man was omphalos and landmark, *axis mundi*, colossus and idol, but his main purpose was to be destroyed. With his tapered limbs and inverted-triangle head he was a caveman's drawing. At night, outlined in green neon, he was reduced to a logo. And in two dimensions—in text messages and on Twitter—he was simply two brackets and an apostrophe:

)'(

The Man was stuffed with burlap soaked in wax. The night before he was due to be burnt, fireworks and explosives would be packed in. Guyed to the ground, the Man was guarded twenty-four hours a day by a detachment of Black Rock Rangers. A few years ago, on a Tuesday afternoon five days before the Man was due to be set alight, smoke was noticed coming from its base. The Man was put out by firefighters before he was destroyed, but still he had to be dismantled and taken down from his platform. The person responsible for setting the fire was a San Francisco playwright named Paul Addis, a long-time Burner unhappy about Burning Man's loss of spontaneity. "This was not an act of vengeance," he said, "it was one of love." Radical self-expression. The Man was rebuilt by the Black Rock Rangers and, five days later, burnt as scheduled. And yet the Man's temporary absence from the city's centre, I was told, had somehow sapped the participants' spirit, as if a cult's idol had been abducted. Addis, meanwhile, had been arrested by Pershing County police and would be charged with arson, destruction of property and reckless endangerment of human life, and sentenced to two years in prison. Three years after his release he killed himself.

In the early 1990s, when numbers were still in the low thousands, you were free to wander where you liked on the playa, and firearms were commonplace. There had been a "drive-by shooting range" where soft toys were lined up as targets. Cars were allowed and people had been mown down in their tents and horribly injured, and light aircraft had crash-landed (Black Rock City now had its own airstrip, overseen by the Federal Aviation Authority). As the city grew, year by year, the available liberties became fewer, but still today Harvey's ten principles are enforced, and the taboo against advertising and other commercial exploitation remains.

I sometimes reread the warning on my ticket: "Risk of serious injury or death." That was partly the point of coming, of course. But what was surprising, given the number of intoxicated young people, and the heat and the sun, and all the bodged-together scaffold towers and gantries, and the mutant vehicles spewing fire, was that, while there was an onsite hospital, there was not a morgue. As far as I knew, only one person had died this year, and he'd had a heart attack. In recent years there had been a scattering of deaths: someone had been killed disembarking from a mutant vehicle, someone had died after deliberately running into a fire, someone had been killed in a plane crash and someone had, somehow, hanged himself in his tent. For a city of more than seventy thousand, the crime rate, excluding drugs offences, was tiny, and violence almost unheard of. The only aggression I witnessed was on the penultimate night, the night the Man burnt, when it seemed like all the generosity and acceptance of the previous week was caused to evaporate.

. . .

AFTER THE OPENING Sunday I quickly lost track of the days. My notebook entries are not chronological but written randomly from the back or the front or the middle, upside down and sideways. I don't always recognise the hand as mine, and often what I have written is illegible or just nonsense. It might, then, have been the next day or the one after, or later, when, sitting in a camp chair spritzing a water-mister into my face, I saw a low cloud carouselling slowly across the playa a kilometre away.

It resolved into two finer threads, whirlwinds, dust devils, willy-willies, which appeared to circle one another, like two figures dancing or fencing. It was a desert phenomenon I had seen before, these min-iature updraughts, but nowhere else had the contrast with the hori-zontal been so extreme. According to Mildred Cable, the Gobi dust devils invariably came like this, in couples, the "male" partner spin-ning clockwise, the "female" anticlockwise. Naturally they were to be understood as *kwei*, demons. "The best for the demon," Cable was told, "is when a living human will let himself be possessed." I stood up and watched them and then found my bike and cycled towards the open playa. One—I couldn't say if it was male or female—had stretched by the time I reached the Esplanade, like clay drawn thin on a potter's wheel, sucking up more dust, and it was now two hundred metres tall, gyrating with what seemed to me a joyous plasticity, and I began to hear *woah*s and *fuck*s as I passed others who'd spotted it. Once I was out of the built city and on the open playa I accelerated, heading towards the larger dust devil as quickly as I could, only to see it wash across the trash fence and out beyond the site, where, deprived of the dust thrown up within the city, it dissolved. Its smaller counterpart was moving more slowly, and I found I could catch up with it and cycle after it at a leisurely pace. But while it was possible to stalk it from a distance of ten metres or so, if you got much closer it became faint against the sky, and if you stood directly under it, in its tail, only a shapeshifting smoke-ring was visible when you looked up, a ghost flourish, and on the ground the faintest of shadows.

Far from anywhere, a three-metre square of playa had been cor-doned off with orange tape, and within this sector three people were on their hands and knees, hatless in the afternoon blaze, scrupulously sweeping up dust with dustpan and brush and tipping the dust into a sack. That it was pointless was the point. When full, the sack of dust was carried a few metres and emptied onto the playa and spread about with a rake. Once this was done, the stakes and cordon marking the swept sector were removed and the three sweepers walked some distance until they apparently agreed on a new location, then re-established the cordon and resumed their work. I was the only spectator, but when I walked away, I looked back and saw that they were still at it. Somewhere, I'd been told, there was a playa-dust vending machine. You were constantly being asked, excitedly, had you seen this or that grand absurdity—the Buddhist stupa, the caviar emporium, the *other* La Mancha's camp, "the guy with two pricks" (him again)—and invariably you hadn't; and the effect was that the already bewildering multiplicity of your own daily experience was infinitely magnified, so that the city began to feel like a place where not only anything could happen, but where everything was happening, and indeed *must* happen.

I spent what seemed like hours following the dust devil—time was harder to keep track of—as it guided me from one side of the city to another, seeming to wait until I caught up again and finally leading me to a beautiful vehicle formed of taut white sails, from whose deck a naked man was lobbing something from a box to a cheering crowd— ice lollies! Cast, it turned out, from a dildo; but no, actually, not a dildo! someone said, the man's own member. "You!" the man called, pointing at me. "You want it! I can tell you want it!" and he arced one into the air and it landed in the dust by my front wheel. A beautiful black woman in a tricorn, Spirit of Fornication, picked it up, licked the dust from it, and handed it to me. "I'm sorry," she said, with a grave little bow, "the head snapped off." It was okay. It was delicious. I rode on, leaving the group of men and women, and a child in his mother's arms, all happily licking their lollies, and out past the man—the Man—and when I had finished my cock-lolly and was wondering where to put the stick, I looked ahead and there was the Temple.

IF THE *AXIS MUNDI* was the Man, its counterpoint at the city's margin was the Temple. The innermost point of the horseshoe-shaped

Esplanade—at "six o'clock"—is known as the keyhole, a symbolic threshold between the city and the playa. From it a straight promenade flanked with ornate lampposts leads to the Man on his platform eight hundred metres away. Follow that line past the Man and you'll reach the Temple site eventually. Beyond the Temple is an expanse of nothing, then the outer fence, then the world.

The Temple was emerging from the dust. This year it was a spiral tunnel, a curling lobster-pot more than sixty metres long and perhaps twenty tall at its entrance, narrowing as you moved from the mouth towards the tail. It resembled an architect's simplified computer model. Hundreds of people could be passing through it at any one time. A certain emotional etiquette was observed: the mutant vehicles kept away, there was no pounding trance music and less nudity. It was ringed by the parked bicycles of those inside. From a distance it was a delicate filigree against the monumentality of the desert. But when you got close it was simple, even crude, like the ribcage of some leviathan dug from the bed of old Lake Lahontan. The arching ribs, laddered together with timber struts, grew narrower as you went deeper. Once you entered, it was too crowded to back out.

The first temple (the design changed each year) had been built in 2000, just another of that year's hundreds of Burning Man artworks. During the course of its construction, one of the builders, a thirty-three-year-old named Michael Hefflin, was killed in a motorcycle accident. The remaining builders, shocked and grieving, decided to continue. The temple when it was completed was dedicated to their friend, and a shrine to his memory was placed within. Those who entered were encouraged to leave messages and tributes, to Hefflin or whomever they chose. The following year the Temple was given its official site by the Burning Man organisers, and along with the Man and the Esplanade and the keyhole and the trash fence, it became part of Black Rock City's cosmology. There was little music here, just some chanting; inside, there was conversation, hushed, and there was intermittent weeping. The occasional louder cry.

"Put your right hand out, that's the person who committed suicide, alone and agonised. Put your left hand close to you. That's the child who died of leukaemia, surrounded by love and support. Now, move

the two hands together and lift them. In this way, those who died amid
love will help liberate those who died in anguish." This was David
Best, the artist who oversaw the Temple's construction each year. The
atmosphere was funereal, and the crowd's pace was that of a military
cortege. There was something about it too of the meat-grinder. The
deeper you went into the Temple's throat and the thickening crowd,
the harder it became not to weep, though to have done so, I felt, would
have been to throw myself off a precipice. You processed into the narrowing tunnel, the weeping becoming louder, the wooden ribs dense
with scrawled messages and artefacts of sorrow and remembrance and
regret pinned and tied on, ribbons and prayer flags flapping in the
wind, photos of the dead, letters to the dead; the toddler dead in a lake,
the lover dead on the highway, the sister who killed herself and the
fiancé shot by police; the beloved cat or dog. Fuck you, cancer, I will
defeat you. Fuck you to my stepmother. Fuck you for raping your son.
Please free my sister from drugs.

Bring your scorn, test it as the tunnel constricts and the weeping
young people lie shuddering on the ground around you. And then be
released into the dazzling whiteness, where you will find a two-metre-
tall teddy bear, who will take you in his arms.

THE EXPLORER JULES REMY, travelling in the Great Basin in 1855,
describes the malady that overcomes one of his party, a former sailor
named George: "It seemed," he writes, "as though the desert had para-
lysed him. He was incapable of thought." Poor George. When I was
ailing—*recrudescent accidie*, let's call it—Brocket took me to a tent a few
streets out from the Gayborhood, where two industrial fans blew ice-
cold vapour onto you as you danced. I stayed there, a foot from one
of the fans, performing a side-to-side camel-shuffle, sucking on the
catheter of my CamelBak, eyes closed into the freezing white, until
I could not feel my face. Then a tap on the shoulder and we were off;
off ice-headed to the next block, where a white ball twenty metres in
diameter bobbed, grounded against its tethers.

It was called the Moon. There was a queue; many of the queuers
were dressed as dogs. To enter, you had to crawl through a hole at

ground level, following someone's tail. And then, when you were inside, it was a new kind of nowhere, the intense sunlight diffused by the walls of the ball, which was really more of a balloon, kept inflated with industrial fans, its underside flat against the ground. The pressure was heightened, you could feel it in your ears. There were dozens of people here, most of them sitting around the edge of the circle, against the wall of the sphere or near-sphere, but some gathered in the centre, playing bongos and singing, enjoying the peculiar abrupt echo that was experienced at that particular point. There were three of them, the bongos-player and another man and a woman, skinny and tanned and dreadlocked, and the woman was leading, improvising a song about Burning Man, about Burners and our beauty, and the beauty of dust, which was the dust of life, life that was only dust, which was beautiful, and the crowd gathered around the edge of the sphere began to clap along, enjoying the blunted acoustic, and the guy with the bongos walked around and handed them to someone, who took over the playing, and then passed them on to someone else, who continued. It didn't matter if they were any good. Brocket, dressed as an orange, pranced around the singer for a while and then lay down on his back beside her, with his head close to her, and began to harmonise, harmonise so sweetly, beginning quietly, carefully, then descending to the lowest of baritones, not singing anything in particular, just articulating sounds, moving the notes around in his mouth and his throat and chest, *ah* and *ooh*, apparently without taking a single breath, relishing the resonance, the volume of his accompaniment growing until his voice, with a laugh, overwhelmed that of the woman (who was delighted), and seemed to fill up the entire vessel, this swooning, swimming plainsong that was at once foghorn and soprano's cry out *into* the fog, and those of us gathered around joined in, not only clapping but singing with him, and some of us danced in couples, with a certain courtly formality, in the space between the walls and the musicians, and it seemed to go on for hours, this languid singing and dancing, for hours as more people slipped in through that narrow diaphragm, and the brightness inside seemed to intensify.

· · ·

I MET AMY at the Earth Guardians camp on the fifth morning. She was from Portland: arch, gently mocking, and it seemed to me glowing with the wellbeing that comes from being constantly loved. Bathing in the hot springs on the edge of the playa had once been part of Burning Man, in the days before the fence; but no longer. Amy and I were being deployed by the Earth Guardians ostensibly to guard these sensitive environments against any Burners who either found them on the way to or from Black Rock City, or somehow escaped during the course of the week. Not that any of these eventualities seemed likely when the spot was many kilometres from the nearest sealed road and even further from the external fence, meaning that in order to reach it any Burner would have to cross not only twenty-five kilometres of shadeless playa, but somehow evade the authorities who were sentried in their Land Cruisers along the perimeter.

A Black Rock Ranger drove us beyond the trash fence across the playa, accelerating until her minivan would go no faster. As we left the city behind at 150 kilometres per hour, you could gain a sense of the vastness of its setting, this monstrous basin filled four thousand metres deep with compacted gravel and dust. The city seemed enormous when you were within it, seemed everything, but it was nothing. We had driven for just ten minutes and Burning Man and its seventy thousand souls were gone; you could come here from the north and never know the event was happening. The playa, just a couple of kilometres away from the trash fence, was oblivious.

The sign in the store in Gerlach had read: WELCOME TO NOWHERE. Imagine the late 1840s, when Gerlach was nothing but a military outpost below towering grey mountains. What must those migrants from the fertile east have made of the playa when they came to it, knowing that it was not endless but with little conception, surely, of what hardship it held? Nothing in their experience, even the deserts they had already crossed, could have prepared them for it. Flatness they knew—they had crossed the Great Plains; but this pallor, this absence of everything *but* pallor? A different order of denudation.

Black Rock Point is a 180-metre-high prominence that marks the southernmost point of a mountain range that cuts into the playa about twenty-five kilometres north-east of the Burning Man site. As we approached it, the surface of the playa became bumpier, and we joined a track that coasted between grey-brown *nebkha* mounds of the kind I had seen in Arabia and the Taklamakan: metre-high hummocks crowned with clumps of iodine bush. The first vegetation we'd seen for nearly a week. Beyond the hummocks, where the ground was sandier, were bushes of greasewood turning yellow with the approach of autumn and salt-grass as rigid as broom-bristles. There were intermittent bursts of yellow-flowering balsamroot. Flowers! And all of this colour and abundance because of the mineral water venting from the fault that ran along the Black Rock Range. The mountains showed the violence of their origins, but this feeling of violence was eased at the playa's edge by the water and greenery. We saw our driver off, and as the noise of her vehicle vanished into the playa's silence, the plume of dust it had sent up was slowly pushed away, until the view to the south and west was clear again, except for the mighty updraught of dust from Black Rock City. The quiet. Just the wind, and when it dropped, our breathing.

The pool fed by the spring was about seven metres across at its widest point, rush-fringed and kidney-shaped, the steaming water surfacing from the volcanic depths at one lobe and growing cooler towards the other. What wasn't clear was whether we too, as the site's supposed guardians, were expected to refrain from entering the clear warm water, having spent five days in the dust and heat with nothing to clean ourselves with but baby-wipes.

Once I met Amy I came to regard the trip as payment for the hours I'd spent in the golf cart with Acumen. We decided to climb Black Rock Point. The Black Rock Desert is sometimes described as Y-shaped, but on maps it looks more like a forked flame. Black Rock Point is the tip of the range that separates its two arms. The climb was perilous; black scree tumbling behind us with every step, every handhold crumbling. Amy strode ahead as if she were climbing a flight of stairs. From 180 metres up we looked out at the playa's western arm stretching thirty kilometres north. The alkali dust from the past five days had dried my hands and feet to husks and clogged my nose. My body reeking under its stale clothes was as pale and crazed as the playa. My beard had grown an uneven canopy of white wires. Never before had my beard grown white. I had been there for less than a week. We found a clutch of casings from a service-issue Smith & Wesson; a memorial scribed in iron and messily cemented into the rock; and small offerings to the dead woman—coloured stones, bullets, dimes, a shard of obsidian. We were not the first to come here, even if we felt a pioneer frisson.

The view seemed to rear up at you. The playa was of polar vastness, scattered with cloud shadows; and of polar whiteness, save for an ingress of dirty green at the mountain's foot, where the spring watered the desert. The air was clear. One kilometre might be twenty. Clear, but for one section, mid-playa, twenty-five kilometres to the south. A tract about three kilometres across was in cloud; but it was not cloud, of course, or smoke, but the upcast dust of Black Rock City. It towered in a tendrilled column a kilometre tall—way above the mountaintops, way above the clouds that sat over the mountains. I thought of the dust storms of Hotan and the Aral Sea, the atomic clouds of Maralinga, and felt the guilt of one who has fled his homeland before its fall. Black Rock City was under siege by the wind, but it was the city itself, with its massed movement, that had unleashed the dust. Black Rock City, the most ironic place on earth.

I had begun to feel, before escaping that morning, that the place was intolerable—or at least that I could tolerate it no longer—and now that I had my freedom, temporarily, the thought of being deported back there was painful. The dust and the constant EDM. The crazed frat-boys, the unrelenting Californian shrieks of "Oh my God!"—a phrase that brooked such a variety of inflections that there was seemingly no circumstance to which it was not the perfect response. Hakim Bey had described the "TAZ" as "a guerrilla operation which liberates an area"; but the desert was already liberated, and there was a sense in which Burning Man deprived it of that liberty.

"I know where I'd rather be," said Amy. Among the dust, she told me, were the tiny eggs of fairy shrimp, which with each flood would hatch and fill the shallow waters with swarming larvae. "Sea monkeys." We were also breathing shrimp eggs, then. For this expedition, where crampons would not have been inappropriate, she was wearing flat-soled plimsolls and harem pants. She found me absurd, naturally. Desert boots. Oh my God. We were getting cold. It was time to go back down; down to the heat. She clambered ahead of me. I watched her

edge down the scree facets and along the ridges of the black *bajadas* and onto the green rim of the playa, where we had set up a sail of cloth as a shade among the *nebkha* mounds. When I reached our small base, she was sitting on the wiry grass beside the wrecked chassis of a nineteenth-century sheep-herder's cart, gnawing on a strip of beef jerky. "I know," she said. "I'm an animal." I looked to the south and the terrible cloud rising from the city.

. . .

IN JUNE 1846 an exploratory party from Oregon, seeking a less hazardous alternative to the established Oregon Trail from Missouri to north-west Oregon, reached the Black Rock Desert. Lindsay Applegate, one of the two brothers leading the expedition, echoed Frémont: the country "had a very forbidding appearance." The party continued south-east to Black Rock Point and eventually discovered a chain of waterholes that connected to the California Trail, establishing a new, shorter route to Oregon. For those migrants travelling to California's Sacramento Valley three years later, however, the route represented

not a shortcut but a three-hundred-kilometre extension to their journey. What prompted so many to take it is unclear, but presumably once
one wagon had turned off many others simply followed. Nose to tail is
how we enter oblivion.

In April 1849, hundreds of wagons bound for California from the
eastern seaboard veered north from the California Trail and followed
the Applegate cut-off towards the Black Rock Desert. The testimony
that exists makes pitiful reading. The party of Alonzo Delano, a dry-
goods merchant from Illinois, had misgivings about the detour, but
"it was decided finally we would go the northern route." They would
regret the decision. "Beyond us, far as we could see, was a barren waste,
without a blade of grass or a drop of water for thirty miles at least.
Instead of avoiding the desert . . . we were in fact on a more dreary and
wider waste." They left the vegetated rim of the playa, and set upon
its cracked surface. "I encountered a great many animals, perishing for
want of food and water, on the desert plain. Some would be gasping for
breath, others unable to stand would issue low moans as I came up, in
a most distressing manner, showing intense agony . . ." A drawing by
one J. Goldsborough Bruff shows the scene his party encountered at
a dry waterhole on the desert's edge in September that year: dozens
of dead and dying cattle; a sky full of "TV's" and, floating above the
mountains, the words "Darkness and harsh mts."

A few miles from Black Rock Spring, Delano came upon a wagon.
Inside was a young woman and a child, both weeping. "Where is your
husband?" he asked. "He has gone on with the cattle," the woman
replied, "and to try to get us some water, but I think we shall die before
he comes back. It seems as if I could not endure it much longer." Giving the pair his remaining water—"'God bless you,' said she, grasping the flask eagerly"—Delano led them north, and the party reached
the springs the following morning, though most of the grass had been
grazed to the root. He climbed to the top of Black Rock Point to gain
his bearings and then descended to bathe in the springs. One James
Bardin, crossing the desert in 1855, warned that the springs were "hot
enough to scald a boy"; Israel Foote Hale, six years earlier, came upon
"an ox that had been scalded to death, his hind part was in the spring
and his forepart on the bank." But Delano "with many others, availed

myself of the opportunity to take a thorough renovation, which we found exceedingly refreshing."

Amy and I stripped and knelt on the small jetty that extended into the water furthest from the vent and dipped our fingers, and then our toes. It was bathwater hot. Slipping off the jetty, we wallowed on our arses, the water up to our necks, sulphuric bubbles siphoning from the disturbed sediment. We were doing no more damage than a pair of hogs. A breeze tousled the rushes and a raven wheeled into the frame and hung above us for a few slow wing-beats, turning its head to eye the creatures lounging below. Mr. W. Hog. Mrs. A. Hog. Mark Twain was right: "nothing helps scenery like ham and eggs." Amy stood up and the bird flew off. I listened for the sound of the city, but all I could hear was the wind in the rushes.

BACK AT BLACK ROCK CITY she said, "You stink of eggs." She had promised to take acid with her campmates that evening. We didn't make plans to meet again, though perhaps we would. By now the air was clear and the sunset over the Calico Mountains was glorious, but on this penultimate day there was a sense everywhere of aftermath: the wind storm we had seen from Black Rock Point had left many of the camps in a state of partial ruin; it was as if the city had been sacked. The contents of my tent, once I got the dust-jammed zip to unzip, lay under a Vesuvian layer of dust, and many of the toggles that secured the communal shade structure had been torn off. I found my campmates slumped silently in a circle of camp chairs in the cabaret tent. They were dazed and covered in dust and they looked at me, without much recognition, from eyes ringed with goggle-marks. "Welcome to the we-don't-want-to-party party," said Brocket. The storm had been horrible. I was scrubbed and pink, and relaxed for the first time in days. Years, it felt like. I had abandoned them during the great battle, and I was glad. From all around, as the sun dipped below the rim of the Calico Mountains, there was a massed howling. It happened every evening at sunset, but tonight it was louder, and it came from far and near. We joined in, first Brocket then all of us, tipping our heads and baying to the sky.

The Man was due to burn at seven. A ring had been established around him containing firefighters and hundreds of fire-jugglers, -breathers and -eaters. The Fire Conclave—among them somewhere was Beaker. As the hour approached, we were no longer Burners but an ordinary civic crowd at a fireworks show or carnival, with all the usual impatience and defensiveness and jostling for position. There was a protocol, it seemed: you were to sit down, so that those behind you could see, even if that meant you could not. Anyone who contravened this was yelled at—"Sit the fuck down, man!"—and this person, the particular one in front of us, aggrieved and exhausted, bellowed back in return, "Dude, *fuck* you!" and the first guy rushed him and there was pushing, and an exchange of doggy-punches.

The Man's arms were winched into the air and the flames took hold, and a crescendo of fireworks emerged from all around him. As the fireworks reached the apex of their intensity two vast explosions engulfed the figure in a hideous plume of flame and his arms dropped to his sides, vanquished. For twenty minutes he remained standing, headless, as he burnt, supported by a steel armature. By the time it all finally gave way, and what remained of the figure came crashing down, the crowd was dispersing.

THE FOLLOWING MORNING the playa was scattered with hundreds of abandoned bicycles. The air reeked of smoke. Where the man had burnt was a smouldering pit of ashes. But that night something of the week's earlier mood returned, a sort of tenderness. By now much of the city had been dismantled. Abandoned by the Man, it was easy to lose your bearings. It was Burning Man's ephemerality that was so remarkable: that it re-formed itself, Brigadoon-like, each year, essentially the same city, and that the playa itself, the ground where the city stood, would be swept clean, and where people had been dancing and laughing and falling in love there would soon be no one and no human things, and the chief point of navigation for those crossing it would not be the Man but, as it had been for the pioneers and the Paiute tribes before them, once again that dark mound of weathered andesite. Black Rock Point had once been the place where your party regrouped, where you met others preparing for the next stage, to California or Oregon; above all, it had been a place of dependable water. It occurred to me how unimaginable to Delano would be the vast voluntary encampment deep in the desert that had caused him such anguish. We do not often hear the stories of those humans who died, some nine hundred bound for California alone; in their suffering, the animals—"gasping for breath," "unable to stand"—must be their proxies. Was it us, Amy and Brocket and Hawthorn and me, for whom Delano and the other pioneers had opened up the desert—to allow his descendants, 150 years later, to abide in the "perfect barren" without risking death; and not only to survive in it, but to play dildo ring-toss and eat *lobster* in it? It looked like a blank, the playa, but it had a history just like anywhere else. Lives had been terribly changed by it; the Black Rock Desert had lodged in the memories of thousands of people as their worst place, a sort of death in life. And yet here we were, in all our frivolity, and it was glorious. This was how America had learned to love the desert—by vanquishing it: squandering its aquifers, exhausting its minerals, destroying its silences; by eating ham and eggs in it.

AROUND THE TEMPLE the following night, as we waited for its destruction, there was again the prohibited ring, again the firefighters in their quilted suits, the tens of thousands of us watching. But there was a subdued quality to the crowd tonight, and the only music was from someone who had taken it upon himself to blow "Amazing Grace" into some bagpipes. A whiff of incense. A procession of torch-bearers approached the Temple. When the first flames had become visible around the Man there was cheering and whooping, but this evening the main sound was the flames.

The tail of the giant spiral was lit first. As the fire took hold, and the flames began to climb the walls of the Temple, you could hear weeping, and someone far away shouted, "I love you, Dad" and someone closer shouted, "Oh *God*, Christine!" and another voice simply repeated, "Love you, love you, love you"—and then, from nearby, a thundering Californian snarl: "Burning-Man-two-thousand-fifteen-make-some-fucking-*noise*!" Nobody made any, apart from some stifled laughter that was almost pitying, and someone who recited, or read, those words of Beckett's about failing better. I thought of all those written messages of love and grief. *One year ago today my mother took her own life. Fuck cancer. Andrew, what happened to you? Travel safely, dear brother.*

Then the only sounds were the intensifying roar of the flames, which had engulfed the whole structure, and the regular stark cracks as timbers snapped; then a muffled *whoomph* and the towering arch of the Temple toppled forward, throwing out a ten-storey wave of heat and sparks. I gazed up at thousands of glowing embers falling amid the stars. *Holy shit, holy shit,* uttered from all around as the inferno's heart glowed red. Dust and smoke were indistinguishable from one another. *Holy shit, holy shit.* Within the inferno a tornado of fire developed, complement to the dust devils that had slinked across the playa. The firefighters were silhouettes, hurrying back and forth. The heat continued to intensify. I looked behind me and scanned the thousands of lit faces—dusty, burnt and weary—and saw that they seemed at peace, and that many of them, like my own, were wet-eyed.

IN SUDAN the Sahara is sometimes called *Bahr bela ma*, "sea without water." Charles Sturt had seen Australia's Stony Desert as a "sandy sea" even while he maintained his belief in the existence of a real sea at the centre of the continent. For Bertram Thomas the Rub' al-Khali was a "troubled sea"; Aurel Stein's Taklamakan was a "choppy sea, with its waves petrified in wild confusion" . . . But looking out with Amy on the great lolloping heaving beast that was the Pacific Ocean, after the exquisite stillness of the Black Rock Desert, I thought the equation forlorn. What made the sea so *awesome*—in the Oxford as well as the Californian sense—was not its vastness or its openness, nor even its depth, but the global energy invoked by its *movement*. It was alive.

We were spending a week on the California coast south of San Francisco, after driving over the Sierra Nevada from Reno. She was still in the harem pants she'd had on when we met. Her hands were coarse as wood. Standing in the garden of a hilltop monastery, slightly nauseated by the smell of flowers, we listened to plainsong coming from the chapel, while far below humpback whales burst their blowhole vapour out of the dark sea. I thought of Lake Lahontan and the Aralkum, and envisaged the Pacific seabed dried out, with distant mobs of camels milling among the hulks of trawlers and the ribcages of whales.

Have mercy on me a sinner, went the monks.

Amy went "Ha!"

We ate colourful thirty-dollar salads at a cliff-edge restaurant then sprinted, drunk on margaritas, into Big Sur's breakers, spluttering, euphoric. There were gulls everywhere, screaming; gulls and butter-flies and dragonflies swarming; and every shrub you brushed against on the way down to the beach threw out a new scent. My skin revived, regained its elasticity; my nostrils lost their lining of dried blood. It was a return to life. Amy began to seem like a genius to me, in her articulation. Thirst and fire can both be quenched.

One evening, sitting on the edge of a motel pool in Carmel, she told me a story, or a parable. "An anthropologist once asked a Hopi Indian why so many of his people's songs were about water," she said. In one hand, as she spoke, she was holding a lemon I'd picked, all rind, big as a grapefruit and hard as a nut. She continued: "'Simple,' says the Indian, 'because water is so scarce ... And why,' he asks the anthropolo-gist, 'are so many of yours about love?'"

A parable it was. I slipped into the water, where we seemed to live, and though I did not say it, I felt that my happiest memories were associated with water.

Within a few days of moving back to Arizona, back to the arid zone, my hands dried out again, like the spent seedcases of some desert plant; they were coarse enough to snag on cotton.

In my casita, the shadows of hummingbirds flitted across the blinds.

The cicadas clicked in the old mesquite tree.

Yellow tomatoes were rotting on the vine.

I kept finding small black lizards in the shower.

On the blank pages at the end of books I scratched away with my pencil. Scratch scratch scratch.

Out in the desert people were still dying.

. . .

GOAT-ISH, QUIXOTE-ISH Jim Corbett believed that the principles of justice, community and sanctuary he espoused in his work with refugees ought to be extended to the nonhuman. The obligation to provide sanctuary, he believed, "extends far beyond Central America and specific human refugees to the need for harmonious community among all that lives." It was a philosophy inspired in part by Aldo Leopold, who in his essay "The Land Ethic" (1949) observed that "there is as yet no ethic dealing with man's relation to the land and to the animals and plants which grow upon it...the land ethic changes the role of *Homo sapiens* from conqueror of the land community to plain member and citizen of it." In Corbett's words, it was about "learning to live by fitting into an ecological niche rather than by fitting into a dominance–submission hierarchy." In 1988 he founded the Saguaro–Juniper Corporation. At the heart of the Saguaro–Juniper philosophy was a "covenant" to hallow the earth, a bill of rights for the environment:

1. The land has a right to be free of human activity that accelerates erosion.
2. Native plants and animals on the land have a right to life with a minimum of human disturbance.
3. The land has a right to evolve its own character from its own elements without scarring from construction or the importation of foreign objects dominating the scene.
4. The land has a pre-eminent right to the preservation of its unique and rare constituents and features.
5. The land, its water, rocks and minerals, its plants and animals, and their fruits and harvest have a right never to be rented, sold, extracted, or exported as mere commodities.

In 1995, it seemed likely that an area close to Corbett's home in Cascabel, sixty kilometres east of Tucson, would be bought by a right-wing militia for automatic-weapons training. Nothing could be more offensive to Corbett. He and others in the community collectively bought up the 180 hectares of rocky desert around Hot Springs Canyon, and founded the Cascabel Hermitage Association.

The strawbale cabin where I went to live after returning to Arizona was built by the association at a location selected by Corbett. There is something about the scenario that reminds me of that other desert pioneer, Brigham Young of the Mormons, arriving in Utah; the prophet striking his staff on the anointed ground: *This is the place!* But Corbett the Quaker was no guru. He had not exactly led, though he had been followed. "To learn why you feel compelled to remake and consume the world," he wrote, "live alone in the wilderness for at least a week. Take no books or other distractions. Take simple, adequate food that requires little or no preparation. Don't plan things to do when the week is over. Don't do yoga or meditation that you think will result in self-improvement. Simply do nothing."

THE SAN PEDRO VALLEY lies in what is known by biologists as the Arizona Upland subdivision, the coolest and wettest part of the Sonoran Desert, an ecosystem dominated by low, green-trunked paloverde trees and saguaro cactus. Saguaros, the pleated, multi-armed cacti of Westerns, grow only in Arizona. The oldest, which might have been growing for two centuries, reach heights of fifteen metres or more. The San Pedro is one of southern Arizona's few "perpetual" rivers, alive where its twin, the Santa Cruz, is largely dead, and flowing for most of the year along its whole course. On the banks, when I passed through Cascabel, asters and sunflowers were blooming in the shade of Fremont cottonwoods. In a shady bosque beside the river I met Daniel, who looked after the hermitage and those who stayed there. He'd studied at a seminary in Chicago and run his own business before moving to Cascabel in 1994. Since then he had mostly lived in a tent on the few hectares he owned in Hot Springs Canyon. He was a model of sanguinity, with a white, untrimmed stubble. He possessed a sort of wayward quietness that was neither guarded nor shy nor remotely aloof. It seemed he was simply allowing me to tell him, by my actions and my words, what sort of person I was, and how he might help me, yet I didn't feel it would be possible to disappoint him. It was the quietness of a person who has spent long periods alone in the wilderness (longer than I ever had); but he wasn't a mystic manqué. He would have hated Burning Man, but he was not (I felt) fearful of the world; he didn't dislike society or humankind, even if he enjoyed the desert more than the city. He was not your dried-out desert rat.

The dry washes east of the river were margined with yellow ragweed. All along the ridges saguaros were lined, arms raised heavenward, watchful. Beside the track as we drove to the hermitage were coils of violet scat, showing that the coyotes' diet extended to the fruit of the low-lying prickly-pear cactus, which was starting to ripen purpley along the ridges. Daniel halted to point out what he thought was a mountain lion's print in the sand alongside the track, a different kind of "cutting sign." When we reached the cabin after forty minutes of driving along dry washes and tracks all but demolished by recent floods, a roadrunner was perched on the roof's ridge like an ornament. It fled as we neared, and I didn't see it again. A few steps from the door was a four-armed saguaro six metres tall. Beside it grew a metre-high paloverde, the saguaro's "nurse tree," whose shade the juvenile cactus depended on. Fifty years later, the saguaro was the biggest living thing for miles. My instinct sometimes was to hug it, never mind the spines. The mesquite nearby attracted bees in such numbers in the late afternoon that at first I thought a swarm had gathered there. Behind the cabin was a mature ocotillo, like a quiver of javelins pointing skyward; sometimes a small dull shrike would sit for a few minutes on the tip of one of these spikes, and sing to me.

Inside the cabin when I arrived, in a corner behind a rolled-up sleeping mat, a nest had been made of carpet fibres, and beside it were two adult mice and, clinging to its mother's rump as she moved away, a baby. Once I'd waved Daniel off, I swept the nest into a dustpan and dumped it outside at the base of the paloverde, and then spent half an hour with the broom shepherding the mice, and two geckoes, out of the door. The baby hid under the cabinet, and I tried to coax it out with the handle of the broom. It was reluctant; I prodded it gently. It stopped moving. So much for the Saguaro–Juniper covenant. Extracting the small body, I realised I had not killed it, not quite: its eyes were open, and I could see its heart beating under its skin. I took it by the tail-tip and laid it outside in the shadow of a rock, either to revive or to be food for something. When I returned, it was still there, still breathing, its useless legs paddling. Still I couldn't do what I ought to have done—crushed its head under my heel or under a rock. That evening it seemed like the mouse's small heart was the engine of all the desert's noise.

Because the desert was not silent. The ridges were richly vegetated and as in every desert, there was wind. In other words the noise was partly the wind acting on the plants, soughing the leaves of the paloverde; shivering the creosote bushes; flowing, hour after hour, over the concertina ribs of the saguaro. The roof of the cabin was sloping tin and resounded like a drum under the movement of the mice and lizards and whatever else was up there. This was the daytime noise; but it was at night, when the desert cooled, that the animal cacophony began. Aside from the mice and lizards tumbling about in the roof, the principal source was the cicada, the thrumming millions of them within hearing range, cranking up as the night deepened, as if compensating with noise for the absent light. Over the cicadas was the intermittent bickering of coyotes from their den in an arroyo a kilometre away; the occasional fox-yowl. And then there were the other sounds, sounds of the semiconscious hours whose provenance it was hard to guess, but which might be, on the one hand, something being eaten alive or, on the other, something relishing its kill. After the first few days I ceased to find anything threatening in these sounds.

I'D DISREGARDED Jim Corbett's advice about bringing books to the desert. In the second-hand bookstore on Fourth Avenue in Tucson—a place where I spent a lot of time—I'd chanced upon a paperback of John C. Van Dyke's 1901 *The Desert*, perhaps the most influential book ever written about arid America. Born to privilege among the lawns of New Brunswick, New Jersey, Van Dyke went on to become chief librarian at the seminary school there, as well as professor of art history at Rutgers College, and among the best-known American art historians of the era.

The journey recorded in *The Desert* began at his brother's ranch in the Mojave, where he had gone in the hope of recovering from a "respiratory disorder" in the dry air. A desire for solitude, for the exclusion of mankind from the desert, extended to his writing: "Heaven knows the literature of humanity is large enough without dragging it into such sublime isolations as the desert." We meet scarcely a single breathing human in all his book's pages: his was an imagined desert, a *desert* in its original sense: not merely unpeopled, but pre-human, post-human. Himself he presents as that rare species, the aesthete-frontiersman, as handy with the rifle as with the pen; notebook in one pocket, hunting knife in the other.

It was not only the clarity of the desert air that made it remarkable. Van Dyke believed "the air itself is coloured," and looking at the Rincon Mountains at dawn I could see what he meant. "It would seem as though the rising heat took up with it countless small dust-particles and that these were responsible for the rosy or golden quality of the air-colouring." Here is what he says about the painter Turner in a letter to a friend: "He carried his nature in his imagination, and he painted his pictures out of his head . . . His landscapes have no existence in nature." There was something of Turner in Van Dyke's own approach: air and light themselves as subjects. *The Desert*'s highlights, small masterpieces of Romantic description, are consecutive chapters entitled "Light, Air and Color," "Desert Sky and Clouds" and "Illusions." For Van Dyke those ephemerals are the desert's foremost attributes. The desert, he writes, is "the most decorative landscape in the world, a landscape all colour, a dream landscape."

> I have seen at sunset, looking north from Sonora some twenty miles, the whole tower-like shaft of Baboquivari change from blue to topaz and from topaz to glowing red in the course of half an hour. I do not mean edgings or rims or spots of these colours upon the peak, but the whole upper half of the mountain completely changed by them. The red colour gave the peak the appearance of hot iron, and when it finally died out the dark hue that came after was like that of a clouded garnet.

The desert failed to cure his respiratory condition. On his return to New Brunswick, furthermore, having been obliged to have his appendix removed, he came down with post-operative pneumonia. "I had always believed that 'back to nature' was a cure for all ills," he wrote; "but, lo! it was not."

FROM THE TOP of the adjoining mesa, a flat-topped hill rising thirty metres, you could gain a sense of the cabin's isolation. It sat alone on a ridge between two washes, in the arena of the degraded alluvial fan formed from the rocks and grit washed down from the Galiuro Mountains thirty kilometres east. From here the cabin was the only human thing visible, like a flake of skin or a single stitch or the dot on an exclamation mark. Sometimes, when I was strolling on the mesa, I would look down to where I had come from and, knowing the building was there somewhere, spend a few pleasant minutes waiting for my eye to find it.

The desert is "timeless"—a platitude worth repeating only because, here, it did not feel that way. I was conscious of its mobility. Which is to say I was conscious of time and geomorphology. This is partly because I was aware of water. The action of water in the desert is not a slow business. It might transform a vista in an hour or two. I'd seen its power in Tucson during the August cloudbursts, and while walking outside Nogales I'd watched a wave moving towards me up a dry wash, implacable, the storm that birthed it visible only as a dark cloud in the distant mountains. It has been said that more die by drowning in deserts than by dehydration. It isn't true, but a true point is being made. I also became aware of slower forces, those we are told are imperceptible. It was partly due to being unaccustomedly still for long periods. I sat for hours, my head wrapped in a damp scarf. It was not, of course, that I sensed the millimetre-per-decade shifting of the mountains or whatever; just that I did not feel that the desert was entirely the moored place it was often thought to be. I was conscious of entropy.

Geologists believe that, prior to the stretching of the mantle that created Nevada, Arizona and the rest of the basin-and-range province, the Sonoran Desert was a tableland, rocky and forested—and largely flat. Since the calming of the basin-and-range disturbance, the chief geological process—I saw it in the Black Rock Desert—has been the erosion of the mountains, their turning into grit and dust, and the slow filling up of the basins with those sediments. And so it can be said, if you are in an idealistic frame of mind, that the state to which the landscape—perhaps all landscapes—aspires, the *ultimate* state, is precisely this flatness, this spatial purity: the mountains, aberrant, are turned to dust, and while they exist, the gaps between them are packed with this dust. And thus a landscape that was previously flat returns to flatness. Water refines the world.

THE DRY WASHES are highways for animals and humans alike: level and flat and largely unvegetated, on account of the floodwaters that periodically surge through them. The walk to Hot Springs Canyon, a walk I came to love, began at the far side of the wash that formed the eastern slope of the cabin's ridge. Take the long-ago-dozered track to the top of the mesa and follow its brink south-west. In places the track had been water-eroded down to hard white calcium-carbonate. Watercourses become human pathways, human pathways watercourses. From the summit of the mesa I could look west and see the green rind of the San Pedro River running along the foot of the Little Rincon Mountains; I could look north-west and see the riddling washes and the pale speck that was the cabin enshadowed by its sentinel saguaro; I could look east and see the range of the Galiuros over which the sun had recently risen. Somewhere, bees were swarming audibly as the air warmed.

Here on the raw heights, creosote bush was dominant. Knee-high, with small waxy green leaves, in the brief moistness of morning it emitted a pleasingly pungent odour. Creosote bush has two names in Spanish: *hediondilla*, or little stinker, on account of its creosote odour; and *el gobernador*, the governor, because of the toxins it emits to impede competition. It is a classic desert strategy, called for by the sparsity of resources: eke out your quadrant of governance and defend it even against your own kind. Here and there, even at this elevation, were the candelabra forms of saguaros, and blocking the path ahead a fallen one, its flesh gone, reduced to a three-metre faggot of woody white ribs. Decay in the desert can be a process as long as life.

The trail-cum-stream ran down, after three kilometres, to a wash parallel (east–west) with the one below the cabin. I turned left, east; then, realising my mistake when the wash ended at a sandstone cliff after five minutes, I turned back, and after *six* minutes realised I'd missed the point where I left the trail. I backtracked, but after several more minutes still had not found the trail. My priority now was just to get back to the cabin. Not entirely lost, not hopelessly—there was a sense that I would look back upon this moment in safety, perhaps describe it—but bewilderment with its tang of adrenaline shot through me like a snakebite. The trailhead was there somewhere, it was only a question of finding it, and trusting memory, and not allowing panic to obliterate that memory. I was conscious of the worst of desert fates: to come endlessly back and back again upon your own footprints. For another ten minutes I walked up and down the wash, slowly, until I identified where the path adjoined it—such a vague incision from this approach, barely visible as a trail at all. I felt slightly nauseous. Before resuming, I found three black rocks and made a cairn of them in the middle of the wash, adjacent to the trailhead. In my notebook, I wrote down the time that elapsed between one point and another; I turned on my heel every few minutes to take a photograph—here, where five saguaros stand together above the wash, this is where you turn; or where a black cave is set high in the cliff-face. With me I had a straight cane of paloverde, around one end of which I had wound a length of surgical tape as a grip. From then on, whenever I took one route rather than another, I used the cane to draw a deep arrow in the grit.

After a few hundred metres, the wash came out at a great dry confluence, a high-walled stadium whose braided grit floor told of dozens of rushing streams. The surface was rilled and islanded and terraced where water had done its folding, planing and carving. Here and there were dumps of sediment and rocks and vegetation—mesquite beans, dry grass, whole dead bushes and the disembodied heads of fifty-year-old saguaros like drowned reptiles. And yet this morning, all that remained of the water, which would have foamed a metre or more deep in places, was a slight darkening under the surface, and an abundance of vegetation. The place was a carnival of birdsong, a reminder that the Sonoran Desert is an extension of the Sierra Madre tropical biome: jungle desert. To negotiate the undergrowth took time, along with a kind of instinct—to detect the narrow, bouldered washes that were easier to walk down and where you were less likely to stumble on a hidden snake. I moved east, into the broader, deeper Hot Springs Canyon, cutting from wash to wash between the zones of scrub and grass, seeking the rocky or gritty ground. I settled on an open passage cut a metre into the surface, where flowing water had graded the grit flat and smooth. The tamarisk shrubs brushing my arms were as even as a suburban hedge. This peculiar orderliness. In the grit at the path's cool margin I noticed a spiral impression ringed by larger stones and wondered if it was drawn by a short-lived whirlpool—before it occurred to me that it was a rattler's waiting place. There was intimacy in that mark, as in any empty bed.

Occasionally, where the wash meandered, the grit coarsened to a stretch of rubble or boulders or was crossed by a small tree washed down from upstream, which had to be climbed over or ducked under. I came to a flat upright triangle of yellow stone, as tall as myself, fallen from the canyon wall. After another kilometre of mazelike corridors I found the way blocked by a linking of branches hung with a web in which was stationed a large black spider. I remove my backpack, slung it under the barrier, and, checking for snakes, crawled after it. For forty minutes I continued, as the canyon walls closed in and became higher, and the air grew cooler. The shadows of dragonflies were busy on the ground. Lizards darted ahead, quick and agile themselves as those dragonfly shadows. Just as I was wondering if the heat would repel me before I reached water, the path (that is what the wash had come to feel like) was glimmering ahead and flowing with shallow water, and there was water's delicious sound, too, and I was elated, shouting with it. I had that dreamy sense of the landscape as chiefly a symbolic realm, a sequence of messages to be interpreted.

I was answered, by the water—and by something other than the water, though its voice did not register. To my left the stream threaded brightly within a broad corridor of grey sediment; to my right it was stiller, deeper—and of course it was this deeper water that attracted me. Still aglow with my arrival, I strode over the cobbled shore, and it rose up and warned me—rattlesnake, rearing sinew ten metres away, in the shadow of its waterside boulder. I stepped back three paces, and watched as it continued to buck and hiss and rattle—that refined, music-less rattle that is higher and more prolonged than the low benign thrum of the cicada. It did not settle until I moved away, and from then on, for the rest of the day, I told myself to watch every step, to watch the ground three metres ahead, and again one metre ahead. After all, what would I do if I was bitten, without antivenin, twenty kilometres from the nearest house—a house whose exact whereabouts was any-body's guess? A down-washed root was a snake; an S-shaped ledge cut into the sand was a snake; the shadow of my own stick ... In the grit I drew a reminder to my returning self:

$$\int$$

After another hour of hyper-alert walking, dousing my wand back and forth ahead of me like a blind man, I came to the place that had been my destination all along, though I hadn't known it was there. It was heralded by a small cyclone of cadmium-yellow butterflies, and high above, two circling eagles. The place was just a green cottonwood tree whose leaves were moved by a continuous breeze, and in its shade a brook knee-deep and on either bank long grass, and midstream a slab of limestone two metres across and almost square. And it was there, on the slab, that I spent the rest of the morning, watching the butterflies, and the dragonflies that baited them; and the pairs of eagles in the blue sky above the canyon walls. I was not impatient to move. For an hour I dozed in the cottonwood's shadow. Why, asked the anthropologist, are so many of your songs about water?

BACK IN THE CABIN was a guestbook. Many of the entries, going back to the 1990s, quoted the Bible or Christian mystics. All shall be well and all manner of thing shall be well. This is a day the Lord has made, let's rejoice and be glad in it. We should put the Bible on the shelf for twenty years and listen to our nature. Solitude is the furnace of transformation. My yoke is easy, my burden light. We are not human beings having a spiritual experience, we are spiritual beings having a human experience. Silence is the home of the word. I, Solitude, am thine own self; I, Nothingness, am thy all; I, Silence, am thy Amen.

Hundreds of words—Julius of Norwich, Teilhard de Chardin, Thomas Merton, Henri Nouwen—precise and loving and fully meant; and yet when I was reading them after returning from my walk they began to liquefy before my eyes. It was as if language was being lost to me, or I to it. Merton's lines alone were an anchor: silence as Amen, nothingness as all. The hike back had taken about three hours. I drank plenty, four or five litres, and had refilled my CamelBak from the stream, but in such heat—I didn't have a thermometer but I'd guess forty-five degrees—fluid is not always enough to regulate the body's temperature. I'd felt woozy since I got back an hour earlier, too woozy to sleep, somehow, though as I flicked through the guestbook I seemed to be on the edge of sleep, the deepest sleep.

I put the book down and sat up, and found that my neck was disinclined to bear the weight of my head. Sick was brewing like an encounter between two inimical gases; I wasn't sure if I wanted to weep or vomit. Or: was I going to shit myself? Life can be exciting.

I stood up, and sensing that I would collapse, sat down. A gust of wind hit the cabin and threw open the door, filling the room with the noonday heat, then slammed it shut again. I thought of W. J. McGee's stages of "thirst": "normal dryness," "functional derangement," "the cottonmouth phase," "the phase of the shrivelled tongue," "the stage of structural degeneration" . . . Sitting on the bed, my head in my hands, I tried once more to remember the song—the song Absalom had played on his defective Samsung on the edge of the Taklamakan a year earlier. I was getting better at remembering how it went; each day a new line:

High on a hill was a lonely goatherd,
Lay-ee-odl-lay-ee-odl-lay-hee-hoo,
Loud was the voice of the lonely goatherd,
Lay-ee-odl-lay-ee-odl-oo . . .

I sat there on the bed and yodelled into my lap, and then I think I passed out.

.   .   .

THE WORD *APOPHASIS* comes from the Greek *phasis*, meaning "image"; and *apo*, meaning "beyond." It is used to describe the unknowability of God and the ineffable character of the divine. In the Old Testament, Moses on Mount Sinai finds that God dwells in "thick darkness." In the New Testament Paul tells us that He "dwells in unapproachable light, whom no one has seen or can see." Evagrius of Pontus, a monastic living in Egypt's Wadi Natrun in the fourth century, counselled supplicants to "strive to render your mind deaf and dumb at the time of prayer, and then you will be able to pray." Abba Pambo, another Desert Father, visited by a prelate seeking spiritual guidance, received him in abject silence: "if he is not edified by my silence, he will surely not be edified by my speech." Abba Agathon of the Wadi Natrun kept a pebble in his mouth to prevent himself from speaking.

It was not until the sixth century that apophasis—also called the *via negativa*—was first articulated as a theological stance, by Pseudo-Dionysius. When we are confronted by God, he wrote, we "find ourselves not simply running short of words but actually speechless and unknowing." Moses himself was able only "to contemplate the place where God dwells."

One of the things that set me off in the first place was that night at the Royal Geographical Society in London; the speaker describing his triumphal procession across the Arabian sands. I had been yearning for retreat—the cure for loneliness, they say, is solitude—but in the wood-panelled lecture theatre it was all I could do to refrain from telling him to put a sock in it. And that was what it came down to: why couldn't we put a sock in it, all of us? Just for a minute. Or not a sock—a pebble, like good Abba Agathon. Pebbles for everyone! Settling down in the London flat under my grave-mound of books, I felt that even *they* were a distraction, the books; that there was nothing they could teach or I could learn from them in a year that was as edifying as a minute's total shtum.

"A time is coming," St. Antony warned, "when men will go mad, and when they see someone who is not mad, they will say, 'You are mad, you are not like us!'"

Jim Corbett's desert unbelief, it seems to me, was a contemporary form of apophasis. "The source of creation is unimageable," he wrote. "The way towards *shalom* ['harmonious community'] is revealed to us in the unclaimed wilderness of Sinai, because it has been and is offered to every people." Solitude, he seems to be saying, is solidarity. This the Desert Fathers understood. Monasticism, the life given up to prayerful resistance, never has been a turning-away from the world, even if it is a turning-away from the word.

The next thing I remember is walking in small circles outside the cabin, as the sun began to go down, in the shadow of the great saguaro. And though it was still hotter outside than in, I was feeling better—the pounding in my head quietened, my vision cleared, my balance returned. I drew some water from the drum and dragged a chair into the shadow of the cabin, and soaked a scarf and wrapped it round my head and neck. From the end of a rafter a lizard watched me. I stood up, naked apart from my boots and the scarf, and sang to him:

> Folks in a town that was quite remote heard,
> Lay-ee-odl-lay-ee-odl-lay-hee-hoo,
> Lusty and clear from the goatherd's throat heard,
> Lay-ee-odl-lay-ee-odl-oo...

It was the closest I could get to psalmody. Away the lizard skittered. It was wonderful, this return of alertness, of language, voice. I wondered if it carried to Daniel down in Cascabel. Rejuvenated, giddy, I went back inside the cabin and sat at the table, and it returned, the nausea, the heaviness. I stopped singing. But it wasn't heatstroke or heat exhaustion or dehydration or "functional derangement." Standing between the storm lantern and the bottle of wine was the camping stove, and its ratcheted black gasket was just off the vertical, slightly open. Ever since I'd brought it back in after making this morning's coffee, butane had been silently filtering into the room, silently gassing me. I opened the windows and propped the door open and sat outside while the cabin aired.

7

THE INNER MOUNTAIN

The Eastern Desert, Egypt

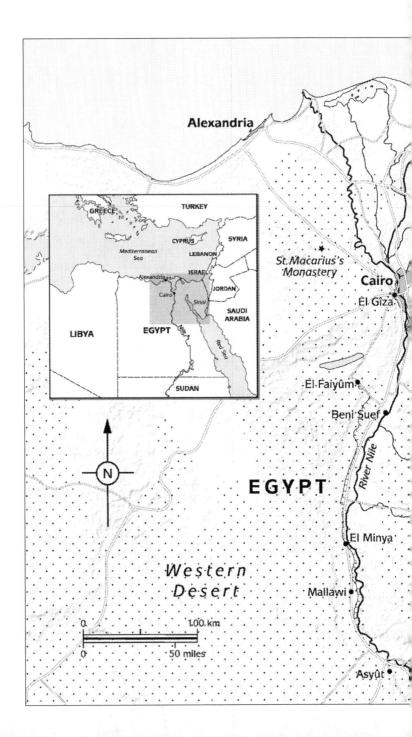

Alexandria

TURKEY

GREECE

CYPRUS

SYRIA

Mediterranean
Sea

LEBANON

ISRAEL

St. Macarius's
Monastery

Alexandria

JORDAN

Cairo

Sinai

SAUDI
ARABIA

Cairo

El Gîza

LIBYA

EGYPT

Nile

Red Sea

SUDAN

El Faiyûm

Beni Suef

River Nile

N

EGYPT

El Minya

Western
Desert

Mallawi

0   100 km

0   50 miles

Asyût

Mediterranean Sea

Port Said

Suez Canal

ISRAEL

Suez

Al'Aqabah

Sinai

Zafarana

St.Antony's
Monastery

Gulf of Suez

St.Paul's
Monastery

Gulf of Aqaba

Ras Gharib

Eastern
Desert

Red Sea

Hurghada

In my cell in the monastery on the edge of Dartmoor, three years ago, was a copy of the Rule of St. Benedict. There are four kinds of monk, it began: coenobites, who live communally under an abbot; sarabaites, who have "been tried by no rule"; anchorites, who reside alone and are "well trained for single combat in the desert"; finally, landlopers, "who keep going their whole life long from one province to another."

I am sitting 3,600 kilometres from Dartmoor, in Egypt's Eastern Desert, in the refectory of St. Antony's Monastery, eating fava-bean stew. Today there is molasses for pudding. Peter, whom I eat most of my meals with, is tall and broad-shouldered and has the sort of luminous complexion you'd expect of a twenty-eight-year-old who practises tae kwon do daily, spends his evenings reading scripture, goes to bed early and consumes nothing that might threaten his body's optimal performance.

His parents moved to Germany from Eritrea before he was born, and though he has visited Eritrea only once, he considers it his motherland and spiritual home. His slightly apologetic English is transformed when he talks about his faith, Jesus Christ, the Antichrist and eternity, and the Eritrean and Ethiopian anchorites he admires above anyone. He shows me a picture on his phone, the way another man might a picture of his wife or children: a beaming Ethiopian monk in bright yellow robes, perched owl-like in a hole in a rock face.

One of the kitchen cats places its paws on his knee for scraps: he scratches its head and imagines aloud its wily voice: "*I don't believe we've met, gentlemen...*" He's capable of this kind of humour. But the devil for him is ever present, a cause of constant anxiety, sadness and pity. He often speaks about the Evil One's instruments and designs: the damage the multinationals have done to Africa, America's illusory democracy, Europe's racist treatment of Eritrean refugees, the barbarism of Israel's actions in Palestine. But what preoccupies him above all is Islam. "The Muslims will cause many problems for Europe," he'll say. Or: "Islam cannot compromise." I'm not to get him wrong—some of his closest friends are Muslims, kids he grew up with in Munich. "They are like brothers to me"—but, he says, they have scarcely read the Koran. They only know what their imam tells them each Friday and what they watch on YouTube. So naturally they are blind to their religion's falsity. Besides, they do not wish to know. "They would never dream of doing violence, but the Koran teaches them to admire men who go to war for Islam."

The refectory is a long room within a larger complex, with a black-and-white tiled floor and tables ranged along each wall. Almost filling the end wall is a framed photomontage twelve metres square showing the gate towers of the monastery overshadowed by an image from an icon: giant, haloed St. Antony, clutching wooden crucifix and tau staff. Lining the entrance hall, and in the corridors that lead from it to the adjoining guest rooms, are fish tanks, eight of them, landscaped with ibex horns and ammonites and rocks from the mountains. Brightly lit, the tanks are perfectly dry apart from one whose few inches of milky water are populated by ten jostling, flaking yellow fish.

The refectory has seating for a hundred, but Peter and I are usually the only ones here, other than the two skinny serving boys always to be found slumped over a table in the adjoining kitchen, waiting—literally slumped—to feed any guests who might arrive, and whose sullenness seems impenetrable until you smile and place your hand on your heart. Then they are glad to see you. Sometimes they excitedly make us fresh lemonade from the small hard lemons that grow in the monastery gardens. We suspect it is a minor infraction, if only of propriety. They are not novitiates, they tell me, just Copts who live in the complex of houses that adjoins the monastery. They admire Peter's tattoos, especially the elaborate Coptic cross on his chest, visible over the neck of his T-shirt. He had it done a couple of years ago, he tells me. The simpler Coptic cross tattooed on the inside of his right wrist is older.

We are sharing the guest apartment and are the only Western visitors. He is ten years younger than me, but I often feel like an apprentice in his company. There's no stridency about him, nor any missionary arrogance; just a simple devout certitude that makes itself known in his fluency. Any anger he has is reserved for the devil. Humankind he only pities. The vast majority of us, after all, are destined for eternal suffering. "Some of them even *know* this—and still they continue to sin!"

For himself, it was three years ago that the Holy Spirit finally entered him, the day he gave up Facebook, movies, TV and music. "My friends thought I was very strange, but my life is better. Purer." He is considering becoming a monk. That is why he is here—to see if this is enough to renounce the world for, and to see if God wants him. "We live for a hundred years, if that is God's will," he says. "But the devil has lived for *thousands of years*, and he uses that experience against us. He watches us. We cannot surprise him! He knows how we will behave in any situation. It is his job. He is very good at it."

"Then the devil is growing stronger?" I say.

"Of course." He stirs his molasses with a scrap of flatbread, but does not eat. "Every day. Everywhere. Even here. People believe the world is ruled by God. But God is not in charge. He did not win!"

It was in this desert 1,700 years ago that St. Antony was tested. The demons assailed him and he suffered the temptations imagined by a thousand artists. We look out of the refectory window at the dry valley of the Wadi Araba, a view Antony knew. An immense shallow depression broken by low hills of dark limestone, the valley traverses the mountainous desert between the Nile and the Red Sea and is a trade route pre-dating even the Roman occupation of Egypt, dividing two ranges of mountains. On its far side, thirty kilometres away, the North Galala Mountains are just visible through the rising dust of morning. Beyond them, 160 kilometres north-west, is Cairo. The South Galala range, which towers behind the monastery, extends hundreds of kilometres to the south towards the border with Sudan, walling off the Eastern Desert from the humidifying effect of the Red Sea.

It was probably the Wadi Araba that Antony followed when he left the Nile Valley. He had been living there at Pispir for twenty years when, frustrated by the acolytes who had joined him, he left in search of greater solitude. Joining a caravan of Saracens he travelled to the South Galala Mountains—Mount Colzim, in St. Athanasius's *Life*. Perhaps he recognised the place as his home as they approached: the shelter promised by the mountains, this raised prospect clear across the desert, and of course the spring at the mountains' foot. The desert might symbolise death but it was the possibility of life that allowed St. Antony to stay here. Water, first and foremost, accounts for the monastery's existence.

It didn't take long before he was sought out by his followers even here, any life in the desert being conspicuous. When Hilarion, the founder of Palestinian monasticism, visited St. Antony, he made his excuses after a couple of months, unable to tolerate the crowds. This is the constant struggle of the Egyptian monk to this day: in his exceptionality he attracts followers. The faithful want to kiss his hand, to receive his blessing, his *baraka*. Merely to know of his existence is not enough; we must bathe in the grace of his presence.

SOME ANCIENT GREEK is helpful. *Monakhós* means "single" or "alone." *Anachorein* means "to withdraw." *Érēmos* is "a wilderness or desert." From the first comes "monk," from the second "anchorite," from the third "hermit."

A centripetal force governed Egyptian monastic life in the years after Antony: to begin with, men (there were a few women too) resided in isolated cells, far from one another; these in turn coalesced over "generations" into *laurae*, small communities whose members came together for meals and prayer. Finally these became formalised monasteries, which at their height each numbered several hundred souls. The life of the anchorite gave way to communal, or coenobitic, monasticism. In a land of little water, where barbarians might attack at any moment, a communal life was only practical. Coenobitism came out of the harshness of the setting, a compromise with its dryness. Nevertheless, some individuals persisted in the solitary life, occupying caves or mud huts beyond the security of the monastery walls. They were the ones Peter most admired.

It is a follower of Antony's, Pachomius, a former Roman soldier, who is usually considered the true founder of coenobitic monasticism. He developed the first written rule, and in around 318 the first planned monasteries. About 380, some twenty-five years after Antony's death, a young monk from Scythia Minor (today's Bulgaria/Romania) visited the desert monasteries around the Wadi Natrun. His name was John Cassian, "John the Ascetic" (he who first described the symptoms of desert accidie). He would return to Europe to found the Abbey of St. Victor in Marseilles, which would serve as a model for further European monasteries. Cassian's written reflections on the lives of the monks of Egypt, the *Conferences of the Egyptian Monks* and the *Institutes of the Monastic Life*, were central influences on Benedict of Nursia. As a hermit living in Subiaco, Italy, Benedict went on to found twelve monasteries. His "Rule," based closely on the writings of Cassian, became the key text of Western monasticism.

The life has not changed substantially since the German theologian and traveller Johann Michael Wansleben visited St. Antony's in 1672: "The rule obliges them to give up marriage, all carnal desires and the relationship to their parents," he writes. "They are not to possess anything; they are to live in the desert, to abstain from meat and wine... They are bound to recite the Canonical Hours, and before retiring at night they prostrate themselves 150 times."

The desert was the matrix in which Christian monasticism was formed. The motives of those who left the cities for the desert were varied, but for monks the desert was no peaceful refuge. On the contrary it was teeming—with satyrs, centaurs and demons and the uncounted millions of the Evil One's foot-soldiers. You went there not only for liberty or meditative quiet, but as to a front line. To take yourself to the desert is not to pursue a new life but to renounce life. An elderly monk I befriend takes me to the concrete ossuary where the remains of the most prominent of St. Antony's fathers are shelved: "We do not say 'he has died'," he tells me. "We say 'he has lain down'. A monk is already dead."

·   ·   ·

AS SOON AS I feel I'm becoming familiar with the monastery—that I know where this passageway or staircase leads, or which alleyway or door I must pass through to reach the old church from the new—I find myself somewhere unfamiliar, and have to retrace my steps. Sometimes it feels like the variety of new places concealed within the maze of alleyways, rooms and corridors is infinite. It is hard to date the monastery's founding, because it evolved piece by piece, accreting shanty-like around a central church. The first record of a monastic establishment at the site dates from around 360, during the reign of Julian the Apostate, just a few years after Antony's death. What we can be sure of is that the monastery's twin hearts, always, were first the spot where that miraculous sweet spring flows out of the mountain, and second the place under the old church where St. Antony's body is said to be interred. Once a wall had been built, the enclave became a citadel and the coenobitic life can be said finally to have prevailed over the anchoritic. Today the monastery still resembles a castle; the architecture of defence is unmistakable. Protruding over the modern gateway is the ancient winch-room. As recently as the 1930s there was no gate, and the only way in was to clamber into a basket and wait for the monks to haul you up. At the centre of the monastery, within the walls, is the *qasr*, a defensive keep for use if the walls were breached, with a wooden drawbridge leading to it from an adjacent building. Above all, belittling everything human, is the most sure wall of all, the South Galala Mountains.

One day after vespers I sit with one of the older monks, Father Samwul, on a bench positioned on the gantry in front of his quarters. The bench is covered with a red rag-rug bleached pink by the sun. We look out at the monastery and the mountains beyond. He's been here for thirty-eight years, he tells me. He must be in his seventies. When he arrived, there were only five monks and the monastery was near-derelict; today there are 130 including novitiates. But he doesn't feel optimistic—which is to say he fears for the future of Christianity in Egypt. I ask him about Abdel Fattah el-Sisi, the new Egyptian president. Surely for Christians he is preferable to the Muslim Brotherhood? "Yes, yes, on the outside," he says. "But inside?" He looks at the monastery walls again. "You in Europe, let me tell you, you're foolish!" He paid a visit to Britain a few years ago and passed through Rotherham. "I saw two churches, close to each other, and you will not believe me, but they were allowing one of them to be used as a mosque! A mosque! Only we, the Copts of Egypt, only we know what Islam truly is. Maybe in ten years you will understand. When London is Muslim."

The outer wall—beyond the original, inner wall—was built only twenty years ago. It's about six kilometres long, an arm reaching out from the mountains to enfold the holy ground. Its purpose, I've been told, is to ensure the "peace" of the desert and keep out the camels (a mob of five or six hangs around a rubbish dump beyond the gates, drawn by the scent of water). But it is also a security measure, even if largely symbolic. Father Samwul, as we look out over the place where he has spent most of his adult life, tells me that ten years ago, while he and the other senior fathers were away at a conference in Alexandria, the army was sent to destroy the wall. The authorities claimed that the land (the empty desert) belonged to the state. "'You haven't paid for the land!' they said. *Paid for the land . . . !* We've been here for fifteen hundred years!" The bulldozers were forced to withdraw before they did any damage. "The law says that any land within 150 metres of a site of antiquity belongs to the owner. Therefore the desert is ours; ours, as it has always been."

In the monastery's gift shop, among the cheaply printed liturgies, I come across a prayer pamphlet in Arabic, with a familiar image on its cover. There is still a market for the orange jumpsuit. A line of men so dressed is being shepherded along a beach by a corresponding line of men, much taller, clad in black from head to foot. In 2015, twenty-one Egyptian Copts working in Libya were seized by ISIS and, as shown in the video from which the image was taken, beheaded on a beach. Blood and sand. A caption on the video called them "The people of the cross, followers of the hostile Egyptian church." The murdered men were made saints by the Coptic Church.

For Copts, the Muslim conquest of Egypt in 641 was less a cause of anxiety than a liberation from the Byzantine Christian rule that had curtailed their religious freedom almost as severely as the Romans.

During the Fifth Crusade, Copts fought alongside Muslims against the Franks. Under the Mamluks in the fourteenth century, however, came a period of ferocious repression during which Coptism withered and the monasteries were abandoned. While this situation improved following the Turkish Ottoman conquest in the sixteenth century, it was not until the early twentieth century that Copts were granted equal rights of national citizenship.

Despite periods in which it flourished, Christianity was consistently viewed as a threat to pagan Rome. A series of anti-Christian persecutions hastened the monastic flight to the desert. The most bloody of these were carried out under the emperors Decius in 250, Diocletian in 303 and Maximinus in 311. So traumatic was Diocletian's reign for Egypt's Christians that the Coptic calendar begins on the day he came to power, the "year of the martyrs," 29 August 284. At the height of Maximinus's persecutions, Antony had yet to enter the inner desert, and was still living close to the Nile at Pispir (today's Deir al-Maymun), the place known as the Outer Mountain. Far from remaining in this sanctuary, however, he was drawn by the slaughter of his coreligionists to temporarily return to the world to confront the regime in Alexandria. "He longed to suffer martyrdom," Athanasius writes. So shaken were the Roman authorities by his fearlessness and zeal, "they commanded no monk should appear in the judgement hall," and the persecutions effectively ceased. They had seen the radical power of the anchorite; it would only be fortified by martyrdom. Antony returned to the Outer Mountain, his faith strengthened, his discipline "much severer...he was ever fasting, and he had a garment of hair on the inside, while the outside was skin...And he neither bathed his body with water to free himself from filth, nor did he ever wash his feet." Two years later, in his early fifties, he went to the Inner Mountain, today's South Galala. While the Inner Mountain remains the spiritual heartland of the Coptic Church, monasticism's coenobitic form was evolved and tested fifteen camel-days away on the edge of Egypt's Western Desert. It was the life refined there that became the model for Coptic monasticism and the traditions that flowed out of Egypt across the world.

.   .   .

BEFORE COMING TO St. Antony's, I travelled from Cairo to the Wadi Natrun, about a hundred kilometres north-west of the city, off the desert road to Alexandria. From the fourth century onwards, it was a centre of monasticism, with thousands of monks inspired by Antony and Pachomius occupying dozens of monasteries and hundreds of isolated cells in the vicinity of the shallow desert valley. Palladius, in 387, reckoned there were five thousand monks living there. The wadi, thirty-five kilometres long and eight wide, is named for the sodium-carbonate salts, natron, harvested from its lakebeds for use as a detergent and later in the chemical industry. The pharaohs used it in mummification on account of its desiccating and bacteriological properties. A few kilometres north were the mountain of Scetis, occupied by monks until the fifth century; and, deep in the Western Desert, Cellia, named for the scattered cells of the monks who held out there. Today, Cellia and Scetis are long abandoned and the natron-processing works founded in the nineteenth century is defunct, but in the Wadi Natrun four monasteries remain: the Monastery of St. Macarius, the Monastery of the Romans, the Monastery of St. Bishoi and the Monastery of the Syrians. It was the first of these that interested me, sacred as it was to the memory of the founder of monasticism in the Wadi Natrun.

Among the most vivid modern travellers' accounts of the region is Constantin von Tischendorf's *Travels in the East* of 1847: "A powerful Arab carried me on his shoulder over the canal," he tells us of his approach to the valley. The baron would have been something of a sight, as he walked (or was hefted) towards the monasteries: "double spectacles, each of which with its four blue glasses, shaded my eyes from the dangerous reflection of the sun on the sand; and my head was decorated with a large straw hat from which hung suspended an ample green veil." He notes the chain of eight salt lakes that ran along the valley bottom, their "obscure reddish-blue waters" and the flamingos that rise from the reeds as his caravan passes. But the desert of those pioneers has gone. Beside the road to Alex, past the prison where the deposed president Morsi is held—"Bad, bad man," says my taxi driver—stands "Wadi Natrun City," dozens of closely built residential tower blocks funded by Sisi. A rutted dirt track leads from it through villages where sacks of fertiliser are heaped outside stores. The people barely raise their heads as we pass: they are used to outsiders. The access road to St. Macarius passes between fields of alfalfa, oranges, pomegranates and beets. We stop, the driver and I, to fill our pockets and the glove compartment with roadside dates. A healing sense of abundance. Birdsong, shrubs cascading with flowers, bright petals in the dust.

The monastic desert, in fact, was never a very distant planet; more a moon circling close to the human world, close enough that it was accessible to the visitor (those nineteenth-century Europeans in their blue shades); close enough, above all, that the world the monks had renounced could not be forgotten. The Wadi Natrun was a prominence from which, on the one hand, to the east, the human world of the Nile and Alexandria continued to register, while, on the other, to the west, you looked out on the Sahara, the limit of the world, and the infinite beyond. In this sense the desert is a stage on which the eternal life of paradise is enacted for a worldly audience. The monks are witnesses to the world but not implicated in it. Hence they are trusted by the people.

It was the Cairo–Alexandria road that transformed the Wadi Natrun, just as the Red Sea highway transformed St. Antony's. The road turned the monasteries into sites of mass pilgrimage, altering the life of the monks forever. In photos taken before the "Alex Desert Road" was built in 1936, the Wadi Natrun monasteries stand in startling isolation, each a fortress on its treeless terrace of gravel and salt-encrusted rock, like a modern army's forward operating base. Despite their isolation and apparent impenetrability, the monasteries were repeatedly sacked by tribes from the oases of the Western Desert. This sense of embattlement, of the monasteries as imperilled wellsprings of the faith, persists.

At the Monastery of St. Macarius I met Father Mercurius. He was about forty, with the usual unkempt wiry black beard of the Coptic monk; the black robe and black skullcap, and the usual subdued voice. Today was neither a feast day nor a holiday, but the monastery was bustling with pilgrims from Cairo and Alexandria, each of them wishing to kiss his hand and receive his blessing as we walked. He never declined; never turned his back. "They believe we are saints," he said.

Children in particular loved the monks: they queued to kiss Mercurius's hand, and to each he proffered first a hand placed on the top of the head then, from some cache secreted in his robe, a boiled sweet, or a prayer card bearing a picture of an icon of St. Macarius. The mutual warmth, so tangible, reminded me of a family reunion; such joy among the visitors, to be luxuriating in the presence of these men they loved, who had guarded the flame of Egyptian Christianity against every attack.

Father Mercurius asked one of the monastery boys to bring us refreshments and led me to a bench shaded by a grape bower where we would not be disturbed by the pilgrims. Glasses of tea arrived on a tray and for a while the only noise was the breeze in the vines and our slurping. He leaned behind us to where a planter stood, and fondled the tender green shoots carpeting its soil. "How I love them! So small!" He stroked a flowering shrub growing beside them. "This I love, too," he smiled; "but these little ones . . . !"

I asked him how long he had been here: "A monk does not measure his life in years, you must understand, but in the quality of his heart." Having donned black, he entered eternity; the years, in principle, ceased to register. But then he smiled: "For five years."

"I have observed," he went on, "the similarities between our life here in Egypt and the life of the Buddhists. I once met a Buddhist monk, a Tibetan who was visiting us here, and I saw that he and I were like brothers. We had no language in common, and yet our lives were the same: solitude, love, self-denial, work, obedience, virginity. Yes, yes, different forms of religion, but our days, our obligations . . .

"There is a story told in our texts. Two monks come to a river and find a girl drowning. Now, you know—everybody knows—that a monk must not touch a girl, whether he is Coptic or Greek or Russian or Buddhist. But one of the monks immediately jumps into the water and rescues her. The other monk, afterwards, says, 'How did you do that? How did you hold that girl? Did it not burn you?' And the monk who went into the water says, '*I* held her only in my arms; *you*,'" Father Mercurius tapped his head twice—"'*you* held her *here*.' And this is what is interesting—" He put his tea down. "I was reading a Buddhist text recently and I found the same story! I don't mean it was similar. It was *identical*. And so I ask myself: which was written first, and how did the story travel so far? Can it be that from similar lives the same stories will always be born?"

It has been suggested that the Egyptian monastic obsession with abstinence, thus with childlessness, was an act of defiance against the Roman occupation. Others have called it an expression of mental crisis. The Alexandrian theologian Origen, like Abraham, resolved the question by bloodily detaching the offending organ from himself. St. Antony "repressed the body and kept it in subjection," Athanasius tells us. Certainly the massed flight to the desert of third- and fourth-century Egypt represented a disruption of the social order—it is partly this that monasticism's critics find objectionable. But abstinence in the service of God was hardly an invention of the Desert Fathers. Didn't St. John believe that union between a man and a woman was a crime? Flesh, being evil, must be broken, and the desert could be a tool in its subdual.

I thought back to those desert-bonneted, piss-drinking Nigels of the early twentieth century: "sexless" Wilfred Thesiger; self-lacerating T. E. Lawrence; the wooden bachelors of Central Asia with their little dogs: half in quest, half in flight, half loving the world and half hating it. Seeking to dissolve the body and become one with the infinite. But I thought about myself, too, and Amy: those days of joyful eating, drinking and swimming in California.

I ASKED Father Mercurius if I could see the library. He fished his iPhone from his gown.

The librarian, Father Cyril, agreed to open it for me. It was not the dusty scriptorium I had expected but a cool, bright hall lined with bookcases and furnished with low institutional armchairs. The books were mostly in French, Arabic and Coptic. A few were in English. On the wall some lines in Coptic were framed (Coptic resembles Greek). I asked Father Cyril to translate. He laughed. "St. Epiphanius said, 'Reading the scriptures is a great safeguard against sin.'" He agreed to let me spend an hour in the library. I took the opportunity to remind myself of the life of the monastery's founder, St. Macarius. According to the *Sayings of the Desert Fathers*, he was a trader of natron, of dubious character, travelling with the camel caravans that plied between the Nile and the Wadi Natrun. He was famous as a "lover beyond all other men of the desert, and had explored its ultimate and inaccessible wastes." One day, arriving at the Wadi Natrun, unpopulated at the time, he was granted a vision in which a cherub told him that he and his followers would one day inhabit this impoverished land. Like Antony a century earlier, Macarius gave his possessions to the poor and settled alone in the desert. Of his appearance we know only what the chronicler Palladius wrote: "The only hair on his face was around his mouth and there was very little on his upper lip, the extremes of austerity to which he had subjected himself inhibiting the growth of beard on his chin."

Upon killing a mosquito, he "made up his mind to stay six whole months, naked and motionless, in one place in a swamp in Scete, situated in a dreary waste, where there are mosquitoes the size of wasps and with stings capable of piercing even the hide of wild boars. He thus reduced his body to such a state that when he returned to his cell everyone thought he was a leper." From a modern-day, let alone secular, perspective his renunciations sometimes seem to descend into competitive farce:

> Learning also that a hermit ate only one pound of bread in a day, he crumbled the pieces of bread which he had and put them into a jar, resolved to take out only as much as he could extract with his fingers. Which is great austerity, for, as he readily explained to us, he could take hold of quite a few pieces but could not get them out, since the neck of the jar was so narrow.

My instinctive response to the more extreme acts of the Desert Fathers has often been a sort of simmering repulsion. I'm not alone in having been stirred to contempt by their self-mortifications. There is vulgarity in self-denial. The anchorites of the Wadi Natrun, it was said, put the proper number of olives to be eaten daily at precisely *seven.* Eight was gluttony; but six was worse, six smacked of pride. Most eloquent among the scorners of the early Christian ascetics is Edward Gibbon, who saw the flight to the desert as a rejection of society and learning, which it was: "They soon acquired the respect of the world, which they despised," he writes; "and the loudest applause was bestowed on this DIVINE PHILOSOPHY, which surpassed, without the aid of science or reason, the laborious virtues of the Grecian schools." And here is a disgusted William Lecky, author of a *History of the Rise and Influence of the Spirit of Rationalism in Europe* (1865):

> There is perhaps no phase in the moral history of mankind of a deeper or more painful interest than this ascetic epidemic. A hideous, distorted and emaciated maniac, without knowledge, without patriotism, without natural affection, spending his life in a long routine of useless and atrocious self-torture, and quailing before the ghastly phantoms of his delirious brain, had become the ideal of nations which had known the writings of Plato and Cicero and the lives of Socrates and Cato.

Many of the most vivid descriptions of life in the Wadi Natrun come from Palladius, who lived there in the early fifth century. Reading his description of Cellia, you might have sympathy for Lecky's characterisation of the movement as an epidemic. The monks' cells, Palladius writes, were "like hyena holes, in which space was so restricted that it was impossible even to straighten out one's legs." Others had less salubrious sleeping arrangements. Father Sisoes "was in the habit of spending the night standing on the very edge of a precipice, so that one moment of unconsciousness would have hurled him to death." Another stood at night with his beard nailed to a rafter, to keep his head from drooping. I pictured hairy-mouthed Macarius, in his hole, hand wedged in a jar—the epitome of the "distorted and emaciated maniac," dignity cast off along with all but the minimum sustenance needful to maintain flesh.

And yet how can we presume to know them, these men of the third and fourth centuries? In the desert—for escaped slave or terrified Christian—it was also surely possible to recover a dignity unavailable in the "world." John Cassian, the monk credited with bringing Christian monasticism to Europe, lived in Scetis for seven years during the fourth century. "We have joy in this desolation, and to all delight do we prefer the dread vastness of this solitude, nor do we weigh the riches of your glebe against these bitter sands."

The desert was not merely tolerated, nor was it only a holy battleground. Take Father Sisoes. Having reluctantly given up the anchoritic life on account of his old age, and moved to a monastery, he is asked: "But what would you do in the desert, now that you are old?" He replies forlornly: "Was not the mere liberty of my soul enough for me in the desert?" The Wadi Natrun is also known as "Wadi Habib": "beloved valley." St. Antony too loved the desert—loved it for what it was and not only for what it was not; for what it gave and not only what it denied. Each evening in his dotage he took a stroll. We can picture him in the blessed twilight of the Eastern Desert, hands clasped behind his back, attended by a couple of ravens.

UNTIL SHELL BUILT the Red Sea highway from Suez to Ras Gharib in 1946, the usual way to St. Antony's was across the Eastern Desert from the Nile, 130 kilometres, and pilgrims were few. In modern times, on a given feast day, two thousand visitors might pass through the gates. Leaving the coast at Zafarana, you follow the highway west along the centre of the Wadi Araba for sixty kilometres. The South Galala Mountains tower ahead of you, though they seem to get no closer. The twin gate-towers of the monastery become visible and you recognise the sheer size of the mountains, how insignificant the monastery is, really. At the centre of the complex, within the inner walls, stands the fifth-century Church of St. Antony, where "the Star of the Desert" is said to be buried. From outside it is unprepossessing among the cluster of pale buildings. Ecclesial grandeur requires an abundance of tall trees. The principal structural material is limestone from the mountains with a thick plaster of lime and gypsum. A little acacia and olive wood inside, carved for decoration. In its comparative lavishness the interior of the Church of St. Antony reminds me of nowhere so much as the Caves of the Thousand Buddhas. For all the austerity of monastic principles, it feels like a cry against the colourlessness of the desert; an illuminated page concealed in a blank manuscript.

Until the wall paintings were renovated in the 1990s, the church was by all accounts a gloomy place; only a few shadowy features could be seen to emerge from walls stained black by smoke—smoke from centuries of candles and oil-lamps and incense, as well as from fires lit by the Bedouin during a period when the monastery was abandoned in the fifteenth century. Today, the smoke stains removed, it is one of the glories of the Coptic Church. Most of the paintings date from around 1232 and are the work of a Master Theodore ("Gift of God"). They represent a genealogy of Coptic monasticism: here, in the nave, is a rank-bearded Macarius accompanied by a being that resembles an owl–toddler hybrid, its wings decorated with eyes—the cherub who called him to abandon his life as a natron trader. Also lined up along the walls are the other founders of the Wadi Natrun monasteries: Maximus and Domitius, Moses the Black, Bishoi the Great, John the Little, Barsuma the Syrian. In the *khurus*, separating the nave from the sanctuary, Abraham, Isaac and Jacob are pictured in paradise, and there is a pleasing addition, as if painted as an afterthought or commentary: outside the frame of the main paintings, a tiny figure of a man aflame, screaming, one hand outstretched in agony or pleading. A label in Arabic identifies him: Nineveh the Unmerciful. "He is begging Abraham for a drop of water," one of the novitiates tells me cheerfully.

Most affecting of all the paintings—it's hard for me to say why I find it so moving—is a kind of double portrait of two old men. On the left is St. Antony, his hands lifted up at shoulder height, his palms facing us; next to him is his friend St. Paul. Antony is robed in black, Paul in dark red, though who knows how the pigments have changed over the centuries. Coptic iconographic convention gives all saints the same small rosebud lips (for silence) and large wide eyes (vigilance). St. Paul occupied a cave on the other side of the South Galala range, fifteen kilometres from the Red Sea. St. Antony's sister monastery stands on the spot today, some fifty kilometres away as the crow flies. St. Jerome's is the most influential version of Paul's story, and was one of Felix Fabri's sources for his twenty-part description of the desert in 1483. In Helen Waddell's translation, Antony one night received a vision: "It was revealed to him that there was deep in the desert another better by far than he, and that he must make haste to visit him." Paul was 113 years old; Antony was ninety-four. "Straightaway as day was breaking the venerable old man set out, supporting his feeble limbs on his staff, to go he knew not whither." But he is directed across the desert by a succession of guides—a "Hippocentaur," a faun, finally a she-wolf who leads him to St. Paul's cave.

Seldom is one saint pictured without the other; and their shared symbol is the creature that hovers above them. "A raven had settled on the branch of the tree, and softly flying down, deposited a whole loaf before their wondering eyes." Behold, Paul tells his visitor: for the past sixty years the bird had delivered to him half a loaf each day—"but at thy coming, Christ hath doubled His soldiers' rations." The raven features in every painting and icon of the two. On the church wall it is as simple as a potato-print: an outline filled with black, its only feature a pale dash marking the eye. In its beak it holds a white disc stamped with a cross like a sacramental wafer.

I wonder about the tenderness I feel towards it. Is it just that they mate for life? It hangs like a child's mobile between the two saints. I remember that Bertram Thomas named his tame raven Suwaiyid, "little black one." The bird in the painting is not only a supplier of sustenance or a symbol of God incarnate. It is also, I can't help feeling, an intermediary, the spirit of communion between these two souls so remote from one another in the intensity of their embodiment.

ADJOINING THE CHURCH of St. Antony is the eighteenth-century Church of the Apostles. You can find it by looking for the dozens of pairs of shoes lined around the door and along the walls nearby. Here three times a week the Divine Liturgy is celebrated. It is also where I attend the Canonical Hours—matins at 4 a.m. and vespers at 5 p.m. The church is large, low and domed. In its openness, and the shoes left at the door, it reminds me of a mosque. Each night at 11 p.m. the monastery's electricity is switched off, and until it is turned on again at 7 a.m. the sole lights are a single floodlight by the gate and those inside the church. As I walk to matins, *tasbiha*, one morning, the monastery

is visible from across the car park only as a distant lit gateway, light
pouring out of it into the darkness. Suddenly the defensive walls are
illuminated too and my shadow staggers ahead of me—it's Peter, coming up behind me, lighting his way with a torch. I wait for him, though
I know that when we enter the church it will be as if we are strangers.
As we pass through the gate into the monastery, the wind picks up, and
there is the mewling of the monastery cats.

The morning service lasts for two hours; you stand throughout.
This is part of the monk's work, this standing for perhaps eight hours
each day. The service is in Arabic with some Coptic. I try to follow the
liturgy and hymns in English but often I don't know what is going on.
In the absence of understanding, the dirge of sung verses and responses
assumes a hypnotic influence. The narthex, where the monks stand, is
divided in two: on the left stand the novitiates in white, on the right
the fathers in black, though there is no strict division and the fathers
mingle among the novitiates. When the singing begins, the novitiates
sing a verse, and this is echoed by the fathers. Antiphonal psalmody.
How do they differ, their voices? I close my eyes: the novitiates' singing is more effortful, self-conscious; the fathers, when it is their turn,
are louder, deeper: it is the difference between a geyser and a waterfall. I open my eyes. The novitiates, few of them older than thirty or
younger than twenty, are glowing and bulky in their white vestments,
the music of the cities still ringing in their ears; the fathers in black are
diminished—diminished by the life: slim but not frail, slightly bent-
backed, slower in their movements. There is something shrivelled
about them. The life of the monk makes one monklike.

Shrivelled, perhaps, but not joyless. What I am most aware of, in
fact, is love: each man touches the hand of every other he meets, to
bless him or take his blessing. There is much warm smiling: a hand on
the shoulder or on the back as words are exchanged. *Agape*: "love," from
the Ancient Greek—the term used by Copts for the shared celebration
of the Christian mysteries.

The Lord's Prayer: "*Abana aladhi fi as-samaawaat...*" Then the Litany of the Sick (I follow the English on an app on my phone): "Those
who are afflicted by unclean spirits, set them all free. Those who are
in prisons or dungeons, those who are in exile or captivity, or those

who are held in bitter bondage, set them all free and have mercy upon
them." The Litany of the Travellers: "Straighten all their ways, whether
by sea, rivers, lakes, roads, air, or by any means, that Christ our God
may bring them back to their own homes in peace ..."

Accompanying the chanting is the quick rhythmic scraping of a
pair of small hand-cymbals and the quick tinny chiming of a triangle. I
remember the plainsong of the Cistercians in that cold abbey on Dartmoor, how it aspired to a choral sweetness, an agile purity of voice.
This is something different. There is nothing musical about it. The
effort of the monks, some of whom will have sung the same verses to
the same tune tens of thousands of times, is tangible: the flagging then
the rallying, a sense of the sheer labour of it. There is no attempt to re-
create the songs of the angels; rather this is physical effort as an expression of praise. There's little beauty in it, but when the cymbals and
the triangle reach a certain crescendo and quickness, and the monks'
voices are raised to the fullness of their passion and volume, the sound
has a power to stir and inspire that exceeds the most exquisite European choral music. A verse will be sung with suddenly renewed vigour,
as if in acknowledgement that the energy was allowed to diminish.

After half an hour of standing, my back is aching; after two hours
it's hard to concentrate on anything but the discomfort. Nor does it
get easier, a novitiate tells me. The pain always. I want to sit down on
the carpet. I'm not sure why I don't. We join in with the *Kyrie eleisons*—
"Lord have mercy"—repeated twenty-five times, the last iteration
drawn out over twenty seconds, like a record played too slow, the
stomach tightening until all breath's gone.

FATHER LUCAS IS in his thirties, I guess; slender in his robe, with a
black beard and a gently professorial air. He trained as a dentist before
taking his vows two years ago. "There are very few dentist-monks," he
says. His surgery is in one of the monastery's fifteenth-century out-
buildings, crammed with state-of-the-art kit—X-ray machine, gleaming autoclave, a new supersonic drill for root-canal jobs. He treats not
only his fellow monks but camel farmers, soldiers and Bedouin from
all over the Eastern Desert. Prayer is not a monk's only obligation. It's

he who tells me about the walk to St. Paul's, the walk that St. Antony undertook when he visited the dying hermit. There are two routes, he explains as we sit in his waiting room drinking tea: the first takes you over the mountains behind St. Antony's; the second, much longer, is the one the elderly Antony probably took. It skirts the highest peaks, following a network of wadis before climbing the mountain above St. Paul's. He warns against the first way at this time of year—too windy on those high peaks, and it's easy to get lost.

He invites Peter and me to attend midnight mass at the cave of St. Antony, the place where the saint is said to have lived during the third century, in the mountainside high above the monastery. At 10 p.m. we hear a honk outside the guest quarters, and he's waiting in his truck. The three of us drive to the foot of the mountain and Peter and I follow Father Lucas up each of the thousand hand-railed steps. It's a climb I know well by now. I often go to the cave after matins, while it's still cool, to watch the sun rise. It was only when I had made the climb a few times that I realised the hillsides of limestone shale through which the path climbs were not bare as I'd assumed. I was reminded of those Rorschach blots where a pattern can emerge from an apparently random arrangement of blobs. The longer you look at the hillsides, the more crosses you become aware of: crosses laid out horizontally on a slope of the same stone from which they were formed. Once you see one you see another, then another—dozens, hundreds, created stone by stone by generations of pilgrims. Halfway up is the tiny modern Church of St. Paul (another St. Paul), its walls coated in Arabic graffiti, and all around it grey bricks—a surplus from its construction— have been stacked in such a way that they too form crosses, these ones standing upright. As you approach the terrace outside the cave, lengths of palm- and acacia-wood have been lashed together and set upright or lodged in natural nooks. The impression is of passing through a great forest or crowd of crosses, crosses of almost infinite number, in fact— the left arm of one being also the right arm of another.

In the darkness I only have a sense of the huge space through which we are clambering; the impression is of ascending a staircase through a void. But the darkness is never absolute, any more than the silence. From some distance away, perhaps a kilometre, there is a murmuring, a human sound, some lone monk in his mountain devotions. There's something terrifying and appalling about the sound, the utter loneliness of it. Though loneliness is surely not what he feels. Father Lucas prefers to walk without torchlight, and so as the three of us climb I am aware only of the swaying black mass of the monk ahead, a blacker black against the black of the mountains. The sound of our breathing, the swish of our hands on the steel handrail. When we stop halfway to rest, Father Lucas utters only one sentence: "Tell me this, is it the man who makes the place holy or the place that makes the man holy?" He is not unhappy with our silence.

When we reach the cave, others are waiting at the entrance, young men, the group lit up with their smartphones' flashlights. On their phones they also carry the three Coptic liturgies of St. Basil, St. Gregory and St. Cyril, the full psalmody and the Agpeya, the cycle of canonical hours. They are pleased to see Father Lucas. He blesses them and tells them to turn off their flashlights; he doesn't like the dazzle.

The Frenchman Jean Coppin, in the seventeenth century, described arriving at the cave, having climbed from the monastery: "The entrance is no more than two feet wide and four and a half feet high. This opening goes for some yards into the rock but does not widen out, so that two men could not pass through it abreast." Three centuries of use has not made it more capacious. Ducking, Father Lucas blesses himself and goes crabwise into the cave, one of the novitiates following with his phone as a light. It's a while before the passage opens out into the main chamber. It smells of incense—years, generations of incense, not sweet, more like the smell of an inactive furnace, at once metallic and earthy and herbal. The very stone is imbued with the fragrance; it is visible as a resinous glaze on the walls' surface and you can scrape it with a nail. The stone is burnished wherever it is accessible to hands—the walls, the low ceiling, millions of caresses. And in every crack and crevice are jammed folds of paper—one cannot praise a saint but one can ask for his favour.

For Copts, merely to be in this place is a form of blessing; holiness is accretive, a function of time, and the ancient soot of incense- and candle-smoke is time and praise substantiated. The twelve of us process down a short flight of steps into a domed pit the size of a garden shed. For those of us who find ourselves positioned at the edge of the chamber, where the roof lowers, it is impossible to stand up straight. At one end is a rock altar adorned with modern icons of St. Antony. This small lightless space is where Antony, so the monks believe, spent the last forty years of his life. Six candles are lit and each one, planted in a drop of its own melted wax, is set in a natural niche or on the edge of one of the stone steps. The chasuble and chalice are taken from a locked cupboard under the rock altar, and wine poured into the chalice, and white vestments quickly pulled on by Father Lucas and his two aides.

I experience a bafflement that I'm becoming familiar with. I am handed a candle as slender as a pencil, which I clutch between two fingers as you would a cigarette, leaving my hands more or less free. I open the Liturgy of St. Gregory on my phone, but soon lose track of what is being chanted, and simply stand, head bowed, listening to the psalmody thrown back and forth between Father Lucas and the novitiates. And as the singing escalates, and the heat within the cave intensifies, I suppress a feeling of panicked claustrophobia. After an hour, I can feel the air thinning, air that is now dense with incense smoke. Just as the candle is burning down to my fingers, the words scatter and slow to an uncertain close. Father Lucas turns, dips his hand in a bowl, and splashes water over us, once, twice, three times, and I look around and everyone is smiling. Sheer relief. Father Lucas's final few utterances are like the last birds of dusk.

The candles are blown out and we file up the steps to the cave's throat, edging out like potholers into the fresh night. Two hours have passed. I feel slightly astonished. Night after night, these eager young men climbing 400 metres and pressing themselves into a hole in the earth for hours at a time, and doing it with joy. They're all but indistinguishable—save for their phones and trainers—from their predecessors of the past fifteen hundred years; and that is at the heart of their pleasure, of course.

We sit exhausted outside the entrance, looking down at the night desert—a single pair of headlights is crossing the Wadi Araba twenty kilometres away—and up at the night sky. The younger boys—not novitiates, just local Copts—have brought water in a three-litre plastic canteen: they hand it to me, it's cold, pieces of ice shucking as I upturn it to my lips. Peter is settling beside me; it's good to see him. He won't have any water. "Drink," I say. He says he's fine. "Do me a favour." He obliges. But he's not exhausted; he's galvanised and newly garrulous; if he were a different sort of person you'd think he'd just eaten a good meal or had sex or watched his football team win. The sky is framed by the arch of the overhang that hoods the cave's entrance, its shape expressed as an absence of stars. "It is so amazing!" he says, lying back. "The greatness of God's work. So great that we cannot imagine it." I ask him if the night skies are like this in Eritrea. "Yes! Yes, exactly the same. Beautiful. In the stars you see the pure breath of God."

TOMORROW IS MY last day before I walk to St. Paul's. Through the church windows this morning the sky has lightened to a pale blue. Soon the sun will touch the tops of the North Galala Mountains, fifty kilometres away across the Wadi Araba, but direct sunlight will not come to the monastery for an hour or more. This is the time I love most, here as in Arizona, the half-hour or so of passive light when night is giving way to the luminous time before the sun hits the ground around you. Today is a national holiday. I had expected to walk out of the monastery into the usual deserted dawn car park, but there are perhaps twenty coaches already idling, and others arriving, bringing pilgrims from Cairo and Alexandria and all along the Nile to start the climb to the cave before the sun rises.

This form of informal pilgrimage, known as *rihla*, is a modern phenomenon facilitated by the desert highways. It's a day out, tourism as much as pilgrimage; but Copts also visit the monasteries to receive the grace, the *baraka*, of the fathers and the place itself, as well as praying before the church altars and making supplications to the remains of saints. Back inside our rooms there is no peace: from outside comes shouting and laughter, the sounding of horns and the revving of engines. The front door rattles and I open it to find two little boys running away, shrieking with laughter. The world. I'm glad to see it— the women and children, especially—but for Peter it's too much. He's putting on his shoes. I fill my water bottle and don my rucksack and together we go out into the smog and the honking.

The trail to St. Antony's cave, visible 1,500 metres away, is thronged, a line of people almost unbroken threading up the steps. We push through the coaches and the crowds—by now there are perhaps five hundred people here, eating breakfast, kicking footballs, hollering to one another—and find our way around the monastery walls to the rear, where the slope to the mountains begins. Here there is no one, only the pale wall behind us and the dark face of the mountain ahead. But the horns are still audible. At the foot of the slope the track that runs behind the monastery has just been tarmacked and our feet stick to the glossy black surface as we cross. I find a trail—human or animal it is hard to say—that runs along an alluvial fan and up the mountainside. The way is rough and demanding, but well used, and not only by ibex and foxes. Close to the top, at about four hundred metres, where the face becomes vertical, a few flights of crude steps have been built, with a scaffold-pole handrail. I notice twin black power cables snaking up from the monastery. It's not clear if we are trespassing; still, there is no question but that we will continue to the top, if only for the view. Once we get there we see that we have reached not the top but the edge of a terrace scattered with towering dunes of limestone rubble intersected by a single winding path, and that the mountains continue to rise beyond this plateau, surging to eight hundred metres or more. "The devil is like a snake or a scorpion," Peter says suddenly, as we walk between two hills of rubble. "We only need to say the name of Christ and it is as if he is crushed under our feet." He is trying to comfort himself: it is not the devil that is preoccupying him but the thought of real snakes and real scorpions. I'm not sure whether his unease is just that of one accustomed to the city or if he recognises these mountains as an extension of the wildernesses of the Old Testament. He has read Athanasius and knows that the Inner Mountain was never a place of tranquillity for St. Antony. Nor was the devil ever subdued for long.

Antony's acolytes, when they visited, "saw the mountain become full of wild beasts, and him also fighting as though against visible beings . . . Almost all the hyenas in that desert came forth from their dens and surrounded him." And as we proceed, following those black power cables, we see that battle is still being joined. Built into a narrow escarpment is a small wooden hut. As we are approaching it, we see another on the other side of the path. It is these that the cables are supplying. They are like sentry houses positioned to guard the passage between the hills, the way to the monastery from which we have climbed. The doors are closed, the windows shuttered. Outside one of them is a wooden bench, but a monk's prayer is done inside his cell, for hours without pause, for days (and who knows what his private devotions might be?), and so we cannot know if the cells are occupied or not, and we daren't approach them for fear of disturbing someone submerged in prayer. We walk on into the maze of hills.

Limestone, I tell him, is a product of the sea; the hardened remains of tiny creatures sunk to the bed and tamped down, layer upon layer, over millions of years. But it is as if Peter, usually such a careful listener, is paying no attention. He stops and stares up at the peaks above us, at their stark line against the blue sky. Then he walks on. Close to the path ahead lie a pick and shovel. An effort has been made to dig a flat shelf from the rock slope, a sleeping place or a platform for a new cell. Where the rock's laminations have been exposed by the digging are dozens of fossil shells. I lever one out and hand it to him. I'm not trying to prove anything. He frowns. He's amazed. "Really? All of this, under the sea?" I pick out some more and put them in his open palm.

"How do you know this?"

I tell him it's just a fact; we forget how we come by certain knowledge.

"You will laugh at me . . ." he says.

"If you say something funny."

"Well," he says. "Perhaps . . . perhaps, the Great Flood? . . . The flood of Noah?"

Yes, I tell him, perhaps that; perhaps the Great Flood—though these mountains are millions of years old.

He's struggling to reconcile biblical time and geological time, but he seems to put it out of his mind as we walk on, into the wilderness. I remember what he said the other night, as he looked up at the stars outside St. Antony's cave, thinking, perhaps, of what he could do to his life—*God's work, so great we cannot imagine it . . .*

It is hard to imagine the monastic tradition being born in any fertile place, in any place of birdsong or children's laughter. Only in the desert does the austerity of the prospect echo the austerity of the existence, only this mineral landscape could speak to a monk's own avowed barrenness. We walk in the mountains for the rest of the morning, and find, lodged here and there among hidden crevasses, further monks' cells, as well as blankets and oil lamps abandoned beneath overhangs. There is a feeling of the mountains as a dormitory. Few live here permanently. High in the mountains we follow a series of small red crosses painted onto a succession of boulders: way-markers.

YOU CAN COME to dread the sun, even when shelter and water are at hand: its heat, but also its light. No sooner has it risen than I long for it to set. That afternoon I retreat to the Church of St. Antony. The pilgrims are gone, and the monastery is quiet once more. Peter has been summoned to help the fathers with some work. Sitting on the floor in one corner is Brother Joachim, the novitiate whose job it is to care for the church. He's an affable, slightly bumptious man, with a moustache that is far thicker than the beard it surmounts. He gets to his feet, glad to see me; I place a hand on my heart, he on his, and he gestures me to sit with him. He's eager to talk (the novitiates often are). He has been here only sixteen months, he tells me. I use the word "amazing" to describe the wall paintings—I mean to put him at his ease, but it's a fool's word. Nevertheless it is this word he picks up, repeatedly, to describe his life here at the monastery, though it seems more the case that it is his being here, living this life, that amazes him, rather than the place or the life itself. He would not be the first to awaken to the reality of his own life with a sense of surprise. "Amazing ... But it is very hard. You can read about the life of the monk, but you cannot understand it until you live it. To leave your family and your friends ..."

He is young, he has not yet taken his vows. He wonders if he has made a mistake—this wondering is the essence of every monk's life's work. And then there are the visitors, those thousands of pilgrims who are the monastery's lifeblood and its burden. "God knows I love you," the fourth-century anchorite Abba Arsenius told his followers, "but I cannot be with God and with men."

"The people think we are perfect. They come to us because they no longer trust the priests," Joachim says. "They tell us this. They even make confession to the fathers. The work of the clergy has fallen upon the monasteries. But a man can live one life only: the life of the monastery or the life of the world."

He lists the three eternal duties of the monk: chastity, poverty, obedience. "When there are many people here, they bring the devil with them. The devil *knows* how to tempt us. Maybe you see a nice car, a BMW: 'Am I wasting my life? Is this all for nothing?' This is how the devil works."

He doesn't mention the women, the silk-haired Cairenes stepping down from coaches, or the bands of roaring twenty-something men in aviator sunglasses, arms around one another's shoulders. He doesn't mention the new silence when the last coach has gone.

He likes novels, he tells me—he mentions Orhan Pamuk and Elif Shafak—and in his old life, during his twenties, he spent much of his time reading. Here, it is true, he is free to read whatever he pleases, whatever he himself deems appropriate. "But we are told that we are not here to learn about the world. We are not here for our education. Knowledge, reading, studying: it is all a distraction from prayer. Some of the best fathers, the old men, they know nothing of the world but scripture."

Despite the monasteries' libraries and scriptoria (the library here remains off-limits to visitors), *reading*—the word—has always been a subject of suspicion among the desert monastics. Athanasius tells us that, even as a boy, St. Antony "could not endure to learn letters," and while claims that he was illiterate are undermined by letters attributed to him, he was no bibliophile: "My book," he said, "is the nature of created things; whenever I want to read the word of God it is always there before me." Joachim goes on, "Our father Antony said, 'In the person whose mind is sound there is no need for letters.'" God, as Moses knew, is "beyond images" and thus beyond words. The desert is not a blank page; it is a library whose shelves have never been occupied.

As I'm getting up, Joachim asks me to stay. "You have an appointment? An important meeting? Stay. Stay for a while. Look." He stands and bends down to lift a corner of the church's red carpet, revealing a pane of dusty reinforced glass covering the ancient crypt. "There are many secret places here, you see; and there are many secrets." But he won't elaborate, he only smiles and holds my gaze as if we both understand. He only means, I think, that the life the visitor sees is not the true life, that there is something of the actor in the public monk.

It's hard to imagine this guy who likes to read Pamuk, whose favourite singer is Susan Boyle, and who is so eager for news of the world, ever reconciling himself to the principles of chastity, poverty and obedience. But then it is not a life to which one is expected to become reconciled. It *is* amazing.

IT HAS BEEN an unusually hot day. This afternoon one of the novitiates came to our quarters and told Peter there was work to do. He, Peter, had been pleading for labour all week. Prayer and fasting were not enough. While some of the monastery's water still comes from the spring that first brought St. Antony here, much of it is piped in. Somewhere out there on the plain of the Wadi Araba the pipe had ruptured, and since Peter was keen to know the monk's life in all its parts, he was to join the work gang.

When I get back from the church he is sitting on the edge of his bed, head in hands. He looks up at me, then places his head in his hands again. "Peter," I say. He looks at me exhausted. I fill a mug and mix some electrolyte powder into it: "Drink." I'm constantly telling him to drink. He drinks. For four hours he's been out in the midday sun, hatless, digging the rocky ground. "They told me I could leave, but I didn't want to." He looks drawn and spacey, his speech is slightly slurred. On his bedside cabinet are the hand-cymbals he uses to accompany his private prayers and a candle burnt down to a nub.

They successfully uncovered the pipe, fixed the leak, filled the hole. But he's dehydrated and I'm worried about heatstroke. I tell him to sleep, but he wants to talk. "The fathers did nothing," he says, "only shouted instructions." He laughs. "It wasn't what I expected!"

"Drink."

"I feel fine."

I go and refill his mug. At dinner in the refectory he is better; his eyes have lost their stickiness, water is doing its work. But his fervour of a week ago is spent. As he and the novitiates dug, dug, fixed, and refilled, he says, the fathers stood around the hole drinking Pepsi and laughing. They had called him "German":

"'Dig, German!'

"Some of the monks are good," he says, "some are bad. You can see—at the morning praises, sometimes only a few of the fathers are there." Maybe they're praying in private, I say, or in one of the monastery's other churches. "I'm not judging them," he replies quickly. "But—would *I* be like that, if I came here? I am not judging them ..." But he goes on: "If you want to live the life of the city, to drink coffee"—and Pepsi—"and meet new people, why not do God's work in the city?"

He is still exhausted, but there is energy in his gaze.

"If we live as Jesus wished, then we will hate the world. God hates the world, because it is evil. Yes, there are some good people, but most people do not live good lives. Evil is there for us to look at. In the Sinai desert the Bedouin kidnap Eritrean refugees and if the family will not pay twenty thousand, thirty thousand dollars, they kill them; then they cut out the heart and the liver and they sell them—"

I interrupt him. "How old are you?"

"You know how old I am. Twenty-eight. When I was nineteen, I hated getting older: 'Oh no, I am twenty! Oh no, I am twenty-one!' ... Since Christ came to me, I *long* to be older! To be fifty, to be sixty, to be close to the end—to paradise. You see? When we are in paradise the pain of this world will be ... oh, like the sting of a mosquito ... or an accident we had when we were a child. Of *course* God hates the world. God did not win."

I am tiring of the Evil One. To doubt the existence of God is one thing, it seems; but to question the reality of Satan? Evil is there for us to look at. Go to YouTube and watch those men in orange jumpsuits being led along a Libyan beach. Google the rate for an Eritrean's heart.

Tomorrow morning I'll leave the monastery for good, and cross the mountains to St. Paul's. Peter's flight is not for another week, but he's made his decision. The hours of digging in the desert, the fathers in black chugging Pepsi—"Dig, German!": a turning point. Perhaps the turning point he was seeking...He will go to his parents' motherland, Eritrea (Eritrea, from where a whole generation longs to escape), where the monastic life is truer to that which St. Macarius and his followers lived—behind walls without gates, or in "hyena holes"; or in caves deep in the desert, *paneremos*, *le désert absolu*, eternally anonymous. It is they who inspire him, those of whom no one will ever know.

On the way back to our quarters we stop in the corridor to watch the fish in their tank. The water hasn't been refilled since yesterday; it evaporates quickly in this dryness, and as it evaporates it becomes cloudier and cloudier. Another day or two and the fish will die. You can barely see them through the murk. Peter goes to the kitchen and returns holding a large tin cooking pot to his chest. Together we lift it and tip the water into the tank. "Drink!" he tells the fish.

THERE ARE NO good maps of the South Galala Mountains—the best I've come across was drawn by British military surveyors in 1891. You'd trust it at your peril. A few years ago, an American expat set out to walk between the monasteries alone. He was found too late, having lost his way and run out of water. Only the Bedouin of the northern Eastern Desert, the Ma'aza, know the mountains, and as a foreigner it is prudent to at least get their consent before setting out. Moussa, an English-speaking Coptic guide, is recommended to me by a friend. He makes contact with Mussalem, a member of the Ma'aza, and Mussalem's cousin Khaled. They were among those who found the American. The journey will take us two days. Khaled will transport our dinner, and our water for the second day, along with my luggage, and meet us at this evening's campsite in his truck.

I attend matins for the last time before we leave. In Greek there is the word *apatheia*, which means something like "the stilling of the passions." It is the most hard-earned of the monks' aspirations. Few achieve it. A state of holy tranquillity that equates to disinterestedness, indifference, detachment. Disinterest not towards duty, but towards social expectation; indifference to the opinion of others; detachment from the laws of the human world: this is *apatheia*. It is related to *apophasis*: you first have to acknowledge the incalculable value of silence. As the theologian Evagrius of Pontus said, "desert *apatheia* has a daughter whose name is love." It is this—love, *agape*—that is visible in the deportment of the older fathers during matins: their reverence for the church and the liturgy and their forebears, their small tendernesses to the other monks and novitiates. The desert, in its harshness, is the external complement of the indifference that love requires.

Moussa, when we meet outside the monastery gates, is boisterous and obliging, with the slightly guarded air of liberation you find in new fathers away from home (his wife's just had their third baby). He's good company even when we are walking in silence. I'm his first client in months, he says. Egypt's tourist industry is all but nonexistent following the war in neighbouring Libya and the bombing of a Russian airliner flying from Sharm el-Sheikh. He was a tour guide in the Sinai desert, but he has had to retrain as a teacher. For him, as a Copt, our journey is in the nature of a pilgrimage. Mussalem, a foot shorter than Moussa, scarcely speaks, and walks ahead—always several metres ahead—navigating the rubble and boulders as if gliding just above the wadi floor. He wears an off-white dishdasha and a white headscarf. Slung across his back are his canvas satchel and a canteen formed from coloured yarn woven snug around a two-litre plastic water bottle. Over one shoulder, all day, he holds a plastic bag containing flatbreads and tubs of halva.

After a morning spent walking the boulder-strewn plain of the Wadi Araba we meet Khaled for lunch under an acacia tree, the only vegetation above ankle-height we've seen since leaving St. Antony's. Having eaten, Moussa and I rest for an hour in its shade while Mussalem and Khaled lie under the truck. A fly's attentions serve as a reminder of what reeks about you: where does it attend? Nostrils, ear-holes, eye-corners, lips; wherever there is fluid. Along one of the acacia's branches a line of ants processes. From another, Khaled has hung a plastic bag. I watch as blood drips from one corner onto the dust by my feet, pools. And yes, as it dries, I see that its colour is not red but grey.

We see Khaled off for the afternoon and turn right, following a wadi into the mountains. There is a feeling of containment after the infinite openness of the plain. Containment and the relief of shade. The only animal life we see are two indignant finches in a solitary wild fig tree. The valley closes in—on either side, ten-metre walls of gravelly conglomerate carved with vertical channels where water has cascaded. The sun is getting low. We've walked about thirty kilometres. On the other side of the wadi we see a white Toyota Hilux moving parallel to us: Khaled.

Once he has lit a fire, Mussalem puts the flame of a lighter to a plastic water bottle and carefully tears off its funnelled top. He pushes one of the monastery's candles into the coarse sand of the wadi floor and fits the half-bottle over it, mouth first, to serve as a wind-break, then lights the candle. He repeats this with our remaining empty water bottles, so that our camp is ringed by flickering, crystalline cones of plastic. After dinner I find a windless spot for my sleeping mat.

It's about three hours later when I'm snapped awake by a noise. I blink and the valley walls are ablaze in shifting, rocking yellow light. Passengers. Mussalem, Moussa and Khaled sit up as headlights dazzle us and a rusted Toyota truck skids to a halt metres from our camp. There's a moment's silence, then a door slams.

Moussa is kneeling in his sleeping bag, one hand visored on his brow. Mussalem is up and shouting at the strangers. The headlights are switched off and I can see nothing. "Who are you?" Mussalem is demanding. "What are you doing on our land?" They shout back; another door slams. The exchange cools. The two men are Ma'aza from another clan, apparently looking for a herd of absconded camels. This is precisely what the men who sped up to our lunch camp in Oman two years ago said. Perhaps it's just the story one feeds strangers after the fact. They have tea with us before returning to their truck.

The engine-growl withdraws and the night is returned to quiet, and I register a sound that is familiar to me now: the sound that is what we call silence: the deep, mysterious internal piping: blood in movement, or the generation of cells, or some discreet regularising of aural pressures.

Yesterday morning, as we were walking to matins, Peter stopped and said, "There: *there* is the best place to be a monk." He was looking at the moon. It is not visible from the valley floor tonight, but its light touches the heights of the mountains.

In *The Desert*, John C. Van Dyke asks: "Have we not proof in our own moon that worlds die? And how came it to die? ... Perhaps it died through thousands of years with the slow evaporation of moisture and the slow growth of the desert." Which leads him, naturally, to ask: "Is then this great expanse of sand and rock the beginning of the end? Is that the way our globe shall perish?" But the ever windless, ever waterless moon is an imperfect analogue for the deserts of earth. In 1911 an American astronomer, seeing the dark lines that appeared to crisscross Mars's surface, postulated that they were irrigation canals constructed by the Martians to bring fertility to the desert planet. Told that the dark ribbons were tens of kilometres across, he responded that of course they were; what was visible were not the canals themselves but the margins of irrigated land lining their banks. Where they intersected, he reasoned, great cities stood. Since *Viking I* and *II* were dispatched to Mars's surface in the 1970s and 1980s, four further vessels have landed on the planet, including two mobile rovers. The images they have sent back show features that would be familiar to the Bed-

ouin: alluvial fans, gibber plains and playas. There are dust devils eight kilometres tall, and seasonal dust storms that engulf the whole planet. On the sweeping northern plains, meanwhile, are monstrous sand seas whose dune formations—rectilinear, longitudinal, transverse, crescentic, barchanoid—are indistinguishable from those of earth.

I wake to the murmuring of prayer: Mussalem kneeling on his rug on the rocky ground as orange sunlight touches the summits. There are yellow-grey clouds, the first clouds I've seen since coming to Egypt. We say farewell to Khaled, whose vehicle can go no further. After breakfast we clamber along crumbling limestone banks above what, in times of flood, would be an immense staircase of waterfalls. It's two years since the last flash floods, Mussalem says. In the pit of every dry falls is an island of acacia and tamarisk. From a wild fig tree I pick a fruit no bigger than a cherry; velvety-soft, pale green, bitter. A leaf, glossy and pliant when I pick it, has crumbled to brown flakes in my pocket a few hours later.

Towards midday, as we continue to climb, there's a sense of approaching a precipice or a summit. A new expansiveness to the light. Moussa shouts back at me, grinning, but his words are inaudible. A single step higher and the wind hits me, snatches my hat and frisbees it into the valley behind us.

Far below, on the other side, is the Red Sea coastal plain, and fifteen kilometres away the thin blue line of the Gulf of Suez. Just visible beyond the water are the mountains of Sinai. And there, nestled in the foothills far below us, a grid of limewashed buildings within a defensive wall.

At the monastery gate a guard is surprised to see anybody other than monks approaching from the mountains. When Moussa tells him where we have come from he laughs and lets us in and goes to fetch one of the English-speaking fathers. Arriving twenty minutes later, he is a man in his thirties, with a hollow, red-cheeked face and large lips dried salt-white by the sun, whiter still against his black beard. A thin, sunburnt Allen Ginsberg, who of course speaks with a soft, east-coast American accent—though he prefers not to tell me where he is from, just as he prefers not to tell me his name. A reluctant docent, not unfriendly. Father Allen.

In the small, dim, half-buried church built over St. Paul's cave, he shows me a wall painting matching the one at St. Antony's: the two saints wide-eyed and small-mouthed in the tradition of Coptic art. Elevated between them is the raven, holding in its beak a round of bread, the bread it brought for St. Paul and the visiting St. Antony. The ravens are a nuisance, Father Allen tells me—they steal dates from the monastery palms and interrupt the liturgies with their cawing. In the old days the monks used to shoot them, despite the service the birds' ancestor did for St. Paul.

We stand and talk in the shade. "My personal view," he says, "is that the clergy exists to speak to the people. *This*"—he means attending to visitors—"is not part of the monk's work. A monk's work is to be hidden."

I think of Peter and his Ethiopian monks lodged happily in their desert holes. Father Allen prefers not to have his photo taken. He prefers not to tell me how long he has been here. Before returning to his cell, he shows us where the spring flows from the foot of the mountain along a narrow channel cut into the stone floor. On a plastic chair lies a steel cup. I crouch and fill it and pass it to Moussa. He drinks, and returns the cup to me. It's sweet, less mineralised than the water at St. Antony's. I refill the cup and drink again; refill it once more—drink.

In a few hours I'll be back in Cairo, with its two million vehicles and their two million horns. We find a taxi and drive towards the Red Sea highway, dropping Mussalem at a junction from where he'll hitch-hike back to his village. A couple of kilometres from Zafarana, near the huge windfarm that fills the Wadi Araba where it meets the Red Sea, I get the driver to pull up at a deserted tourist restaurant beside one of the Russian-owned resorts. While he and Moussa have coffee, I cross the hundred metres of hard brown sand. It's not a tourist beach and there's a smell of engine oil, but the sea looks clean enough. I strip in the shade of a fisherman's hut and pick my way towards the water.

ACKNOWLEDGEMENTS

The people and organisations to whom I'm most indebted are mentioned in the text, though not always under their real names. My gratitude to them is beyond measure.

At Faber I'm grateful to my editor Lee Brackstone, Ella Griffiths, Lizzie Bishop, Samantha Matthews, Lauren Nicoll, Ruth O'Loughlin, Dan Papps, Donna Payne and Kate Ward. At Doubleday I'm indebted to my editor, Gerald Howard, and to Michael Goldsmith, Nora Grubb and Lauren Weber; thanks, also, to Doug Pepper and Louis Dennys at Signal/Knopf, Canada; to Alan Horsfield for the maps; and to Lucy Ridout, who copyedited the book.

I owe a great debt to my friend and agent Patrick Walsh, and to other friends, allies, supporters and inspirations: Stuart Evers and Lisa Baker, Stephanie Cross, Lucy Abraham and Neil Cameron, Betsy and Thomas Cameron, Guy and Alanna Griffiths, Ellen Blythe, Judith Adams and Simon Warner, John Ash, Simon Baker and Hilda Breakspear, Maryann Bylander, James Cowan, Catherine Eccles and Joe Gannon, William L. Fox, Peter Gale, Andrew Goudie, Philip Hoare, Nick Holdstock, Brad Holland, Gregory McNamee, Megan Miller, Richard Muir, Elna Otter, Daniel Baker and James McPherson, Daniel Pinchbeck, Owen and Catherine Sheers, Rhonda Walker, Michael Welland and Carol Welland, Susan Whitfield, Joy Williams, the Yateses (especially Charlie and Evie), Chris and Angus Patterson, and Chloe, Katherine, Keith and Gill Atkins.

I'm grateful to Arts Council England for a grant; to Gladstone's Library, Hawarden, for a residency; and particularly to Philip Davies and the Eccles Centre for American Studies, for the gift of an Eccles British Library Writer's Award.

TEXT ACKNOWLEDGEMENTS

Lines from *Don Quixote* by Miguel Cervantes, trans. John Rutherford, reproduced by permission of Penguin Random House. Lines of Taras Shevchenko's verse translated by Pavlo Zaitsev, from *Taras Shevchenko: A Life*, reproduced by permission of the Shevchenko Scientific Society, New York; lines from "The Lonely Goatherd" © 1959 by Richard Rodgers & Oscar Hammerstein II. Copyright Renewed. International Copyright Secured. All Rights Reserved. Used by Permission of Williamson Music, a Division of Rodgers & Hammerstein.

IMAGE ACKNOWLEDGEMENTS

p. 10: *Saint Antony Abbot with Saint Paul the Hermit*, lithograph by F. Blanchar after J. de Madrazo after Velazquez, copyrighted work available under Creative Commons Attribution only licence CC BY 4.0, Wellcome Library.

p. 19: *The Temptation of St. Antony*, follower of Hieronymus Bosch, Public Domain via Wikimedia Commons.

p. 48: Bertram Thomas and Retinue © Royal Geographical Society (with IBG).

p. 90: Marcoo nuclear test © Newspix.

p. 114: From Mildred Cable, *The Gobi Desert*.

p. 120: Bishop Wang (by Aurel Stein) © Bridgeman Images.

p. 148: From Sven Hedin, *Through Asia*.

p. 183: Taras Shevchenko, *Burning Steppe*, reproduced by permission of Taras Shevchenko Museum, Canada.

p. 191: Taras Shevchenko, Untitled, reproduced by permission of Taras Shevchenko Museum, Canada.

p. 197: Taras Shevchenko, Untitled, reproduced by permission of Taras Shevchenko Museum, Canada.

p. 209: From *Harper's Magazine*, May 1957.

pp. 268–69: J. Goldsborough Bruff, *The Rabbit-hole Springs* © Huntingdon Library.

p. 325: "High Dune," Mars, from the mast camera of NASA's Curiosity rover. Part of the "Bagnold Dunes" field of active dark dunes along the north-western flank of Mount Sharp © NASA/JPL-Caltech/MSSS.

Bibliography

GENERAL

E. F. Adolph, *Physiology of Man in the Desert* (New York: Interscience Publishers, 1947)

W. H. Auden, *The Enchafèd Flood; Or the Romantic Iconography of the Sea* (New York: Random House, 1950)

R. A. Bagnold, *Libyan Sands: Travel in a Dead World* (London: Hodder & Stoughton, 1935)

——, *The Physics of Blown Sand and Desert Dunes* (London: Methuen, 1941)

Jean Baudrillard, *America* (London: Verso, 2010)

Ron Cooke, Andrew Warren, Andrew Goudie (eds), *Desert Geomorphology* (London: UCL Press, 1993)

Isabelle Eberhardt, *The Oblivion Seekers* (London: Peter Owen, 1988)

Uwe George, trans. Richard and Clara Winston, *In the Deserts of This Earth* (New York: Harcourt Brace Jovanovich, 1977)

Andrew S. Goudie, *Arid and Semi-Arid Geomorphology* (Cambridge: Cambridge University Press, 2013)

Roslynn D. Haynes, *Desert: Nature and Culture* (London: Reaktion, 2013)

Anton Imeson, *Desertification, Land Degradation and Sustainability* (Oxford: Wiley-Blackwell, 2012)

Robert Irwin, *Camel* (London: Reaktion, 2010)

Edmond Jabès, trans. Keith Waldrop, *If There Were Anywhere But Desert* (Barrytown: Station Hill Press, 1988)

——, trans. Pierre Joris, *From the Desert to the Book* (Barrytown: Station Hill Press, 1990)

Sven Lindqvist, trans. Joan Tate, *Saharan Journey* (London: Granta, 2012)

Pierre Loti, trans. Jay Paul Minn, *The Desert* (Salt Lake City: University of Utah Press, 1993; originally published in French in 1896 as *Le Désert*)

Gregory McNamee (ed.), *The Desert Reader: A Literary Companion* (Albuquerque: University of New Mexico Press, 2003)

Antoine de Saint-Exupéry, trans. Lewis Galantière, *Wind, Sand and Stars* (London: Heinemann, 1939)

————, trans. Stuart Gilbert, *The Wisdom of the Sands* (London: Hollis & Carter, 1952)

Paul Bigelow Sears, *Deserts on the March* (Norman: University of Oklahoma Press, 1935)

Paul Shepard, *Nature and Madness* (San Francisco: Sierra Club Books, 1982)

David S. G. Thomas (ed.), *Arid Zone Geomorphology* (Chichester: Wiley, 2011)

———— and Nicholas J. Middleton, *Desertification: Exploding the Myth* (Chichester: Wiley, 1994)

Yi-Fu Tuan, *Topophilia: A Study of Environmental Perception* (Englewood Cliffs, NJ: Prentice-Hall, 1974)

————, *Landscapes of Fear* (Oxford: Blackwell, 1980)

————, *Romantic Geography* (Madison: University of Wisconsin Press, 2013)

Michael Welland, *The Desert: Lands of Lost Borders* (London: Reaktion, 2015)

Peter Wild, *The Opal Desert: Explorations of Fantasy and Reality in the American Southwest* (Austin: University of Texas Press, 1999)

1 THE DESERT LIBRARY: THE EMPTY QUARTER, OMAN

David C. Arkless, *The Secret War: Dhofar 1971* (London: Kimber, 1988)

John Beasant: *Oman: The True-life Drama and Intrigue of an Arab State* (Edinburgh: Mainstream, 2002)

Peter Brent, *Far Arabia: Explorers of the Myth* (London: Weidenfeld & Nicolson, 1977)

Bill Broyles et al., "W. J. McGee's 'Desert Thirst as Disease'," *Journal of the Southwest* 30, no. 2 (1988): 222–27. McGee's essay was originally published in *Interstate Medical Journal* (see below)

Richard Burton (trans.), *The Book of the Thousand Nights and a Night*, 16 vols. (London: Kama Shastra Society, 1885–88)

Mark Cocker, *Loneliness & Time: British Travel Writing in the Twentieth Century* (London: Secker & Warburg, 1992)

Charles Montague Doughty, *Travels in Arabia Deserta* (Cambridge: Cambridge University Press, 1888)

Felix Fabri, *Wanderings in the Holy Land* (London: Palestine Pilgrims' Text Society, 1892)

K. W. Glennie, *Oman's Geological Heritage* (Muscat: Petroleum Development Oman, 2006)

T. E. Lawrence, *Seven Pillars of Wisdom* (London: Penguin, 2000)

Alexander Maitland, *Wilfred Thesiger: The Life of the Great Explorer* (London: Harper Perennial, 2007)

Arthur Mangin, *The Desert World: The Scenery, Animal and Vegetable Life and Physical Character of the Wilderness and Waste Places of the Earth* (London: T. Nelson and Sons, 1872)

W. J. McGee, "Desert Thirst as Disease," *Interstate Medical Journal* 12 (1906): 1–23

James Morris, *Sultan in Oman* (London: Faber & Faber, 1957)

William Harman Norton, "The Influence of the Desert on Early Islam," from *The Journal of Religion* 4, no. 4 (July 1924): 383–96

Harry St. John Philby, *The Empty Quarter* (London: 1933, Constable)

Andrew Taylor, *Travelling the Sands: Sagas of Exploration in the Arabian Peninsula* (Dubai: Motivate Publishing, 1995)

Wilfred Thesiger, *Arabian Sands* (London: Longmans, Green, 1959)

———, *The Life of My Choice* (London: HarperCollins, 2000)

Bertram Thomas, *Alarms and Excursions in Arabia* (London: Allen & Unwin, 1931)

———, *Arabia Felix* (London: Jonathan Cape, 1932)

Tetsuro Watsuji, trans. Geoffrey Bownas, *Climate and Culture* (Tokyo: Hokuseido Press, 1971)

2 FIELD OF THUNDER: THE GREAT VICTORIA DESERT, AUSTRALIA

Lorna Arnold, *Britain, Australia and the Bomb: The Nuclear Tests and Their Aftermath* (Basingstoke: Palgrave, 2006)

Daisy Bates, *The Passing of the Aborigines* (London: John Murray, 1938)

Len Beadell, *Blast the Bush* (London: Angus and Robertson, 1967)

———, *Beating About the Bush* (Adelaide: Rigby, 1976)

Julia Blackburn, *Daisy Bates in the Desert* (London: Secker & Warburg, 1994)

Geoffrey Blainey, *The Tyranny of Distance: How Distance Shaped Australia's History* (Melbourne: Macmillan, 1975)

Paul Carter, *The Road to Botany Bay* (London: Faber & Faber, 1987)

David Day, *Claiming a Continent: A New History of Australia* (Sydney: Harper-Perennial, 2005)

Charles Duguid, *Doctor and the Aborigines* (Adelaide: Rigby, 1972)

Edward John Eyre, *Journals of Expeditions of Discovery into Central Australia* (London: T. and W. Boone, 1845)

John Greenway, *The Last Frontier* (London: David-Poynter, 1973)

Roslynn D. Haynes, *Seeking the Centre: The Australian Desert in Literature, Art and Film* (Cambridge: Cambridge University Press, 1998)

Michael Hughes, *Spectre of Maralinga* (London: W. H. Allen, 1985)

Sven Lindqvist, trans. Sarah Death, *Terra Nullius: A Journey Through No One's Land* (London: Granta, 2007)

Christobel Mattingley and Ken Hampton (eds), *Survival in Our Own Land: "Aboriginal" Experiences in "South Australia" Since 1836* (Adelaide: Wakefield Press, 1988)

Robert Milliken, *No Conceivable Injury: The Story of Britain and Australia's Atomic Cover-up* (London: Penguin, 1985)

Ferenc Morton Szasz, *The Day the Sun Rose Twice: The Story of the Trinity Site Nuclear Explosion, July 16, 1945* (Albuquerque: University of New Mexico Press, 1984)

Penny Van Oosterzee, *The Centre: The Natural History of Australia's Desert Regions* (Chatswood: Reed, 1991)

Kingsley Palmer and Maggie Brady, *Diet and Dust in the Desert: An Aboriginal Community, Maralinga Lands, South Australia* (Canberra: Aboriginal Studies Press, 1991)

John Pilger, *A Secret Country* (London: Jonathan Cape, 1989)

Royal Commission into British Nuclear Tests in Australia, *The Report of the Royal Commission into British Nuclear Tests in Australia*, 3 vols. (Canberra: Australian Government Publishing Service, 1985)

Adrian Tame and F. P. J. Robotham, *Maralinga: British A-Bomb Australian Legacy* (Melbourne: Fontana, 1982)

W. H. Tietkens, *Journal of the Central Australian Exploring Expedition*, 1889 (Adelaide: C. E. Bristow, 1891)

Frank Walker, *Maralinga* (Sydney: Hachette Australia, 2014)

Don Watson, *The Bush* (Melbourne: Penguin, 2014)

Michael Williams, *The Making of the South Australian Landscape* (London: Academic Press, 1974)

Yalata and Oak Valley Communities with Christobel Mattingley, *Maralinga: The Anangu Story* (Sydney: Allen & Unwin, 2009)

3 TROUBLEMAKERS: THE GOBI DESERT
AND THE TAKLAMAKAN DESERT, CHINA

Neville Agnew (ed.), *Conservation of Ancient Sites on the Silk Road* (Los Angeles: Getty Conservation Institute, 1997)

Ai Chen Wu, *Turkistan Tumult* (London: Methuen & Co, 1940)

Linda K. Benson, *Across China's Gobi: The Lives of Evangeline French, Mildred Cable and Francesca French of the China Inland Mission* (Norwalk: Eastbridge, 2008)

Charles Blackmore, *The Worst Desert on Earth: Crossing the Taklamakan* (London: John Murray, 1995)

Gardner Bovingdon, *The Uyghurs* (New York: Columbia University Press, 2010)

Tania Branigan, "China Charges Uighur Scholar Ilham Tohti with Separatism" *Guardian*, 30 July 2014

Chris Buckley, "Xinhua Details Charges in Case Against Ilham Tohti," *New York Times*, 25 September 2014

Mildred Cable with Francesca French, *The Gobi Desert* (London: Hodder & Stoughton, 1942). Reprinted, with an introduction by Marina Warner (London: Virago, 1984)

———, *Through Jade Gate and Central Asia: An Account of Journeys Through Kansu, Turkestan and the Gobi Desert* (London: Hodder & Stoughton, 1937).

——— and Evangeline French, *A Desert Journal: Letters from Central Asia* (London: Constable, 1934)

———, *Something Happened* (London: Hodder & Stoughton, 1933)

Simon Denyer, "Bullet Trains Tighten China's Embrace of Restive Xinjiang," *Washington Post*, 10 September 2014

Michael Dillon, *Xinjiang: China's Muslim Far Northwest* (London: Routledge-Curzon, 2004)

Ding Xiao Lun (ed.), *Entering Xinjiang* (Urumqi: Xinjiang Art & Photography, 2006)

David Eimer, *The Emperor Far Away: Travels at the Edge of China* (London: Bloomsbury, 2014)

Peter Fleming, *News From Tartary* (London: Jonathan Cape, 1936)

Sven Hedin, *Through Asia* (London: Methuen, 1898)

Nick Holdstock, *China's Forgotten People: Xinjiang, Terror and the Chinese State* (London: I. B. Taurus, 2015)

Peter Hopkirk, *Foreign Devils on the Silk Road* (London: John Murray, 1980)

Justin Jacobs, "Confronting Indiana Jones: Chinese Nationalism, Historical Imperialism, and the Criminalization of Aurel Stein and the Raiders of Dunhuang, 1899–1944," in Sherman Cochran and Paul G. Pickowicz (eds.), *China on the Margins* (Ithaca, NY: Cornell East Asia Program, 2010)

Jun Ma, *China's Water Crisis* (Norwalk: EastBridge, 2004)

Jonathan Kaiman, "Chinese Media Reports Fifty Killed in Xinjiang in Revision of Death Toll" *Guardian*, 26 September 2014

Ellsworth Huntington, *The Pulse of Asia: A Journey in Central Asia* (New York: Houghton, Mifflin & Co, 1907)

W. E. Johns, *Biggles in the Gobi* (London: Hodder & Stoughton, 1953)

Owen Lattimore, *The Desert Road to Turkestan* (New York: Little Brown, 1929)

Ma Jian, *Red Dust: A Path Through China* (London: Chatto & Windus, 2001)

Ella Maillart, trans. John Rodker, *Turkestan Solo* (New York: Putnam, 1935)

Mao Tse-Tung, *Selected Works* (Peking: Foreign Language Press, 1967)

James A. Millward, *Eurasian Crossroads: A History of Xinjiang* (London: Hurst, 2007)

William James Platt, *Three Women: Mildred Cable, Francesca French, Evangeline French* (London: Hodder & Stoughton, 1964)

Eva May Sawyer, *Mildred Cable* (London: Pickering & Inglis, 1962)

Vikram Seth, *From Heaven Lake: Travel Through Sinkiang and Tibet* (London: Chatto & Windus, 1983)

Judith Shapiro, *Mao's War Against Nature: Politics and the Environment in Revolutionary China* (Cambridge: Cambridge University Press, 2001)

Aurel Stein, *Ruins of Desert Cathay: Personal Narrative of Explorations in Central Asia and Westernmost China* (London: Macmillan, 1912)

———, *Sand-Buried Ruins of Khotan: Personal Narrative of a Journey of Archaeological and Geographical Exploration in Chinese Turkestan* (London: T. Fisher Unwin, 1903)

Phyllis Thompson, *Desert Pilgrim: The Story of Mildred Cable's Venture for God in Central Asia* (London: China Inland Mission, 1957)

Colin Thubron, *Shadow of the Silk Road* (London: Chatto & Windus, 2006)

Rian Thum, *The Sacred Routes of Uyghur History* (Cambridge, Mass.: Harvard University Press, 2014)

Jeremy Tredinnick, *Xinjiang: China's Central Asia* (Hong Kong: Odyssey, 2012)

Christian Tyler, *Wild West China: The Taming of Xinjiang* (London: John Murray, 2003)

Joanna Waley-Cohen, *Exile in Mid-Qing China* (New Haven, Conn.: Yale University Press, 1991)

Jonathan Watts, *When a Billion Chinese Jump* (London: Faber & Faber, 2010)

Roderick Whitfield, Susan Whitfield and Neville Agnew, *Cave Temples of Dunhuang: Art and History on the Silk Road* (London: British Library, 2000)

Susan Whitfield, *Life Along the Silk Road* (Berkeley: University of California Press, 1999)

Sally Hovey Wriggins, *The Silk Road Journey with Xuanzang* (Boulder: Westview, 2004)

Xuncheng Xia, *Desertification and Control of Blown Sand Disasters in Xinjiang* (Beijing: Science Press, 1993)

Xuanzang, trans. S. Beal, *Buddhist Records of the Western World* (London: Truebner's Oriental Series, 1884)

Yi-Fu Tuan, *China* (Harlow: Longmans, 1970)

4 BASTARD STURGEON: THE ARALKUM, KAZAKHSTAN

Chingiz Aitmatov, trans. John French, *The Day Lasts More Than a Hundred Years* (London: Macdonald and Co., 1986)

Tom Bissell, *Chasing the Sea* (New York: Pantheon Books, 2003)

Leonid Brezhnev, *The Virgin Lands* (Moscow: Progress, 1978)

Alexey Ivanovich Butakov, "Survey of the Aral Sea," in *Journal of the Royal Geographical Society* 23 (London, 1823): 93–101

Rob Ferguson, *The Devil and the Disappearing Sea: A True Story About the Aral Sea Catastrophe* (Vancouver: Raincoast Books, 2003)

Michael H. Glantz (ed.), *Creeping Environmental Problems and Sustainable Development in the Aral Sea Basin* (Cambridge: Cambridge University Press, 1999)

Peter Hopkirk, *The Great Game: On Secret Service in High Asia* (London: John Murray, 1990)

George Luckyj, *Shevchenko's Unforgotten Journey* (Toronto: Canadian Scholar's Press, 1996)

Patrick Marnham, *Snake Dance: Journeys Beneath a Nuclear Sky* (London: Chatto & Windus, 2013)

Philip Micklin et al. (eds.), *The Aral Sea* (Berlin: Springer, 2014)

David Moon, *The Plough that Broke the Steppes: Agriculture and Environment on Russia's Grasslands, 1700–1914* (Oxford: Oxford University Press, 2013)

G. I. Reznichenko, *The Aral Sea Tragedy* (Moscow: Novosti, 1992)

Maria Shahgedanova (ed.), *The Physical Geography of Northern Eurasia* (Oxford: Oxford University Press, 2002)

Struan Stevenson, *Stalin's Legacy: The Soviet War on Nature* (Edinburgh: Birlinn, 2012)

Chokan Chingisovich Valikhanov, trans. John and Robert Mitchell, *The Russians in Central Asia* (London: Edward Stanford, 1856)

Pavlo Zaitsev, *Taras Shevchenko* (Toronto: University of Toronto Press, 1988)

Peter Zavialov, *Physical Oceanography of the Dying Aral Sea* (New York: Springer, 2005)

Igor S. Zonn et al. (eds), *The Aral Sea Encyclopaedia* (Berlin: Springer, 2009)

5 BETWEEN GREAT FIRES: THE SONORAN DESERT, USA

Edward Abbey, *Desert Solitaire: A Season in the Wilderness* (New York: McGraw-Hill, 1968)

————, *Confessions of a Barbarian: Selections from the Journals of Edward Abbey* (London: Little Brown, 1994)

————, *The Best of Edward Abbey* (San Francisco: Sierra Club Books, 2005)

John Alcock, *Sonoran Desert Summer* (Tucson: University of Arizona Press, 1990)

John Annerino, *Dead in Their Tracks: Crossing America's Desert Borderlands* (New York: Four Walls Eight Windows, 1999)

Mary Austin, *The Land of Little Rain* (New York: Houghton, Mifflin, 1903)

————, *Stories from the Country of Lost Borders* (New Brunswick: Rutgers University Press, 1987)

Reyner Banham, *Scenes in America Deserta* (Salt Lake City: Gibbs M. Smith, 1982)

Julio L. Betancourt and Robert H. Webb, *Requiem for the Santa Cruz: An Environmental History of an Arizona River* (Tucson: University of Arizona Press, 2014)

Charles Bowden, *Blue Desert* (Tucson: University of Arizona Press, 1986)

————, *Red Line* (New York: W. W. Norton & Company, 1989)

————, *Desierto: Memories of the Future* (New York: W. W. Norton & Company, 1991)

————, *The Sonoran Desert* (New York: H. N. Abrams, 1997)

————, *Trinity* (Austin: University of Texas Press, 2009)

Jim Corbett, *The Sanctuary Church* (Wallingford: Pendle Hill Publications, 1986)

————, *Goatwalking* (New York: Viking Penguin, 1991)

Miriam Davidson, *Convictions of the Heart: Jim Corbett and the Sanctuary Movement* (Tucson: University of Arizona Press, 1988)

Patrick W. Ettinger, *Imaginary Lines: Border Enforcement and the Origins of Undocumented Immigration, 1882–1930* (Austin: University of Texas Press, 2009)

Linda M. Gregonis, *The Hohokam Indians of the Tucson Basin* (Tucson: University of Arizona Press, 1979)

W. Eugene Hollon, *The Great American Desert* (New York: Oxford University Press, 1966)

William Temple Hornaday, *Camp-Fires on Desert and Lava* (London: T. Werner Laurie, 1908)

Edmund Carroll Jaeger, *The California Deserts* (Stanford: Stanford University Press, 1955)

Jason de León, *The Land of Open Graves: Living and Dying on the Migrant Trail* (Oakland: University of California Press, 2015)

Aldo Leopold, *A Sand County Almanac* (New York: Oxford University Press, 1949)

Michael F. Logan, *The Lessening Stream: An Environmental History of the Santa Cruz River* (Tucson: University of Arizona Press, 2002)

———, *Desert Cities: The Environmental History of Phoenix and Tucson* (Pittsburgh: University of Pittsburgh Press, 2006)

Barry Lopez, *Desert Notes* (Kansas City: Andrews McMeel, 1976)

David E. Lorey, *The U.S.–Mexican Border in the Twentieth Century* (Wilmington: Scholarly Resources, 1999)

Carl Lumholtz, *New Trails in Mexico: An Account of One Year's Exploration in North-western Sonora, Mexico, and South-Western Arizona, 1909–1910* (London: T. Fisher Unwin, 1912)

Gary MacEoin (ed.), *Sanctuary: A Resource Guide for Understanding and Participating in the Central American Refugee Struggle* (San Francisco: Harper & Row, 1985)

William E. Martin et al., *Saving Water in a Desert City* (Washington: Resources for the Future, 1984)

Gregory McNamee, *Blue Mountains Far Away: Journeys into the American Wilderness* (New York: The Lyons Press, 2000)

John McPhee, *Basin and Range* (New York: Farrar, Straus and Giroux, 1981)

Joseph Nevins, *Operation Gatekeeper* (London: Routledge, 2002)

———, *Operation Gatekeeper and Beyond* (London: Routledge, 2010)

Bruce M. Pavlik, *The California Deserts* (Berkeley: University of California Press, 2008)

Steven J. Philips and Patricia Wentworth Comus (eds.), *A Natural History of the Sonoran Desert* (Tucson: Arizona-Sonora Desert Museum Press, 2000)

John Wesley Powell, *Report on the Lands of the Arid Region of the United States, with a More Detailed Account of the Lands of Utah* (Washington, D.C.: Department of the Interior, 1878)

Marc Reisner, *Cadillac Desert* (London: Pimlico, 2001)

Amanda Rose, *Showdown in the Sonoran Desert: Religion, Law, and the Immigration Controversy* (New York: Oxford University Press, 2012)

Rachel St. John, *Line in the Sand* (Princeton: Princeton University Press, 2011)

Rebecca Solnit, *Savage Dreams: A Journey into the Hidden Wars of the American West* (Berkeley and Los Angeles: University of California Press, 2014)

Aron Spilken, *Escape!* (New York: Signet, 1983)

6 MATTER OUT OF PLACE: THE BLACK ROCK DESERT, USA

Alonzo Delano, *Life On the Plains and Among the Diggings* (New York: Miller, Orton & Co, 1857)

Brian Doherty, *This is Burning Man* (New York: Little, Brown, 2004)

William L. Fox, photographs by Mark Klett, *The Black Rock Desert* (Tucson: University of Arizona Press, 2002)

——, *Playa Works: The Myth of the Empty* (Reno: University of Nevada Press, 2002)

John Charles Frémont, *Narrative of the Exploring Expedition To the Rocky Mountains* (New York: Appleton, 1846)

Peter Goin, *Black Rock* (Reno: University of Nevada Press, 2005)

Rose Houk, *Sonoran Desert* (Tucson: Southwest Parks and Monuments Association, 2000)

Samantha Krukowski (ed.), *Playa Dust: Collected Stories from Burning Man* (London: Black Dog, 2014)

Thomas Merton, *The Wisdom of the Desert: Sayings from the Desert Fathers* (Norfolk: James Loughlin, 1960)

Allan Nevins, *Frémont, Pathmarker of the West* (Lincoln: University of Nebraska Press, 1992)

Daniel Pinchbeck, *Breaking Open the Head: A Chemical Adventure* (London: Flamingo, 2004)

Scott Slovic (ed.), *Getting Over the Colour Green* (Tucson: University of Arizona Press, 2001)

David W. Teague, *The Southwest in American Literature and Art: The Rise of a Desert Aesthetic* (Tucson: University of Arizona Press, 1997)

David W. Teague and Peter Wild (eds.), *The Secret Life of John C. Van Dyke: Selected Letters* (Reno: University of Nevada Press, 1997)

Barbara Traub, *Desert to Dream* (San Francisco: Immedium, 2011)

Stephen Trimble, *The Sagebrush Ocean: A Natural History of the Great Basin* (Reno, Nev.: University of Nevada Press, 1989)

John C. Van Dyke, *The Autobiography of John C. Van Dyke* (Salt Lake City: University of Utah Press, 1993)

——, *The Desert: Further Studies in Natural Appearances* (New York: Charles Scribner's Sons, 1901). Reprinted with an introduction by Peter Wild (Baltimore: Johns Hopkins University Press, 1999)

Bert Webber, *Over the Applegate Trail to Oregon in 1846* (Medford: Webb Research Group, 1996)

Sessions S. Wheeler, *The Black Rock Desert* (Caldwell: The Caxton Printers, 1978)

7 THE INNER MOUNTAIN: THE EASTERN DESERT, EGYPT

Sahar Abdel-Hakim and Deborah Manley (eds.), *Travelling Through the Deserts of Egypt: From 450 BC to the Twentieth Century* (Cairo: The American University in Cairo Press, 2009)

St. Antony, trans. Derwas J. Chitty, *The Letters of St. Antony the Great* (Oxford: SLG Press, 1975)

St. Athanasius, trans. Edward Stephens, *The Life of St. Antony* (London: The Author, 1697)

———, trans. Robert C. Gregg, *The Life of Antony and the Letter to Marcellinus* (New York: Paulist Press, 1980).

———, trans. E. A. Wallis, *The Paradise or Garden of the Holy Fathers* (London: Chatto & Windus, 1907)

M. R. Balme (ed.), *Martian Geomorphology* (London: Geological Society, 2011)

Elizabeth S. Bolman (ed.), *Monastic Visions: Wall Paintings in the Monastery of St. Antony at the Red Sea* (New Haven, Conn.: Yale University Press, 2002)

David Brakke, *Athanasius and the Politics of Asceticism* (Oxford: Clarendon Press, 1995)

Peter Brown, *The Body and Society: Men, Women and Renunciation in Early Christianity* (London: Faber & Faber, 1989)

Edward North Buxton, *On Either Side of the Red Sea* (London: Edward Stanford, 1895)

Christian Cannuyer, *Coptic Egypt: The Christians of the Nile* (London: Thames & Hudson, 2001)

Douglas E. Christie, *The Blue Sapphire of the Mind: Notes for a Contemplative Ecology* (New York: Oxford University Press, 2013)

Isabel Colegate, *A Pelican in the Wilderness: Hermits, Solitaries and Recluses* (London: HarperCollins, 2002)

James Cowan, *Desert Father: A Journey in the Wilderness with Saint Antony* (Boston: New Seed Books, 2006)

Robert Curzon, *Visits to Monasteries in the Levant* (London: George Newnes, 1897)

William Dalrymple, *From the Holy Mountain* (London: Flamingo, 1998)

Andre von Dumreicher, *Trackers and Smugglers in the Deserts of Egypt* (London: Methuen & Co, 1931)

Gawdat Gabra, *Coptic Monasteries: Egypt's Monastic Art and Architecture* (Cairo: American University in Cairo Press, 2002)

Nelson Glueck, *Rivers in the Desert: The Exploration of the Negev* (London: Weidenfeld & Nicolson, 1959)

Mark Gruber, *Sacrifice in the Desert* (Lanham, Md.: University Press of America, 2003)

Martin Hense and Steven E. Sidebotham, *The Red Land: The Illustrated Archaeology of Egypt's Eastern Desert* (Cairo: American University in Cairo Press, 2008)

Vivian Ibrahim, *The Copts of Egypt* (New York: I. B. Tauris, 2013)

David Jasper, *The Sacred Desert: Religion, Literature, Art and Culture* (Oxford: Blackwell, 2004)

Jill Kamil, *Christianity in the Land of the Pharaohs: The Coptic Orthodox Church* (London: Routledge, 2002)

O. H. E. Khs-Burmester, *A Guide to the Monasteries of the Wadi'n-Natrun* (Cairo: Société d'Archéologie Copte, 1954)

Jacques Lacarriere, *The God-Possessed* (London: Allen & Unwin, 1963)

Belden C. Lane, *The Solace of Fierce Landscapes: Exploring Desert and Mountain Spirituality* (New York: Oxford University Press, 1998)

Percival Lowell, *Mars and Its Canals* (New York: Macmillan, 1906)

Sara Maitland, *A Book of Silence* (London: Granta, 2008)

Michael W. McClellan, *Monasticism in Egypt* (Cairo: American University in Cairo Press, 1998)

Otto F. A. Meinardus, *Monks and Monasteries of the Egyptian Deserts* (Cairo: The American University in Cairo Press, 2003)

H. V. Morton, *Through Lands of the Bible* (London: Methuen & Co, 1938)

Henri J. M. Nouwen, *The Way of the Heart* (New York: Daybreak, 1990)

Palladius, trans. W. K. Lowther Clarke, *The Lausiac History of Palladius* (New York: Macmillan, 1918)

Samuel Rubenson, *The Letters of St. Antony: Origenist Theology, Monastic Tradition and the Making of a Saint* (Lund: Lund University Press, 1990)

Evelyn Dorothea Russell, *Medieval Cairo and the Monasteries of the Wadi Natrun* (London: Weidenfeld & Nicolson, 1962)

Samuel al Syriany, *Guide to Ancient Coptic Churches and Monasteries in Upper Egypt* (Cairo: Institute of Coptic Studies, 1990)

E. Tawadros, *Geology of Egypt and Libya* (Rotterdam: A. A. Balkema, 2001)

Martyn Thomas (ed.), *Copts in Egypt* (Zurich: G2W-Verlag, 2006)

Constantin von Tischendorf, *Travels in the East* (London: Longman, 1847)

Leon Arthur Tregenza, *The Red Sea Mountains of Egypt* (London: Oxford University Press, 1955)

Helen Waddell, *The Desert Fathers* (London: Constable, 1936)

Johann Michael Wansleben, Englished by M. D., *The Present State of Egypt; Or, A New Relation of a Late Voyage into That Kingdom, Performed in the Years 1672, and 1673, Wherein You Have an Exact and True Account of Many Rare and Wonderful Particulars of That Ancient Kingdom* (London: John Starkey, 1678)

James Wellard, *Desert Pilgrimage: A Journey into Christian Egypt* (London: Hutchinson & Co, 1970)

Index

Page numbers in *italics* refer to pages with illustrations

Printed in the United States
by Baker & Taylor Publisher Services